P9-BZU-261

The World's Health Care Crisis

The World's Health Care Crisis

From the Laboratory Bench to the Patient's Bedside

By

Ibis Sánchez-Serrano

AMSTERDAM • BOSTON • HEIDELBERG • LONDON • NEW YORK • OXFORD
PARIS • SAN DIEGO • SAN FRANCISCO • SINGAPORE • SYDNEY • TOKYO

Elsevier
32 Jamestown Road, London, NW1 7BY
225 Wyman Street, Waltham, MA 02451, USA

First edition 2011

British Library Cataloguing-in-Publication Data
A catalogue record for this book is available from the British Library

Library of Congress Cataloging-in-Publication Data
A catalog record for this book is available from the Library of Congress

ISBN: 978-0-12-391875-8

For information on all Elsevier publications visit our website at www.elsevierdirect.com

This book has been manufactured using Print On Demand technology. Each copy is produced to order and is limited to black ink. The online version of this book will show color figures where appropriate.

I dedicate this book to my family, with all my love. Like any Latin family, they have been there for me in the joyful moments and in the difficult times, feeling always very proud of whatever I did, even if they did not quite understand what I was doing. And to my friend Daniel Morand, who has been not only a friend, but also an older brother to me. He has done for me what few people nowadays are capable of doing for others.

When you set out on your journey to Ithaca,
pray that the road is long,
full of adventure, full of knowledge.
The Lestrygonians and the Cyclops,
the angry Poseidon—do not fear them:
You will never find such as these on your path,
if your thoughts remain lofty, if a fine
emotion touches your spirit and your body.
The Lestrygonians and the Cyclops,
the fierce Poseidon you will never encounter,
if you do not carry them within your soul,
if your soul does not set them up before you.
Pray that the road is long.
That the summer mornings are many, when,
with such pleasure, with such joy
you will enter ports seen for the first time;
stop at Phoenician markets,
and purchase fine merchandise,
mother-of-pearl and coral, amber and ebony,
and sensual perfumes of all kinds,
as many sensual perfumes as you can;
visit many Egyptian cities,
to learn and learn from their sages.
Always keep Ithaca in your mind.
To arrive there is your ultimate goal.
But do not hurry the voyage at all.
It is better to let it last for many years;
and to anchor at the island when you are old,
rich with all you have gained on the way,
not expecting that Ithaca will offer you riches.
Ithaca has given you the beautiful voyage.
Without her you would have never set out on the road.
She has nothing more to give you.
And if you find her poor, Ithaca has not deceived you.
Wise as you have become, with so much experience,
you must already have understood what Ithacas mean.
—Konstantinos P. Kavafis, *Ithaca* (1911)

Contents

Preface

> *This is, precisely, the gravest thing ... There are too many intelligent people all over the world who only talk about our problems, but who do not act. If our goal is to save the world, then we need to start a crusade. So, it is not only about publishing a summary of all our ills, but about finding remedies for them. It is about providing the layperson access to a more noble and dignified concept of humankind.*
>
> **—*Georges Mathieu (French painter), interviewed by novelist Vintila Horia* (Viaje a los centros de la tierra, *1971*)**

Over the last couple of years, many people have asked me, "Ibis, what are you doing with your life?" To this question, I have always replied unequivocally (and not without a grain of self-defensiveness), "I am writing a book on the biopharmaceutical industry!"

I found it very interesting that most people, many of them with advanced degrees (including physicians) and hailing from several different countries, would invariably bombard me with the following comments after hearing my response:

> *You know, the pharmaceutical industry is a mafia ... you are lucky to be alive if you are writing a book about it!*
>
> *Do you know that they spend more money lobbying in Washington, D.C., in marketing, and in lavish promotion than they do in R&D? Do you know how powerful they are and how they work in combination with the government and insurance companies?*
>
> *I am sure you are aware of how they manipulate the scientific and clinical data so that they can pass their drugs through the regulatory systems.*
>
> *Of course, pharmaceutical companies do not like to talk about prevention; in fact, they don't want to cure diseases, because for them it is more profitable to treat them as chronic ailments.*
>
> *Do you know all the big pharmaceutical companies do in Africa and how they experiment with people? Are you aware of the horrible nature of those experiments, especially in patients with HIV/AIDS? Haven't you seen the movie [fill-in-the-blank]?*

Even the recent (and mysterious) outbreak of so-called swine flu, caused by the A(H1N1) virus, has led to speculation on the Internet as to all sorts of conspiracy theories, primarily the theory that this virus was prepared by the pharmaceutical industry to create a pandemic for which they would find the cure and, as such, make massive amounts of money and improve their ailing finances.[1]

Although these are some of the main (and at times, the only) ideas that many people all over the world have about the pharmaceutical industry, I need to say, right from the start, that this book is neither a corroboration nor a rejection of these ideas. Rather, it is something quite different: *this book is an attempt to understand how the biopharmaceutical industry works and how it affects society when it comes to health care and health care interventions.*

Thus, my goal in writing this book, which is aimed toward a wide international audience of educated laymen, scientists, businessmen, and politicians, is threefold. First, I would like to provide my readers with a guide to understanding the biotech and pharmaceutical industries (otherwise known as the biopharmaceutical industry) and introduce them to this important industry's incredible potential and titanic challenges, given that this fascinating topic has long been neglected and never presented in a book format for the general public—at least not objectively, in my opinion. Second, this book is a journey through the process of making medicines and the importance that this process has in the overall shaping of health care provision, since an overview of the role of the biopharmaceutical industry within the context of the global health industry is probably not available. There are critiques of the productivity of research and development (R&D), which is the subject of Chapter 5 of this book, but not an analysis of the totality of health care and the pharmaceutical role within it. Third, this book offers concrete solutions to some of the most important problems that the biopharmaceutical industry is facing today and, hence, to some of the most immediate issues of the global health care crisis we currently must live with.

Health care is a tremendously important subject, as evidenced in our daily lives when we or our loved ones become affected by a particular disease and need immediate health care attention and medicine; or when we pay for taxes, Social Security, and health insurance; or when we think of the enormous amount of news (notably, concerning the Obama administration's struggles to pass legislation to provide affordable health insurance to Americans) and research articles on health care issues. Nevertheless, to my knowledge, no single book has addressed all these issues in a coherent and comprehensive manner, and more important, no book has *established* the crucial connection between good organization and management of R&D at the pharmaceutical and academic levels *and* the shaping of health care policy prescriptions: the gray zone in which the solutions to the world's health care crisis are to be found. I must say that this is not surprising because not only is the amount of information available on the subject extremely vast, but given the many and interesting topics that fall within the health care category, finding a unifying leitmotif and the appropriate angle from which to target these issues makes the process of writing this kind of book most difficult.

This book has its origin in an article I published in 2006 in *Nature Reviews Drug Discovery* titled "Success in Translational Research: Lessons from the Development of Bortezomib." In this piece, I dissected the key factors that led to the approval, in record time, of an anticancer drug, Velcade, created by a Harvard University spinoff company called Myogenics/ProScript and further developed and marketed by Millennium Pharmaceuticals (now part of Takeda Pharmaceuticals) for the treatment of multiple myeloma. The story of how this drug was developed and came to the market was extremely unusual and illustrates that if performed correctly, collaboration between academia and industry, and between the public and private sectors, can create extraordinary health care benefits for society. As a result, many lessons, including an organizational model based on the trade of assets between the academic and private sectors, which I named the "core model," to improve effectively the drug discovery and development process were learned.

Then, my good friend Daniel Morand of Switzerland—someone who, like me, has no links whatsoever to the pharmaceutical industry, academia, or politics—proposed that I write a book on drug discovery and development for a much broader audience, with his philanthropic support, based on the number of positive letters and reviews I received from specialists in the field the world over. I gladly accepted his proposal, having no idea that this would represent the greatest physical and intellectual challenge of my life. Since then, every day has been a constant struggle to get to the core of the health care crisis that has become an epidemic in the world, but at the same time, every day enriched my knowledge and understanding of this topic. So this challenge made me all the more responsible for presenting the public with a panoramic and comprehensive view of the biopharmaceutical industry, which is at the center of our discussion (and any discussion) regarding health care. I think that it is important to emphasize that although general areas within health care—such as public and private health care insurance and the current efforts of the Obama administration to overhaul the U.S. health care system—are discussed here, the focus of this book remains the drug industry because in my opinion, everything revolves around it.

This assertion, however, does not mean that I fail to acknowledge that lack of access to general health care due to not being insured or to not having general health care available (as in some developing nations) is a primary cause of morbidity and mortality both in the developed and developing nations; nor do I wish to deny that prevention programs, having access to clean water, stop smoking, eating healthily, etc., also have a place in reducing morbidity and mortality: quite the opposite! But at the end of the day, it is having or not having access to the right medicine that makes the difference between staying healthy or not; between being able to tolerate and "live with" a chronic disease or not; between living and dying. And this is valid for any person in any country in the world.

In fact, at one point during the preparation of this book, someone made the following observation to me:

> *[Ibis,] the assertion that fixing the pharmaceutical industry will [help] fix the world's health care needs is a massive overstatement and if not carefully handled will lose credibility of serious readers. You will turn off all 'pharma' execs, for example. In India, generic drugs are already dirt cheap, but 60% (sic) of the population can't read, has no electricity and no easy access to health care infrastructure. Provision of cheap and effective drugs does nothing to improve diagnosis, patient compliance and monitoring. This is true of much of Latin America and Africa, etc.*[2]

My answer to this observation was:

> *Yes, in countries such as India, as well as in many African and Latin American nations, a number (only a number) of commonly used generic drugs are 'dirt' cheap, but only in absolute terms (for the wealthy in those countries and for a naïve observer in the developed world), but not in relative terms (for the middle class and for the poor there), if we consider incomes and purchasing power in these countries; if we take lack of safety and efficacy compliance into consideration; if we add*

into the equation that hundreds of millions of these people cannot even afford to eat or to live like human beings; if we remember that they are more vulnerable to complications, infectious diseases and other ailments that are not present in the rich nations, and for which there is no cure, etc. Furthermore, not having access to clean water, infrastructure and electricity, etc., is intrinsically an international economic development problem with an impact on health care and public health, but not the other way around. Even if the provision of cheap and effective drugs did 'nothing' to improve diagnosis, patient compliance and monitoring, as you say—and with which I strongly disagree—this does not mean that these people should be abandoned to their own fate, allowing them to suffer and die in pain, when a great deal can be done for them, and when enormous wealth is generated by developing pharmaceuticals in a commercial way. So, having access to medicines is a very immediate, huge, and pervasive issue worldwide, and while the pharmaceutical industry cannot provide the solutions to lack of infrastructure, lack of diagnostics, lack of follow up, etc., it is within the pharmaceutical industry's realm, as the maker of medicines, to contribute to the solution of the world's health care ills by correcting deficiencies in pharmaceutical innovation, by making drugs more accessible and affordable worldwide, by fostering emphasis on the need of prevention, diagnostics and the creation of health care infrastructure, and by creating new drugs and vaccines in therapeutic areas where there is only emptiness.[3]

According to the World Health Organization (WHO), 90–95% of the developing world's health care problems can be solved with generics to which people presently do not have access.

The link between fixing pharma and fixing health care may seem, at first glance, not only audacious and bold, but also far-fetched for an unsympathetic critic in the developed world. Nonetheless, this relationship becomes all the more evident if we think about several facts:

- Pharma market value represents about 75% of *global* health care value (for quoted companies).
- These companies generate more profit than any other constituency in health care.
- The price of prescription medicines has not only increased hugely in the last couple of decades, but it has done so faster (and at least twice as much) as general inflation.
- The U.S. Food and Drug Administration (FDA) has become very politicized and desperate to keep drugs with side effects off the market, which means that the safety hurdles are so high that potentially good drugs are not available to the public. It can cost $2 billion to do a phase 3 trial in a cardiovascular drug and show non-inferiority to a generic!
- Without the benefit of friendly regulatory and political agencies, this industry could be "toast."

All these factors have a tremendous impact on the way drugs are priced and in determining who in the world will benefit from them. Thus, the crucial role of pharmaceutical development in global health care is undeniable.

The book is organized into five major parts and a conclusion. Part I (Chapters 1 and 2) presents a worldwide panoramic picture of the health care crisis that we are living with and of its components and introduces the reader to the pharmaceutical industry.

Part II (Chapters 3–6) deals with the biopharmaceutical industry and today's regulatory environment. Specifically, Chapter 3 introduces the reader to a brief historical survey of the pharmaceutical and biotechnology industries so that people familiarize themselves with the major industrial players and, more important, gain a historical perspective of today's state of affairs. Knowing the past of this industry will allow us to understand better its present position and foresee its future. Chapter 4 is an analysis of the pharmaceutical industry and its current problems, whereas Chapter 5 explores the whole process of drug discovery, development, and marketing, which is important in understanding how the industry works. Chapter 6 discusses what the regulators are doing to deal with the problems related to drug approval.

The third part of the book (Chapters 7–10) deals with innovation and R&D in academia and in the industrial sector. Accordingly, Chapter 7 concerns the major challenges and benefits of the academia–industry relationship, which is at the center of scientific innovation. Chapter 8 discusses the translation of academic innovation into health care and economic benefits, and Chapter 9 analyzes the biotechnology industry and its challenges, which, in many respects, are different from the pharmaceutical industry's mainstream problems. Finally, Chapter 10 explores the reasons for the current lack of R&D productivity in the pharmaceutical industry.

Part IV (Chapters 11 and 12) is dedicated to the health care imbalance that exists between the developed and underdeveloped world and what can be done to bridge the gap between them. Part V (Chapter 13) proposes and discusses some strategies for change in the public and private sectors that may have a positive impact on both the biopharmaceutical industry's R&D productivity and global health care reform.

The audience at which this volume is aimed includes both the general layman and the specialist. Accordingly, I try not to assume familiarity with all the intricacies of scientific research and the process of drug discovery and development, nor with the concepts and theoretical models in biology. I try to avoid jargon as much as possible; however, when complex concepts are introduced, which is unavoidable when writing about science, I clearly explain them. Because the United States is the largest pharmaceutical market and the world leader in this sector, the reader will notice that at times, such as in Chapter 1, there will be greater emphasis placed on what happens in the United States. Nonetheless, I believe that a great deal can be learned from the United States' successes and failures; besides, what happens in the United States is indicative of what will happen in the rest of the world, at least in the pharmaceutical field. If big changes (good and bad) are going to take place, they will begin in the United States.

Any single author who attempts to cover the entire spectrum of drug discovery and development is quickly made aware that in matters of detail, he or she is at an enormous disadvantage in comparison with scholars who have specialized in individual subjects. By compensation, a book of this nature written by a single, *Latin American,* hand may be able to emphasize features on drug discovery and development, with important health care managerial and public policy implications, that are less obvious in a compilation made by specialists, just as a distant view of a canvas may bring out features of a painting that are almost invisible to those close to it.

— Ibis Sánchez-Serrano
Santiago de Veraguas and Panamá City, Panamá; London, UK;
and Boston, MA, U.S.A.

Notes

1. Del Moral, T., 2009. Explicaciones no comprobadas. La Prensa de Panamá, May 28. http://mensual.prensa.com/mensual/contenido/2009/05/28/hoy/panorama/1796067.asp.
2. Words from a critic, London, UK, Fall 2010.
3. Ibis Sánchez-Serrano, Santiago de Veraguas, Panamá, Fall 2010.

Acknowledgments

This book would never have been written in the first place if Daniel Morand, a private philanthropist, did not believe in me, come up with the idea, show enough patience to deal with this very expensive project, and encourage me to keep going, especially at times when I felt physically exhausted.

In writing this book—a process that has consumed five years of my life—I have interviewed a significant number of leading global figures in the biopharmaceutical world, both in the United States and Europe, such as industry managers, scientists, public health scholars, regulators, bankers, managers in the not-for-profit world, and others. To all of these people, I give my gratitude for their generous time and valuable insight. I would like to single out, in no particular order, the following people, who in one way or another have contributed to the realization of this book:

- Roy Vagelos, retired chairman and CEO, Merck;
- Thomas Lönngren, former executive director, European Medicines Agency (EMEA);
- Steven Paul, retired executive vice president and science and technology president, Lilly Research Laboratories;
- Julian Adams, president of R&D and chief scientific officer, Infinity Pharmaceuticals;
- Janet Woodcock, director, FDA Center for Drug Evaluation and Research;
- Tom Maniatis, former Jeremy R. Knowles Professor of Molecular and Cellular Biology, Harvard University (now Isidore S. Edelman Professor of Biochemistry and Chairman, Dept. of Biochemistry and Molecular Biophysics at Columbia University);
- Jo Walton, pharmaceuticals equity research analyst at Lehman Brothers (now pharmaceuticals analyst, Credit Suisse, London);
- Martin Wood, Medical Research Council Technology;
- Robert Lang, director, Corporate Resources, Medical Research Council Technology;
- Richard N. Seabrook, head of business development, technology transfer, The Wellcome Trust;
- Sam Williams, CEO, Modern Biosciences;
- Zina Affas, former principal, Atlas Venture (now partner at Orion Healthcare Equity Partners);
- Tom Hockaday, managing director, Isis Innovation, The Technology Transfer Company of the University of Oxford;
- Teri Willey, CEO, Cambridge Enterprise;
- Jackie Hunter, senior vice president for Science Environment Development, GlaxoSmithKline;
- Anita Kidgell, vice president, Corporate Strategy, GlaxoSmithKline;
- Susan Gasser, director, Friedrich Miescher Institute for Biomedical Research;
- Mark McGrath, former head of patents and licensing, Friedrich Miescher Institute for Biomedical Research, Switzerland (now head of search and evaluation, Cardiovascular and Metabolism, Novartis, Switzerland);

- Jeremy M. Levin, former global head of strategic alliances, Novartis Institutes for Biomedical Research (now senior vice president of external science, technology, and licensing, Bristol-Myers Squibb);
- Lembit Rago, director, health technology and pharmaceuticals, World Health Organization (WHO);
- Peter Kirkpatrick, chief editor, *Nature Reviews Drug Discovery*;
- Barbara Marte, senior editor, *Nature*;
- Christopher Milne, assistant director, Tufts Center for the Study of Drug Development, Tufts University;
- Anne Boulay, Friedrich Miescher Institute for Biomedical Research; and
- Timothy Wright, senior vice president, global head of Translational Sciences at Novartis.

I would also like to give special thanks to Roy Vagelos, Thomas Lönngren, Janet Woodcock, Julian Adams, and Daniel Morand for their useful comments on the first draft of the book. Similarly, I would like to thank Holly Thesieres Monteith for preparing the first copyedited version of this book and for her valuable editorial comments, to my friend David Frías for his Spanish hospitality in London, and to Mr. and Mrs. Peter and Elizabeth Thomson for their kind hospitality and warmth in Boston. Finally, my thanks go to Harvard Medical School's Francis A. Countway Library of Medicine.

Introduction

Today's patient is far from yesterday's stereotype, who was docile, uninformed, and in a relatively weak position compared to that of the doctor. The characteristics of the new consumer are dramatically different. Today's patients are well-informed and demanding. They think critically, and they are building powerful networks.

***—Johan Hjertqvist*[1]**

Though we are constantly being informed about the approval of medications or of major setbacks when developing them, we rarely hear that the pharmaceutical industry is having a hard time coming up with truly innovative and effective drugs, which has led to a productivity crisis in this sector—a crisis that has been downplayed by the pharmaceutical companies in their press releases for several years and that the industry has camouflaged by increasing the price of pharmaceuticals to consumers all over the world, among other strategies. In other words, patients have to pay for all the inefficiencies that take place at the pharmaceutical-industry level.

The actual situation in this industry is, indeed, very complex, as shown by the fact that disappointing productivity performance, in recent years, has been accompanied by the massive expiration of best-selling drugs and scandals associated with the safety, or lack of safety, of some medications. Though many industry observers (both in the private and public domains) are alarmed by these facts—and reasonably so—one should say that rarely does this alarm take the form of a careful examination to get to the roots of the pharmaceutical industry's problems—something that I attempt to do in this book. And needless to say, a crisis at the pharmaceutical-industry level exacerbates the crisis that already exists in the globally crippled health care systems: As medicine prices continue to increase, it becomes more and more difficult for these systems to afford them. Therefore, a book of this scope and ambition cannot fail to address some of the most important and sensitive health care issues that affect the world today such as (1) the inadequacy of most health care systems worldwide to provide patients with satisfactory health care attention; (2) the significant number of unmet medical needs that prevail both in developed and underdeveloped countries; (3) the lack of access in developing countries to the cheap drugs that we take for granted in our "developed" society and that would solve more than 90% of the health problems that afflict underprivileged countries; and (4) the need to take severe and effective measures against the commercialization of counterfeit drugs worldwide, among many other issues.

In fact, I think that the lack of a comprehensive and coherent analysis of the drug industry (and of its research and development, R&D) not only is limiting significantly our ability to implement effective policies to reform health care but is also limiting our ability to design adequate strategies for making important personal health care decisions, and in the case of the biopharmaceutical industry and investors, to deal appropriately with the industry's productivity problems. Framed in a different manner, how can we attempt to reform health care—how can we strive for the production of better, safer, and more effective drugs—if we lack a basic understanding of the causes of the global health care crisis, from the laboratory bench to the patient's bedside?

It is not surprising, amid so much confusion and the omnipresence of scandalous reports on the pharmaceutical industry's practices—some of them accurate, others exaggerated—that many patients, the general public, and biopharmaceutical industry critics react so bitterly, just like an immunological response to a viral infection, when they hear the term *pharmaceutical industry*, as illustrated in the preface to this book. It is my hope, then, that in tackling the causes of these problems, I am able to create a platform that will lead to more productive and objective discussions on all these issues, which will lead eventually to more effective ways, both at the commercial and public policy levels, to bring drugs to the market more efficiently. This also leads, in this way, to a win–win situation for the public and private sectors alike. In fact, one of the major obstacles in trying to reform a health care system is maintaining a balance between public and private interests.

To accomplish these goals, this book dissects all the elements that play an important role in the process of drug discovery and development: (1) an industrial base, constituted by drug companies ("big pharma" and "biotech"); (2) a regulatory infrastructure, embodied principally by the U.S. Food and Drug Administration (FDA) and the European Medicines Agency (EMEA); (3) an academic/innovative base, comprising universities and research centers; (4) a financial/investment platform, represented by private investors (such as venture capitalists and institutional investors); and (5) a public base such as government-sponsored research agencies [i.e., the National Institutes of Health (NIH) and the U.K. Medical Research Council], philanthropic organizations, and advocacy groups. Unlike what it is usually assumed—that drug development is the sole role of the pharmaceutical industry—I must say that each one of the sectors mentioned here performs a vital role in drug discovery and development, and without one of them, the drug creation machinery would not function.

Even though the patient is and should be at the center of any discussion on medicine, tacitly or explicitly, my approach in this work emphasizes the nature of scientific research and how basic scientific discoveries are translated into health care and economic benefits for society and how this feedback-loop mechanism works—a perspective that is all too often neglected. Once we understand how drugs move from the laboratory bench to the bedside and what obstacles have to be overcome to accomplish this, it will be possible to draw general conclusions on how the process of drug development and the actual delivery of medications to patients—all over the world—could be improved effectively, which should also lead to lower medicine prices.

I personally believe that regardless of the economic recession in which we are currently immersed, the set of challenges that the pharmaceutical industry faces right now represents a critical inflection point in its history, probably the end of a path and the beginning of a new phase, especially if we consider that the industry is confronted by the daunting task of integrating and assimilating an unprecedented amount of knowledge, technology, and information, as epitomized by constant breakthroughs in the biomedical sciences made possible through biotechnology, genomics and postgenomics (proteomics), computational biology, nanotechnology, and so on. I believe that a great future lies ahead of us in terms of better, safer, and more effective and affordable medicine. But unfortunately, the biopharmaceutical industry (and investors) has been more focused on the financials inherent to its endeavor than on a long-term vision of productivity, high-quality research, product safety, social weal, and, of course, transparency and integrity.

Note

1. Quote is from "Perspectives on the European health care systems: Some lessons for America," Heritage Foundation, Lecture 711, July, 9, 2001. http://www.heritage.org/research/healthcare/hl711.cfm.

Part I

The Global Health Care Crisis

1 The World's Health Care Crisis: The United States' Leadership

If this is the best of all possible worlds, what must the other worlds be like?
—Voltaire, Candide, ou l'Optimisme (1759)

Finding effective ways to provide and pay for health care (in particular, for medicines) is no longer a problem exclusive to the less-developed countries—such as African nations, large parts of Asia, and some parts of Latin America—but is also a great challenge even in the world's richest countries: the United States, European nations, Canada, Japan, and Australia. Although the economic, political, and cultural differences that exist between poor, middle-income, and wealthy nations are enormous, all nations have to deal with serious health care issues of one sort or another, regardless of whether their health care systems are universal. In fact, the world is going through a health care crisis—that is, a *financial* crisis in which countries cannot successfully meet the twenty-first century person's access to medicine due to the rising cost of health care services and, more importantly, of pharmaceuticals. This was not the case a few decades ago, especially in the wealthier nations. Not surprisingly, people all over the world have expressed great dissatisfaction and concern about this situation, which is generally perceived as unsustainable in the near future. This health care crisis is worsened by rising age-dependency ratios and aging populations in these countries; and it then competes with the pension crisis for the money and political will that are needed to solve these problems. It is ironic that one of the most remarkable conquests of the past century was to provide humans with the opportunity of living longer when this great privilege has not necessarily resulted in living a healthier, more fulfilling, and happier existence.

Though a health care crisis is more evident in the developing world and the United States—the country with the worst health care system in the industrialized world,[1] as embarrassedly evidenced during the 2008 US presidential campaign and also by statistical measures (see the later discussion)—it is also affecting Europe, which, in opposition to the United States, has a long tradition of institutionalized social welfare. In many European countries, national health systems were developed to create social safety nets for all citizens. In fact, health care costs in Europe have continued to rise in recent years, and to keep costs low, in addition to pharmaceutical price controls, a variety of payment and reimbursement systems (i.e., copayments, reference pricing,[2] differential pricing,[3] and others) have been created.[4] Although health care systems and procedures to set prices and reimbursement levels vary from country to country on the European continent, the ways in which most European countries generally achieved price controls have been by setting prices at a level

The World's Health Care Crisis. DOI: 10.1016/B978-0-12-391875-8.00001-9

that may not reward financially pharmaceutical innovation to the same degree as in the United States, and by delaying decisions about reimbursement. In part, this fact explains why the largest European pharmaceutical companies have developed strong research and operational bases in the United States—the world's largest pharmaceutical market. Other countries that have very socially conscious health care systems, such as Canada, Japan, and Australia, are struggling to find ways to deal with rising health care and medicine costs.

Facing severe criticism in the United States, where there are no "official" drug price controls (unlike in Europe and other regions), the pharmaceutical industry, which, between 1995 and 2002, was the most profitable industry in the United States (and still remains among the top three most profitable businesses in the country, with profits as percentage of revenues of 19.3% and with returns on shareholders' equity of 23%[5]), has had to defend itself against "abuse" charges for the way in which it prices medicine. They claim that in the United States (a country where doctors' and health care services' fees are the most expensive and profitable in the entire planet[6]), pharmaceuticals account for *only* 10–12% of total health care costs, with the remaining 88–90% of costs shared among hospitals, doctors, and insurance companies[7] (see Figures 1.1a and b). Though this is in striking contrast to most countries, where medical services are not nearly as expensive as in the United States owing to several factors, such as universal (or close to universal) health care coverage and the fact that doctors' salaries are significantly much lower than in the United States, 10–12% is still a high number in both relative and absolute terms. In addition, this statistical figure fails to reflect the challenges that individuals with low or even average incomes face in accessing medications, which are sometimes priced in the tens of thousands of dollars a year, that they need to survive. Furthermore, seen from a global perspective, these figures take on a different significance when we consider that pharmaceutical market value represents about three quarters of the world's health care value for quoted companies alone, and that these companies generate more profit than any other constituency in health care.

Though an institutional health care crisis has been discussed for many decades in the United States, nothing really significant resulted from this debate until the Obama administration signed into law a health care reform bill in March 2010. However—and it is extremely important to say this—this reform is centered around issues such as extending health insurance coverage to many uninsured US citizens, which is only the tip of the iceberg, rather than on facilitating *easier* and *more affordable* access to *better* and *safer* medicines. This latter problem is the greatest challenge and the common denominator among all countries, as we shall see later, in Chapter 2. Even prominent US economists who admire the European and Canadian universal health care systems and have proposed the implementation of a similar system in the United States fail to realize that even universal health care coverage (or something close to it[8]) is not a solution to the problem. Not only is the history of the European and Canadian health care systems dramatically different from the history of health care in the United States, proving such systems unsuitable for adoption by the United States, but, as we shall see in the next chapter, even countries with universal health care coverage, such as France and Canada, confront serious problems

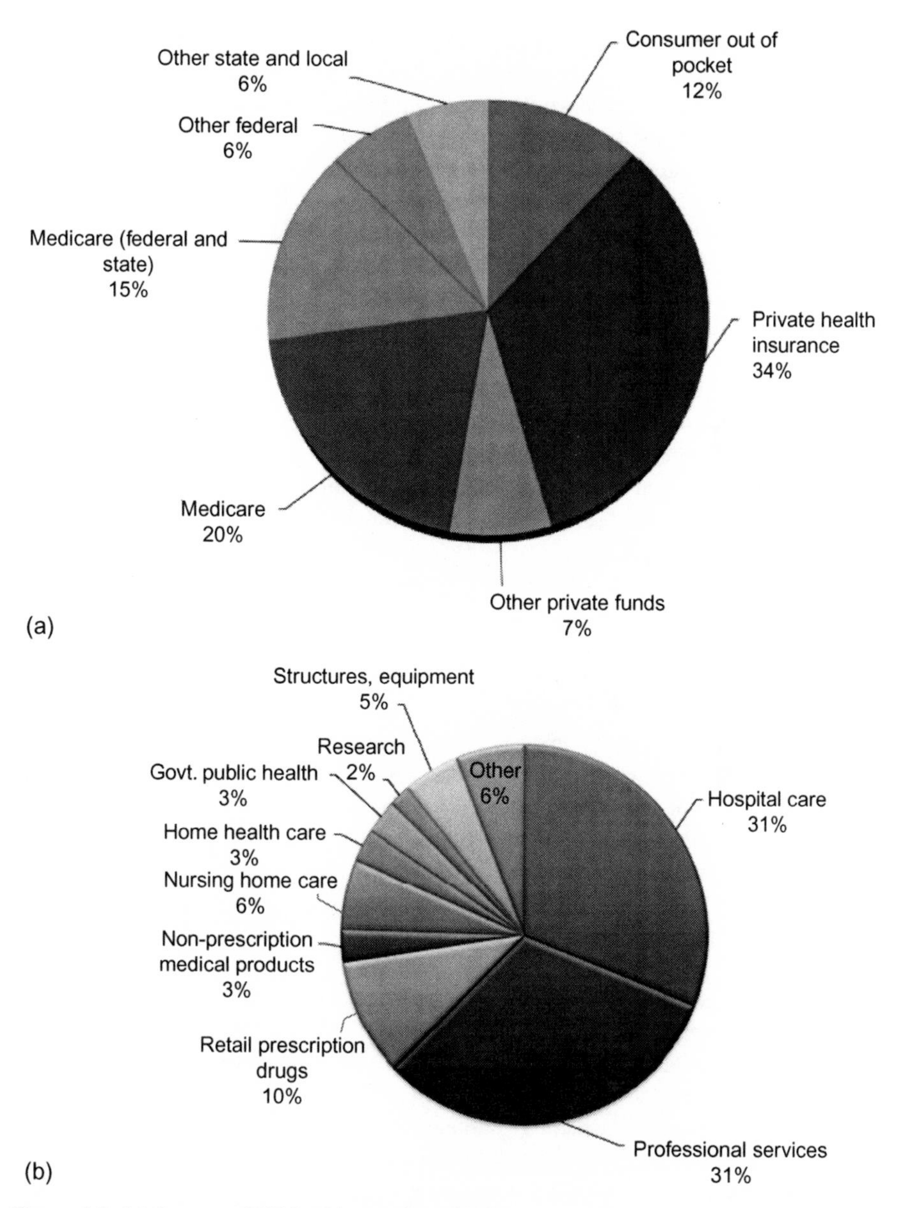

Figure 1.1 (a) Sources of US health spending, 2008.
Source: Truffer, C.J., Keehan, S., Smith, S., Cylus, J., Sisko, A., Posial, J.A., Lizonitz, J., Clemens, M.K., 2010. Health spending projections through 2019: the recession's impact continues. Health Affairs, March. © Health Affairs. Reprinted with permission. All rights reserved. http://content.healthaffairs.org/cgi/content/abstract/hlthaff.2009.1074v1.
(b) Where the US health care dollar went, 2008.
Source: Hartman, M., Martin, A., Nuccio, O., Catlin, A., the National Health Expenditure Accounts Team, 2010. Health spending growth at a historic low in 2008. Health Affairs, January. © Health Affairs. Reprinted with permission. All rights reserved. http://content.healthaffairs.org/cgi/content/abstract/29/1/147

in providing citizens with the best medicines for a wide range of maladies. Not only that, universal coverage is on the verge of collapse in these other nations.

Some questions that immediately come to mind are the following: can the pharmaceutical industry justify the high prices of medicines? Is there anything that can be done to obtain better access to pharmaceuticals? If drug prices continue to increase, who is going to be able to afford them, and what is going to happen to those who cannot afford them? Has the pharmaceutical industry realized that increasing medicine prices may backfire in the future, especially if the world's economic situation continues to worsen at some point?

Although none of these questions has an easy answer, I shall explore throughout the rest of the book what is driving this crisis in the development of pharmaceuticals and how this crisis is affecting global health care, so that we can attempt to answer them. For now, let us become familiar with the shape of the global health care crisis and its magnitude. To avoid overwhelming the reader with too much information, this first chapter summarizes the US health care situation in the last few decades, and in the next chapter, I will discuss what is happening in other industrialized countries, as well as in the developing world.

The US Health Care Crisis

Back in the early 1990s, Bill Clinton promised that one of the things he would do if elected president of the United States would be to reform the US health care system and address some of the critical issues related to rising health care costs by creating a system of universal health care.[9] But Clinton's plans failed for many reasons, among the most cited of which were other politicians' unwillingness to confront both the insurance and pharmaceutical lobbies and a temporary remission in the growth of health care spending brought about because health management organizations (HMOs) briefly managed to limit cost increases.[10] That remission did not last long, however, and soon rising health care costs again became a source of news. The figures speak for themselves: in 1960, the United States spent 5.2% of its gross domestic product (GDP) on health care, but by 2008, it was spending 17% of its GDP on health care, one third of which went to waste.[11] In 2008, Barack Obama promised, as part of his successful presidential campaign, to make health care insurance affordable to every US citizen and committed his administration to lowering health care costs.[12] Accordingly, on February 4, 2009, President Obama signed the Children's Health Insurance Bill,[13] which mandated health insurance coverage for low-income children. Throughout the first half of 2009, his health insurance plan proposed severe cost-control measures that would lower premiums so much that the uninsured could afford them, and it also asked employers to either provide "meaningful" coverage or contribute to a public plan. In addition, he proposed increasing taxes on the incomes of affluent people (i.e., individuals with an adjusted gross income of $280,000 a year or couples filing joint returns with an adjusted gross income of $350,000 or more a year) to help pay for his plan to make health care more accessible and affordable.[14]

These revenues would account for about half of a $634 billion "reserve fund" that President Obama would set aside in his budget to begin addressing health care, while the other half would come from Medicare savings, derived in part from putting an end to billions of dollars in subsidies to insurance companies under the Medicare Advantage program and making other possible tax law changes.[15] A further $80 billion contribution, over a period of 10 years, by the pharmaceutical industry was pledged to improve drug benefits for seniors on Medicare and to defray part of the cost of President Obama's health care legislation,[16] in exchange for some very important concessions from the government that would spare the industry from having to consider some very threatening issues that could have caused major structural changes.[17]

However, by September 9, 2009, the date of the president's second address to the nation pushing his health care reform agenda, his so-called universal, government-sponsored health care plan had metamorphosed into the following (which includes some of the health care reform proposals put forward by his presidential campaign opponent, Senator John McCain):

1. The hundreds of millions of Americans who already have health insurance through Medicare, Medicaid, the Veterans Association, or their employer would not have to change what they already had. What Obama's new plan would do is make the insurance that they already had worked better for them because it would be against the law for insurance companies to deny coverage to patients because of a preexisting condition. Likewise, insurance companies would no longer be able to place an arbitrary cap on the amount of coverage that patients could receive in a given year or over their lifetimes. In addition, the government would place a limit on how much a patient could be charged for out-of-pocket expenses because, in Obama's words, in the United States of America, "no one should go broke because he or she gets sick." Finally, insurance companies would be required to cover routine checkups and preventive care like mammograms and colonoscopies at no extra charge.
2. The millions of Americans who do not currently have health insurance, as well as those who lose or change their jobs and those who start a new business, would receive coverage at an affordable price. The way to do this would be through the creation of a new insurance exchange; i.e., "a marketplace where individuals and small businesses will be able to shop for health insurance at competitive prices." As a result, according to Obama, "insurance companies will have an incentive to participate in this exchange because it lets them compete for millions of new customers. As one big group, these customers will have greater leverage to bargain with the insurance companies for better prices and quality coverage." For those individuals and small businesses who still could not afford the lower priced insurance available in the exchange, the government would provide tax credits, the size of which would be based on a person's or a business's specific needs.
3. Under this new health care plan, individuals would be required to carry basic health insurance, just as most states require people to carry auto insurance. In a similar fashion, businesses would be required either to offer their workers health care or to chip in to help cover the health care costs of their workers. There was a hardship waiver for those individuals who still could not afford coverage, and 95% of all small businesses, because of their size and narrow profit margins, also would be exempt from these requirements.[18]

The president promised, "I will not sign a plan that adds one dime to our deficits—either now or in the future. Period."[19]

After much debate and heated confrontation between the Democratic and Republican parties, two major health care reform proposals were considered by the US Congress: the Affordable Health Care for America Act, 220-215 (the House bill, passed on November 7, 2009), and the Patient Protection and Affordable Care Act, 60-39 (the Senate bill, passed on December 24, 2009).[20] Both bills had varying degrees of similarities and differences on a wide range of issues, including the type of financing to be used, the presence of insurance exchanges, the existence of a public option, the level of Medicaid eligibility, and the coverage of abortion and illegal immigrants.

As of the end of January 2010, however, no consensus had been reached by the members of the US Congress about what shape the final health care reform bill should take, and great, seemingly irreconcilable divisions remained between and among the Democrats, Republicans, and independents. The matter became even more complicated when Republican Scott Brown, who pledged to oppose the Democratic Party's health care reform bill, unexpectedly won the late Ted Kennedy's Massachusetts senatorial seat in a special election in January 2010. His victory over his Democratic opponent, Martha Coakley, who like Kennedy favored health care reform, was a turning point in the health care battle. Before Brown's election, the Democratic coalition (which included two independent senators) had 60 members—enough to block a Republican filibuster and pass a health care reform bill in the Senate. But after Brown was elected, the number of Republican senators changed to 41, and the Democratic Party no longer held a filibuster-proof majority.

This major setback prompted Obama to challenge Republicans for a televised debate on health care (scheduled for February 25, 2010) and to issue, on February 22, 2010, his own version of a health care overhaul—which turned out to be largely based on the Senate version passed on December 2009, but offering some concessions to the House bill.[21] The goal of this action was to lay down the groundwork for a complicated political maneuver called "reconciliation," in which a health care bill could be passed on a simple majority vote, which the Democrats could still win. In fact, it was through reconciliation that on March 21, 2010, the Democrats passed a health care overhaul bill without a single Republican vote.

Though some parts of the health care bill are going to come into effect before 2014 (and in fact, some have already taken effect), it is expected that some of the most important health care reforms will become effective in 2014.[22] But this battle still seems to be far from over: ever since the Democrats lost the majority of seats in the House of Representatives (which has control over the US budget) during the 2010 midterm elections, Republicans have vowed to overturn or severely cut back the Democrats' health care reform effort championed by President Barack Obama and the Democratic-controlled Congress.

The question I pose is the following: how will the Obama administration be able to accomplish its promised health care reform goals and create a sustainable health care system in the *long run* (notwithstanding whether it is fiscally, politically, and legally possible to do so in all states[23])? The answer remains a mystery to me, because fixing the messy financial crisis left behind by the George W. Bush administration will take a significant amount of time, great political maneuvering, and trillions of dollars. It is, indeed, quite concerning that most of the current efforts to reform the US health care system and to deal with a number of complex health care problems are focused on cost reduction rather than on more solid, radical, and sweeping initiatives that would *really* represent a so-called overhaul! Though we should not be pessimistic, we need to remember that the collapse of recent attempts at health care reform in California, in which the government could not provide health care insurance to all its uninsured citizens without going bankrupt, and many problems encountered in Massachusetts, where there were more uninsured people than originally believed and where there is a shortage of funds to cover all the uninsured people, are telltale signs of what might lie ahead when reforming the US health care system.

The case of Massachusetts, whose budget falls quite short of the funds needed to cover the uninsured, is particularly interesting because this was initially the model that proponents of a more affordable health care system were using to create a health care reform system for the nation.[24] As has been noted elsewhere, "the impacts of going uninsured are clear and severe. Many uninsured individuals postpone needed medical care, which results in increased mortality and billions of dollars lost in productivity and increased expenses to the health care system. There also exists a significant sense of vulnerability to the potential loss of health insurance, which is shared by tens of millions of other Americans who have managed to retain coverage."[25] And in fact, every American, no more and no less than any other person in the world, deserves to be covered by a health insurance plan that satisfies at least his or her basic needs. But the real and pragmatic question is: is this possible in the depredatory capitalist system that characterizes the United States and that differentiates it from all other countries on earth?

The US Health Care System

An important characteristic of the US health care system is that it is more privatized than it is in any other country in the world, yet almost half of its health care spending is subsidized by the government through Medicare, an insurance program for qualified elderly, and Medicaid, an insurance program for the poor. Those who do not qualify for either Medicare or Medicaid[26] may, in some cases, obtain health coverage through their employers, as has historically been the case since the end of World War II.[27] As of 2007 (the latest available data), there were around 46.6 million uninsured persons in the United States, representing approximately 18% of the total population under 65 years old.[28] More than two thirds of uninsured adults in the United States worked in 2005[29]; in other words, there were 39.8 million US workers who had no health care—more than the population of Canada.

The US health care system, as it is right now, is indubitably the most inefficient in the industrialized world, as demonstrated by basic measures of health performance. It spends more on health care than any other advanced nation, but it ranks near the bottom of industrialized countries on healthy life expectancy (age 60 years), which means that Americans spend more years living in poor health resulting from chronic illness or disability. In addition, of the 23 industrialized countries, the United States has the highest infant mortality rate (see Table 1.1).[30] It is also true that excessive administrative expenses, inflated prices, poor management and inappropriate care, waste, and fraud significantly increase the cost of medical care, health insurance for

Table 1.1 International Health Comparisons, 2007

Country	Life Expectancy	Infant Mortality Rate (Deaths/ 1,000 Live Births)	Physicians per 1,000 People	Nurses per 1,000 People	Per Capita Expenditure on Health (USD)	Health Care Costs as a Percentage of GDP	% of Government Revenue Spent on Health	% of Health Costs Paid by Government
Australia	81.4	4.2	2.8	9.7	3,137	8.7	17.7	67.7
Canada	80.7	5.0	2.2	9.0	3,895	10.1	16.7	69.8
France	81.0	4.0	3.4	7.7	3,601	11.0	14.2	79.0
Germany	79.8	3.8	3.5	9.9	3,588	10.4	17.6	76.9
Japan	82.6	2.6	2.1	9.4	2,581	8.1	16.8	81.3
Norway	80.0	3.0	3.8	16.2	5,910	9.0	17.9	83.6
Sweden	81.0	2.5	3.6	10.8	3,323	9.2	13.6	81.7
U.K.	79.1	4.8	2.5	10.0	2,992	8.4	15.8	81.7
US	78.1	6.7	2.4	10.6	7,290	16.0	18.5	45.4

Life expectancy versus health care spending in 2007 for OECD countries. The data source is http://www.oecd.org (publicly available data). http://en.wikipedia.org/wiki/Health_care_system.

employers and workers and affect the security of families,[31] but these facts alone are not creating the health care crisis experienced in the United States.

Nobel laureate Paul Krugman and Robin Wells have pointed out that "the key problem with the US health care system is its fragmentation. A history of failed attempts to introduce universal health insurance has left [Americans] with a system in which the government pays directly or indirectly for more than half of the nation's health care, but the actual delivery both of insurance and of care is undertaken by a crazy quilt of private insurers, for-profit hospitals, and other players who add cost without adding value."[32] The authors waste no time in proposing the adoption of a Canadian-style single-payer system, in which the government provides insurance directly to the consumer, which they claim is a cheaper and more effective model than the current health care system in the United States.

Krugman and Wells also point out that "American health care tends to divide the population into insiders and outsiders. Insiders, who have good insurance, receive everything modern medicine can provide, no matter how expensive. Outsiders, who have poor insurance or none at all, receive very little."[33] Though the second part of their statement, that the uninsured in the United States receive very little health care, is cruelly accurate, the first part, that the insured "receive everything modern medicine can provide, no matter how expensive," unfortunately no longer holds. And this is not surprising because in their analysis, the authors forgot to include a crucial, perhaps even the most important, component of health care coverage: medications. If the United States were to adopt a universal health care coverage system (or its equivalent), wholly or mostly subsidized by the government, or if the United States were to implement a health care system in the way recently proposed by President Obama—which, needless to say, has many gaps and on which no feasibility study has been performed—it is necessary to ask this question: who would pay for highly expensive medicines to treat diseases such as cancer, whose treatment could cost beyond $100,000 a year for medicines alone? This does not even include the even more expensive drugs that are used to treat severe chronic ailments and rare disorders, nor does it take into account doctors' high salaries and hospitals' huge fees. After all, the purpose of not having drug price controls in the United States and of having a privatized health insurance system is to create incentives for the pharmaceutical and investment industries to take the high risks that are involved in producing innovative, better, and safer drugs and to allow very ill patients to access those medicines through their private health insurance. In addition, we need to consider that this deficiency in bringing novel, safer, and more effective medicines to the market creates a "domino effect" that necessarily leads to longer (and sometimes inadequate) treatments, hospitalizations, surgical procedures, decrease of labor productivity, decrease in the quality of living, psychological and emotional distress, more visits to the doctor, higher doctor's fees, more clinical tests, higher morbidity and mortality, more paperwork, higher health insurance premiums, etc. All of these factors have a direct and powerful impact on the increase in overall health care costs and, needless to say, a very detrimental effect upon society as a whole.[34]

In other words, medicines are to a health care system like the foundation is to a house. The foundation does not represent the biggest nor the most visible part of the house (very often, in fact, it is the invisible part), but if the foundation is not planned and built correctly, the overall house will not be stable and could simply collapse under any stress. So a universal health care system (or a single-payer system) in the United States would necessarily imply large rationing, as happens in Europe; a much larger health care budget; a significant change in the US health care infrastructure; major changes in the US medical education system that would make it more focused on social welfare and less centered on money; the collapse of the health insurance industry[35]; the imposition of drug price controls; huge cuts in research and development (R&D); a threat to innovation; and the subsequent collapse of the biopharmaceutical and financial systems, resulting in worldwide chaos. Certainly, the combined collapse of Enron, Fannie Mae, Freddie Mac, AIG, Lehman Brothers, and General Motors would serve as only a mild foretaste of the real global nightmare that such a change in the US health care system would entail.

On the other hand, one wonders how effective and sustainable the cooperative system proposed by President Obama in his health care reform plan (which was actually a proposal championed by Democratic senator Max Baucus, the chairman of the Finance Committee) will be—if it can even survive without going bankrupt—if we consider the fact that many patients will be medicated with highly expensive drugs. In fact, there is growing evidence that the costs of US health care reform will be higher than expected.[36]

Since 2006, when Krugman and Wells published their article, much has changed in the US economic and political arenas, and a major change took place in the health care domain with the introduction of Medicare Part D, which has had a tremendous impact on people who do not qualify for Medicare or Medicaid. Let me elaborate on this because it is paramount.

Beginning on January 1, 2006, Medicare Part D became effective in the United States. This program was enacted by the Bush administration as part of the Medicare Prescription Drug, Improvement, and Modernization Act of 2003, with the overarching goal of subsidizing part of the costs of prescription drugs for beneficiaries of Medicare—the US government's health insurance program for people aged 65 and older or who meet other special criteria.[37,38]

The original Medicare program, which was created back in 1965 when people took considerably fewer and cheaper medications, consisted of three parts (A, B, and C), none of which provided prescription drug benefits (see Table 1.2). The addition of Medicare Part D sought to mitigate the burden of purchasing prescription drugs by allowing patients to choose from a wide array of private insurance plans that are reimbursed by the Centers for Medicare and Medicaid Services (CMS). As of 2008, there were more than 1,824 stand-alone Part D plans available,[39] providing participants in Medicare Part D with the opportunity to choose a plan that—in compliance with the formulary classes and categories established by the US Pharmacopeia—would, in theory, best meet their individual needs.[40]

The general idea was that, typically, each plan's formulary would be organized into tiers, and each tier would be associated with a set copay amount. In fact, most formularies have between three and five tiers, and the lower the tier, the lower the copay amount. For example, Tier 1 might include all the plan's preferred generic drugs, and each drug within this tier might have a copay of $5–10 per prescription.

Table 1.2 Medicare Before Medicare Part D

- Medicare Part A covered hospital insurance
- Medicare Part B helped to pay for medical services not covered by Part A
- Medicare Part C (also called Medicare Advantage) provided beneficiaries who had Parts A and B the option of receiving all their health care through a provider organization, like an HMO.

Source: Centers for Medicare and Medicaid Services (CMS) (publicly available data).

Tier 2 might include the plan's preferred brand drugs with a copay of $20–30, while Tier 3 may be reserved for nonpreferred brand drugs that are covered by the plan at a higher copay level—perhaps $40–50. Tiers 4 and higher typically contain specialty drugs, which have the highest copays because they are generally quite expensive. In theory, standard benefits per year (which increase annually), as of 2009, should cover 75% of drug costs between $295 and $2,700 (the initial coverage limit); 0% of costs between $2,700 and $6,154 (the coverage gap, also known as the "doughnut hole"); and 95% of costs above $6,154 (the catastrophic coverage threshold). The "doughnut hole" is the difference between the initial coverage limit and the catastrophic coverage threshold, and within this coverage gap, the patient is responsible for all prescription drug costs without any aid from the Medicare Part D plan.[41] But the fact is that many seniors have trouble understanding these benefits, and this poor knowledge limits their ability to manage their medication needs and costs.

Before Medicare Part D was proposed, there was a strong outcry, especially by senior citizens in the United States, regarding the high price of prescription drugs, which led many of them to organize trips to Canada and Mexico to purchase cheaper drugs in these countries or to buy them through online pharmacies, raising great concerns for the pharmaceutical industry because of potential revenue losses. With the establishment of Medicare Part D, the outcry diminished as a significant portion of the participants' drug expenses became subsidized by the government. According to the CMS, 40 million seniors now have prescription drug coverage,[42] and some data show that seniors in Part D plans filled about 486 million prescriptions in 2006, boosting the use of the most profitable chronic disease drugs, such as drugs for high blood pressure and high cholesterol, which accounted for 122 million prescriptions. More than 20 million prescriptions were for drugs to treat diabetes, pain, cancer, and ulcers, and rounding out the list of top items were antibiotics, hormones, blood thinners, and drugs for seizures and psychiatric disorders.

The problem is that though the program has benefited patients who are better off, it has failed to protect low-income Americans from high out-of-pocket costs for their medications.[43] Furthermore, program costs—which critics had feared would exceed government projections by as much as $750 billion by the end of the decade—have materialized sooner than expected.[44] In an attempt to fix the problem, the Bush administration proposed cuts in Medicare spending of $196 billion over the next 5 years and increases in Medicare premiums for those earning more than $82,000 a year.[45] It is believed that the implementation of Medicare Part D was an irresponsible political maneuver by the Bush administration to win reelection in 2004 that has been costly and inefficient and that has enriched the drug companies and the insurance industry at the expense of seniors and taxpayers. In addition, since 1997, Congress has cut Medicare payments to doctors (physicians could face a cumulative 40% reduction in Medicare payments by 2015 if no congressional action takes place[46]), raising fears that an increasing number of them will stop seeing Medicare patients.[47]

Concerns have intensified all the more as it has become clear that drug makers, ever since the inception of Medicare Part D, took this opportunity to raise their prices even more—something that had been forewarned by many observers as the legislation was debated. One of the problems is that under the provisions of President Bush's Medicare reform plan, Medicare is barred from using its powerful purchasing power to negotiate steeper discounts with manufacturers. At the same time, it is to reimburse expensive "me-too" drugs—i.e., drugs that are structurally very similar to already known drugs, with only minor differences—as well as more cost-effective drugs. These provisions also banned pegging drug prices to average wholesale prices, as used to be done in hospitals.[48]

In a study published in March 2008 by the AARP (formerly known as the American Association of Retired Persons),[49] brand-name drugs most commonly prescribed to the elderly under Medicare Part D rose by an average of 7.4% in 2007—i.e., nearly 2.5 times the rate of general inflation. The watchdog report produced by AARP's Public Policy Institute studied the prices of 220 brand-name drugs from 2002 through 2007 and found that 216 of these drugs underwent a price increase.[50] Specifically, the study looked at the prices charged to wholesalers and noted that the price increases have been significantly greater since the Medicare drug benefit began on January 1, 2006. In the 4 years prior to the benefit's initiation, wholesale prices rose between 5.3% and 6.6% a year. Nearly all increases exceeded the rate of general inflation. The report found that the average treatment cost exploded from $80 per year per prescription in 2002 to $151 in 2007. According to the report, an older American who took three brand-name prescriptions to treat a chronic condition over this period of time, for example, saw an increase in his or her costs of more than $1,600 between 2002 and 2007.

In August 2010, the AARP published another study demonstrating that pharmaceutical firms raised their wholesale prices for 217 brand-name prescription drugs widely used by Medicare beneficiaries by about 8.3%, which was notably higher than the rate of increase observed during any of the prior 4 years (i.e., 2005–2008), which ranged from 6.0% to 7.9%. In contrast, the rate of general inflation was −0.3% over the same period (see Figure 1.2).[51]

Among all the drugs included in the study, the prostatic hypertrophy agent Flomax (Boehringer Ingerheilm) had the largest price increase, at 24.8%, followed by the analeptic Provigil (Cephalon), with a 22.7% increase, the open-angle glaucoma or ocular hypertension treatment agent Alphagan P (Allergan), with an increase of 21.5%, and the antacid reflux disease medication Prevacid (Takeda), with an increase of 21.3%. Popular drugs, such as the sleep aid Ambien (Sanofi-Aventis), antidemential drugs (e.g., for the treatment of Alzheimer's disease) such as Aricept (Eisai), and AztraZeneca's Seroquel, for the treatment of schizophrenia and bipolar disorder, showed dramatic increases as well. Prices also increased for three of the four top-selling brand-name products that recently faced their first generic

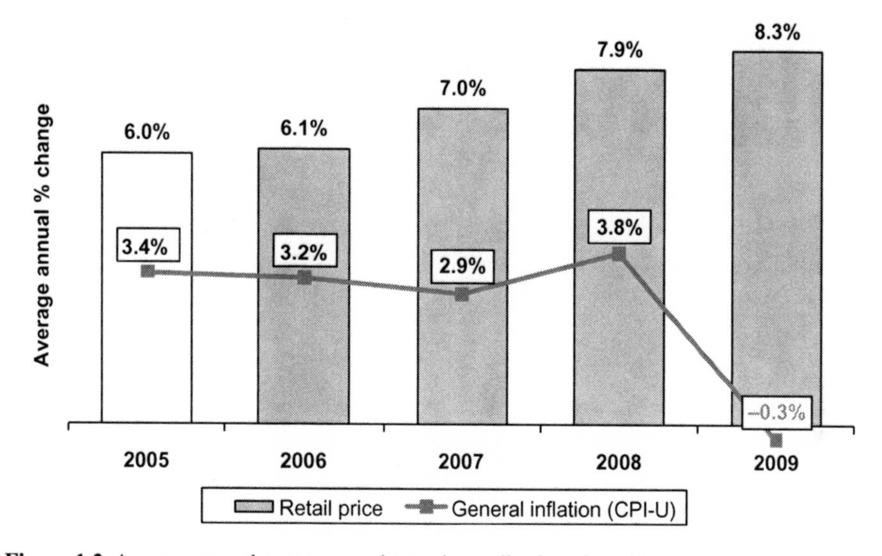

Figure 1.2 Average annual percentage change in retail prices for widely used brand-name prescription drugs continue to grow in 2009.
Note: Calculations exclude Zyrtec 10 mg tablets, which began to be sold over the counter (that is, without a prescription) in January 2008. Calculations also exclude Risperdal 0.25 mg tablets and Risperdal 4 mg tablets due to insufficient price data. Shaded bars indicate years when Medicare Part D was operational. Prepared by the AARP Public Policy Institute and the *PRIME* Institute, University of Minnesota, based on data from Thomson Reuters MarketScan® Research Databases.
Source: AARP Public Policy Institute, 2010. Trends in retail prices of brand name prescription drugs widely used by Medicare beneficiaries 2005–2009. Rx Price Watch Report. AARP Public Policy Institute, Washington, DC. http://assets.aarp.org/rgcenter/ppi/health-care/rxpricewatch.pdf.

competitors: Wyeth's Protonix 40 mg tablets EC (generic first available in January 2008), Pfizer's Norvasc 5 and 10 mg tablets (March 2007), and Takeda's Prevacid 30 mg DR capsules (November 2009). Price increases for these drugs ranged from 4.3% to 8.8% in 2009 (see Table 1.3). It is ironic that while health care reform is aiming at saving $8 billion in costs a year, this recent increase in prices by the pharmaceutical industry—the highest since 1992—adds an additional $10 billion to the US drug bill, which, in 2009, was more than $300 billion.[52] It is suspected that this dramatic rise in prescription drug pricing has been implemented in anticipation of the upcoming US health care reforms, and as such, it is being subjected to further investigation by the US federal government[53]—and rightly so.

Because Medicare cannot negotiate prices directly with drug manufacturers, companies have found an interesting alternate strategy: increase prices to wholesalers and other direct purchasers. This is important because overall, the manufacturer's wholesale price is the most substantial component of a prescription drug's retail price. It is true that insurance companies, such as those that cover Medicare beneficiaries, could negotiate confidential rebates from the manufacturer and that plans could cancel out a higher wholesale price by negotiating a steeper discount with the manufacturer or

Table 1.3 Retail Price Increases for the Top 25 Brand-Name Prescription Drugs in 2009

Rank by Sales among Study Market Basket[a]	Product Name, Strength, and Dosage Form	Package Size	Manufacturer	Therapeutic Class	Retail Price per Day	Annual Percentage Change in Retail Price
1	Nexium 40 mg capsule	30	AstraZeneca	Ulcer drugs (PPIs)	$5.40	6.0%
2	Plavix 75 mg tablet	90	Bristol-Myers Squibb	Anticoagulants	$5.06	8.8%
3	Prevacid 30 mg DR capsule	100	Takeda	Ulcer drugs (PPIs)	$5.50	7.0%
4	Protonix 40 mg tablet	90	Wyeth	Ulcer drugs (PPIs)	$4.21	6.8%
5	Lipitor 20 mg tablet	90	Pfizer	Cholesterol agents (HMG CoA)	$4.03	4.1%
6	Lipitor 10 mg tablet	90	Pfizer	Cholesterol agents (HMG CoA)	$2.84	4.2%
7	Aricept 10 mg tablet	30	Eisai	Antidementia agents	$6.59	10.8%
8	Fosamax 70 mg tablet	4	Merck	Osteoporosis agents	$2.92	3.4%
9	Norvasc 10 mg tablet	90	Pfizer	Antihypertensives (CCBs)	$2.66	4.4%
10	Advair Diskus 250-50 mist	60	GlaxoSmithKline	Respiratory agents	$6.65	5.8%
11	Lipitor 40 mg tablet	90	Pfizer	Cholesterol agents (HMG CoA)	$4.03	4.1%
12	Actonel 35 mg tablet	4	Warner Chilcott Pharm	Osteoporosis agents	$3.44	8.1%
13	Norvasc 5 mg tablet	90	Pfizer	Antihypertensives (CCBs)	$1.95	4.3%
14	Celebrex 200 mg capsule	100	Pfizer	Anti-Inflammatory agents	$3.72	4.4%

15	Namenda 10 mg tablet	60	Forest	Antidementia agents	$5.80	8.5%
16	Singulair 10 mg tablet	30	Merck	Respiratory agents	$3.85	8.1%
17	Flomax 0.4 mg capsule	100	Boehringer Ingelheim	Prostatic Hypertrophy agents	$4.09	24.8%
18	Zetia 10 mg tablet	30	Merck/Schering-Plough	Cholesterol agents (HMG CoA)	$3.42	9.3%
19	Lexapro 10 mg tablet	100	Forest	Antidepressants (SSRIs)	$2.86	5.7%
20	Lantus 100/ml inj	10	Sanofi-Aventis	Antidiabetics (Insulins)	$8.95	8.5%
21	Zocor 20 mg tablet	30	Merck	Cholesterol agents (HMG CoA)	$4.84	2.3%
22	Ambien 10 mg tablet	100	Sanofi-Aventis	Sedatives	$5.11	13.1%
23	Seroquel 200 mg tablet	100	AstraZeneca	Antipsychotics	$8.29	13.0%
24	Zocor 40 mg tablet	30	Merck	Cholesterol agents (HMG CoA)	$4.84	2.3%
25	Avandia 4 mg tablet	30	GlaxoSmithKline	Antidiabetics (Oral)	$3.86	8.6%
General rate of inflation (as measured by growth in CPI-U)						−0.3%

Source: AARP Public Policy Institute, 2010. Trends in retail prices of brand name prescription drugs widely used by Medicare beneficiaries 2005–2009. Rx Price Watch Report. AARP Public Policy Institute, Washington, DC. http://assets.aarp.org/rgcenter/ppi/health-care/rxpricewatch.pdf. © AARP. Reprinted with permission. All rights reserved.
Prepared by the AARP Public Policy Institute and the *PRIME* Institute, University of Minnesota, based on data from Thomson Reuters MarketScan® Research Databases.
[a]Ranking based on prescription payments made by the Medicare Part D plan provider during 2006.

by lowering their reimbursement rates to pharmacies; nevertheless, a change in the wholesale price generally leads to a similar percentage change in the price of most prescriptions because an individual plan's power to negotiate is rather limited compared to the U.S. Department of Veterans Affairs, which can negotiate very steep discounts. So in the end, it is the consumer who ultimately gets stuck with the bill.

Theoretically, with Medicare Part D, the plans would shift people to lower-cost generic drugs, which, according to government economists, account for two thirds of all prescriptions.[54] But the savings from people shifting to generics—approximately 59% of all prescriptions of the Medicare Part D plan and 23.9% of drug expenditures—is, of course, being offset by the higher prices for brand-name drugs, which account for 41% of all prescriptions of the Medicare Part D plan and 76% of drug expenditures.[55] So while Medicare is helping millions to afford prescription drugs, the continuous rise in price of brand-name drugs increases the likelihood of higher insurance premiums and the threat that consumers will fall into the Medicare coverage gap increasing the out-of-pocket expenses of those who find themselves in the doughnut hole.[56] In fact, in October 2009, federal officials announced that in 2010, basic Medicare premiums will increase by 15%, affecting 12 million people, or 27% of Medicare beneficiaries.[57]

But this is not the whole story. One of the major complications brought up by the tiered system established by Medicare, and by the increasing cost of brand-name drugs, is that overall, health insurance companies are rapidly adopting the new pricing system for very expensive drugs, asking patients to pay hundreds and even thousands of dollars for prescriptions for medications that may save their lives or slow the progress of serious diseases. With the new pricing system, insurers abandoned the traditional arrangement that had patients pay a fixed amount, such as $10, $20, or $30, for a prescription, no matter what the drug's actual cost. Instead, they are charging all patients a percentage of the cost of certain high-priced drugs, usually 20–33%, which can amount to thousands of dollars a month. This means that affording medications is not only a problem for the poor—now, even the insured are affected by the burden of very expensive health care. For instance, Tier 4, which began in earnest with Medicare drug plans and which is incorporated into 86% of Medicare health insurance plans, is now showing up as part of insurance plans that people buy on their own or acquire through employers, and it is the fastest-growing segment in private insurance.[58] A few years ago, that tier was virtually nonexistent in private plans, but now, 10% of private plans have Tier 4 drug categories that correspond to so-called specialty drugs. In the case of some medicines and so-called orphan drugs, which are drugs used to treat patients with illnesses that affect 200,000 people or less in the United States,[59] some programs have even higher copayments—a level that is known as Tier 5. Private insurers began offering Tier 4 plans in response to employers who were looking for ways to keep costs down. Though people who need Tier 4 drugs pay more for these medicines, other subscribers in the plan pay less for their coverage.

Though the exact number of patients affected by this system is still unknown, the truth is that many drugs (called specialty drugs)—many of which are biotechnology products—used to treat diseases such as multiple sclerosis, rheumatoid arthritis, hemophilia, hepatitis C, some cancers, and human growth hormone deficiency, among other conditions, belong to this category and are extremely expensive (see Tables 1.4 and 1.5

Table 1.4 Biotech Drugs Routinely Quoted in Price Controls

Product	Company	Indication	Approximate Average Monthly Cost[a] (US$)
Zevalin (Ibritumomab tiuxetan)	Spectrum Pharmaceuticals	B-cell non-Hodgkin Lymphoma	24,000–30,000
Cerezyme (Imiglucerase)	Genzyme	Gaucher disease	16,000
Avastin (Bevacizumab)	Genentech/Roche	Colorectal cancer	4,400–8,333
Zavesca (Miglustat)	Actelion	Gaucher disease	4,200
Herceptin (Trastuzumab)	Genentech/Roche	Breast cancer	3,250
Enbrel (Etanercept)	Amgen and Wyeth	Rheumatoid arthritis	2,187
Rebif (Interferon beta-1a)	EMD Serono and Pfizer	Multiple sclerosis	3,292
Erbitux (Cetuximab)	ImClone and Bristol-Myers Squibb (and Merck in the rest of the world)	Colorectal cancer	10,000–17,000
Humira (Adalimumab)	Abbott	Rheumatoid arthritis and Crohn's disease	2,122
Gleevec (Imatinib)	Novartis	Leukemia and gastrointestinal stromal tumor	4,702
Epogen (Epoetin alfa)	Amgen	Anemia of chronic renal disease	704
Nexavar (Sorafenib)	Bayer Pharmaceuticals	Advance renal carcinoma/advanced hepatic carcinoma	6,000–8,000
Revlimid (Lenalidomide)	Celgene	Multiple myeoloma/ Myelodysplastic syndrome	6,000–8,000
Rituxan (Rituximab)	Genentech	B-cell non-Hodgkin lymphoma, Leukemia	4,200–13,000

Source: Multiple Internet and other sources.
[a]Dosing duration of all medicines is highly variable, but most regimes require at least one month.

Table 1.5 The World's Most Expensive Biotech Drugs

Brand-Name Drug	Company	Indication	Wholesale Price (WSP) (US$)	Dosage	Approximate Average Annual Cost[a] (US$)
Soliris (Eculizumab)	Alexion Pharmaceuticals	Paroxysmal nocturnal hemoglobinuria disease (PNH)	SOL, IV (PF) 10 mg/ml, 30 ml = 6,3000	The usual starting dose of Soliris is 600 milligrams (mg) every 7 days for the first 4 weeks, followed by 900 mg for the fifth dose 7 days later, then 900 mg every 14 days thereafter.	409,500
Elaprase (Idursulfase)	Shire Pharmaceuticals	Hunter syndrome	SOL, IV (PF) 2 mg/ml, 3 ml = 3,153.84	The recommended dosage of Elaprase is 0.5 mg/kg of body weight given every week through intravenous infusion.	375,000
Naglazyme (Arylsulfatase B)	BioMarin Pharmaceuticals	Maroteaux-Lamy syndrome	SOL, IV (PF) 1 mg/ml, 5 ml = 1,956	The recommended dosage regimen of Naglazyme is 1 mg/kg of body weight administered once weekly as an intravenous infusion.	365,000
Cinryze (C1-inhibitor)	ViroPharma	Hereditary angiodema (HAE)	C1 esterase inhibitor, human PDS, IV, 500 u, e.a. = 2,520.38	A dose of 1,000 Units Cinryze can be administered every 3 or 4 days for routine prophylaxis against angioedema attacks in HAE patients.	350,000
Myozyme (Alglucosidase alfa)	Genzyme	Pompe disease	PDS, IV (PF) 50 mg, e.a. = 720.00	The recommended dosage regimen of Myozyme is 20 mg 2.2 pounds of body weight, every 2 weeks as an intravenous (IV) infusion. The total volume is determined by body weight and should be given over approximately 4 h.	300,000

Arcalyst (Rilonacept)	Regeneron	Cryopyrin-associated periodic syndromes (CAPS)	PDS,SC (PF) 220 mg, 4 s e.a. = 24,000.00	The usual dosage of Arcalyst is 320 mg given as two injections of 160 mg each on the same day at two different sites. Dosing should continue with a once weekly injection of 160 mg.	250,000
Fabrazyme (Alpha-galactosidase)	Genzyme	Fabry disease	PDS, IV (PF) 35 mg, e.a. = 5,403.60	The recommended dosage of Fabrazyme is 1.0 mg/kg of body weight administered every 2 weeks as an intravenous infusion.	200,000
Cerezyme (Imiglucerase)	Genzyme	Gaucher disease	PDS, IV (Vial) 400 u, e.a. = 1,903.20	Dosage of Cerezyme should be individualized to each patient. Initial dosages range from 2.5 U/kg of body weight 3 times a week to 60 U/kg once every 2 weeks. 60 U/kg every 2 weeks is the dosage for which the most data are available.	200,000
Aldurazyme (Iduronidase)	Genzyme/ BioMarin Pharma	Hurler syndrome	Sol, IV (PF) 0.58 mg/ml, 5 ml = 840.00	The recommended dosage regimen of Aldurazyme is 0.58 mg/kg of body weight administered once weekly as an intravenous infusion.	200,000

Sources: Red Book (2010 Ed.), PDRHealth, RxList, Forbes.
Dosing duration of all medicines is highly variable, but most regimes require at least one month.
Estimated cost for a typical adult patient. Dosage may vary based on a patient's weight and other factors.
[a]According to Forbes (2010).

for a summary of biotech products that are routinely quoted in price control debates). There are no cheaper equivalents for these drugs, so patients are forced to pay the price or simply forgo treatment. Therefore, it is surprising that insurers claim that the new system of reimbursement keeps everyone's premiums down at a time when some of the most innovative and promising new treatments for conditions like cancer, rheumatoid arthritis, and multiple sclerosis can cost $100,000 or more a year, discounting the remaining medical expenses, which, in a country like the United States, can be astronomical. The reality is that many patients end up spending more for a drug than they pay for their mortgages and, in some cases, more than their monthly incomes. It is estimated that 1.85 million Americans are driven to bankruptcy every year by health care bills,[60] and the number continues to increase. It is estimated that medical bills account for more than 62% of bankruptcies filed in the United States.[61]

Traditionally, the idea of insurance was to spread the costs of paying for the sick among a wide population. But now, the situation is inverted: the more the sick person pays, the less the healthy person pays. As a result, those beneficiaries who bear the burden of illness also bear the burden of huge bills, and private insurers can, with no advance notice, legally change their coverage to one in which some drugs are Tier 4. Examples of drugs classified as Tier 4 include Sprycel, for the treatment of chronic myelogenous leukemia, which costs more than $13,500 for a 90-day supply. Another is Tykerb, used in the treatment of metastatic cancer, that costs, $3,480 for 150 tablets, which may last a patient 21 days.[62] And these are only examples of Tier 4 drugs in the mid-price range.

How could an uninsured person or someone living on Social Security disability or on Medicaid, for example, pay for those drugs when the Medicaid program, which assumes the tab of 40–60% of the poor, has severe coverage limitations and is currently under intense political attack?

The problem of affording health care is most acute for people with no insurance, who represent a group of approximately 50 million in the United States. With the economic slowdown of recent years, the number of people without health insurance has increased and millions of additional people are threatened with the loss of insurance. But these people find that coverage is too limited or that they cannot afford to pay their share of medical costs, and therefore they deal with the issue of paying for very expensive drugs. Many of the 158 million people in the United States covered by employer health insurance are struggling to meet medical expenses that are much higher than they used to be—often because of some combination of higher premiums,[63] less extensive coverage, and greater out-of-pocket deductibles and copayments. As of mid-2008, 57 million Americans were living in families struggling with medical bills, and the vast majority of them—43 million—had insurance coverage.[64]

Since the recession began in 2001, an employee's average cost of annual health care premiums for family coverage has nearly doubled—to $3,354, up from $1,800—while incomes have come nowhere close to keeping up. The total annual cost for family coverage now averages $12,680, up 5% from 2007.[65] Taking into consideration other out-of-pocket medical costs, the portion of the average American household's income that goes toward health care has risen about 12% and is now approaching one fifth of the average household's spending. These are staggering numbers when one considers that only 7% of people in the United States feel financially prepared for their future health care needs.[66] It is no wonder, then, that poll after poll reflects that the majority of the people in the United States no longer trust and respect their government's health care policies or the drug or insurance companies. Nearly one of every five families had problems paying medical bills in 2007. More than half of these families said that they borrowed money to pay these expenses, and nearly 20% of those having difficulty said they contemplated declaring personal bankruptcy as a result of their medical bills.[67]

As said before, it is often claimed that prescription drugs account for only 10–12% of total health care costs.[68] However, given the economic slowdown, the financial disasters that struck the world in 2008, and the fact that many people have to pay a large portion of medical costs out of pocket, 10–12% is still a large percentage. In the United States, the percentage of people aged 50 or older has increased significantly because the baby boom generation is beginning to reach that age, and statistical analyses project that from 2000 to 2030, the number of Americans over age 65 will double to around 71.5 million.[69] Unfortunately, the very unhealthy lifestyle of the United States is increasing the incidence of many chronic disorders, such as diabetes, atherosclerosis, and hypertension, which will continue to increase health costs to the point of bleeding state and federal budgets and creating great disincentives for private companies to provide health insurance coverage. The drugs used to treat such chronic conditions are very costly, and millions of people are struggling with these costs, not only in the United States, supposed to be the most powerful nation on the planet, but globally as well.

On the basis of all we have considered in this chapter, there is no doubt that the United States desperately needs health care reform. But is the US government health care reform plan, as it is now designed, heading in the right direction, or is it heading for a major disaster? Before attempting to answer this question, let us take a look at what is happening in the rest of the world—the scenario there is no less dismal.

Notes

1. This has been publicly acknowledged by the US Secretary of Health and Human Services, Kathleen Sebelius, in an interview by *The Wall Street Journal* published at the end of 2009. Sebelius, K., 2009. Laying the groundwork. The Wall Street Journal, November 23. http://online.wsj.com/article/SB100014240527487042043045745440638910 42666.html.
2. Reference pricing is defined as any reimbursement rule used by a third-party payer or regulator that sets the maximum reimbursement for one product by referring to the price of some other comparable product in the same market. Danzon, P.M., 2001. Reference pricing: theory of evidence. Wharton School, University of Pennsylvania, May 22, 2001. http://hc.wharton.upenn.edu/danzon/PDF%20Files/barcelonaEditfinal%20.pdf.
3. With differential pricing, identical products are priced differently for different types of customers, markets, or buying situations. See Danzon, P.M., Towse, A., 2003. Differential pricing for pharmaceuticals: reconciling access, R&D and patents. International Journal of Health Care Finance and Economics 3, 183–205.

4. Kaplan, W., Laing, R., 2004. Priority Medicines for Europe and the World. World Health Organization, Geneva, p. v.
5. Fortune 500, The most profitable industries, May 4, 2009. http://money.cnn.com/magazines/fortune/fortune500/2009/performers/industries/profits/.
6. US health care: world's most expensive. Voice of America, February 28, 2006. http://www.voanews.com/english/archive/2006-02/2006-02-28-voa59.cfm?CFID=107577751&CFTOKEN=98766785&jsessionid=de30ff6f1cbbfd2762492e5d535227661b66.
7. Herrera, S., 2006. Price controls: preparing for the unthinkable. Nature Biotechnology 24, 257–260.
8 Here, I differentiate between universal health care and its equivalent based on Trudy Lieberman's observation that "both [Hillary Clinton and Barack Obama] have used the word 'universal' to describe a potpourri of options that could bring coverage to some portion of the population currently not covered while keeping commercial insurance in the game." Lieberman, T., 2008. Cautionary healthcare tales from California and Massachusetts. The Nation, March 25, 2008. http://www.thenation.com/doc/20080407/lieberman.
9. Toner, R., 1993. Clinton's health plan; poll on changes in health care finds support amid skepticism. New York Times, September 22, 1993.
10. Krugman, P., Wells, R., 2006. The health care crisis and what to do about it. New York Review of Books, March 23, 2006. http://www.nybooks.com/articles/18802.
11. National Coalition on Health Care. Health care costs. http://www.nchc.org/documents/Fact%20Sheets/Fact%20Sheet%20-%20Cost%208-10-09.pdf.
12. The Obama plan. http://www.barackobama.com/issues/healthcare/.
13. Pear, R., 2009. Obama signs children's health insurance bill. New York Times, February 4, 2009. http://www.nytimes.com/2009/02/05/us/politics/05health.html?_r=1&hp.
14. Herszenhorn, D.M., Pear, R., 2009. Democrats may limit tax increase for health plan. New York Times, July 20, 2009. http://www.nytimes.com/2009/07/21/health/policy/21health.html?_r=1&scp=1&sq=nancy%20pelosi%20health%20care%20surtax&st = cse.
15. Calmes, J., Pear, R., 2009. Obama budget taxes richest to help pay for health care. New York Times, February 26, 2009. http://www.nytimes.com/2009/02/26/us/politics/26budget.html?_r=1&hp.
16. Espo, D., 2009. Drug industry agrees to improve benefits for seniors. Boston Globe, June 21, 2009. http://www.boston.com/news/nation/articles/2009/06/21/drug_firms_agree_to_improve_benefits_for_seniors/.
17. According to Standard and Poor's (June 3, 2010):

    "Early on, the US-based pharmaceutical industry recognized the potentially unfavorable ramifications of many of the healthcare reforms being proposed by President Obama and Congressional Democrats. Acting through its Washington-based lobbying arm, the Pharmaceutical Research and Manufacturers of America (PhRMA), and under the leadership of its president, Billy Tauzin, PhRMA took a proactive role in reaching a deal with the Obama Administration on a version of healthcare reform that included some compromises—agreeing to some significant concessions, while successfully blocking some of the more threatening issues.

    Proposals that were blocked included several that could have caused damaging major structural changes to the industry. These included measures such as the public option, which would have established a government-run insurance program to compete with private sector plans; the reimportation of inexpensive drugs from Canada and other foreign countries; and mandating rebates on drugs used by indigent seniors covered by either Medicare or Medicaid (known as 'dual eligible' rebates). However, probably the most damaging from the industry's perspective would have been a directive for the federal government to negotiate Medicare Part D drug pricing directly with pharmaceutical manufacturers. Under the present law, negotiations must be handled through managed care organizations and other private sector buyers.

Another potential negative for the pharmaceutical industry that did not appear in final healthcare reform legislation was a proposal to eliminate the present deferral of US taxes on foreign earnings of multinational corporations. President Obama's initial 2010 budget proposal included a provision to save $210 billion from 2010 through 2019 by 'implementing international enforcement, reform deferral, and other tax reform policies,' which many believed was a reference to removing the tax deferral in foreign earnings.

Under current law, those earnings are not taxed until they are repatriated back to the United States. For the large capitalization US-based pharmaceutical companies, which generate close to two fifths of revenues from international sales, new US taxes on foreign profits would materially affect earnings. We estimate that such a change would have raised Big Pharma's estimated average tax rate to 35%, from 23%, and reduced industry profits by more than 15%. While indicating that this proposal would not be implemented at the present time, President Obama did not rule our revisiting it at some future date.

The new healthcare reform law also left out a proposal that would have prohibited branded/generic patent settlements—agreements whereby branded drugmakers to pay or otherwise compensate generic producers for keeping generics off the market. The Federal Trade Commission (FTC) under Jon Liebowitz has been staunchly opposed to these deals, which are considered anticompetitive and detrimental to consumer interests, because they delay the entry of cheaper generics into the market for several years. We believe the issue may also be revisited in the future, given its prior support by President Obama and its consumer friendly theme." Standard and Poor's, 2010. Industry surveys. Health care: Pharmaceuticals, June 3, 2010, 1–2.

18. Abridged from "Obama's health care speech to Congress," September 9, 2009. http://www.nytimes.com/2009/09/10/us/politics/10obama.text.html.
19. According to Rep. Charles Boustany, the Obama health care proposal "creates 53 new government bureaucracies, adds hundreds of billions to our national debt, and raises taxes on job-creators by $600 billion" and also "cuts Medicare by $500 billion, while doing virtually nothing to make the program better for our seniors." Boustany, C. Response to Obama's health care speech, September 9, 2009. http://abcnews.go.com/Politics/HealthCare/charles-boustany-republican-rebuttal-obama-health-care-speech/story?id=8527214.
20. Pear, R., 2009. Senate passes health care overhaul bill. New York Times, December 24, 2009. http://www.nytimes.com/2009/12/25/health/policy/25health.html?_r=2&hp.
21. Stolberg, S.G., Herszenhorn, D.M., 2010. Obama's health bill plan largely follows Senate version. New York Times, February 22, 2010. http://www.nytimes.com/2010/02/23/health/policy/23health.html?pagewanted=1&hp.
22. According to Moody's Investors Service (June, 2010): "[This is exactly] when the pharmaceutical industry will start to benefit from the [health care reform] law. Expansion is to be achieved through employer mandates to provide coverage, individual mandates to purchase coverage, government subsidies for lower-income individuals, and broader eligibility criteria for the state-based Medicaid programs." This means that although the pharmaceutical industry will be slightly affected by the Obama health care reform law between 2010 and 2013 due to concessions on the pharmaceutical industry's part, such as higher Medicaid rebates (starting in January 1, 2010, the minimum rebate for drugs funded by the Medicaid program has been increased from 15.1% to 23.1%); new user

fees (effective January 1, 2011, the branded drug industry will begin paying a non-tax-deductible user fee, allocated based on market share in government-funded benefit programs. The user fee totals $2.5 billion in 2011 and steadily rises, peaking at $4.1 billion in 2018 before declining to $2.8 billion annually thereafter); and Medicare doughnut hole discounts (beginning January 1, 2011, branded drug companies will have to offer 50% discounts for seniors in Medicare Part D plans that are affected by the "doughnut hole"), it will more than make up for this "investment," beginning in 2014. Moody's Investors Service. Industry Outlook: Global Pharmaceuticals, June, 2010, pp. 7–8.

23. Sack, K., 2010. Judge voids key element of Obama health care law. New York Times, December 13, 2010. http://www.nytimes.com/2010/12/14/health/policy/14health.html?hp.
24. Lieberman. Cautionary health care tales.
25. National Coalition on Health Care. Health care costs.
26. According to some estimates, Medicaid consumes 22% of the average state budget, paying 40–60% of the tab for their poor. Harris, G.G., 2005. Fixing welfare seemed like a snap. New York Times, June 16, 2005.
27. This has been discussed by Julius Richmond and Rashi Fein, The Health Care Mess, as cited by Krugman and Wells, "The health care crisis."
28. DeNavas-Walt, C.B., Proctor, B.D., Smith, J., 2008. Income, poverty, and health insurance coverage in the United States: 2007. US Census Bureau, August 2008. http://www.census.gov/prod/2008pubs/p60-235.pdf. See also census data from August 2006.
29. Fast facts on the US health care crisis. ABC News, October 13, 2006. http://abcnews.go.com/WNT/PrescriptionForChange/story?id=2563381.
30. Organisation for Economic Co-Operation and Development, 2006. Commonwealth Fund: Results from a Scorecard. OECD, Paris.
31. National Coalition on Health Care. Health care costs.
32. Krugman, Wells. The health care crisis.
33. Ibid.
34. This is more evidence of the influence that pharmaceutical development has on health care.
35. Unless major measures are implemented to prevent "crowd-out"; that is, that public insurance premiums must be priced comparably to private market coverage so people will not be tempted to use the state's plan instead of buying from an insurance company.
36. Moody's Investors Service. Teleconference, June 9, 2010.
37. Certain people younger than age 65 can qualify for Medicare, too, including those who have disabilities and those who have permanent kidney failure or amyotrophic lateral sclerosis (Lou Gehrig's disease).
38. Medicare is financed by a portion of the payroll taxes paid by workers and their employers. It is also financed in part by monthly premiums deducted from Social Security checks. The Centers for Medicare and Medicaid Services is the agency in charge of the Medicare program, but patients apply for Medicare at their local Social Security office.
39. Summer, L., *et al.*, 2008. Medicare Part D 2009 Data Spotlight: Low-Income Subsidy Plan Availability. Henry J. Kaiser Family Foundation, November. http://www.kff.org/medicare/upload/7836.pdf.
40. These plans are not required to pay for all covered Part D drugs, and they can change the drugs on their formularies during the course of the year with 60 days' notice to affected parties. So with Part D, more seniors have drug benefits but, at the same time, an overwhelming number of plan choices, something not easily managed by a senior person. Once beneficiaries are in a plan, they face complex and high-level cost sharing and formulary structures and therefore have a substantial financial stake in their decision whether to start or stop a medication and in determining which medications offer the greatest value to them. See http://www.cms.hhs.gov/home/medicare.asp.

41. The structure of this reimbursement system (including the doughnut hole) was created by Congress to allow greater coverage to patients without making the system go broke over the ensuing years. This part of Medicare Part D has created great controversy in the United States.
42. http://www.cms.hhs.gov/home/medicare.asp.
43. According to a 2007 survey of 16,000 seniors by the Kaiser Foundation, Commonwealth Fund, and Tufts–New England Medical Center. Andreopoulos, S., 2008. Medicare Part D threatens program budget. San Francisco Chronicle, February 27, 2008, Section B-9. http://articles.sfgate.com/2008-02-07/opinion/17142487_1_drug-benefits-drug-coverage-seniors-and-taxpayers.
44. Editorial. Medicare's financial woes. New York Times, March 28, 2008. http://www.nytimes.com/2008/03/28/opinion/28fri2.html?ref=opinion.
45. Reinberg, S., 2008. Bush's budget proposal would cut Medicare spending. Washington Post, February 5, 2008. http://www.washingtonpost.com/wp-dyn/content/article/2008/02/04/AR2008020402490.html.
46. Democrats push to reverse Medicare payment cuts to doctors, October 21, 2009. http://edition.cnn.com/2009/POLITICS/10/20/health.care/index.html.
47. Andreopoulos. Medicare Part D threatens program budget.
48. Angell, M., 2004. The Truth about the Drug Companies: How They Deceive Us and What to Do about It. Random House, New York.
49. AARP Public Policy Institute, 2008. Trends in Manufacturer Prices of Brand Name Prescription Drugs Used by Medicare Beneficiaries 2002 to 2007. Watchdog Report. AARP Public Policy Institute, Washington, DC. No matter what type of measures one uses to evaluate brand-name drug prices, the average increase in prescription drug prices by and large outstrips inflation. It is estimated that 70% of the population over age 50 is having problems paying for prescription drugs, according to John Rother, director of policy and strategy of the AARP. Rother is correct when he says that "some of these [drugs] are wonder drugs, but they can't realize their potential if people can't afford to buy them."
50. Ibid.
51. AARP Public Policy Institute, 2010. Trends in Retail Prices of Brand Name Prescription Drugs Widely Used by Medicare Beneficiaries 2005 to 2009. Rx Price Watch Report. AARP Public Policy Institute, Washington, DC. http://assets.aarp.org/rgcenter/ppi/health-care/rxpricewatch.pdf.
52. Wilson, D., 2009. Drug makers raise prices in face of health care reform. New York Times, November 15, 2009. http://www.nytimes.com/2009/11/16/business/16drugprices.html?_r=1.
53. Wilson, D., 2009. Rising prices of drugs lead to calls for inquiry. New York Times, November 18, 2009. http://www.nytimes.com/2009/11/19/health/policy/19drugs.html?src=linkedin.
54. Ibid.
55. Ibid.
56. Beginning January 1, 2011, branded drug companies offer 50% discounts for seniors in Medicare Part D plans that are affected by the "doughnut hole."
57. Pear, R., 2009. Medicare premiums to rise 15 percent as costs jump. New York Times, October 19, 2009. http://www.nytimes.com/2009/10/20/health/policy/20health.html?_r=1&hpw.
58. Kolata, G., 2008. Co-payments soar for drugs with high prices. New York Times, April 14, 2008. http://www.nytimes.com/2008/04/14/us/14drug.html?pagewanted=1.
59. In Europe, an orphan disease is one with an incidence of 5 in 10,000 people.
60. National Coalition on Health Care. Health care facts: costs. http://www.nchc.org/facts/cost.shtml.

61. Tamkins, T., 2009. Medical bills prompt more than 60 percent of US bankruptcies. CNN, June 5, 2009. http://www.cnn.com/2009/HEALTH/06/05/bankruptcy.medical.bills/index.html. This is based on a Harvard study by Steffie Woolhandler, published in August 2009 in the *American Journal of Medicine*.
62. Kolata. Co-payments soar.
63. For instance, in February 2010, Anthem Blue Cross, a California-based unit of WellPoint, a major health insurance company, informed subscribers in California that premiums for individual insurance policies would rise an average of 25%, with some rates going up as much as 39%. Pear, R., 2010. Health executive defends premiums. New York Times, February 24, 2010. http://www.nytimes.com/2010/02/25/health/policy/25health.html?ref=politics.
64. Abelson, R., 2008. Health care costs increase strain, studies find. New York Times, September 24, 2008. Section C4. http://www.nytimes.com/2008/09/25/business/25health.html.
65. Ibid.
66. Ibid.
67. Ibid.
68. Herrera. Price controls.
69. Administration on Aging. Statistics on the aging population. US Department of Health and Human Services, 2009. http://www.aoa.gov/AoARoot/Aging_Statistics/index.aspx.

2 The Health Care Crisis in Other Parts of the World

What he felt was a satisfaction of a sufferer who has always known only shame and the bite of conscience for hiding the suffering that cold, hard life brings, and who now, suddenly [...] receives elemental, formal justification for having felt such suffering in this world—in the best of all possible worlds, which by means of playful scorn was proved to be the worst world imaginable.

—Thomas Mann,* Buddenbrooks *(1901)

European health care has been traditionally characterized as a socialized, supportive, publicly funded welfare system in which national health care is administered and provided for by the government. In fact, for decades, advocates of socialized medicine in the United States and Canada have maintained that health care systems financed by taxes and under government control, such as European ones, are more efficient than private sector models in their ability to control costs and maintain the quality of health care. Although European health care systems are certainly more egalitarian (and health care services are cheaper) than their US counterpart, most European countries are facing tremendous problems that make these systems no longer sustainable as they are at present. Furthermore, it is very difficult to equate all European health care systems because one can observe remarkable differences from country to country.

One of the major problems facing Europe, and which, in many ways, is exacerbating the health care crisis there, is its rapidly aging population and low fertility rates, which are creating a demographic imbalance, especially as life expectancy has continued to increase. The imbalance between the young and the old is particularly marked in countries such as France, Germany, and Italy, and it is certainly creating much more pressure on their health care systems than those of countries such as the United States and Canada. Because state-funded and managed health care is financed in Europe on a pay-as-you-go basis (i.e., funds are spent as they come, leaving no room for capital reserves for the future), young people today pay for the health care needs of sick, and usually older, people and rely on future generations to do the same thing for them. The problem is that as the number of young people in European society declines, and as the world economy worsens and life becomes more expensive, the economic burden on the younger generation becomes unbearable and the government's only option is to reduce the quality of health care. Moreover, introducing further economic and social reforms would be quite difficult, if not impossible, on a continent such as Europe, with long-established countries where change is not welcome. However, as we shall see, some important health care changes are slowly taking place in countries such as the Netherlands, Germany, and Switzerland.

The World's Health Care Crisis. DOI: 10.1016/B978-0-12-391875-8.00002-0

To keep costs under some control, European countries have created a variety of payment and reimbursement systems that include rationing, copayments, reference pricing, differential pricing, delays in decisions regarding the introduction and reimbursement of novelty drugs, and some horrendous rationing measures, such as denying treatment to insured patients if they are over a certain age or if they are afflicted by a specific disease—or if they purchase additional insurance, as is the case in Great Britain. Within this rationing scheme, it is not surprising to hear stories of public hospitals and clinics treating the elderly with old drugs that are known to cause deleterious secondary effects, such as deafness, so that the best and most effective medical and pharmaceutical resources are saved for younger people. Accelerating death if a person is too frail and sick, just to save money, as was known to happen in Belgium in 2001 in a process known as economic euthanasia,[1] is not part of a horror novel: this is a reality in Europe, the most civilized continent on the planet.

After many decades of mismanagement, European health care funds have reached their nadir: the demand for services and medicines is high, while the supply is nowhere close to meeting it. The difference between economically prosperous Western Europe and Eastern Europe is remarkable. Although we cannot discuss every European health care system here, two of the most powerful countries in Western Europe in particular face serious challenges that, if not resolved soon, will head to even greater socioeconomic problems: France and the United Kingdom. Let us discuss these nations now because their problems are representative of all that is taking place, both in Western and Eastern Europe.

The French Health Care System

The French universal health care system dates back to 1945, just after the end of World War II.[2] Health care in France is nonnegotiable: Compulsory health insurance covers the entire population, although in theory, to qualify for health coverage in France, it is necessary to have paid social insurance contributions, which are charged as a percentage of income (12.8% by the employer and 0.75% of salary plus 7.5% of whole income by the employee).[3] Fees, which are generally modest, are paid by the patient upon treatment and then claimed back from the state-run insurer, which makes no differentiation between private and public hospitals (half of all France's hospitals are state owned).[4] About 7 million people in France, those who meet the criteria of being poor, are exempt from paying fees.

The assumption underlying the French health care system is that people are unable to afford health care and that the government must assume all the burdens of the entire health care system. This is a system based on solidarity and personal responsibility, in which patients should be allowed to select what they believe best satisfies their needs. In fact, the French are allowed to consult as many doctors as they wish, regardless of whether the doctors are general practitioners or specialists,[5] whenever they wish (which implies a large consumption of medicine), and they still receive a refund of between 70% and 100% of their medical expenses by the government.[6] Any unpaid balance is taken up by the mutual companies to which most employers are subscribed, so health care and medicine are almost "free." Almost 90% of people in France have supplemental insurance, which is often paid in full or in part by employers. The problem is, as French economist Philippe Manière has pointed out, "when the demand for doctor care is met by a guarantee of unlimited services, with no costs and no constraints, the result, of course, will be a boom in health care consumption"[7]—in other words, overconsumption, which is exactly what France has experienced for many years now and which has put the system in danger of going bankrupt.

In fact, health care cost expenditures in France have been increasing at the alarming rate of 5–8% every year[8] over the past few years, and although it had a moderate growth of 3.8% in 2008, France has one of the largest percentages of health care expenditures among the industrialized countries (more than 11%).[9] Such figures are preoccupying as unemployment has increased, with less taxes being infused into the health care system as a result. Besides abuse, fraud and waste are other problems that have plagued the system for many years.

To keep medicine costs under control, the French government has demanded that pharmaceutical manufacturers indiscriminately cut their prices by a certain set percentage[10] (usually 5%). In addition, the pharmaceutical industry in France is heavily regulated by the Pharmaceutical Sector Agreement and by complex procedures necessary to gain approval for reimbursement. The regulations involve, among several other things, drug evaluation by the Transparency Commission and price regulation by the Economic Committee. The appendix of the Pharmaceutical Sector Agreement lists the rates of growth by therapeutic class that are allowed by the government. Companies can either negotiate and sign a "convention" agreement with the Economic Committee, or they can have their drug prices fixed, and probably reduced, by public decree. Interestingly, if sales exceed the target, companies have to make "penalty payments" of at least 25% of the excess. These penalties are called "quantity discounts for everybody"; in other words, companies can be punished for selling too much of a product.[11] Not surprisingly, this set of regulations has created a nightmare for the pharmaceutical industry in France.

One of the areas that has been severely affected, because of shortages of cash that is consumed elsewhere in the health care chain, is investment in research and development (R&D) in pharmaceuticals. Why is this? As soon as a new drug hits the market, health care organizations in France begin negotiations to determine the rate of refund that the health care body will accept. The issue is that, compared to other European countries, France's rate of refund for prescription drugs is very low, and pharmaceutical companies have no incentives to invest heavily in R&D. It is no wonder, then, that the pharmaceutical industry in France, which was at the forefront of innovation several decades ago, has not produced a single cutting-edge product in years, and because of low investment by the government in this sector, and because of the lack of economic incentives, it is quite unlikely that the situation will improve any time in the foreseeable future.

The French national health care system is currently on the verge of going bankrupt: In 2008, it had a deficit of over €10 billion (about US$15 billion) and was expected to reach €15 billion in 2009,[12] which, for the time being, the French government has financed with debt. The French health care system is no longer sustainable as it is, and major reforms are needed, as President Sarkozy has recently proposed, whether people like it or not.

The UK Health Care System

The situation in the United Kingdom is quite a different story. Great Britain is an industrialized country with a universal health care system that may well be the most inefficient in Western Europe. In the United Kingdom, the National Health Service (NHS) was created in 1948 to provide all its citizens with access to health care and medicines. But the system fell short from the very beginning: after the first year, the operating costs of NHS were £52 million higher than original estimates.[13] After many decades of severe limitations by this saturated system, such as extremely long waiting lists, shortages of doctors and resources, lack of access to medicines, and overall inefficiency, the British government allowed the introduction of some market-based health care competition to British citizens in 1989.[14] Even so, the situation in Britain remains quite dire.

Recently, a great scandal exploded in the United Kingdom when several NHS beneficiaries, currently under cancer treatment, are taking legal action against NHS for denying them treatment, including all the care associated with cancer such as scans, the cost of the administration of chemotherapy, radiotherapy, consultation with doctors, and blood tests,[15] after they purchased medicine out of pocket that doctors recommended as better treatment options, such as Avastin, Tarceva, Nexavar, and Tyverb, which are commonly prescribed in the United States for the same cancers. This plan of action would mean that once a patient pays privately for a drug, he or she has to pay privately for everything else as well, which could total a sum around £10,000 (or US$20,000) a month, if not higher, and that is not even including the medicine. These cancer patients have felt not only very disappointed but betrayed that after having paid taxes into the health service system during their adult lives, not only is it not there for them when they need it, but it is actually punishing them for doing what they think is best for themselves.

According to Alan Johnson, during his tenure as health secretary, "the government policy of denying NHS treatment to patients who pay for private medicines is necessary to prevent a two-tier NHS, with those receiving top-up medicines being treated on the same ward as those who must make do with standard health service medicines." But patients legitimately ask, "How can they say this policy is far more important than somebody's life?"[16] This policy is not an aberration of what tax-funded insurance should be about; it represents a real monstrosity.

Not surprisingly, Britain has among the worst cancer survival rates in Europe, and doctors argue that the policy of denying NHS patients the right to buy the most effective drugs is contributing to that record. In fact, cancer patients in the United Kingdom have to struggle with knowing that the United Kingdom is lagging behind other Western countries in its use of new cancer drugs.[17] Even France, despite all its problems, is, with Switzerland and the United States, a leader in using new cancer drugs. The problem with the United Kingdom is that, as it is presently funded, the NHS is unlikely to be able to afford many new and expensive drugs (see Table 2.1 for a list of cutting-edge anticancer drugs not yet approved by the NHS).

But cancer is not the only disease for which Britons have to fight for access to medicines: hundreds of patients with a rare lung disease, pulmonary hypertension, a condition that affects approximately 4,000 people in the United Kingdom, will be sentenced to death by plans by the National Institute for Health and Clinical Excellence (NICE)—the NHS rationing body, established in 2000 to evaluate medical technologies, especially new and expensive ones—to stop doctors prescribing a range of drugs through the NHS because they are too expensive.[18] Only a quarter of these patients actually need the most expensive level of treatment, yet NICE's plans mean that no life-extending therapies will be available to new patients because the cost of the most expensive medicines exceeds its threshold of £30,000 per person. Only the cheapest drug used to combat the condition, Revatio (also known as Sildenafil and Viagra), will remain available for patients, and, in over a quarter of the patients suffering from pulmonary hypertension, the drug is ineffective. Lung specialists currently combine it with inhaled or infused drugs such as prostacyclins for the most seriously affected patients, which can add £40,000 to the £12,000 annual cost. Another group of drugs, endothelin receptor antagonists, are also under threat. Additionally, studies show that though more than 50% of patients in the United States receive the latest, most effective pharmaceuticals for arthritis, they are available to only 15% of patients in the United Kingdom.

Table 2.1 Cutting-Edge Medicines Not Yet Approved by the United Kingdom's National Health Service as of 2010

Bevacizumab (Avastin)

For bowel cancer. Licensed for colon cancer in January, 2005, but turned down on the grounds of cost-effectiveness in January, 2007 and in November 2010. Avastin was also rejected by NICE for kidney cancer, in August 2009, and for breast cancer in July 2010.

Erlotinib (Tarceva)

For non-small cell lung cancer. Licensed in September 2005, approved by the Scottish Medicines Consortium in June 2006, and rejected by NICE in March 2007 on the grounds that it was not clinically or cost effective. The drug's manufacturer, Roche, appealed the decision, and the drug was rejected again in June 2010.

Sorafenib (Nexavar)

For the treatment of liver cancer. NICE rejected this drug in May 2010, on cost-effectiveness grounds. NICE's decision was final.

Lapatinib (Tyverb)

For the treatment of breast cancer. NICE rejected this drug in June 2010 on the grounds that the drug was not a good value when compared with treatment alternatives.

Source: *The Telegraph*, FiercePharma.

The imposition of a national policy for new technologies—the Health Technology Assessment, implemented by NICE to make reimbursement decisions, among other things[19]—represents a real disaster for the United Kingdom. First, as has been mentioned elsewhere,[20] it is based on the assumption that all relevant evidence on the effects of a specific technology can be assembled at an early stage in the life cycle of the new therapy, which is impossible. Second, if NICE recommends delaying the use of technologies because it believes that "all" the evidence is not available, as it has done in its appraisal of the cancer drugs listed in Table 2.1 and of beta interferon for the treatment of multiple sclerosis, the United Kingdom is essentially taking a free ride, waiting for other countries to do the studies and the hard work for them. As the British scholar David Green has pointed out, "the British government is taking too narrow a view of cost-effectiveness ... Many new technologies may bring corresponding savings elsewhere in the NHS or in the economy, but others simply add to total costs by permitting patients to benefit in entirely new ways."[21]

More important, NICE may also slow down the process of scientific discovery because many pharmaceutical companies and biotech startups may not develop certain products, even if they have the capacity to do so, if they think that NICE may not reimburse these drugs. At present, the British system, in contrast to the French one, gives each pharmaceutical company a target profit for all its sales to the NHS. In addition, by discouraging doctors from allowing patients to seek a second opinion, and through NICE, the British health care system ensures that there are measures to reduce demand.

The current state of the British health care system is reaching its maximum level of intolerance: too-severe rationing is blocking those who most need the system from having access to better drugs. At the same time, consumers are unable to escape this single-payer system, a system riddled by inefficiency and bad service and that lacks all incentives to improve and to raise its standards, without deleterious consequences.

It is not difficult to see the results of Britain's ill health care policies: babies born to poor families now have a 17% higher than average chance of dying, compared to a 13% higher than average chance 10 years ago.[22] The life expectancy of people living in poverty, particularly women, has fallen further below average than it was around the time of Tony Blair's election in 1997. One in eight NHS hospital patients still has to wait more than a year for treatment.[23] A UK Department of Health analysis of 208,000 people admitted to a hospital in March 2008 showed that 48% were wheeled into the operating theater within 18 weeks of a general practitioner sending them for hospital diagnosis. But 30% of patients waited more than 30 weeks, and 12.4% waited more than a year.[24]

Jo Walton, a leading pharmaceutical analyst (now at Credit Suisse) based in London, summarizes the British situation in the following way:

> *The issue is that we have made the societal choice, for example, that if you are over seventy and your kidneys fail, you just won't get to the top of the kidney transplant list. Let's say that you are given points for being young; but if you are seventy, you don't get those points, you never get enough points to get to the top of the list. So we have a longevity-based system here, which says we'll pay more to treat younger*

persons, to cure them because they then have another twenty years. ... In the States, where the older have voting power, you couldn't do that! So you will give an eighty-year-old a kidney transplant in the U.S. Here, in the U.K., if I get five years of life, an eighty-year-old person would get only one. So I think that NICE is making a societal-based decision cleverly without mentioning the word rationing, *but that's what they are doing! Well, they have to, because in Europe we expect health care to be funded out of our taxes, so the bill for health care can go up only as much as our taxes go up. It's as simple as that. I mean, if our tax revenue goes up 3 percent per annum, then our health care bill will only go up 3 percent per annum, or else we get to spend less on policemen, firemen, and teachers.*[25]

Private Insurance Use in Europe

Perhaps one of the biggest issues that Europe is confronting now is access to new medicines, which are doubtless a crucial component of health care. However, in most European Union (EU) countries, patients have to wait years before these innovative drugs become available. Besides obtaining approval by the European Medicines Agency (EMEA), pharmaceuticals need to obtain approval from the country's national department of health and obtain pricing and reimbursement approvals before they can be introduced into the market. All this, obviously, can result in long delays, estimated to average 18 months, which means that many breakthrough drugs are simply not available in Europe for a significant amount of time. Of course, some European governments may have no incentive to accelerate this process; in fact, quite the opposite is true because new medicines are considerably more expensive than older ones, and by delaying access to the new drugs, they save money. In fact, cutting drug expenditures, as opposed to cutting service costs across the health care sector, is relatively faster, cheaper, and easier. This strategy is currently being adopted in countries such as Spain, Greece, the United Kingdom, and even Germany, and is expected to spread soon to other European nations (see Table 2.2).

But as I hinted earlier, because the socialized health care systems in Europe are no longer sustainable as they are at present, some signs of change toward privatization are becoming evident in some countries. In other words, in addition to the official health insurance provided by the state, an increasing number of Europeans are purchasing private insurance to cover medical treatment that is not provided by the statutory system. Hence, a two-tiered health care system is developing in some of these countries. The first tier includes people who can afford to pay twice for health care, via their income taxes or payroll contributions and via premiums to a private insurer, and the second tier includes those who have to deal with the official system and its poor quality.

Two countries in Europe, Germany and the Netherlands, allow their citizens to opt out of the official system altogether and use the taxes or wage contributions that they would make to the official system to purchase private insurance on the health care market, so citizens do not have to pay twice for insurance. In the case of Germany, citizens whose income is above a certain level opt out of that system and are no longer obliged to pay a percentage of their wages to the sickness fund. However, they

Table 2.2 Recent Initiatives for Drug Price Cuts in Europe and Japan

Country	Initiative
Germany	The German government presented earlier in 2010 a white paper containing several proposed changes: (1) Increase of the rebate that pharmaceutical companies have to offer to the statutory health insurance to 16% from 6%; (2) Freezing prices until 2013, using prices as of August 1, 2009 as the basis; (3) Higher threshold for reimbursement in that new drugs will have to demonstrate differentiation to obtain premium pricing; (4) Negotiations over prices for differentiated drugs in between manufacturers and insurers 1 year after market launch. The German Health Ministry hopes to create cost savings of around €2 billion annually through these initiatives.
Spain	Out of the large European countries, Spain is among those spending the highest share of its total public health care budget (around one third) on pharmaceuticals. The government launched earlier in 2010 a plan for cost containment to materialize through a combination of price cuts (up to 23%) on drugs not included in the reference-price system as well as an average price reduction of 25% for generic drugs. A more restrictive policy of reference pricing for drugs that already have a generic approved shall also be put in place. The recently introduced measures aim to cut €1.3 billion of Spain's expenditures on pharmaceuticals.
Greece	While representing only a limited share of revenues, the significant reduction of prices averaging around 21.5% may have wider implications as Greece may be used as a basis for reference prices in other European countries and cause a negative domino effect. Furthermore, price cuts of such magnitude are also likely to stimulate parallel importation by pharmaceutical wholesalers.
Japan	Under the national health insurance system, revision of ethical drug prices occurs every 2 years based on the difference between market prices and official prices. A new pricing system was introduced effective April 2010. Normally, ethical drug prices for both in-patent and generic drugs are reduced under this pricing system. However, the 2010 changes included the following: (1) drugs that have been listed less than 15 years and not subject to generic competition will receive a less severe price cut or, in some cases, may maintain the current price; (2) branded drugs with expired patents and with generic availability will receive more substantial price cuts. The new pricing system aims to promote greater use of generics while providing good incentives for branded drug companies to develop innovative drugs. On a relative basis, companies that have more in-patent products fare better under the new pricing rules. Companies that do not have strong late-stage pipelines will eventually face further revenue pressure. On an overall basis, the April 2010 price cuts—applicable until March 2012—are generally consistent with those of prior years. However, if the Japanese government significantly changes the drug price revision system in April 2012, the impact on branded drug companies could be more severe. Over the medium term, the government aims to raise generic penetration ratio to at least 30% from the current 17%; progress toward this goal will influence future government pricing actions.

Source: Industry Outlook: Global Pharmaceuticals, June 2010, p. 9.

must use that money to buy private health insurance.[26] Over 10% of the German population has opted out of the public system, and premiums are set at the time of purchasing the plan. They are calculated not on the basis of personal health risks but rather according to the average health risk of a patient's age group (in 5-year cohorts), and this remains so even as the person ages. The premium can be raised only to reflect general increases in health care costs affecting all age groups. The problem with this system, which is pay-as-you-go, is that there are no financial reserves.

In the Netherlands, people also can opt out of the official health care system once they earn more than a certain amount of income, or they are excluded automatically from the public insurance system if they reach a certain level. However, the income threshold in the Netherlands is lower than in Germany, so a larger portion of the population (one third) is insured by the private sector. Private insurance is affordable to almost anyone in the Netherlands because the highest risks are covered by a separate insurance system. It is interesting that the Dutch system has a separate insurance system for very expensive and long-term treatment, called "catastrophic health care needs," which is mandatory and paid for by income taxes proportionally to the level of income (the government is the single payer). Noncatastrophic expenses are paid by the official national insurance.[27]

Switzerland, on the other hand, relies entirely on private health insurance. In 1995, the Swiss government made health care insurance mandatory, and people pay premiums and modest copayments, although the government subsidizes poor individuals by paying part of their premiums or one third of health care funding by the Swiss Confederation.[28] People can choose from a variety of insurance companies, each with different coverage packages and premiums, although all packages have to include the basic coverage stipulated by the health insurance law. Insurers, on the other hand, are required to set some capital aside in a central fund to avoid falling into the pay-as-you-go trap and to handle financial risk.

The insurance system in Switzerland encourages people to save for future emergencies and to adopt a healthy lifestyle because they themselves are liable for parts of the costs of treatment and hospitalization, via copayments and deductibles. The system has seemed to work well for a number of years, but lately, Switzerland's hospitals, considered the envy of the world, have been facing limitations in their capacities and shortages of personnel that have led to increasing wait times for operations to take place.[29] In addition, rising health service costs and costs for medicines are increasingly putting the system under strain, which has led to severe budget cuts in health care and higher health insurance premiums in recent years.

Another country that is following a privatization path is Sweden, Europe's most heavily socialized Scandinavian state. For decades, this country has relied on an underperforming civic health service monopoly characterized by long waiting lists, chronic overspending, and flagging quality. But currently the health care system is undergoing some degree of privatization. It remains to be seen how this is going to play out in the future.

Though not within the scope of this chapter, Eastern Europe faces even greater challenges than Western Europe. And if changes are going to take place in Europe, they will surely begin in Western Europe.

Other Industrialized Nations

Of the other industrialized countries with universal health care, Canada faces similar issues to Europe. The Canadian parliament unanimously passed the Canada Health Act in 1984, which established a single-payer, publicly financed health care system. To ensure a true government monopoly, private health insurance was outlawed. As a result, Canada is in the same trap as Europe, with high inefficiency, long waiting lists, a lack of access to the most innovative drugs, and in some cases, people dying as they wait to receive appropriate treatment.

Japan, which also has a universal health system, faces problems similar to the ones in Europe—or even worse: it has been suggested that 50% of suicides in Japan are linked to medical problems.[30] The Australian mixture of public and private health care insurance seems to be working relatively well, but it is not without some challenges, especially with regard to having access to new drugs, which, as in the rest of the world, are very expensive.

As we have seen thus far, even the richest nations in the world are facing a health care crisis. And we have also seen that universal health care (or its equivalent) is far from being the way to get access to better health care services and medicines.

If the current health care situation in the developed world—the best of all possible worlds, paraphrasing Voltaire—seems to be straight out of a horror movie, how fares the situation in the developing and underdeveloped world?

The Developing World: In Search of Hope

The overall view in the developed world is that most people in tropical countries and in other less-developed nations die mostly of diseases such as malaria, AIDS, sleeping sickness, elephantiasis, tuberculosis, and other infectious diseases that are not endemic to the rich nations. A great deal of the international aid that developed nations and even the pharmaceutical industry provide to these countries is allocated to these types of diseases. But the reality is that in addition to these illnesses, people in the developing countries are stricken by the same diseases common to the developed world, plus malnutrition, a lack of money and infrastructure, and, in places such as Africa and parts of India and China, inhuman living conditions. In these regions, as more vaccines, antibiotics, and medicines to treat infectious diseases such as AIDS become available, more people survive infections, diarrhea, pneumonia, tuberculosis, malaria, birth complications, and other causes of a quick and early death, only to die slowly of cancer; suffer terribly from central nervous system disorders such as Alzheimer's disease, Parkinson's disease, and depression; and endure complications from cardiovascular diseases.

Although the extent to which people suffer because of health ailments varies significantly among Africa, Asia, and Latin America, the health care problems in the United States and Europe generally pale in comparison (see Figure 2.1a and b for a comparison of health care spending as a percentage of GDP among poor, middle-income, and wealthy nations). The World Health Organization (WHO) has estimated that in

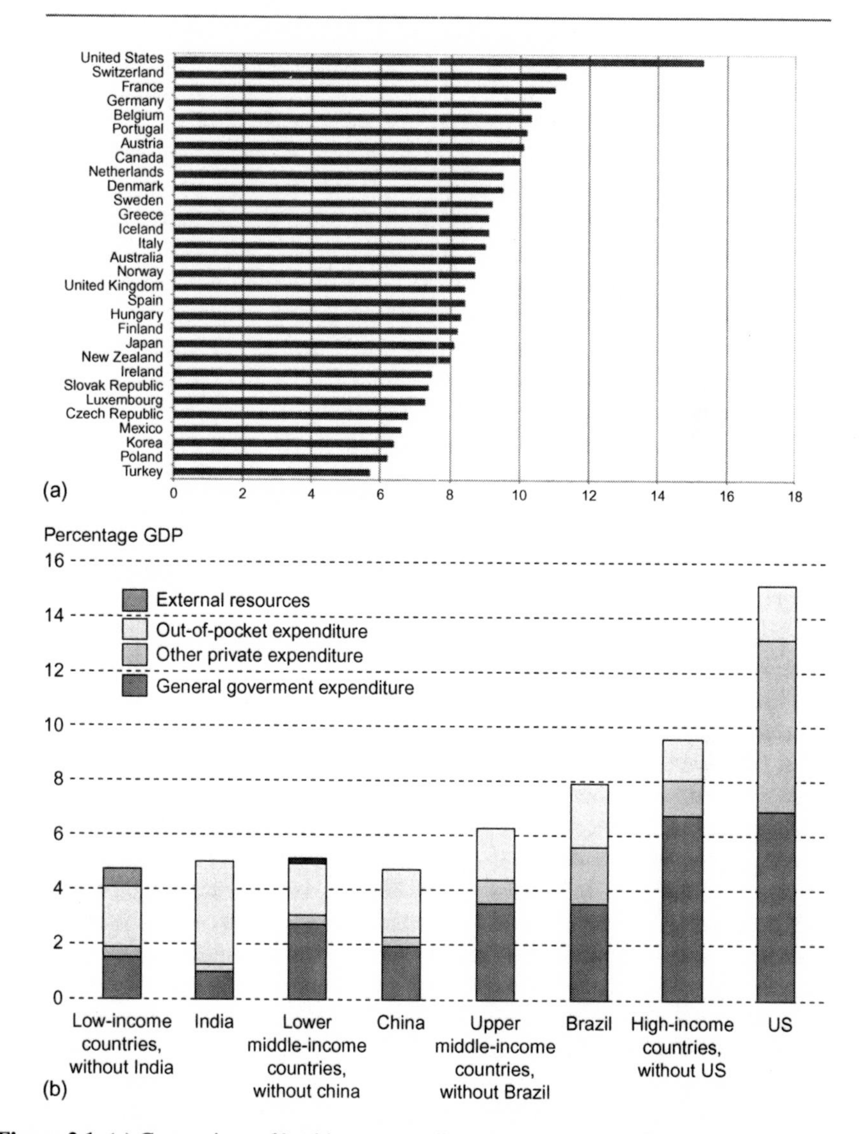

Figure 2.1 (a) Comparison of health care spending as percentage of GDP among OECD countries in 2008.

Source: Organization for Economic Cooperation and Development, OECD Health Data, 2008 (Paris: OECD, 2008). http://en.wikipedia.org/wiki/Health_care_in_the_United_States (publicly available data).

(b) Comparison of health care spending as percentage of GDP among poor, middle-income, and wealthy nations.

Note: As can be deduced from this graph, there is great out-of-pocket health care expenditure in developing countries.

Source: World Health Organization Report, 2008, p. 82. © World Health Organization. Reprinted with permission. All rights reserved. http://www.searo.who.int/LinkFiles/Reports_whr08_en.pdf.

the next 10 years, there will be an increase of 17% in the incidence of noninfectious diseases, such as diabetes, heart disease, central nervous system disorders, and cancer, worldwide.[31] Countries in Africa will see an increase of 27%; countries in Asia will see an increase of 20%; and countries in Latin America will see an increase of 17%.[32] In emerging economies, where most people still cannot afford the most innovative and effective medicines (some of which are actually cheap), millions of people in the world's poorest countries are destined to die in pain, without having access to the drugs that they need and that we take for granted in the United States and Europe.

In 2005, 7.6 million people died of cancer, out of 58 million deaths worldwide. More than 70% of all cancer deaths occurred in low- and middle-income countries, where resources for the prevention, diagnosis, and treatment of cancer are limited or nonexistent. On the basis of projections, cancer deaths will continue to rise to an estimated 9 million people in 2015 and 11.4 million in 2030.[33]

The WHO estimates that more than 4.8 million people a year with moderate to severe cancer pain receive no appropriate treatment, nor do another 1.4 million with late-stage AIDS; in addition, for other causes of lingering pain, such as burns, car accidents, gunshots, diabetic nerve damage, and sickle-cell disease, millions of people go untreated. In fact, statistics from the United Nations International Narcotics Control Board reveal that citizens of rich nations suffer less.[34] Six countries—the United States, Canada, France, Germany, the United Kingdom, and Australia—consume 79% of the world's morphine, a cheap and effective drug, according to a 2005 estimate. Poor and middle-income countries, where 80% of the world's people live, consume only about 6%[35] of this drug. About half of the almost 8 million cancer deaths in the world are in poor countries, and most diagnoses are made late, when death is unavoidable. Of course, before the end, there is pain, agony, and misery: 80% of all cancer victims suffer severe pain, as do half of those dying of AIDS.[36]

"Poverty is the world's deadliest disease," according to Hiroshi Nakajima, former director of the WHO, because "it wields its destructive influence at every stage of human life, and for most of its victims, the only escape is an early death." Unfortunately, poverty provides that escape window because though life expectancy has increased significantly in the most developed countries, the opposite is happening in some of the poorest ones. Nakajima adds that "for many millions of people for whom survival is a daily battle, the prospect of a longer life may seem more like punishment than a prize."[37] In fact, many doctors from Africa and other poor areas in the world describe patients whose pain is so unbearable that they find a radical way out—hanging themselves from trees or throwing themselves in front of trucks, to shed, once and for all, the burden of living.[38]

One of the major issues with diseases such as cancer is that in some cases, an earlier diagnosis, which would have probably changed the fate of many patients, is out of the question in less-developed countries. In the absence of enough funds and a functional infrastructure, hospitals do not have the sophisticated equipment that is taken for granted in the developed world. In some instances, only one private hospital in a country offers chemotherapy drug treatment, as is the case in Sierra Leone.[39] Even in countries with such facilities, such as Brazil, Mexico, and China, resources are always on a shoestring.

Globally, cardiovascular diseases are the number one cause of death and are projected to remain so. An estimated 17.5 million people died from cardiovascular disease in 2005, representing 30% of all global deaths. Of these deaths, 7.6 million were due to heart attack and 5.7 million were due to stroke. About 80% of these deaths occurred in low- and middle-income countries. If current trends are allowed to continue, an estimated 20 million people will die from cardiovascular disease (mainly from heart attack and stroke) by 2015.[40] While cardiovascular diseases, cancer, and communicable diseases are the leading causes of death in the world, disorders of the central nervous system are the most disabling afflictions, and little treatment exists for them.

As the world becomes smaller, thanks to transportation improvements, infectious diseases are now spreading geographically much faster than at any time in history. The WHO reports that 2.1 billion airline passengers traveled in 2006[41]; this means that an epidemic outbreak in any one part of the world can become a pandemic threat in any other area in just a matter of hours, as we saw with the swine flu (A[H1N1]) pandemic that appeared in 2009. Ever since the 1970s, almost every year, a newly emerging disease is identified somewhere in the world: nearly 40 new diseases exist today that were unknown a generation ago. Besides this, more than 1,100 epidemic events have been recorded worldwide in the last 5 years. One of the major threats that the world is facing is that gains in many areas of infectious disease control become compromised quickly and seriously by the spread of antimicrobial-resistant strains such as drug-resistant tuberculosis (XDR-TB). Not only has TB (and HIV) become drug resistant but so have some diarrheal diseases, hospital-acquired infections, malaria, meningitis, respiratory tract infections, and several sexually transmitted diseases. It is just a matter of time before the world becomes stricken by another pandemic that will most likely be more severe than the swine flu, or worse, by a plague of one sort or another. On the basis of the disastrous way in which the A(H1N1) crisis has been handled worldwide, is it still correct to say that these pandemic threats are only the problems of so-called Third World countries?

The Pharmaceutical Industry

While many people, including this writer, firmly believe that morally, politically, and economically, it is necessary to make advanced medicines available much more cheaply to poor countries, it is also necessary to identify the roots of the problems in developed countries first and then find ways to help less-privileged nations use their own resources to their betterment. This can be done through education, prevention, sanitation, better diet, clean water, better public health policies; through the creation of a health care infrastructure and a health care market that respects intellectual property; and most important, through significant investment in R&D.

Although health care systems around the world are unable to meet the demands of the twenty-first century, health care reforms, like the hasty ones that are being proposed in the United States, will not be fully effective if major changes in the way medicines are produced do not take place—if better, safer, and more affordable medicines are not readily available to patients everywhere. So, rather than rushing to implement health care system reforms without having all the necessary resources (and information) in place and without being fully conscious of the unwanted consequences that these reforms may bring, one of the fundamental steps toward getting out of the current global health crisis is to find more efficient ways to develop safer and more effective drugs, but in such a way that they become more accessible to the market. The pharmaceutical industry's role in this, as in the preservation of human health, is quintessential. But unfortunately, this industry, owing in part to how terribly the United States and Europe run their health care systems, and thanks to the complicity of investors and the corruption of governments—as if there were no tomorrow—has become a money-making enterprise first and foremost, at the expense of quality and productivity.

How can it be that a course of some biotechnology-derived drugs, such as Avastin and Erbitux, is priced at $50,000–100,000 to give an average prolongation of life in metastatic colorectal cancer of 2–4 months, when there are at least three to five unpatented drugs that can do the same? Obviously, the prices of such medicines are completely unrelated to the *value* they deliver to patients. Such prices cannot be justified and, from an economic view, are unsustainable. According to Roy Vagelos, the luminary former CEO of Merck, "the industry is suicidal in respect to gaining support and admiration from the general public with this strategy. High prices are, perhaps, justified [in the United States] in cases such as combination therapy for HIV infection, about $20,000 a year, but the *value* delivered is excellent, as patients who would otherwise be sentenced to death can live a relatively normal life after treatment. In such cases, the prices are easily justified based on R&D expenses *and* the patient outcomes."[42]

Criticisms of the biopharmaceutical industry are becoming even sharper nowadays, not only because of safety issues, such as the Vioxx scandal among myriad others, and for its incapacity to bridge important unmet medical needs, but because some recent studies have suggested that the industry spends almost *twice* as much on promotion as it does on R&D, which runs contrary to the industry's claim that the reason that medicines are so expensive is that the industry spends heavily on R&D.[43] These criticisms come during a period in which the pharmaceutical industry is struggling to bring innovative products to the market while facing serious competition from generics as a result of the massive expirations of drugs: perhaps the greatest crisis in the industry's 150-year history.

Understanding the pharmaceutical industry and getting to the root of its crisis will certainly empower humankind to find realistic and practical solutions to its health care problems. This perspective shall occupy us throughout the rest of this book.

Notes

1. Belien, P., quoted in "Perspectives on the European health care systems: some lessons for America," Heritage Foundation, Lecture 711, July 9, 2001. http://www.heritage.org/research/healthcare/hl711.cfm.
2. Brunner, S., 2004. The French health care system. Medical News Today, June 27, 2004. http://www.medicalnewstoday.com/articles/9994.php.

3. Green, D., Irvine, B., 2001. Health Care in France and Germany: Lessons for the UK. Institute for the Study of Civil Society, London. http://www.civitas.org.uk/pdf/cs17.pdf; see also Belien, as quoted in "Perspectives on the European health care systems."
4. Ibid.
5. There is no gatekeeping between the patient and the specialist, so the patient can go directly to the specialist.
6. In the 1970s, the French government began to cut expenditures. In the 1960s, about 30% of French citizens paid privately for supplemental insurance; in the 1970s, 50% did so; whereas nowadays, 85% purchase supplemental health insurance. Belien, as quoted in "Perspectives on the European health care systems."
7. Ibid.
8. Ibid; see also Dormont, B., Huber, H., 2006. Causes of health expenditure growth: the predominance of changes in medical practices over population ageing. Annales D'Econommie et de statistique 83/84. http://annales.ensae.fr/anciencs/n8384/vol8384-08.pdf.
9. Dépenses de santé en France: une croissance 'modérée' de 3,8% en 2008. MyPharma Editions, September 10, 2009. http://www.mypharma-editions.com/depenses-de-sante-en-france-une-croissance-«-moderee-»-de-38-en-2008.
10. International Trade Administration, 2004. Pharmaceutical Price Controls in OECD Countries: Implications for US Consumers, Pricing, Research and Development, and Innovation. US Department of Commerce, Washington, DC. http://www.trade.gov/td/health/DrugPricingStudy.pdf.
11. Belien, as quoted in "Perspectives on the European health care systems."
12. Reuters, 2009. French government to tackle surging health care deficit. National Post, September 7, 2009. http://www.nationalpost.com/life/health/story.html?id=4132e453-5c91-4401-9b9e-59767f074b3b; also Lopes, C., 2007. Health care in France: facing hard choices. Canadian Medical Association Journal 177. http://www.cmaj.ca/cgi/content/full/177/10/1167?ck=nck.
13. Wollstein, J.B., 1992. National health insurance: a medical disaster. The Freeman, October 1992. http://www.thefreemanonline.org/columns/national-health-insurance-a-medical-disaster/.
14. Doyal, L., Doyal, L., 1999. The British National Health Service: a tarnished moral vision. Health Care Analysis 7, 363–373.
15. Templeton, S.-K., 2008. Cancer patients "betrayed" by NHS. Sunday Times, June 1, 2008. http://www.timesonline.co.uk/tol/life_and_style/health/article4040168.ece.
16. Ibid.
17. The study, published in the cancer journal *Annals of Oncology*, was compiled by Dr. Nils Wilking, clinical oncologist at the Karolinska Institute in Stockholm, Sweden, and Dr. Bengt Jönsson, director of the Centre for Health Economics at the Stockholm School of Economics; Wilking, N., Jönsson, B., 2005. A Pan-European comparison regarding patient access to cancer drugs. Karolinska Institutet, Stockholm. http://ki.se/content/1/c4/33/52/Cancer_Report.pdf.
18. Hope, J., 2008. Lung patients "condemned" to death as NHS withdraws their too expensive drugs. Daily Mail, March 24, 2008. http://www.dailymail.co.uk/health/article-544112/Lung-patients-condemned-death-NHS-withdraws-expensive-drugs.html.
19. Taylor, R., Taylor, R., 2009. What is health technology assessment? April 2009. http://www.medicine.ox.ac.uk/bandolier/painres/download/whatis/What_is_health_tech.pdf; Stevens, A., Milne, R., 2004. Health technology assessment in England and Wales. International Journal of Technology Assessment in Health Care 20, 11–24.
20. Green, D., in "Perspectives on the European health care systems."
21. Ibid.

22. O'Dowd, A., Coombes, R., 2008. Government will not meet its health inequalities targets in England. British Medical Journal 336, 633; see also Sparrow, A., 2008. Health inequality has got worse under Labour, says government report. Guardian, March 13, 2008. http://www.guardian.co.uk/politics/2008/mar/13/health.health.
23. O'Dowd, A., Coombes, R. Government will not meet.
24. Carvel, J., 2007. One in eight patients waiting over a year for treatment, admits minister. Guardian, June 8, 2007. http://www.guardian.co.uk/society/2007/jun/08/health.politics.
25. Interview with Jo Walton, then at Lehman Brothers, now at Credit Suisse, London, May 2007.
26. Belien, in "Perspectives on the European health care systems"; also Schneider, M., 2003. Structure and Experience of German Opt-Out System of Statutory Health Insurance (GKV). World Bank, Washington, DC. http://194.84.38.65/files/esw_files/gkv_health_eng.pdf.
27. Belien, in "Perspectives on the European health care systems."
28. Reinhardt, U., 2004. The Swiss health system: regulated competition without managed care. Journal of the American Medical Association 292, 1227–1231.
29. Hospitals on the verge of a breakdown. Swiss Info, July 24, 2003. http://www.swissinfo.ch/eng/index.html?siteSect=105&sid=4059652; see also The Swiss health care system. Civitas, 2002. http://www.civitas.org.uk/pdf/Switzerland.pdf; and Crisis looms for Swiss hospitals. Swiss Info, September 5, 2009. http://www.swissinfo.ch/eng/front/Crisis_looms_for_Swiss_hospitals.html?siteSect=105&sid=11172320&cKey=1252148886000&ty=st.
30. Freire, C., 2007. Japan's suicide rate remains high. Newsvine, November 9, 2007. http://www.newsvine.com/_news/2007/11/09/1084313-japans-suicide-rate-remains-high.
31. OMS: Muertes por enfermedades no transmisibles aumentarán 17%. La Prensa de Panamá, July 8, 2009. http://mensual.prensa.com/mensual/contenido/2009/07/08/uhora/salud_2009070811482468.asp.
32. World Health Organization, 2009. World Health Statistics Report. World Health Organization Press, Geneva.
33. Boyle, P., Levin, B., 2008. World Cancer Report 2008. World Health Organization Press, Geneva.
34. United Nations, 2009. International Narcotic Board Report. United Nations, New York.
35. Ibid.
36. McNeil Jr., D., 2007. Drugs banned, many of world's poor suffer in pain. New York Times, September 10, 2007. http://www.nytimes.com/2007/09/10/health/10pain.html.
37. Nakajima, H., 1995. World Health Organization Annual Report 1995. World Health Organization, Geneva.
38. McNeil, Drugs banned.
39. Ibid.
40. World Health Organization, 2007. Cardiovascular diseases. Fact Sheet 317, February 2007. http://www.who.int/cardiovascular_diseases/en/.
41. World Health Organization, 2007. World Health Statistics Report. World Health Organization, Geneva.
42. Interview with Roy Vagelos, New York, June 2009.
43. Big pharma spends more on advertising than research and development, study finds. Science Daily, January 7, 2008. http://www.sciencedaily.com/releases/2008/01/080105140107.htm.

Part II

Understanding the Biopharmaceutical Business

3 A Brief Commercial History of the Biopharmaceutical Industry up to the Year 2000*

I have always told you that History is boring!

— ***Indro Montanelli,* Storia d'Italia**[1]

In English and some other languages, the word *drug* probably derives from the Dutch/Low German word *droog*, which means "dry,"[2] perhaps because in the past these substances were obtained from dry plants. In chemical and medicinal terms, a drug is the active ingredient of a medicine or another substance that is present therein, when the active ingredient has not been purified. Drugs are used to alter biochemical processes in the body with the objective of treating an illness, relieving a symptom, enhancing a performance or an ability, or altering a person's state of mind.

The use of plants, narcotics, purgatives, and minerals for curative, palliative, or hedonistic purposes has been documented extensively since ancient times, either as part of medicine or as an important component of some ritual ceremonies, magic, or religious/initiation practices. However, drug research as a scientific discipline is a remarkably recent phenomenon. Its origins date to the second half of the nineteenth century, mostly in Europe,[3] after the establishment of long-lasting scientific principles in the fields of chemistry, physiology, pharmacology, bacteriology, and immunology. Drug research allowed scientists and physicians to acquire an unprecedented understanding of how living organisms are structured and how they function, which subsequently led, indirectly and directly, to the creation of a drug industry.

The precise date and place of birth of the pharmaceutical industry cannot be established easily because there were several different lines of pharmaceutical development and a convergence of scientific findings on many different fronts, both in Europe and in the United States. However, it is safe to say that Germany contributed most to the rise of the pharmaceutical industry as we know it today via the chemical and dyestuff industries. The creation of an industrial drug base was something quite different from the already existing business of apothecaries, druggists, and

* The history of the pharmaceutical and biotechnology industries has been documented extensively. In conducting research for this chapter, I referred to a large number of works, among which I would like to recommend the following: Weatherall, M., 1990. *In Search of A Cure: A History of Pharmaceutical Discovery*. Oxford University Press, New York; Singer, C., Underwood, A., 1962. *A Short History of Medicine*. Oxford Clarendon Press, Oxford; Chandler, A.D., 2005. *Shaping the Industrial Century: The Remarkable Story of the Evolution of Modern Chemical and Pharmaceutical Industries*. Harvard University Press, Cambridge, MA; and Lesch, J.E. (Ed.), 2000. *The German Chemical Industry in the Twentieth Century*. Kluwer Academic, Netherlands. The companies' official Web sites were also very useful.

The World's Health Care Crisis. DOI: 10.1016/B978-0-12-391875-8.00003-2

wholesalers who specialized for centuries in the preparation of chemicals and the production of age-old preparations and remedies that were used to treat and cure human diseases, such as the drug wholesale family business of Heinrich Emanuel Merck (H. E. Merck) in Germany. This company dated back to 1668 from apothecary Friedrich Jacob Merck's (F. J. Merck) business in Darmstadt and is the direct ancestor of Merck & Co., which, beginning in 1827, began producing purified drugs from the recently discovered alkaloids and developed the skill of applied chemistry.[4] Although such a type of business existed in other European countries, the United States, Canada, and Japan, their contribution to the pharmaceutical industry took place after Germany had set an industrial model to follow.

The Pharmaceutical Industry Begins

In 1856, Briton William Henry Perkin, stimulated by his mentor, the German chemist August von Hoffmann, tried to synthesize (i.e., create artificially) quinine, a drug that had already been isolated by Pierre Pelletier and Joseph Bienaimé Caventou in 1820 from cinchona bark. Quinine, whose use by South American Indians was recorded around 1630 by Spanish conquistadors, was in great demand in Europe for the treatment of malaria and other fevers.[5] However, cinchona bark grows in mountainous regions of South America, and at that time, the supplies of this plant in Europe were very scarce while the demand was high. Given the progress that had taken place in synthetic chemistry, it was thought that this substance, whose chemical formula was known ($C_{20}H_{24}N_2O_2$), could be produced synthetically in a laboratory or chemical factory. So there was a great commercial and economic incentive to pursue this idea. Perkin tried to synthesize quinine by coal-tar distillation because through this method, it is possible to obtain several intermediate compounds such as benzene, toluene, naphthalene, and anthracene—to mention only four important substances—which are the starting point for countless other products.[6] But to his own surprise, Perkin initially obtained a dark precipitate that was certainly not quinine. After subsequent distillations, he managed to extract from benzene a brilliant purple dye, subsequently named "mauveine" or "aniline blue." From aniline, Perkin obtained the first artificial dyestuff ever produced. His manufacture of this and other aniline dyes was a great commercial success. Single-handedly, he secured funding and went on to create the modern synthetic dyestuffs industry, introducing a new range of colors used for many applications such as in photography and microscopy. In the latter, it was used to stain specimens and reveal structures that otherwise would have been invisible to the human eye.

Given the numerous types of compounds that could be derived from coal-tar, parts of this industry widened their range of interest to other fine chemicals. For instance, dyes gave rise to the manufacture of sulfuric and nitric acids and caustic soda; in turn, these led to the creation of artificial fertilizers, explosives, and chlorine. They could also give rise to medicines because coal-tar contained many of the aromatic and aliphatic building blocks that became the toolkit of medicinal chemistry. After a series of distillations, chemical derivatives similar to the ones already characterized in some medicines could be obtained, which was exactly what Perkin had in mind when he attempted to synthesize quinine from coal-tar. In spite of the technological limitations and dearth of available information at the time, in creating and studying new drugs, scientists used analogies with existing agents, whose entire or partial compositions were known, as an important guide to the development of new medicines. This was also a period of self-experimentation, and there was no industry regulation, so those compounds that seemed interesting and potentially useful were simply tested directly on human subjects to evaluate their effects. Needless to say, a large number of these drugs made patients very sick and had to be withdrawn or improved, but several useful drugs were also discovered in this heuristic manner and became effective in relieving headaches and minor pains (called *analgesics*, meaning "against pain") or in reducing the temperatures of fevered patients (called *antipyretics*, "against fever"). In the 1870s, clinical thermometers and temperature charts were introduced,[7] and in this way, the development of new drugs was greatly facilitated because now there was a diagnostic tool to measure a decrease in temperature in patients. Therefore, at the base of commercial applications lay basic scientific and diagnostic tools as well.

Some alert individuals quickly saw that producing medicines out of coal-tar derivatives would become a very profitable activity. However, none of the existing institutions where the seminal drug experimentation efforts took place—pharmacies, university laboratories, hospitals, and the chemical companies that produced dyes from natural sources—represented suitable platforms for the emerging drug research that was driven primarily by chemistry. However, by the 1880s, drug research was increasingly controlled by the new disciplines of pharmacology, the clinical sciences, physiology, immunology, and bacteriology. Therefore, new institutions that would support interdisciplinary drug research and development had to be created and made functional.

Though the dyestuff industry began in England, it was in Germany that some dyestuff and chemical firms began to embark on drug production in a strictly commercial fashion, either by purifying them from natural sources or by synthesizing them from coal-tar derivatives, as described earlier. The industrial platforms for the mass production of drugs began to take place either in pharmacies, such as at H. E. Merck, which was to become a world leader in the production of pharmaceuticals, or in the pharmaceutical divisions of chemical or dye companies. During the second half of the nineteenth century, substantial chemical factories had been built in Germany to extract essential ingredients for the synthesis of a variety of products. Thus, the newly founded industry, embodied by several leading firms—Hoechst, a dye company founded in 1863 as Teerfarbenfabrik Meister; Lucius & Co. in Höchst, near Frankfurt, which later changed its name to Teerfarbenfabrik Meister Lucius & Brüning; Bayer, a chemical and pharmaceutical company founded in northeast Germany in 1863; and Agfa, founded in 1867 to commercialize dyes—began to make and sell new kinds of drugs. Hoechst, for instance, began as a company that consisted only of a 3-HP steam engine and a small boiler, in which aniline oil, arsenic acid, and boiling water produced synthetic fuchsia dye. But by 1874, it had already become a chemical plant, and by 1883, the company was already involved in the production of drugs. The year 1883 was very important for Hoechst because it was then that a chemist in the firm working with quinine discovered Antipyrin, which became a popular and important analgesic. This event was the starting point of the subsequent unrivaled success of the company. Hoechst's secret lay in its ability to secure strong ties with academia and academic scientists—such as Robert Koch, who discovered the tuberculosis-causing agent (Koch's or tubercle *bacillus*), and Paul Ehrlich, who postulated the theory of receptors[8]—to produce drugs such as Novocaine, a local anesthetic, and salvarsan, a chemotherapeutic agent used for the treatment of syphilis, among many other drugs, as we shall see later. This asset gave the company a degree of technical expertise unrivaled in the world for well over a century.

The creation of an industrial infrastructure to commercialize chemical and pharmacological findings, such as synthetic coal-tar derivatives used as antipyretics and painkillers and, to some extent, chemotherapeutics, was only preparation for what was yet to come: the incorporation of physiology, bacteriology, immunology, and the clinical sciences into pharmaceutical research and development (R&D). The basic and applied work of men of the stature of Louis Pasteur, the great French chemist and microbiologist; German physician Robert Koch, who isolated the bacteria responsible for cutaneous anthrax, tuberculosis, and cholera; German physiologist Emil von Behring, who discovered the diphtheria antitoxin and developed a serum therapy against diphtheria and tetanus; and the great German immunologist and hematologist Paul Ehrlich, who postulated the theory of receptors, coined the term *chemotherapy*, found a cure for syphilis, and carried out impressive studies on autoimmunity, had a far-reaching impact that not only consolidated the pharmaceutical industry in the 1880s and 1890s but also created a strong R&D industry in Europe. In fact, there was a need to capitalize in a large-scale, efficient, and standardized manner on the discoveries of these men in bacteriology and immunology, specifically in the production of vaccines and serum antitoxins.

Of particular importance was the creation of the Pasteur Institute in Paris in 1887 and of the Koch Institute in Berlin, created in 1891 as the Royal Prussian Institute for Infectious Diseases. Both of these organizations addressed the issue of applying basic scientific findings in bacteriology and immunology to the treatment of human diseases. German companies such as Hoechst became very interested in commercializing this kind of research—which nowadays would be considered translational research (in other words, the application of basic academic findings to humans)—and to a large extent played an important role in funding the work of first-rate scientists such as Emil von Behring, Paul Erhlich, and others. Unlike the Pasteur Institute, the Koch Institute had as a goal the commercialization of its scientific research.

In Germany, the chemical industry, having secured strong academic connections, was prepared to manufacture antitoxins on a commercial scale. The work was undertaken by the Hoechst factory. This was a remarkable and risky undertaking for a chemical business because it required extremely high standards of care and management of the animals in which antitoxin was raised, but the undertaking was achieved successfully thanks to the company's supreme quality control (the quality of the product was subject to external quality control, in which Koch and the Koch Institute played an important role) and talented staff.

Together with Hoechst, Bayer was a leading chemical company in Germany. Bayer was founded in 1863 in Barmen (now Wuppertal) by Friedrich Bayer, a chemical salesman, and Johann Friedrich Weskott, the owner of a dye company. Initially, the company manufactured dyestuffs. In 1899, Bayer introduced its trademark for aspirin, or acetylsalicylic acid, a drug rediscovered by researcher Arthur Eichengrün and research assistant Felix Hoffmann at Friedrich Bayer & Co. It is interesting that many drugs that had great potential as therapeutic agents remained largely unappreciated and abandoned for a long time; this was the case with aspirin, which remained abandoned on a chemist's shelf for many years. This drug was initially synthesized in 1853 by the French chemist Charles Gerhardt, but its medicinal properties were not recognized until the end of the nineteenth century by Eichengrün and Hoffmann. In all likelihood, this was because of its chemical resemblance to salicylic acid, derived from willow bark and used to relieve fever and rheumatic pains (Hoffmann successfully treated his father, who suffered from arthritic pains, with aspirin).

Once commercialized in 1899, Bayer aspirin became an instant success: it was the most widely used of all synthetic medicines in the Western world, whose only competitor was paracetamol (acetaminophen), the chief survivor of the coal-tar antipyretic analgesics. Bayer also commercialized new analgesics such as heroin (discovered by Hoffmann soon after aspirin was rediscovered), lycetol (a uric acid solvent), and salophen (an antirheumatic and antineuralgic), among several others. Some hypnotics appeared during this period, and the fact that their effects were quickly observable facilitated their clinical use. In 1904, Bayer introduced the "Bayer cross" as its corporate logo (and registered it worldwide), consisting of the horizontal word *BAYER* crossed with the vertical word *BAYER*, both words sharing the *Y*. This logo was actually imprinted on the company's aspirin tablets.

By the late nineteenth century, some German companies, such as Hoechst and Bayer, had built very strong marketing organizations in the United States. By 1905, Bayer was already producing drugs in the United States (in New York State). It was Hoechst, however, that maintained the lead in the production of new pharmaceuticals, and its organizational base served as a model for other companies worldwide.

The success of Germany in becoming the indisputable leader in the newly founded pharmaceutical industry depended both on its heavy industrialization and its economic growth, which afforded the creation of several industries (dyestuffs, chemicals, and pharmaceuticals) from scratch, and on the fact that the chemical industry there had strong ties with academia, where men of science, such as Justus von Liebig, tirelessly and vigorously promoted the industrial applications of scientific findings. Without the existence of a major and capable chemical manufacturing industry in Germany, the development of the pharmaceutical industry would have been quite different and more limited.

The Swiss Pharmaceutical Industry

As the Germans became leaders in the production of chemicals and pharmaceuticals, their Swiss neighbors did not want to be left behind. In Switzerland, firms such as Ciba, Geigy, Sandoz, and F. Hoffmann–La Roche immediately became world leaders in the commercialization of sera for diphtheria, vaccines for tetanus and cholera, analgesics such as phenacetin, painkillers such as Novocaine, and even salvarsan, a chemotherapeutic discovered and developed by Ehrlich for the treatment of syphilis. As said already, medicines during this period were used and tested directly on patients in a trial-and-error fashion, as the concept of clinical trials (by today's standards) was nonexistent. (The first regulatory agency in the world regarding pharmaceuticals was not introduced until 1906 with the Food and Drug Act in the United States, which prohibited interstate commerce in falsely labeled and adulterated food, drink, and drugs.)

Of the Swiss companies that entered pharmaceuticals during the second half of the nineteenth century, Geigy was the oldest. This company dated back to 1758 and began as the shop of chemist and druggist Johann Rudolf Geigy in Basel. For over a century, this firm was run as a family-owned dye business, and by 1868, it had become a prosperous dyestuff company. At the end of the century, Geigy began producing drugs. Another company that was to play an important role in the Swiss chemical and pharmaceutical business was Ciba, whose history goes back to 1859, when it began to manufacture the synthetic dye fuchsine in Basel. In 1900, Ciba began the production of pharmaceuticals and was, by that time, Switzerland's largest chemical company. Another Swiss company, Sandoz AG, was founded in 1886 in Basel by Alfred Kern and Edouard Sandoz to make synthetic dyes, but in 1895, it began making pharmaceuticals, most notably the fever-reducing drug antipyrin.

An interesting company which, unlike the German and other Swiss companies, did not begin as a chemical or dyestuff business was F. Hoffmann–La Roche. This firm was founded in 1896 by Fritz Hoffmann (the "La Roche" part of the name comes from the last name of his wife, Adele La Roche) after he acquired experience in pharmacy and the chemical trade in Basel, Switzerland. Hoffmann's goal was producing and commercializing standard medical preparations. Initial products developed by F. Hoffmann–La Roche included aiodin, a thyroid preparation; Airol, a wound antiseptic; Allonal, an analgesic sedative and hypnotic and the first Roche product to use compounds produced by synthetic chemistry; Sirolin, a nonprescription cough syrup marketed for over 60 years; and Pantopan, a remedy for pain, colic cough, and anxiety (still sold in several countries and the longest-selling Roche product). From the very beginning, this has been a most successful enterprise, due in great part to the company reinvesting its profits (and the family's wealth) in internal development and in the acquisition of companies in closely related industries.

The English Pharmaceutical Players

The evolution of the pharmaceutical industry in European countries other than Germany and Switzerland was very different. Among the firms that played an important role in shaping the pharmaceutical industry and that maintained a close relationship with academic centers and research institutes from the beginning, some British pharmaceutical companies, such as Burroughs Wellcome (a leading research pharmaceutical company by the first half of the twentieth century), Glaxo, and the Beecham Group, deserve special mention. Burroughs Wellcome was founded in London in 1880 by Henry S. Wellcome and Silas W. Burroughs, both graduates of the Philadelphia School of Pharmacy. This company introduced the selling of medicine in tablet form (which is different from a pill, which preceded the tablet) to England under the 1884 Tabloid trademark; prior to that, medicines were sold mostly as powders, liquids, or pills. In addition, Burroughs Wellcome introduced direct marketing to doctors, giving them free samples. In 1894, Burroughs Wellcome set up the company's Physiological Research Laboratory, the first of its kind in Britain, which played a very important role (especially under the direction of the eminent physiologist Henry Dale) in understanding many physiological events related to human disease.

In 1895, Silas Burroughs died, and the company passed to Henry Wellcome. As the firm flourished, Wellcome set up several research laboratories linked to the drug company, and within a few years, it began its expansion by establishing a subsidiary in South Africa in 1902. This was followed shortly thereafter with one in Italy, one in Canada, and one in the United States in 1906, and then in China, Argentina, and India. There is speculation that Wellcome's model for this expansion was Parke Davis (created in 1885), the first US company to build a comparable global enterprise during the 1890s and which, for many years, was a model of research-oriented pharmaceutical enterprise in the United States.

The history of Glaxo goes back to 1873, when English-born Joseph Nathan founded Joseph Nathan & Co. in New Zealand, a business trading in a range of goods as diverse as whale teeth and patent medicines. After acquiring the rights on a process for drying milk, the company focused on the production of dried milk in Bunnythorpe, New Zealand, and found a good market in baby food. The company soon moved to London, where it became a prosperous business and important UK-based manufacturer of baby food products. The company became popular because of its slogan "Builds Bonnie Babies," but it was not until 1924 that Glaxo produced its first pharmaceutical product, the vitamin D preparation *Ostelin*. After this point, the company expanded and created the Glaxo Laboratories in London in 1935.[9]

Before its merger with SmithKline in 1989, Beecham's Group Ltd was the oldest of the British pharmaceutical companies. Beecham's Group Ltd derives from Beecham's Pills, a company founded in 1842 by Thomas Beecham, a chemist and druggist who sold medicines and remedies. In 1859, the company opened the world's first factory built exclusively for the purpose of making medicines at St. Helens in England. Its most notable product became a laxative pill that became very popular in the United Kingdom. Soon after, the company was exporting its products as far away as Australia.

So even though the dyestuff industry began in England, the pharmaceutical industry in Britain emerged from quite different sources. It was based more on physiological research and on the traditional pharmacy/apothecary business; in other words, the British pharmaceutical industry, unlike in Germany and Switzerland, originally was not based on coal-tar derivatives.

The United States Enters the Scene

The Germans were indisputably the leaders in the new pharmaceutical industry. They used organic chemistry to synthesize new drugs, which were initially named "ethical" drugs (to be used for specific purposes, as labeled, and as time passed, sold only with a physician's prescription, originating the term *prescription drugs*), and developed vaccines and serum antitoxins. But the United States decided to enter the industry, too.

As has been remarked,[10] the pharmaceutical industry in the United States developed primarily from the already existing wholesaler-producer business that packaged and marketed already existing drugs, standard preparations, and age-old remedies derived from natural sources (botanical, animal, and mineral). These so-called branded drugs, which used the manufacturer's copyright name and were packaged and distributed throughout the nation to apothecaries, pharmacists, and other retailers, were sold to a mass market without a physician's prescription; in other words, they were sold over the counter (OTC). In addition, these US wholesalers–producers pioneered the development of pills (the pill-making machine was invented in 1885 by a physician in Michigan), which allowed for the precise specifications and dosages of mixed-drug preparations and their standard production on a large scale. Over time, these wholesaler enterprises entered the field of newly developed, ethical drugs.

Needless to say, low-tech OTC medicines gave rise to an advertising-intensive pharmaceutical industry in the United States, while the prescription drug path led to a research-intensive type of industry in Europe. Whereas the impulse that moved the German pharmaceutical industry forward was a response to the convergence of many discoveries in basic research and the close relationship with academia, in the United States[11] technological developments in means of transportation (coal locomotion) and communication (the telephone and telegraph) greatly facilitated the commercialization of pharmaceuticals and other products. Not surprisingly, the pharmaceutical industry was one of the first to take advantage of these new developments. Initially, during the second half of the nineteenth century, small companies such as Eli Lilly, Abbott, SmithKline, Bristol-Myers, Upjohn, and Squibb pioneered the creation of an infrastructure that bore fruit a few decades later. Of these companies, only Eli Lilly and Abbott have remained unmerged since their foundation. The others have either merged and survived or disappeared (after several mergers).

Eli Lilly was founded in 1876 when pharmacist Colonel Eli Lilly, a Civil War veteran, started a manufacturing and marketing pharmaceutical enterprise in Indianapolis, Indiana. Its initial success resulted from an innovative process of gelatin coating pills, which the firm still uses today. Soon after, this company was commercializing drugs based on natural and then synthetic organic sources, which included several analgesics and barbiturates, cough drops, and other OTC drugs. But it was not until many years later that this company emerged as an important pharmaceutical player. In 1919, Lilly hired biochemist George Henry Alexander Clowes as director of biochemical research. Clowes was a key figure in negotiations with Frederick Grant Banting and his colleagues at the University of Toronto regarding the large-scale commercialization of insulin, which they had discovered in 1921 and had begun large-scale production of in 1923. The success of insulin enabled the company to attract well-respected scientists, expand its research capabilities (a large research complex was created in 1934, and an office opened in England that same year), and, with them, make more medical advances. By the end of the 1930s, Lilly's prescription drugs included a liver extract for pernicious anemia, sedatives (Seconal), and drugs for heart disease.

Abbott Laboratories was founded in 1888, when Dr. Wallace C. Abbott established the Abbott Alkaloid Company in Chicago with the objective of using a new technique for the preparation of drugs—precipitating them into solid extracts and then selling them in granules, which were named "dosimetric granules." This innovation gave this wholesaler firm a competitive edge because it provided a more accurate and effective dosing mechanism for patients than other treatments available at the time. The firm continued prospering and was incorporated in 1900. By 1906, it had increased its sales force to reach doctors, and by 1910, it had opened its first European agency in London and branches in New York, San Francisco, Seattle, Toronto, and Mumbai, India. In 1916, the company acquired its first synthetic medicine, an antiseptic agent called Chlorazene, which was used extensively on the battlefields of World War I to clean wounds. It opened its headquarters in Chicago in 1920.

Owing to the limited space available for this chapter, it is impossible to discuss the other companies mentioned earlier, such as Squibb, Upjohn, and Bristol-Myers, but the examples of Lilly and Abbott provide an idea of the line of development that these companies followed. I would like to close this section on US pharmaceutical companies by briefly mentioning two companies that, as the twentieth century progressed, became leaders in the industry: Merck & Co. and Pfizer.

Two US Pharmaceutical Giants

Merck & Co. was created in New York City in 1887 as the US marketing subsidiary of the Merck company. By 1903, this subsidiary was producing plant, narcotics, bismuth salts, iodine, and other chemicals in its plant in Rahway, New Jersey, and was to act as a role model for American companies in the coming decades.

Pfizer was established in 1849 in Brooklyn as Chas. Pfizer and Company, Inc., by Charles Pfizer and his cousin, Charles Erhart, two German immigrants. Initially, the company produced iodine preparations, refined camphor, borax, and tartar, which it sold to pharmacists and drug companies. The company's first medicinal product was santonin, a remedy used against parasitic worms. At the beginning of the twentieth century, Pfizer's main product was citric acid, which was used in several industrial applications, especially in food flavoring. Starting in 1917, Pfizer chemists developed a new process of fermentation based on black bread mold, which allowed the production of citric acid on a large scale. This made the company the largest producer of citric acid in the United States by the 1930s.

Most US firms, which are so familiar to us today, did not become major pharmaceutical players until the advent of World War I. Let us examine why in the following section.

Impact of World War I (1914–18)

By the time World War I ended in 1914, German companies, most notably Hoechst and Bayer, had become the world's chemical and pharmaceutical leaders. The United States felt great resentment for these companies, not so much because of their success but because they, together with the German chemical company BASF, established a fierce price war against the US dye industry using a series of tactics such as "dumping" (selling chemicals below cost to eliminate competitors) and forming trusts that impeded the development of the US chemical industry.[12] The situation was aggravated during World War I, during which the US chemical industry was at a disadvantage to the German industry.

Before the advent of the nuclear bomb during World War II (1939–45), it was the chemical industry that produced weaponry such as gunpowder, mustard gas, and synthetic substitutes for organic materials. Once World War I started, the German chemical and pharmaceutical industry produced inorganic chemicals, pharmaceuticals, explosives, and photographic chemicals, among other agents. The embargoes that were instituted by European countries created a shortage of supplies in the United States, and this forced the United States to manufacture its own products. During World War I, the United States no longer imported German products, and it was forced to develop its own industrial capabilities at a level that matched the levels of European companies to supply national and international markets with chemicals and prescription medicines. US companies that succeeded in doing so included Eli Lilly, Abbott Laboratories, SmithKline, Upjohn, Squibb, and Parke-Davis. Furthermore, two US subsidiaries of German companies, Merck and Schering, imported the capabilities and organizational structures of their sponsor companies and used them in the United States very successfully. During this period, Merck's US branch began the production of coal-tar–based synthetic intermediates, which it had received from its German parent company. After the United States entered the war in 1917, the US government confiscated 80% of the subsidiary's common stock, which was held by George Merck, president of the subsidiary and grandson of the modern German company's founder. However, in 1919, the 80% share held by the alien property custodian was bought back, and the subsidiary was registered as a US enterprise called Merck & Co.

Once the war was over, Merck & Co. continued to have close personal and technical relationships with its former parent company, which was very important for the new company because it was developing its own technical and functional capabilities. Merck & Co. began its pharmaceutical research after building a large laboratory in the early 1930s. Soon after, it began to commercialize vitamins: B_1, at first, then B_2, followed by B_6, C, and K, and culminating in 1944 with vitamin B_{12}, a treatment for pernicious anemia. By the end of World War II, Merck was the leading company in the production of vitamins in the United States and the second largest worldwide, after F. Hoffmann–La Roche.

After the war, most of the other US pharmaceutical companies continued to be focused on OTC drugs and concentrated on developing their marketing capabilities, taking advantage of the recently developed radio networks of the 1920s to reach a mass market, which was to have a great impact in the years to come. Among the leaders in the advertising-intensive sector of the pharmaceutical industry were Bristol-Myers, Warner, Plough, and American Home Products.

Though World War I was very profitable for Hoechst and Bayer in Germany, these companies, together with other German companies, lost their share of the US market and their entire US assets. In spite of this, the organizational capabilities of these companies in the United States remained intact, which allowed them to reenter the US market after World War I. For example, Bayer (which, during World

War I, did not retrieve its trademark for Bayer's aspirin) and Hoechst reentered the US market through a 50% interest in Sterling-Winthrop. The United States, then, created a series of protectionist policies for its chemical and pharmaceutical industries, while Germany reacted by creating a cartel in 1925 named Interessen Gemeinschaft Farbenwerke, better known as IG Farben.[13] The leaders of the cartel were none other than Hoechst and Bayer. It has been speculated that it was Wall Street—in particular, J. P. Morgan—who financed IG Farben, which in turn brought Adolf Hitler to power and was involved in countless crimes.[14] In fact, the interwar period was a very dark period in the history of the chemical and pharmaceutical industries, owing to their close association with and support of all sorts of atrocities.

IG Farben was not the only cartel to be formed during this period. In 1918, Ciba, Geigy, and Sandoz formed the Interessengemeinschaft Basel (Basel Syndicate), or Basel IG, to compete with the German chemical industry. In 1929, the Basel IG joined with IG Farben to form a dual cartel. French dyemakers joined soon after to form a tripartite cartel. In 1932, the British cartel Imperial Chemical Industries joined the group to form a Quadrapartite cartel, which lasted until the outbreak of World War II in 1939. IG Farben existed until 1945, when it was disintegrated by the Allies.[15] Basel IG survived the war, but it dissolved in 1951, partly out of regard for US antitrust legislation.

Impact of World War II (1939–45)

Like World War I, World War II had important implications for the pharmaceutical industry in Europe and the United States. In Europe, the German industry suffered the same effects of World War I, and companies lost their patents, yielding significantly to the US firms. In contrast, for US and, to some extent, English firms, this period represented a great opportunity, especially owing to the multiple programs in academic and industrial settings to carry out more research on drugs that could be used during the war.

In England, the discovery of sulphonamides (c. 1935) and penicillin (early 1940s) coincided with the war, which created the necessity of producing penicillin on a large scale. The academic group at Oxford University, where penicillin was discovered, created a small factory for further experimental work and to treat some special cases with the antibiotic and proved that the drug was efficacious against infections. Unlike England, the United States was not yet at war, and the Oxford researchers, led by the actual discoverers of penicillin, Walter Florey and Ernst Chain, presented their data to US authorities. Thus, large-scale commercial production was undertaken first in the United States, and then by the United Kingdom. In the United States, this work was led by companies such as Pfizer and Merck. These companies engaged in the production of large quantities of penicillin (Pfizer) and other antibiotics, such as streptomycin (Merck),[16] which gave them great opportunity to grow and restructure in the afterwar years. The production of antibiotics enabled these companies to expand their core facilities and take advantage of the most sophisticated science of the time. As a result, these companies grew rapidly, but they lacked a strong sales force and marketing structure and had to develop them. To accomplish this, Merck merged with Sharp and Dohme, a smaller business with a remarkable reputation in the production of sera and vaccines as well as alkaloids and other drugs and which possessed an experienced sales force. Pfizer accomplished this goal by internal investment and by developing its own core capabilities, which included the creation of a strong marketing structure to reach doctors and hospitals. Soon after, other US companies followed suit, such as American Home Products, which, up to that point, was a much-diversified company, and American Cyanamid, a strong player in the chemical industry. Both companies turned to antibiotics and the development of prescription drugs.

As mentioned earlier, owing to war conflicts, England could not develop antibiotics initially, but after US companies began producing them, British companies began to follow suit. Among the companies that took the lead in this respect were Glaxo, Imperial Chemical Industries (ICI), and Beecham, which until that point was Britain's major producer of OTC drugs. Glaxo became Britain's designated leader of the government's wartime penicillin program. Due to these demands, Glaxo's pharmaceutical unit became central to the development of the entire company's strategy and organizational structure. Around this time, the company decided to create a pharmaceutical department, organized into a subsidiary named Glaxo Laboratories Ltd. By 1944, Glaxo, using Pfizer's fermentation process, had built four factories, which produced about 80% of Britain's total penicillin output. After the war, Glaxo remained Britain's leader in penicillin and other antibiotics, while expanding its vitamin lines (it isolated vitamin B_{12} simultaneously with Merck). Glaxo, like most US companies of its kind, diversified into related product lines, which included veterinary products and medical instruments, and it acquired a drug distribution company. In this way, the company grew in the 1950s through acquisition and consolidation. In the 1950s and 1960s, the company took immediate advantage of academic work on hormones, and soon it was developing Britain's first commercial cortisones and a series of corticosteroids (e.g., Betnovate) through licensing agreements with Schering United States.

The production of antibiotics was also paralleled by the rapid growth and development, at least in the United States, of the health care insurance industry[17] and employer-based medical insurance, which became established in the United States after World War II. At that time, a shortage of labor compelled employers to attract workers by providing them with health care benefits (which were not regulated) even as employers were subject to controls that prevented them from attracting workers by offering higher wages.[18] The impact of such developments can be illustrated easily by the numbers: in 1929, sales of prescription drugs accounted for nearly one third of all consumer expenses for medical drugs; by 1969, however, this figure accounted for more than four fifths of it.[19]

Another important episode that occurred slightly before World War II and that was to have tremendous consequences for society and the drug industry was the creation of a drug regulatory agency. In 1938, in response to a number of deaths from the use of a poisonous solvent called diethylene glyclol in a new sulpha drug, the US Congress decided to create the Food and Drug Administration (FDA) to protect the public and assigned it the specific task of requiring drug companies to prove that their products were safe before they could be sold.[20]

By the early 1950s, Merck and Pfizer emerged as the leading US pharmaceutical firms and turned to the development of other antibiotics and prescription drugs. With a strong marketing organization in place, they continued in the late 1950s and early 1960s to produce fine chemicals and enlarged their production of vitamins, vaccines, antibiotics, and other drugs. In 1963, Merck, Sharpe, and Dohme marketed Diuril (chlorothiazide), an important diuretic for treating high blood pressure, and later, another diuretic, Hydrodiuril. Subsequently, the company commercialized several other products, including the nonsteroidal drug Indocin, for the treatment of arthritis; two antidepressants; and Aldomet, another new treatment for high blood pressure. Pfizer, like most companies of the time, adopted the strategy of unrelated diversification and acquired companies producing OTC consumer remedies (such as Ben-Gay and Visine) as well as toiletries (Barbasol shaving cream), cosmetics, and fragrances (Coty). At the end of the 1960s, the company had become a conglomerate of unrelated products by acquiring companies that made specialty metals and materials, including high-temperature cement and linings for steel-producing furnaces.

In the rest of Europe besides Britain, the situation was different. As mentioned earlier, before World War II the European market was dominated by the German industry (IG Farben) and, to some extent, the Swiss (and to a lesser extent, US companies had a share, too). Owing to military conflicts, German and French companies (notably Rhône-Poulenc, which was France's most important pharmaceutical firm, specializing in the production of vaccines) fell behind, and Swiss companies were unable to export their products because they were landlocked. During the 1950s and 1960s, after a series of major institutional and organizational restructurings, Hoechst and Bayer rebuilt their drug and chemical facilities domestically and abroad. Of the largest German companies that, on the breakup of the IG Farben cartel, received their pre-1925 holdings, Hoechst grew fastest owing to heavy internal investment and because, unlike the other German companies, it did not invest in expensive petroleum projects; instead, it purchased oil and gas through long-term contracts. In the case of Hoechst, its worldwide (exclusive of the United States) manufacture of polyester and then its incursion into polyethylene and polyolefins in the early 1950s gave it a strong competitive edge. In the 1960s, Hoechst had already recovered. Bayer, on the other hand, used a different strategy: it reached recovery through a series of acquisitions in related fields into the 1970s, providing the company with strong learning bases.

During the 1940s and 1950s, F. Hoffmann–La Roche did not take part in the development of antibiotics; however, in 1952, it launched the antituberculosis drug Rimifon. Beginning with Rimifon, Roche became a leader in antimicrobial chemotherapy. In the 1960s, Hoffmann–La Roche, together with Ciba-Geigy and Sandoz, paved the way for the commercialization of benzodiazepines (tranquilizers). In 1960, Hoffmann–La Roche introduced librium for the management of emotional, psychosomatic, and muscular disorders, and in 1963, as a follow-up, came valium, a sedative and anxiolytic drug belonging to the benzodiazepine family. Librium was a top-selling drug, but it was surpassed by valium, which, up until 1981, was the world's best-selling drug.

By the 1960s, the production of new drugs reached a plateau, and the threat of price controls loomed on the horizon in the United States. Therefore, most of the leading US companies opted for diversification as a growth strategy, entering aggressively into consumer chemical and advertising-intensive areas such as soaps, cosmetics, cleaners, household goods, and in some cases, food and drink.

In the 1970s, while European companies continued to be focused on the prescription drug path and on the chemical business, in the United States, the advertising-intensive firms realized that going beyond consumer chemicals produced lower revenues, and especially lower net incomes, than the prescription and OTC paths.[21] Thus, many of the advertising-intensive firms decided to become exclusively prescription drug companies before the 1970s were over. For these companies, the only way to do this was by merging with prescription and research-based pharmaceutical companies. Simultaneously, the research-intensive companies in the United States realized that their income as percentage of revenue was much higher for prescription drugs than for research-intensive health care products.

During the 1970s, companies such as Merck and Lilly, which heavily strengthened and upgraded their prescription drug capabilities by increasing their R&D expenditures, became leading pharmaceutical companies in shaping the new-product development process. Their areas of focus included the use of structure-based molecular design (i.e., discovery by design), and because they implemented novel project management techniques, they were able to translate these efforts effectively into an increased flow of drug production in the late 1970s and early 1980s. These companies were in a much better position than any other US firms to exploit the revolutionary discoveries that were produced in the 1970s in the field of biotechnology, which was to revolutionize the pharmaceutical industry and medicine.

The Biotechnology Era

The biotechnology industry was born in the United States in the mid-1970s as a result of the commercialization of the nascent cloning and recombinant DNA (rDNA) techniques. In 1973, Stanley Cohen of Stanford University and Herbert Boyer of the University of California, San Francisco (UCSF), invented the cloning technique and performed the first rDNA experiments using bacterial genes. In 1975, two major breakthroughs took place that would have a tremendous impact on the development of biotechnology in the years to come. The first was the creation of a method to produce monoclonal antibodies (MAbs); that is, the artificial creation of antibodies (molecules that react solely with a specific antigen such as a blood cell surface receptor) derived from a single clone of cells by Georges Kohler (1946–95) and César Milstein (1927–2002) in Cambridge. The second was the invention of DNA sequencing by Frederick Sanger.

Kohler and Milstein fused myeloma cells with B-lymphocytes to create a hybrid cell (the hybridoma) that produced antibodies. In doing this, a single and specific antibody could be produced in vast amounts. Frederick Sanger, on the other hand, discovered a mechanism for breaking up DNA molecules to analyze their base pair sequences, which is essential for predicting the sequence of proteins. In 1976, another landmark event took place: Har Gobind Khorana and his team at the Massachusetts Institute of Technology (MIT) synthesized the first artificial gene capable of working in bacteria (in 1970, he had synthesized the first artificial gene). This breakthrough had an enormous impact on basic research and opened the floodgates to the creation of myriad therapeutics, among many other applications.

By 1976, biotechnology was ripe for commercialization, especially in the United States, the country of its birth, even if a great deal of the basic research and mechanistic models that led to the invention of this technique was actually undertaken in Europe, particularly in Britain and France.[22] It is interesting that as soon as the new cloning methods were disclosed publicly, a series of concerns, debates, and discussions took place in the United States, which led to the establishment of regulatory policies that permitted a better understanding of this revolutionary technology, steps that were crucial in securing funding and support for further research in the public and private domains.

After Boyer and Cohen developed the rDNA technique, a young venture capitalist and entrepreneur named Robert Swanson became fascinated with the new technology and approached Boyer to propose its commercialization. Boyer became interested, and a company called Genentech was created in 1976 with the goal of developing "a new generation of therapeutics created from genetically engineered copies of naturally occurring molecules important in human health and disease."[23]

The company began with a staff of five people. By 1977, Genentech had produced the first human protein (somatostatin) in *E. coli*, and by 1978, it had already produced the first human insulin product from genetically engineered bacteria, which was followed in 1979 by human growth hormone (hGH). In 1978, Genentech then established development contracts with Eli Lilly, to which Genentech licensed recombinant insulin for an 8% royalty (it was called Humulin, for "recombinant human insulin"), and with the Swedish firm Kabi, to commercialize hGH technology for a smaller and much more specialized market than insulin. The company went public in 1980. In 1982, Humulin was approved, first in the United Kingdom and then in the United States, for the treatment of diabetes. It was the first rDNA drug to be marketed. In 1990, F. Hoffmann–La Roche acquired a majority of shares of Genentech (55%) for $2.1 billion.

In the late 1970s and early 1980s, a series of biotechnological start-ups proliferated, especially in the United States, and an industrial infrastructure called *commercial biotechnology* was created—just as had occurred a century earlier in the pharmaceutical industry. Commercial biotechnology represented a challenge both to the already established pharmaceutical industry, which had to adapt its existing infrastructure to the new but powerful technologies, and in particular to the biotechnology start-ups, which had to start almost everything from scratch and build strong product development and marketing bases to be able to commercialize their products. Notable examples of other companies that, like Genentech, jumped onto the biotechnology bandwagon included Amgen, Biogen, Genzyme, Chiron, Centocor, and the Genetics Institute.

It is important to highlight that Genentech was not the first pioneering biotechnology company. In fact, early in the 1970s, several already established companies that in one way or another had a link to the pharmaceutical industry became interested in exploiting the new basic findings in molecular genetics. Instrumentation firms, such as New Brunswick Scientific, Dynatech, and Flow General; research companies like Cetus, Bioresponse, Biotech Research Laboratories, Native Plants, and Agri Genetics; and enzyme fermentation specialists such as Novo Laboratories were looking for ways to establish a platform for the new and fast-growing discipline. Several other companies, mostly in the United States, were also interested in the new field.

Biogen was started in 1978 by Walter Gilbert (who won the Nobel Prize in chemistry in 1980). Biogen survived in its early years on the basis of royalty income from licensing its work on immune-system proteins called *interferons*. Merck and SmithKline licensed the technology to commercialize hepatitis B vaccines; Abbott did the same for developing hepatitis B diagnostics, and Eli Lilly for human insulin. In addition, Schering-Plough's investment of $8 million enabled Biogen its initial entry into molecular genetic engineering and permitted it to become a leader in alpha interferon products. The company overexpanded immediately by establishing research facilities and offices in England, Switzerland, Belgium, and Germany, and soon it had cash flow shortages, which became an overpowering reality by 1985. To keep Biogen solvent, Gilbert sold 90% of its patents, and later in the year, the board took drastic measures to save the company, including replacing Gilbert as CEO, selling plants in European countries, and reorganization. The new CEO, James L. Vincent, an accomplished executive from Abbott, was in great part responsible for these new changes, and was instrumental in renegotiating Gilbert patent agreements, so that the company would receive new royalties, which allowed the company to survive.

Amgen, whose name stands for "Applied Molecular Genetics," was founded near Los Angeles in 1980 by venture capitalists and a group of biologists from the University of California, Los Angeles. The company started with very little financial resources, but by 1985, it had five genetically engineered drugs undergoing human testing. Two of these showed remarkable promise: erythropoetin (Epogen) and a related protein, a granulocyte colony-stimulating factor called Neupogen (Filgrastim). The first was designed to fight anemia, the second to offset the effects of radiation and chemotherapy in patients treated for cancer. Epogen was approved by the FDA in 1989, and Neupogen was approved in 1991. Needless to say, the basic research and mechanistic studies behind these breakthrough drugs had been carried out in academia years earlier.

Genzyme was founded in Boston in 1981 by Henry Blair. The company's objective was to make products based on breakthrough enzyme technologies. The company secured venture capital funding and purchased two companies. The first was Whatman Biochemicals Ltd, which became Genzyme Biochemicals, and the second was Koch-Light Laboratories, an English catalog firm specializing in providing supplies to the pharmaceutical industry and whose pharmaceutical division (Koch Laboratories) became Genzyme Pharmaceuticals in 1986. Blair hired Henri Termeer, a former executive vice president at Baxter International, as president (and elevated him to CEO in 1985). Soon after his arrival, Termeer began securing funding and bringing in prominent scientists from MIT to the Scientific Advisory Board of Genzyme to identify some promising areas for product development. The company then began building its infrastructure and recruited its salaried personnel, and it adopted the strategy of producing products, based on the modification of enzymes and carbohydrates, that were relatively easy to make and sell while it developed longer-term products. For instance, Genzyme first marketed an enzyme called cholesterol oxidase, including an enzyme that was an active agent in cholesterol tests. In 1986, Genzyme became a public company, raising $28.2 million. It opened a subsidiary in Japan, financed by sales in that country, and then built a small production facility in

Cambridge, Massachusetts, for the production of so-called medical-grade hyaluronic acid. After this point, the company entered the production of genetically engineered hyaluronic acid–based drugs, such as Ceredase, and raised $10 million to develop these drugs through a limited partnership. At each step along the way, the company manufactured and marketed its own products.

Amgen and Genzyme succeeded on their own by using the strategy of producing and commercializing high-priced orphan drugs; that is, products that treat a rare disease affecting fewer than 200,000 Americans (the Orphan Drug Act was signed into law in the USA on January 4, 1983, which granted companies such as Amgen and Genzyme, great benefits, such as tax breaks, exclusive marketing rights for seven years, etc., see later discussion in this chapter). These companies then focused on small and specialty markets while keeping control of their licenses.

Like Lilly with Genentech, Merck was one of the first pharmaceutical companies to create an infrastructure to develop further the new findings in molecular biology and genetic engineering. For instance, in the late 1970s, Merck's research laboratories, in search of a vaccine for hepatitis B, sent their hepatitis team to UCSF, a pioneer institution in biotechnology, to work with William Rutter, the head of its Department of Biochemistry and Biophysics. As a result of their cooperative efforts and those of Benjamin Hall of the University of Washington, they were able to develop a means for expressing a hepatitis B antigen in *E. coli*. Then, UCSF licensed the basic process to Merck on the basis of a contract that Rutter and colleagues formed in 1981 with Chiron, which quickly became a leading biotechnology research company. It is important to mention that Merck was not only involved in the discovery itself, but it also conducted the research necessary to develop a practical vaccine, organized the clinical trials, and designed and scaled the manufacturing processes and marketing—an excellent example of how a basic science finding can translate into a commercial product. Chiron learned how to bring a drug to market, while this opportunity allowed Merck to build an important and solid in-house biotechnology and genetic engineering platform. In 1986, the FDA and the West German government approved Recombivax HB, the first genetically engineered vaccine for humans, to protect against the hepatitis B virus. This is a great example of the potential power of the academia–industry relationship.

Although biotechnology did not begin in Europe as in the United States, several established European companies, such as F. Hoffmann–La Roche, Ciba-Geigy, and then Glaxo, created an important platform for the US biotechnology industry by supporting biotech start-ups and by showing them the ropes, through joint partnerships and exchange of scientists and materials and, importantly, through the marketing of some new biotech-derived products. Unlike Hoechst and Bayer, Ciba-Geigy and Sandoz took advantage of genetic engineering at an early stage and focused sooner on pharmaceuticals than did Bayer and Hoechst. It is estimated that between 1984 and 1999, at least 20 such contracts were carried out by Ciba-Geigy alone, which included one with Genentech in 1984, three with Chiron in 1986, one with Biogen the same year, and the remaining with smaller companies.[24] Ciba-Geigy's strategy ended in 1990 with the acquisition of 60% of Chiron, one of the leading US companies in genetic engineering. In April 2006, Novartis bought the rest of the company.

During the early 1980s, Pfizer decided to enhance its prescription drug capabilities in the 1980s by increasing its R&D expenditures and broadening its therapeutic lines (cutting down on antibiotics while increasing its focus on cardiovascular and anti-inflammatory drugs), keeping, however, some of its older product lines. However, Pfizer, unlike Merck and Lilly, failed in building the necessary technical and functional capabilities based on biotechnology and in establishing a broader and closer set of collaboration agreements and relationships with universities and research institutions, where innovation *really* was. In fact, by the time Pfizer began to make licensing and other arrangements with start-ups such as Genzyme, Moleculom, Neurogen, and Cell Tech in 1987, this company had little in-house capability to commercialize biotechnology products. For this reason, it fell behind Merck and Lilly in this field.

Regulatory Pathways for Biotechnology

The set of techniques and discoveries that biotechnology brought forth in the 1970s and 1980s in the United States as well as several federal and institutional arrangements, most notably the Bayh-Dole Act of 1980 and the Hatch-Waxman Act of 1984 (both of these laws are discussed later in the book, in Chapters 8 and 5, respectively), represented a stupendous opportunity for growth and restructuring in the pharmaceutical industry. One reason for this was that as basic discoveries in biochemistry and the clinical sciences provided a better understanding of the nature of diseases at a molecular level, a new and more specific approach to drug discovery took place—namely, discovery by design. In other words, based on biochemical and crystallographic studies, scientists would design drugs that would interact specifically with the active site of molecules inside the body involved in a specific malady. A second reason was the full maturity of genetics and the blending of genetics, microbiology, biochemistry, and molecular biology into biotechnology and the clinical sciences. As these new learnings were evolving, it became necessary not only to invest heavily in them and to create new strategies to fully exploit them from a commercial point of view, but also to hire a highly specialized and trained scientific staff (and supportive staff), to adopt new ways to perform R&D and to create different marketing strategies.

In the early 1980s, four events took place that facilitated the speedy progress to biotechnology. The first of these was the recognition of patent rights on genetically altered life forms in 1980 by the US Supreme Court in the case *Diamond v. Chakrabarty*. The second was the granting of patent rights on gene cloning to Cohen and Boyer that same year by the US Trade and Patent Office. This development had a great impact on the scientific world because it stimulated research with the objective of commercializing scientific ideas. This also stimulated costly investment in the biotech industry, especially in the medical and agricultural areas, as applied ideas were duly protected by intellectual property rights laws. The number of university spin-offs and the amount of investment in biotechnology has exploded ever since, in spite of the costs and risks associated with this business.

The third was the creation of the Bayh-Dole Act of 1980, which entitled US universities to intellectual property rights from research financed by federal funding and which had a great impact on the creation of academia-based biotech start-ups to commercialize academic research—which, as we shall see later in Chapter 7, has greatly benefited the pharmaceutical industry as well. The fourth was the approval in 1983 by the FDA of the Orphan Drugs Act, designed for rare diseases within patient populations of fewer than 200,000 individuals. This law provides research grants, tax breaks, exclusive marketing rights for 7 years, and other benefits for companies that develop these kinds of drugs. Companies such as Amgen and Genzyme, which found a niche market in the orphan drug category, achieved success in this way, in great contrast to most other biotech start-ups, which built their strategies with great grandiosity, only to see their dreams vanish. By the end of the 1980s, orphan drugs allowed the start-ups the necessary time to create fully integrated functional infrastructures.

By the 1990s, the following scenario in the drug industry was developed: already established pharmaceutical firms used new techniques in biotechnology to commercialize new drugs in large markets, while the smaller biotechnology firms focused on highly specialized technologies to produce specialty and expensive drugs for small markets.

The 1990s presented significant challenges for both the pharmaceutical and the biotech industries. For instance, on the pharmaceutical side, many companies had to assimilate the new technologies and also compete with long-established chemical companies that had entered the pharmaceutical field. For the biotech sector, many companies could simply not afford by themselves the astronomical costs of R&D, product development, clinical trials, and manufacturing and marketing. It is, therefore, no surprise that only a small handful of such biotech companies have succeeded in seeing sustained profitability (see Table 3.1).

Also, since the 1990s, the prescription-path pharmaceutical companies have been challenged by four sets of competitors: in the United States, Johnson & Johnson (which entered pharmaceuticals from medical accessories and which has become one of the top 10 leading pharmaceutical companies in terms of sales) and Procter & Gamble (which entered from consumer goods) became strong competitors. Johnson & Johnson entered the prescription drug path initially via the industry's advertising-intensive medical products path, followed by research-intensive paths. Subsequently, this company started to establish close relationships with innovative biotech start-ups (in the same way that Merck, Eli Lilly, and Abbott had done before in commercializing rDNA drugs)—a strategy that has proven successful. Procter & Gamble, on the other hand, entered the OTC drug path first in the early 1980s and then, in 1982, into prescription drugs primarily by acquisition (a strategy also adopted by Eastman Kodak, which failed in doing so). The other set of companies includes the long-established Japanese firm Takeda—a firm that, after World War II, established relationships with US and European producers through buying and selling licenses, marketing agreements, or joint ventures to introduce new products. In 1997, Takeda decided not to renew its long-term agreement with Abbott Laboratories, but instead to create an integrated overseas subsidiary with its own development—and which continues to capture a large market at present (in fact, in April 2008, it acquired the US-based biotech company Millennium Pharmaceuticals for $8.8 billion). It was joined by German firms E. Merck, Schering AG, and Boehringer-Ingelheim, which, in the 1980s, began to concentrate on the strategy of replacing their chemical business with prescription drugs. Another set of competitors comprised the biotechnology start-ups that began after the biotechnology

Table 3.1 List of the Top 10 Biotech Companies R&D Expenditures and Revenues as of 2010 (in millions of dollars, ranked by 2009 R&D expenditures)

Company	R&D Expenditures			Revenues			R&D as % of Revenues	
	2008	2009	% CHG.	2008	2009	% CHG.	2008	2009
Amgen	3,030	2,864	(5.5)	15,003	14.642	(2.4)	20.2	19.6
Biogen-Idec	1,097	1,283	17.0	4,098	4,377	6.8	26.8	29.3
Gilead Sciences	733	940	28.3	5,336	7,011	31.4	13.7	13.4
Genzyme	1,308	865	(33.9)	4,605	4,516	(1.9)	28.4	19.2
Celgene	2,671	795	(70.2)	2,238	2,677	19.6	119.4	29.7
Cephalon	404	442	9.3	1,975	2,192	11.0	20.5	20.1
Vertex Pharmaceuticals	360	401	11.3	176	102	(41.9)	205.4	393.8
Regeneron Pharmaceuticals	278	399	43.4	238	379	59.1	116.6	105.1
Exelixis	257	235	(8.8)	118	152	28.8	218.4	154.7
Amylin Pharmaceuticals, Inc.	293	185	(36.9)	840	758	(9.7)	34.9	24.4

Source: Standard & Poor's, Industry surveys: Biotechnology. August 19, 2010, p. 19.

revolution. Finally, we must consider the galaxy of generics companies in the industry, of which it is noteworthy to mention the Israeli firm Teva Pharmaceuticals, the largest generics company in the world, and the Indian firm Dr. Reddy's Laboratories, which, as we will see, has become an important pharmaceutical player.

By the 1990s, most large pharmaceutical companies had fully embraced the prescription drug path. This represented an insurmountable challenge to many companies—such as the OTC US ones and all large European pharmaceutical companies except Roche—because this made their sales dependent on their innovativeness. As a result, the 1990s saw an international wave of mergers and acquisitions that created a new set of super-giant companies (see Tables 3.2, 3.3, and 3.4) that, in the 2000s, have dominated the biopharmaceutical industry. Many early mergers were driven less by pipelines and more by the need for a strong US presence, where most of the money was made. At the same time, there was a massive push into "me-too drugs," which were easier to develop than completely novel products. The huge wave of "me-too-drugs" in various therapeutic categories distorted the finances of the industry and also its priorities, emphasizing sales and marketing at the expense of R&D. This wave of products is now losing patents, so a huge loss of income is the result. Many companies are pushing into generics, OTC, diagnostics, emerging markets, and other areas as a way of mitigating these losses. The US price increases may be explained by this as well.

For over a century, Hoechst and Bayer were the world leaders in the chemical and pharmaceutical industries, despite their different strategies and paths. However, transitioning into the life science pharmaceutical business, which was inevitable, was very difficult for both companies, especially for Hoechst, due primarily to their large diversification and slowness in assimilating and integrating the new ideas coming from US universities. By the late 1990s, these companies had fallen behind smaller US and Swiss companies—ironically, in the areas in which they always had been world leaders. Also, by the early 1980s, German universities, which had been extremely instrumental in the success of German companies, had fallen behind US ones, where the most sophisticated and innovative research was being produced. Hoechst, then, made efforts to establish close relationships with leading US universities, such as its relationship, in the early 1980s, with Massachusetts General Hospital (MGH), a Harvard Medical School affiliate, but it failed to repeat this successful formula with other academic institutions and biotech start-ups in the United States. As a result, Hoechst's performance in the 1980s and early 1990s in the pharmaceutical field was rather unremarkable.

Although the history of the scientific developments that eventually found their way to the clinic will not be discussed here, it is necessary to say that the creation of and progress in both the pharmaceutical and biotechnology industries led to the effective translation of basic, mostly academic discoveries into commercial applications. In this sense, most of the initial and important targets and the understanding of the mechanisms involved in disease were developed in academic centers and research institutes. For 150 years, the success of the pharmaceutical industry has depended on a close, symbiotic relationship with academia to develop its drugs; however, without a commercial pharmaceutical infrastructure and strong financial

Table 3.2 List of the Top 10 Pharmaceutical Companies in 1998 (ranked by worldwide sales, in billions of dollars)

Company	Sales
Novartis	10.6
Merck	10.6
Glaxo Wellcome	10.E
Pfizer	9.9
Bristol-Myers Squibb	9.8
Johnson & Johnson	9.0
American Home Products	7.8
F. Hoffmann–La Roche	7.6
Eli Lilly	7.4
SmithKline Beecham	7.3

Source: Standard & Poor's, Industry surveys. Health care: Pharmaceuticals. December 16, 1999, p. 10. With consent from IMS Health, Inc.

Table 3.3 List of the Top 10 Pharmaceutical Companies in 2002

	2002 Sales (US$ Billions)	Percentage Growth Year-Over-Year
1. Pfizer	19.5	12.8
2. GlaxoSmithKline	17.3	10.8
3. Johnson & Johnson	12.7	18.9
4. Merck & Co.	12.7	4.5
5. AstraZeneca	10.9	10.6
6. Bristol-Myers Squibb	8.8	−13.2
7. Novartis	8.0	19.4
8. Wyeth	7.4	7.8
9. Pharmacia	7.2	12.8
10. Lilly	6.7	−10.2
Total	111.2	7.8

Source: IMS Retail and Provider Perspective™, January 2003.

Table 3.4 Leading Pharmaceutical Companies in 2007*

Pharmaceutical Sales Only					
Company	**Sales (bil. $)**				
	2003	**2004**	**2005**	**2006**	**2007**
1. Pfizer	29.3	31.1	27.3	26.3	23.5
2. GlaxoSmithKline	18.5	18.9	20.0	21.3	20.1
3. Merck	14.0	15.3	15.4	16.7	17.6
4. Johnson & Johnson	15.4	10.7	16.0	16.1	16.3
5. AstraZeneca	10.1	11.5	12.7	14.7	15.5
6. Amgen	7.7	9.7	11.9	14.5	14.3
7. Novartis/Sandoz	10.5	11.6	13.0	13.9	13.9
8. Hoffman–La Roche	5.3	6.2	8.2	10.4	12.3
9. Sanofi-Aventis	9.0	10.2	11.1	11.0	10.9
10. Lilly	7.7	3.2	8.7	9.2	10.3
Total, top 10	127.5	139.4	144.3	155.1	154.7
Total US market	219.6	239.9	253.9	276.1	286.5

Source: Standard & Poor's, Industry surveys. Health care: Pharmaceuticals. April 24, 2008. Copyright © Standard & Poor's Financial Services LLC, a subsidiary of The McGraw-Hill Companies, Inc. Reprinted with permission. All rights reserved. With consent from IMS Health, Inc.

*Leading pharmaceutical companies after the wave of mergers of the late 1990s/early 2000s and before the wave of mergers of 2009.

backup and marketing channels, most of the basic scientific discoveries emerging from academia that could lead to potential drugs would have remained, like aspirin, shelved on a research bench, depriving society of great benefits.

In the next chapter, let us explore what shape the biopharmaceutical industry has taken in the first decade of the twenty-first century.

Notes

1. Montanelli was an eminent Italian journalist, historian, and novelist. He is using irony in this expression to denote that there is nothing new in human history, yet we make the same mistakes time and again because we fail to learn from the past.
2. It is interesting, and amusing, that in Spanish the word *droga* (drug) comes from the Hispanic Arabic word *hatrúka*, which literally means "*charlatanería*" (charlatanism).
3. Some important research was taking place in the United States and Japan as well.
4. Weatherall, M., 1990. In Search of a Cure: A History of Pharmaceutical Discovery. Oxford University Press, New York.

5. Cinchona bark's medicinal uses were discovered by the Peruvian Quechua Indians. Through the Jesuit Order, the root made its way to Europe in the early seventeenth century, where it was used to treat malarial fevers. Singer, C., Underwood, A., 1962. A Short History of Medicine. Clarendon Press, Oxford. See also Weatherall, M., 1990. In Search of a Cure: A History of Pharmaceutical Discovery. Oxford University Press, New York.
6. Gardner, W.M., 1915. The British Coal-Tar Industry: Its Origin, Development, and Decline. William and Norgate, London.
7. Singer, C., Underwood, A., 1962. A Short History of Medicine. Oxford Clarendon Press, Oxford.
8. Ehrlich, P., in Gesammelte Arbeiten, cited by Drews, J., 2000. Drug discovery: a historical perspective. Science 287 (5460), 1960–1964. See also Weatherall, M., 1990. In Search of a Cure: A History of Pharmaceutical Discovery. Oxford University Press, New York.
9. GlaxoSmithKline, Our History. Available from: http://www.gsk.com/about/history.htm.
10. Chandler, A.D., 2005. Shaping the Industrial Century: The Remarkable Story of the Evolution of Modern Chemical and Pharmaceutical Industries. Harvard University Press, Cambridge, MA.
11. Ibid.
12. Ibid.
13. Lesch, J.E. (Ed.), 2000. The German Chemical Industry in the Twentieth Century. Kluwer Academic, Dordrecht. This cartel was later to support Hitler and the Nazis and was involved in many crimes.
14. See http://www.fdrs.org/ig_farben_quotes.html and http://www.whale.to/b/war_q.html.
15. After this period, a new era of reorganization and growth took place at Hoechst, as discussed later in the chapter. In 1918, Ciba, Geigy, and Sandoz formed a cartel, the Interessengemeinschaft Basel (Basel Syndicate), or Basel IG, to compete with the German chemical cartel IG Farben. In 1929–32, Basel IG joined with IG Farben and French and British chemical firms to form the Quadrapartite Cartel, which lasted until the outbreak of World War II in 1939. Basel IG survived the war, but it dissolved in 1951 partly out of regard for US antitrust legislation.
16. It was through Rutgers University, specifically through the work of Dr. Selman Waksman, who discovered streptomycin, that Merck joined the antibiotic revolution. Thus, Merck agreed to manufacture and distribute the new drug with the patents assigned to the Rutgers Research Foundation.
17. See Note 10.
18. Richmond, J., Fein, R., 2005. The Health Care Mess: How We Got into It and What It Will Take to Get Out. Harvard University Press, Cambridge, MA.
19. See Note 10.
20. It was not until 1952, however, that Congress decided that a doctor's prescription would be necessary to purchase drugs that could not be used safely without medical expertise. In 1962, another requirement was added: drug companies had to prove that their products were not only safe, but also effective. That mandate soon gave rise to rules for carrying out clinical trials—the only way to show safety and effectiveness unequivocally.
21. See Note 10.
22. Such as the discovery of the DNA structure (Watson and Crick in the United Kingdom) and the Operon model (Jacobs and Monod in France).
23. Genentech, available from: http://www.gene.com/gene/about/corporate/history/.
24. See Note 10.

4 The Biopharmaceutical Industry in the Twenty-first Century: Titanic Challenges Ahead

As of today, the pharmaceutical industry represents a global market of approximately $837 billion,[1] of which by far the largest market share belongs to the United States (36%), followed, in order of market share size, by Europe (31.5%), Asia-Africa-Australia (12.7%), Japan (11.3%), and Latin America (5.7%) (see Table 4.1.) Even if most large pharmaceutical companies are European in origin, the United States represents their largest market owing to several factors, particularly the lack of official price controls, a very stringent drug regulatory system, a large population, a very rewarding financial and insurance market, and many incentives at the public and private levels to pursue innovation, notwithstanding the large amounts of funding and resources that the US government invests in basic research in universities and research institutes. Not surprisingly, for many years, the pharmaceutical industry positioned itself as the most profitable of all industries in the United States; that situation has varied over recent years, though it continues to be among the top three most powerful industries, as was mentioned in previous chapters.

Ever since 1999, the year in which the sales of pharmaceuticals reached its highest growth level, global pharmaceutical sales have decelerated continuously, a fact that has become more evident in the last few years. For example, between 2002 and 2004, the compound annual growth rate (CAGR) of the industry was about 8.1%.[2] It then dropped to 7% in 2005, to 6.6% in 2006, and to 6.4% in 2007, and in 2008, it reached a level of 4.5% to 5.5%.[3] In 2009, the CAGR slowed even further, to a rate of 4.5%.[4] From a financial point of view, especially after the 2008 collapse of the world financial markets, a growth slowdown of the pharmaceutical industry's sales has preoccupied investors and, of course, industry managers. But discounting the impact that the 2008 crisis had (and continues to have) in the world, and seeing things from a broader perspective, the continuous decline in the sales growth rate of the pharmaceutical industry is symptomatic of something deeper that may be eroding the industry (see Table 4.2 for a list of the top 10 pharmaceutical companies as of 2009).

One of the most obvious problems that the pharmaceutical industry is confronting is that in spite of the ever-increasing spending on research and development (R&D) over the last decades, the number of new molecular entity (NME) approvals has declined significantly (see Figure 4.1a and b). An NME is an active ingredient that has never before been marketed in the United States in any form.[5] It is estimated that it takes an average of approximately $0.8–1 billion and 10–15 years to bring a new drug to market.[6,7] In 2007, the pharmaceutical industry alone spent

The World's Health Care Crisis. DOI: 10.1016/B978-0-12-391875-8.00004-4

Table 4.1 Leading Global Regional Markets for Pharmaceutical Sales

	Global Pharmaceutical Sales, by Region				
	Sales[a] ($ Billions) 2009	**Market Share (%) 2009**	**% CHG. 2008–09**	**CAGR % 2004–09**	**Forecast % Growth 2009–10**
US and Canada	323.8	38.7	5.5	5.2	3–5
Europe	263.9	31.5	4.8	6.6	3–5
Asia, Africa, Australia	106.6	12.7	15.9	13.9	13–15
Japan	95.0	11.3	7.6	3.9	0–2
Latin America	47.9	5.7	10.6	10.9	10–12
TOTAL	837.3	100.0	7.0	6.7	4.6

Source: Standard & Poor's, Industry surveys. Health care: Pharmaceuticals. June 3, 2010, p. 9. © Standard & Poor's Financial Services LLC, a subsidiary of The McGraw-Hill Companies, Inc. Reprinted with permission. All rights reserved. With consent from IMS Health, Inc.
CAGR-Compound annual growth rate.
[a]In constant dollars, using Q4 2009 average exchange rates.

Table 4.2 Top 10 Pharmaceutical Companies in 2009

	US Pharma Sales ($ Billions)				
Company	**2005**	**2006**	**2007**	**2008**	**2009**
1. Pfizer	34.3	34.2	31.4	27.7	27.8
2. Merck	18.7	20.6	21.9	20.1	19.8
3. AstraZeneca	12.4	14.5	15.2	16.1	18.3
4. GlaxoSmithKline	17.0	18.7	18.3	16.5	15.0
5. Hoffman–La Roche	8.0	10.2	11.9	12.6	14.3
6. Novartis	12.6	13.6	13.5	12.2	13.4
7. Lilly	8.9	9.7	10.7	12.0	13.2
8. Johnson & Johnson	15.6	15.7	15.9	15.6	12.8
9. Amgen	11.6	14.2	13.6	12.8	12.5
10. Teva Pharmaceuticals	7.3	9.0	9.8	11.2	12.1
Total, Top 10	146.4	160.4	162.2	156.8	159.2
Total, US Market	247.3	270.3	280.5	285.7	300.3

Source: Standard & Poor's, Industry surveys: Pharmaceuticals. June 3, 2010, p. 9. © IMS Health, Inc. Reprinted with permission. All rights reserved.

more than $60 billion in R&D (twice as much as the National Institutes of Health), which constituted roughly 10% of its global sales, yet only 16 NMEs and 2 biologic license applications (BLAs)[8] were approved, which is less than half of what was approved a decade ago and the lowest number of approved NMEs since 1983, when

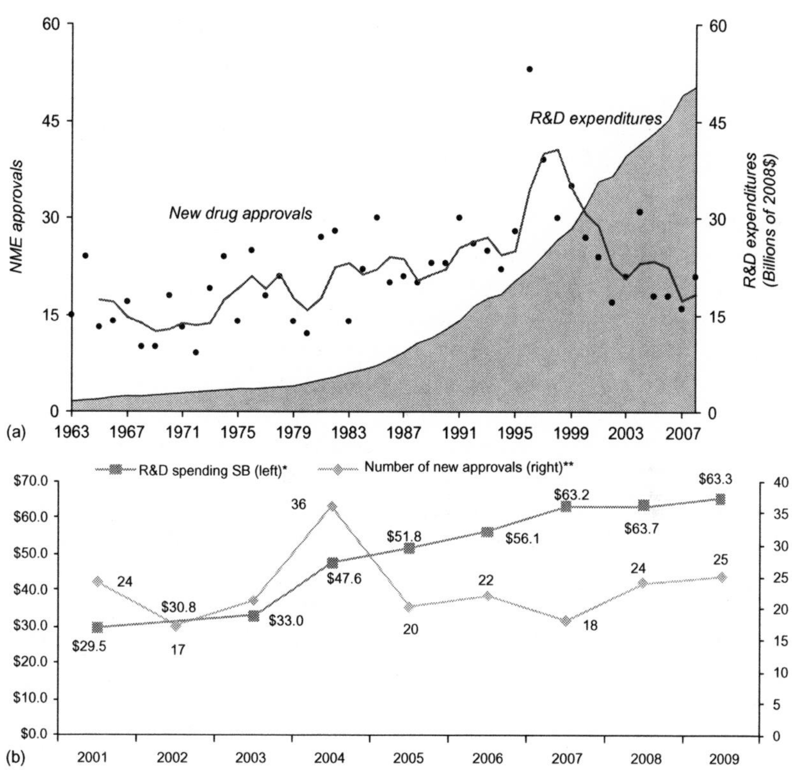

Figure 4.1 (a) New drug approvals are not keeping pace with research and development. *Source*: Tufts Center for the Study of Drug Development (TCSDD) Approved NCE Database, PhRMA, 2007. Courtesy TCSDD. © Tufts Center for the Study of Drug Development. Reprinted with permission. All rights reserved.
(b) New FDA approvals and R&D spending by year (2001–2009).
Source: Moody's Investors Service. Global Pharmaceutical Outlook, June 2010, p. 4. © Moody's Investors Service, Inc. and/or its affiliates. Reprinted with permission. All rights reserved.
*PhRMA Industry Profile 2010 and Moody's estimates.
**FDA gov; includes approvals of New Molecular Entities (NME's) and Biologics Licensing Applications.

the US Food and Drug Administration (FDA) approved only 14 NMEs. But in contrast to 2007, the amount invested by industry in R&D in 1983 was only $3.2 billion.[9] Furthermore, none of the approvals could be considered breakthrough drugs. It is estimated that the amount invested in R&D by the pharmaceutical industry alone exceeded $65 billion in 2009.[10]

In 2008, the FDA approved 21 NMEs and 3 BLAs, which were evaluated by the Center for Drug Evaluation and Research (CDER).[11] In 2009, the FDA approved 25 NMEs in total (19 NMEs and 6 BLAs)[12]—a slight improvement over 2008, but one that still fell far short of the approval rate seen in the 1990s. As has been remarked, the fact that a slight improvement takes place in 1 year should not be interpreted as a trend or a consequence of the FDA speeding up or slowing down the drug approval process, because some applications that met the standards for approval in 2008 and 2009 went through only one cycle, but others were applications that were submitted years ago and that required multiple cycles. Interestingly enough, 2010 witnessed another reversal in drug approval because only 21 NMEs were approved.

Though a few potential "blockbuster" drugs won approval in 2010, some of the most highly anticipated new products got delayed into next year or even beyond. Some of the most important approvals in 2010 include Amgen's Prolia, a drug that is injected twice yearly to treat osteoporosis in postmenopausal women; Genentech's Actemra, a drug that is administered intravenously to treat rheumatoid arthritis; Boehringer Ingelheim's Pradaxa, a new type of blood-thinning drug to prevent strokes in patients with irregular heart rhythms; Novartis's Gilenya, an oral product for the treatment of multiple sclerosis; and Acorda Therapeutics's Ampyra, a drug to improve walking in multiple sclerosis patients. Some of the major 2010 setbacks include AstraZeneca's blood-thinning drug Brilinta, when the FDA asked in December 2010 for more information about a study backing this application; and Amylin Pharmaceuticals/Eli Lilly's Byetta, when the FDA also rejected a long-acting version of this diabetes drug on the grounds that more clinical data were needed to address cardiovascular safety concerns.[13]

As the pharmaceutical industry struggles to bring new drugs to the market, it faces another major problem related to product underperformance: the massive number of patent expirations of the industry's best selling drugs. Pharmaceutical companies are awarded 20 years of market exclusivity once a patent is granted, from which they need to discount the time required for the development of the drug and to bring it to the market—approximately 12 years, on average. Once a drug goes off patent, it becomes a generic drug, and slightly before the patent expiration date, generics companies challenge the innovator's patent. As a result, within 2 years, brand-name sales erode as much as 80% of the original price. Because of their large size and the fact that the drug industry spends a great deal of resources and funding (amounting to more than 20% of its global sales) on marketing and promotion, companies need a huge amount of cash in revenue to compensate for losses due to patent expirations, which has become a heavy burden. The conglomerate value of brand-name drugs continues to increase year after year: from $12 billion in 2005 to $15 billion in 2006, $18 billion in 2007, and about $25 billion in 2008 and 2009.[14] This situation is expected to continue until 2011, when the largest number of patents will expire; Tables 4.3, 4.4, and 4.5 list the number of drugs that will be expiring in 2008 and 2009. It is projected that by 2016, medicines worth $140–200 billion will lose patent protection.[15]

The patent expiration problem is exacerbated by the fact that some of the most popular (which also means profitable) areas have been affected, such as the lipid regulators and antihypertensive therapeutic classes, which alone are responsible for an erosion of 35% of brand-name sales.[16] Pfizer, the largest pharmaceutical company in the world, has been hit particularly hard by the expiration of five of its best selling drugs in the last couple of years (including its hypertensive Norvasc, at $2.7 billion in sales in 2006, and Zyrtec, at $1.5 billion in sales[17]), which together accounted for 21% of the company's revenues in 2006. Sleeping disorder drugs constitute one of

Table 4.3 Major Patent Expirations by 2009[c]

Brand Name	Generic	Company	Indication	2005 US Sales[b] ($ Billions)	Expiration Date[a]
Zocor	Simvastatin	Merck	Hyperlipidemia	4.4	June 2006
Prevacid	Lansoprazole	TAP	Duodenal ulcers	3.8	Nov. 2009
Zoloft	Sertraline	Pfizer	Depression	3.1	June 2006
Effexor XR	Venlafaxine	Wyeth	Depression	2.6	June 2008
Norvasc	Amlodipine	Pfizer	Hypertension	2.6	Sept. 2007
Risperdal	Risperidone	Janssen	Schizophrenia	2.3	Dec. 2007
Fosamax	Alendronic acid	Merck	Osteoporosis	2.0	Feb. 2008
Pravachol	Pravastatin	Bristol-Myers Squibb	Hyperlipidemia	1.7	April 2006
Ambien	Zolpidem tartrate	Sanofi-Aventis SA	Insomnia	1.6	April 2007
Zyrtec	Certrinzine HCL	Pfizer	Allergies	1.4	Dec. 2007
Zofran	Ondansetron HCL	GlaxoSmith-Kline PLC	Chemotherapy-induced nausea	1.3	Dec. 2006
Toprol XL	Metoprolol XL	AstraZeneca PLC	Hypertension	1.1	Sept. 2007
Lamisil	Terbinafine	Novartis AG	Antifungal	0.7	June 2007
Proscar	Finasteride	Merck	Prostate cancer	0.4	June 2006

Source: Standard and Poor's, "Industry Surveys. Health care: Pharmaceuticals," 2009. © Standard & Poor's Financial Services LLC, a subsidiary of The McGraw-Hill Companies, Inc. Reprinted with permission. All rights reserved. With consent from IMS Health, Inc.

[a]Both actual and potential dates are listed. Some expiration dates are subject to change as a result of court rulings and deals struck between pharmaceutical and generics companies; among those vulnerable are Risperdal and Prevacid. (A federal court upheld Risperdal's patent in October 2006; expiration date is likely to stand unless decision is appealed.)

[b]Sales based on prescription drug purchases at wholesale prices by various channels; includes retailers, food stores, hospitals, clinics, etc., among others.

[c]Due to lose patent protection by 2009, ranked by 2005 sales.

the fastest growing drug categories, with sales accounting for 31.5% of pharmaceutical spending in 2005, and several drugs in this class are going off patent, of which the Sanofi-Aventis insomnia drug Ambien ($2.2 billion in sales in 2006), which went off patent in 2007, is a prominent example; there has been fierce competition among generics companies to share that market.[18] This loss of revenue owing to generics competition makes the pharmaceutical industry's leaders and investors nervous, especially because it is expected that the revenues generated by near-term new

Table 4.4 Some Potential Patent Expirations for 2010–2012

Possible Patent Expiration[a]	Brand Name (Generic Name), Manufacturer/ Marketer	Uses	2009 US Retail Sales (SM)
2010	*Effexor XR*® (venlafaxine extended-release), Wyeth	Depression, anxiety, panic disorder	$2,554
	Flomax® (tamsulosin),[b] Boehringer Ingelheim	Benign prostatic hypertrophy	$1,718
	Aricept® (donepezil), Pfizer	Alzheimer's disease	$1,464
	Cozaar® (losartan), Merck	High blood pressure	$771
	Arimidex® (anastrozole), AstraZeneca	Breast cancer	$697
	Hyzaar® (losartan/HCTZ), Merck	High blood pressure	$584
	Mirapex® (pramipexole), Boehringer Ingelheim	Parkinson's disease, restless legs syndrome	$417
	Aldara® (imiquimod topical cream), Graceway	Actinic keratosis, genital warts, skin cancer	$412
	Differin® (adapalene topical),[b] Galderma	Acne	$282
	Asterlin® (azelastine nasal spray), Meda	Allergic rhinitis	$209
	Fosamax® *Plus D* (alendronate/cholecalciferol), Merck	Osteoporosis	$123
2011	*Lipitor*® (atorvastatin), Pfizer	High cholesterol	$6,053
	Zyprexa® (olanzapine), Lilly	Schizophrenia, bipolar disorder	$1,968
	Xalatan® (latanoprost ophthalmic solution), Pfizer	Glaucoma, ocular hypertension	$519
	Protonix® (pantoprazole), Wyeth	Stomach ulcers, GERD	$497
	Femara® (letrozole), Novartis	Breast cancer	$461
	Caduct® (amlodipine/atorvastatin), Pfizer	High blood pressure and high cholesterol	$362
	Patanol® (olopatadine ophthaimic solution),[b] Alcon	Allergic conjunctivitis	$256
	Accolate® (zafirlukast),[b] AstraZeneca	Asthma	$44
2012	*Plavix*® (clopidogrel), Sanofi-Aventis	Prevention of arterial thrombotic events	$4,562
	Seroquel® (quetiapine), AstraZeneca	Schizophrenia, bipolar disorder	$3,482

Singulair® (montelukast), Merck	Asthma, allergic rhinitis	$3,465
Actos® (pioglitazone),[b] Takeda	Type 2 diabetes	$2,782
Lexapro® (escitalopram), Forest	Depression	$2,554
Levaquin® (levofloxacin), Ortho-McNeil	Bacterial infections	$1,632
Diovan® (valsartan), Novartis	Hypertension, CHF	$1.469
Diovan HCT® (valsartan/HCTZ), Novartis	Hypertension	$1,376
Tricor® (fenofibrate), Abbott	High triglycerides	$1,350
Lovenox® (enoxaparin), Sanofi-Aventis	Treatment/prevention of venous thromboembolism	$1,245
Lidoderm® (lidocaine) patch, Teikoku	Postherpetic neuralgia	$1,064
Viagra® (sildenafil), Pfizer	Erectile dysfunction	$1,000
Geodon® (ziprasidone), Pfizer	Schizophrenia	$975
Provigli® (modafinil), Cephalon	Narcolepsy, idiopathic hypersomnolence	$966
Lunesta® (eszopliclone), Sepracor	Insomnia	$804
Avandia® (rosiglitazone), GlaxoSmithKline	Type 2 diabetes	$436
Avapro® (irbesartan), Sanofi-Aventis	Hypertension	$413
Avalide® (irbesartan/HCTZ), Sanofi-Aventis	Hypertension	$359
Avandamet® (rosiglitazone/metformin), GlaxoSmithKline	Type 2 diabetes	$207
Clarinex® (desloratadine), Schering	Allergic rhinitis	$207
Atacand® (candesartan), AstraZeneca	Hyprtension CHF	$162
Atacand HCT® (candesartan/HCTZ), AstraZeneca	Hypertension	$77

Source: Graph from Medco's Drug Trend Report, 2010, p. 43.

[a]Availability dates for first-time generics are subject to significant change as a result of multiple patent protections, patent litigation, pediatric or other exclusivities, at-risk launches, and delays between patent expiration and launch of first-time generics.

[b]Possible patent expiration assumes a pediatric extension.

Table 4.5 Selected Companies' Exposure to Patent Expirations and Challenges

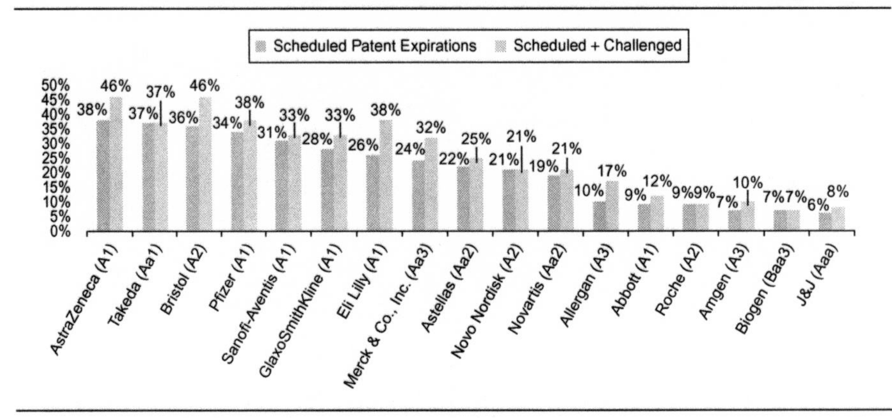

Source: Moody's Investor Service. Industry Outlook: Global Pharmaceuticals. 2010, p. 4.

approvals, which, by now, should be in Phase II clinical trials, will not be enough to offset these hemorrhaging losses.[19] (Table 4.6 shows the most recently approved drugs, whereas Table 4.7 shows how some major pharmaceutical companies are refilling their pipelines.) Furthermore, it takes a few years for most drugs to build a strong market.

In the meantime, the branded drug–generic drug interface has become a battlefield of legal litigation because as generics companies challenge brand-name drugs by bringing generic versions to market earlier than expected, the branded drug companies fire back. Generics are an evolving sector (in 2007, the sector grew 7.9%, faster than branded drugs, reaching a global generics market of $90.7 billion in 2007, although it dropped to 3.6% in 2008),[20] the generic market gained momentum again in 2009 with 7.7% growth and total global sales of $84 billion[21] and has been enhanced by the rapid loss of patent protection of branded drugs. However, the profitability of generics companies is rather small compared to the profitability of branded pharmaceutical companies, which is in the hundreds of billions of dollars every year (e.g., the United States, which constitutes 42% of the global generics market, attained generics sales worth $34 billion in 2007, $33 billion in 2008, and $34 billion in 2009, compared to approximately $250 billion in sales every year, in branded drugs, during the same time frame).[22]

Because generics companies need to keep costs down to survive—once a drug becomes generic, the spoils of the war against brand-name companies are split among many different players—they face significant challenges such as pricing pressures and lack of trust. This is especially true because many patients associate generics with safety scandals and a lack of stringent regulation, as evidenced by some products manufactured in China and India that, unfortunately for many other high-quality generics, stained the reputation of generics in general. It is believed that generics constitute about three fourths[23] of all prescriptions in the United States. In Europe, because of

Table 4.6 Recent New Molecular Entities Approved*

Trade Name	Generic Name	Applicant	Therapeutic Potentials	Approval Date
Votrient	Pazopanib	GlaxoSmithKline	S	10/19/09
Folotyn	Pralatrexate	Allos Therapeutics	PO	9/24/09
Telavancin	Telavancin	Theravance	S	9/11/09
Bepotastine Besilate	Bepotastine Besilate	Ista Pharmaceuticals	S	9/8/09
Sabril	Vigabatrin	Lundbeck	SO	8/21/09
Saphris	Asenapine	Organon	S	8/13/09
Livalo Tablets	Pitavastatin	Kowa Research	S	8/3/09
Onglyza	Saxagliptin	Bristol-Myers Squibb	S	7/31/09
Effient	Prasugrel	Eli Lilly	P	7/10/09
Multaq	Dronedarone hcl	Sanofi-Aventis	P	7/1/09
Besifloxacin Hcl	Besifloxacin	Bausch & Lomb	S	5/28/09
Samsca	Tolvaptan tablets	Otsuka America	S	5/19/09
Fanapt	Iloperidone	Vanda Pharmaceuticals	S	5/6/09
Ulesfia	Benzyl alcohol	Sciele Pharma	S	4/9/09
Coartem	Artemether 20 mg/ lumefantrine 120 mg	Novartis	PO	4/7/09
Affinitor	Everolimus	Novartis	P	3/30/09
Uloric	Febuxostat	Takeda	S	2/13/09
Savella Tablets	Milnacipran hcl tablets	Cypress Bioscience	S	1/14/09

Source: Standard & Poor's, Industry surveys. Health care: Pharmaceuticals. June 3, 2010, p. 16. © Standard & Poor's Financial Services LLC, a subsidiary of The McGraw-Hill Companies, Inc. Reprinted with permission. All rights reserved.

*Excludes diagnostic NMEs. P-Priority review: significant improvement compared with marketed products in the treatment or prevention of a disease. S-Standard review: drug appears to have therapeutic qualities similar to those of one or more already marketed drugs. O-Orphan drug.

governmental intervention, especially in countries such as Germany, Italy, and Spain, growth in this industry is expected to take place in upcoming years.[24] Table 4.8 shows the top generics companies in the world, of which Teva (Israel), Mylan (United States), and Sandoz (a branch of Novartis AG, Switzerland) are the leaders, and their corresponding market shares.[25]

Trying to balance revenue losses due to patent expirations of best selling drugs by bringing a new array of blockbuster drugs to the market has been quite difficult for most companies because of major setbacks that took place when high-profile and potentially highly profitable products were denied approval by regulators or when

Table 4.7 New Product Pipelines at Top US Pharmaceutical Companies as of 2010

Company	Name of Compound	Pharmacologic Class	Treatment	Status	EST. 2015 Sales (MIL. $)
Abbott Laboratories	ABT-874	Human monoclonal antibody	Crohn's disease		500
	Certriad	Fibrate and stain combination	Cholesterol/tryglycerides regulation	Filed	400
	Flutiform	Beta2 agonist	Asthma	Filed	200
	Vicodin CR	Hydrocodone/acetaminophen	Pain	Filed	350
Brristol-Myers Squibb	Apixaban (partnered with Pfizer)	Factor Xa inhibitor	Thrombosis	Phase III	1,100
	Belatacept	Anti-b7 integrin Mab	Immunosuppression	Phase III	800
	Dapaglifloxin	Selective SGLT2 Inhibitor	Diabetes	Phase III	750
	Ipilimumab	Human monoclonal antibody	Melanoma	Phase III	500
	Onglyza	Dipeptidyl peptidase IV (DPP-IV) inhibitor	Diabetes	Approved	1,600
Eli Lilly & Co.	Ramucirumab	Anti-VEGFrMAb	Breast cancer	Phase III	400
	Bydureon	Glucagon-like peptide 1 (GLP-1) agonist	Diabetes	Filed	1,100
	Effient	Platelet ADP antagonist	Acute coronary syndrome	Approved	950
	Enzastaurin	Protein kinase C (PKC) inhibitor	Cancer	Phase III	250
	Solaneuzumab	Monoclonial antibody	Aizheimer's disease	Phase III	200
	Teplizumab	Monoclonal antibody	Diabetes	Phase III	225
	Semagacestat	y-secretase inhibitor	Alzheimer's disease	Phase III	240

Johnson & Johnson	Ceftobiprole	Cephalosporin	Bacterial infections	Filed	850
	Bapineuzamab (partnered with Pfizer)	Anti-beta amyloid Mab	Alzheimer's disease	Phase III	1,100
	Dapoxetine	SSRI	Premature ejaculation	Filed	300
	Dacogen	Pyrimidine analogue	Cancer	Phase III	150
	Rilpivirine	Reverse transcriptase inhibitor	HIV	Phase III	350
	Simponi (partnered with Merck)	Anti-TNFa Mab	Rheumatoid arthritis	Approved	2,600
	Stelara	Anti-IL-12 & IL-23 MAb	Psoriasia	Filed	780
	Telaprevir	Protease inhibitor	Hepatitis C	Phase III	1,250
	Xareito	Factor Xa inhibitor	Thrombosis	Phase III	1,500
	Abiraterone	Abiraterone acetate	Prostate cancer	Phase III	350
Merck & Co.	Bocepravir	HCV protease inhibitor	Hepatitis C	Phase III	790
	Deforolimus (MK-8669)	Rapamycin analogue (mTOR)	Cancer	Phase III	200
	MK-0524B	Tredaptive with simvastatin	Cholesterol regulation	Phase III	800
	MK-0822	Cathepsin K inhibitor	Osteoporosis	Phase III	600
	Org 36286	Corifollitropin alfa	Infertility	Phase III	200
	Preladenant	Adenosine A2 antagonist	Parkinson's disease	Phase II	300
	Saphris	5HT-2/D2 antagonist	Schizophrenia	Approved	600
	Simponi (partnered with J&J)	Anti-TNFa MAb	Rheumatoid arthritis	Approved	2,600
	Bridion	Selective relaxant binding agent	Novel anesthetic	Phase III	650
	Telcagepant	CGRP antagonist	Migraine	Phase III	700

(Continued)

Table 4.7 (Continued)

Company	Name of Compound	Pharmacologic Class	Treatment	Status	EST. 2015 Sales (MIL. $)
	TRA	Thrombin receptor antagonist	Acute coronary syndrome	Phase III	2,100
	Tredaptive	Nicotinic acid/Laropiprant	Cholesterol regulation	Filed	750
	V710	Staphylococcus	Vaccine	Phase II	1,150
Pfizer, Inc.	Apixaban (partnered with Bristol-Myers Squibb)	Factor Xa inhibitor	Thrombosis	Phase III	1,100
	Aprela	Oestrogen agonist & SERM	Osteoporosis & menopause	Phase III	200
	Axinitib	VEGF inhibitor	Cancer	Phase III	550
	CP-69D550	JAK-3 inhibitor	Immunosuppressive	Phase III	1,200
	Bapineuzamab (partnered with J&J)	Humanized monocional antibody	Alzheimer's	Phase III	1,100
	CP-675	Monocional antibody	Skin cancer	Phase III	550
	CP-751	IGF-IR monocional antibody	Cancer	Phase III	200
	Fesoterodine	Antimuscarinic agent	Incontinence	Approved in Europe	500
	Prevnar 13	Pneumococcal 13-valent	Vaccine	Phase III	4,500
	Pristiq	Desvenlafaxine	Depression	Approved	200
	Pristiq	Desvenlafaxine	Vasomotor symptoms	Approvable	150
	Relistor	Mu opioid antagonist	Constipation	Filed	400
	Viviant	SERM	Osteoporosis	Approvable	150
	Xiaflex	Collagenase clostridium	Peyronie's disease	Phase III	320

Source: Standard & Poor's, Industry surveys. Health care: Pharmaceuticals. June 3, 2010. © Standard & Poor's Financial Services LLC, a subsidiary of The McGraw-Hill Companies, Inc. Reprinted with permission .All rights reserved.

Table 4.8 Leading Generics Companies in the World

Company	Annual Sales (in Millions)	Market Share %
Teva Pharmaceuticals (Israel)	6,956	21.8
Mylan, Inc. (United States)	3,620	11.3
Sandoz (generic arm of Swiss Novartis; Germany)	2,494	7.8
Watson Pharmaceuticals (United States)	2,000	6.3
Greenstone (Part of Pfizer; United States)	1,721	5.4
Par Pharma (United States)	1,319	4.1
Hospira (United States)	1,061	3.3
Apotex (Canada)	879	2.8
Mallinckrodt (United States)	860	2.7
Dr. Reddy's Laboratories (India)	834	2.6

Source: Fierce Pharma: http://www.fiercepharma.com/special-reports/top-10-generic-drug-companies-2010. (Publicly available data on the Internet.) http://pharmexcil.org/data/media_files/Top10GenericDru_media_file_792.pdf.

regulators requested additional information before approval was granted. As an example of this, the drug company Wyeth (now part of Pfizer) tried to offset hemorrhaging revenue losses stemming from the patent expiration of its best selling Effexor, an antidepressant ($3.7 billion in sales), and the gastrointestinal drug Protonix (due to expire in 2010–2011; $2 billion in sales) by bringing to market Pristiq, a treatment for menopausal symptoms and depression that the company had hoped to become a $2 billion drug. However, the drug initially failed to gain FDA approval, and though it was approved later for the treatment of depression, it was with a more limited application, with an estimated market of only $200–500 million by 2012.[26] Wyeth also faced regulatory delays from the FDA with two of its other drugs: Bifeprunox, for schizophrenia, and Vivant, for osteoporosis. Another disappointing example came in early 2008 when it was found that comparison trials between the anticholesterol drug Vytorin (Schering Plough Corp./Merck) and the generic drug simvastatin yielded no advantages for Vytorin.[27]

Safety concerns have intensified over recent years, especially in the United States, ever since Merck's painkiller drug Vioxx, a first-in-class COX-2 inhibitor, made world headlines in September 2004 when it was found to increase the risk of stroke and heart attack in patients who used it for the treatment of arthritis. This finding cost the company as much as a capped $4.25 billion in plaintiff settlements and legal fees so far,[28] and this number is likely to continue to rise amid recently filed lawsuits in Australia in 2009.[29] More recently, the erythropoietin stimulating agents (ESAs) used for the treatment of anemia in kidney dialysis and cancer patients; the selective serotonin reuptake inhibitors (SSRIs, antidepressants); and the gliatazones (for type

2 diabetes) have come under fire. This is not good news for the pharmaceutical companies that commercialize these multibillion-dollar products. Even children's cold and cough syrups have come under scrutiny. Because of increasing pressure from the public, regulators are now setting stronger safety warnings on the labels of these drugs, which are already on the market.

It is interesting that many drug companies, such as Merck with Vioxx, and in fact even the FDA in the case of Vioxx and other drugs, allowed them to reach the market even though they knew they had serious safety issues, taking lightly the consequences that this behavior would have for public health, not to mention the tremendously negative images and economic impacts that would follow from such actions. For companies, expenses from litigation fees and compensation to plaintiffs are not as damaging as actually "killing" products. In other words, had Merck done Vioxx studies correctly before bringing it to market, the company might have made less profit, but it also might still have benefited patient populations and kept first-class drugs alive that could have been used for the treatment of other medical conditions.

From a commercial viewpoint, safety issues, or the lack thereof, have a very unwanted effect for pharmaceutical companies: they can affect reimbursement as well as erode sales. For instance, before the ESAs—the market of which is dominated by Amgen, the largest biotechnology company in the world, and Johnson & Johnson—came under public scrutiny between November 2006 and early 2007[30] after several published studies suggested that high doses of ESA therapy in patients with kidney disease could lead to serious cardiovascular complications, including death, and that in the case of cancer patients, these medicines could lead to a worsening of disease. In 2006, ESA sales in the United States alone were $10 billion, but by 2007, their sales had dropped by 9%.[31] In particular, this affected Amgen's Procrit (US sales of $2.9 billion in 2006), a medicine used to increase red blood cell production in the treatment of fatigue and anemia associated with cancer chemotherapy, and two of Amgen's other best selling drugs: Epogen, used for patients on dialysis with anemia (US sales of $3.2 billion in 2006), and Aranesp (US sales of $3.9 billion in 2006), indicated for the treatment of anemia associated with chronic renal failure. An advanced form of Epogen with a lower dosage was also affected. The FDA recommended carrying out additional clinical trials to assess the safety of ESAs, which obviously had an impact on reimbursement. In July 2007, the Centers for Medicare and Medicaid (CMS) tightened significantly its criteria for the reimbursement of ESAs, limiting its coverage to patients with high hemoglobin levels below 10, even though the FDA-approved indication is higher. Furthermore, the CMS indicated that it would no longer cover the product for off-label uses, which represented an increasingly important part of the market for the drugs. Not surprisingly, the companies involved did not welcome the CMS's decision because the CMS spends several billion dollars each year on ESAs, and other third-party payers base their reimbursement decisions on the decisions of the CMS, as discussed in Chapter 1. In response, ESA-producing companies, advocacy groups, and even the government have demanded that the CMS reverse its decision.

For companies, the economic effects were felt immediately. For Amgen, US sales of Procrit fell 13.6%, to $1.4 billion, while overseas sales of Johnson & Johnson's Exprex profits rose only 2.2%, to $900,000, in 2007.[32] The ESA scandals have raised serious criticisms about the standards used to approve such types of medicines. Accordingly, European regulators are also looking into reevaluating ESA reimbursement.

Another safety scandal broke in 2007, when cardiologist Steven Nissen and colleagues, from the Cleveland Clinic, published a study in the *New England Journal of Medicine*[33] suggesting that GlaxoSmithKline's Avandia (US sales of $3.2 billion in 2006), which lowers blood sugar levels in type 2 diabetes, increases the risk of heart attack by 43% compared with other oral antidiabetic medications. In 2006, Avandia and its major competitor, Takeda's Actos (US sales of $2.6 billion in 2006), had an even share of the US market for glitazones, a particular kind of oral type 2 diabetes drug, but because Actos has not been associated with heart attacks, its market share has increased. In fact, Avandia's share of the US market plunged to 33% by July 2007, while Actos's share rose to 67%. GlaxoSmithKline reported that global sales of its Avandia franchise (Avandia, Avandamet, and Avandaryl) fell 22% in the second quarter of 2007, to $705.2 million. As a result, the company reorganized and cut its US sales force, which now totals 9,000 representatives.[34] In late March 2008, the FDA announced that GlaxoSmithKline did not include multiple postapproval studies, as required in periodic and annual reports about the drug.[35] That same day, Glaxo's shares fell 3.8% to $43.32 in morning trading on the New York Stock Exchange. In June 2009 another study was published (results of the RECORD trial) suggesting that Avandia does not increase the risk of overall cardiovascular morbidity or mortality compared with standard glucose-lowering drugs,[36] giving rise to more controversy.[37] By the end of February 2010, the FDA remained internally divided on whether Avandia should be removed from the market or not.[38] Some FDA officials believed that there are safer alternatives to Avandia, while others believed that the scientific evidence did not establish that Avandia increases heart attacks and that the entire issue has been overstated. For this reason, the FDA decided to assemble another advisory committee during the summer of 2010 to make its recommendations on whether Avandia should be sold. However, there have been increasing political pressure in the United States to have the drug withdrawn from the market,[39] and therefore the sale of Avandia was restricted in the United States to patients with type 2 diabetes who do not respond to any other therapy. Avandia's sale has been suspended in Europe and in many other countries.

Another example is illustrated by the finding of contaminated heparin, a blood thinner that is made from pig intestine, coming from China and that was in use in the United States, Europe, and Japan. At the beginning of 2008, the contaminated batches were removed from these markets.[40] This, together with the finding of children's milk and milk products contaminated with melamine, a white powder used to make plastic that some unscrupulous people add to watered-down or substandard milk to make its protein levels appear higher than what they actually are,[41] have focused attention on how inadequate FDA surveillance is, especially of products coming from China and other regions.

The issue of medicines not having sufficient label warnings about their risks and benefits, even if they are approved by the FDA for a particular indication, came to the forefront recently in the case *Wyeth v. Levine*, in which a patient in the United States who was injected with Phenergan to treat nausea symptoms (an FDA-approved application) lost one arm. The Supreme Court upheld a jury verdict of $6.7 million in favor of a patient on the basis that Wyeth failed to provide a strong and clear warning about the risks of quickly injecting the drug into a vein, a method called *IV push*. Gangrene is likely if the injection accidentally hits an artery—which is precisely what happened to this patient.[42] In June 2009, the FDA came up with a list of two dozen drugs, including weight-loss medicines and sleep disorder pills, which may be involved in potential safety problems. Among these medicines are Pfizer's smoking cessation drug Chantix, for possible risk of accidental injury, vision impairment, and other issues; and Cephalon's sleep disorder drugs Nuvigil and Provigil, for a potential for serious skin reactions. Roche's Orlistat, a weight-loss drug sold by Roche as the prescription product Xenical and by GlaxoSmithKline as the over-the-counter drug Alli, was also included.[43]

Even leadership within the industry has been affected by these calamities. In 2007, Peter Dolan, the CEO of Bristol-Myers Squibbs, was fired for his inability to deal with the challenge presented by the generics company Apotex, which brought Bristol-Myers Squibb's blood thinner Plavix to the market as a generic much earlier than expected, which led to an erosion of 80% of the drug's sales. Henry McKinnell, Pfizer's CEO, also lost his position in 2005, the year before his retirement, due to the company's disappointing performance. Similarly, in 2005, Merck's CEO was forced into early retirement in 2005, following failures of several promising products in late stages of development and, more importantly, due to the Vioxx debacle that led Merck to withdraw this painkiller in September 2004.

As a result of such troubles, some leading pharmaceutical companies have, in recent years, announced severe cutbacks to their sales forces and a reorganization of their R&D bases. For example, Johnson & Johnson announced in July 2007 that it would cut its workforce by 3–4% to save $1.3 billion to $1.6 billion in 2008, partially in response to disappointing ESA sales and also because of issues with its drug-eluting stent device business.[44] In anticipation of what would happen when its leading drugs Risperdal (for schizophrenia) and Topamax (epilepsy) went generic in 2008 and 2009, respectively, the company announced in October 2007 that it would take a restructuring charge of $528 million in the third quarter. The company also announced a $10 billion share buyback program to boost its stock price.

Another example of a company that has been forced to reduce its sales force is Pfizer, which has been particularly affected by R&D underperformance, regulatory setbacks, and looming generics competition. In January 2009, it announced that it would lay off 800 researchers,[45] that is, 8% of its global research staff of approximately 10,000 researchers in addition to the ones it had laid off in 2007 and 2008. The company has also seen several R&D setbacks, including its decision in late 2006 to stop work on a high-profile new cholesterol drug, torcetrapib, which was in late-stage development. Further, the company's most important drug, in terms of sales, Lipitor, has faced pressure from therapeutic substitution in the United States since 2006, when competitors' brand-name drugs went off patent. This development forced a fall in Pfizer's sales of 8% in the first half of 2007 and 5% by the end of the year. GlaxoSmithKline, among other notable pharmaceutical giants, followed the same path in 2008 and 2009.[46] At the end of 2010, Swiss companies Novartis and Roche announced severe cost-cutting plans.[47,48]

More important, all this, together with the world financial crisis, has driven further the depression of pharmaceutical stocks, but stock underperformance was there before the financial markets collapsed. For instance, as of late March 2008, price-to-earnings (P/E) ratios, according to Standard and Poor's (S&P),[49] for the large capitalization pharmaceutical group averaged a near record low of 13 times, based on estimated 2008 operating earnings per share (EPS); this represented about a 15% discount to the overall market, as measured by the S&P 500 index. Sector dividend payouts, yielding over 4%, also exceeded average S&P 500 yields. (A decline in stock prices causes yields to rise.)

Interestingly, during turbulent financial times, investors have moved toward the pharmaceutical sector because overall, the pharmaceutical sector has been considered to be shielded from economic downturns; however, this idea has not been clearly valid since 2008. And in addition to all that has been discussed, the possibility that further restrictions on the pharmaceutical industry may be imposed in an attempt to reform the US health care system—after all, Republicans, who oppose the current Obama health care reform law, won the majority of seats in the House of Representatives during the 2010 mid-term elections—may not be good news for the pharmaceutical and health insurance industries at all. So the fears are there; they are latent, but omnipresent.

The Biotechnology Business Crisis

Biotechnology, despite sales of $87 billion in 2008 and a growth of 20% above the pharmaceutical industry, also faces serious challenges, not only because its sales declined in 2009, as a result of Roche's acquisition of Genentech, which accounted for 20% of the industry's revenues, but also because most biotechnology companies are considered money losers and, in some people's opinion, unsuccessful, even though success in the biotech world is a relative construct more than an absolute one. In fact, of the 313 US-listed public biotech companies as of the end of 2009 (in contrast to 366 listed in 2008), only 10 or 11 account for the majority of the industry's sales (around $38 billion from the total).[50] The largest biotech companies, such as Amgen, the former Genentech, Gilead Sciences, and Genzyme, among others (see Table 4.9, with a listing of the major biotech companies and their sales), have had consistent profitability and a sustained revenue stream in the last few years. But the commercial potential of biotech drugs approved since January 2006 has been lower than the approvals recorded between 2001 and 2004.[51] In 2007, only four new biotechnology-based approvals took place: Soliris (Alexion Pharmaceuticals), for the treatment of rare blood cell destruction caused by bone marrow disorders and which is priced at more than $389,000 a year (78 vials, each costing $4,992)[52]; Letairis (Gilead Sciences), for the treatment of pulmonary arterial hypertension; Renvela (Genzyme), for kidney phosphorus control; and Cephalon's Nuvigil, for the treatment of daytime sleepiness. In 2008, only three biotechnology-based products were approved: Arcalyst (Regeneron), an interleukin-1 blocker for the treatment of

Table 4.9 R&D Expenditures at Leading US Biotechnology Companies*

Company	R&D Expenditures			Revenues			R&D as % of Revenues	
	2008	2009	% CHG.	2008	2009	% CHG.	2008	2009
Amgen	3,030	2,864	(5.5)	15,003	14,642	(2.4)	20.2	19.6
Biogen-Idec	1,097	1,283	17.0	4,098	4,377	6.8	26.8	29.3
Gilead Sciences	733	940	28.3	5,336	7,011	31.4	13.7	13.4
Genzyme	1,308	865	(33.9)	4,605	4,516	(1.9)	28.4	19.2
Celgene	2,671	795	(70.2)	2,238	2,677	19.6	119.4	29.7
Cephalon	404	442	9.3	1,975	2,192	11.0	20.5	20.1
Vertex Pharmaceuticals	360	401	11.3	176	102	(41.9)	205.4	393.8
Regeneron Pharmaceuticals	278	399	43.4	238	379	59.1	116.6	105.1
Exelixis	257	235	(8.8)	118	152	28.8	218.4	154.7
Amylin Pharmaceuticals, Inc.	293	185	(36.9)	840	758	(9.7)	34.9	24.4

Source: Standard and Poor's, Industry surveys: Biotechnology. August 19, 2010, p. 19. ©Standard & Poor's Financial Services LLC, a subsidiary of The McGraw-Hill Companies, Inc. Reprinted with permission. All rights reserved.
*In millions of dollars, ranked by 2009 R&D expenditures.

Cryopyrin-associated periodic syndromes, including familial cold autoinflammatory syndrome and Muckle–Wells syndrome; Cimzia (UCB), a tumor necrosis factor blocker, for the treatment of Crohn's disease; and Nplate (Amgen), a thrombopoietin receptor agonist, for the treatment of thrombocytopenia in patients with chronic immune (idiopathic) thrombocytopenic purpura.

More important, with the financial credit crunch that we are experiencing and that has hit investors severely, many early-stage biotech companies in the United States and, to a greater extent, in Europe have been particularly affected, and many of the most cash-hungry enterprises ran out of cash by the end of 2010. As a result, many of the less-mature firms have had to cut staff and terminate projects to stretch their rapidly dwindling cash supplies.

This situation prompted the 2009 request by a group of high-profile figures associated with the UK biotech industry for a government bailout through the establishment of two UK£500 million funds, which, according to this group, would preserve a host of biotech companies.[53] In the United States, where biotech companies have traditionally been more sheltered than in Europe from financial shortages, it was reported at the end of 2008 that more than 100 public US biotech companies had less than 6 months' worth of cash left. In the period between 2008 and 2009, in the United States and Canada, several biotech companies were delisted from the Nasdaq market only a few months after going public.[54]

But despite significant advances, most biotech companies continue to struggle financially. Those without products close to commercialization are particularly vulnerable, but even those that have a successful commercial product need to demonstrate their ability to produce additional products if they are to maintain the confidence of investors. Even so, companies still struggle to bring a second product to market. In fact, some companies, such as ImClone Systems and OSI Pharmaceuticals, became successful in bringing their first products to consumers, but they had difficulties bringing a second product to sustain their growth. As such, the ImClone Systems was bought from market by Eli Lilly in October 2008 for $6.5 billion.[55]

Follow-on biologics, or biosimilars, presently represent a major threat for the US biotechnology industry, especially now that President Barack Obama signed an abbreviated approval pathway for biosimilars into law in March 2010, as part of the "Patient Protection and Affordable Care Act", called "Biologics Price Competition and Innovation Act" (BPCI Act), even though the FDA has yet to lay down the rules for its implementation. Follow-on biologics are so-called generic versions of biotechnology products that are similar in structure and efficacy to biotechnology products. Though the generics industry and payers would like to see some biosimilars emerge in the United States, especially now that significant number of highly profitable biotech products are approaching patent expiration (see Table 4.10), the biotechnology industry is eager to block any efforts to do so because many biotech drugs are approved for niche market indications at very high prices, but these products gradually become important products and a source of great profit as additional research data enable biotech manufacturers to obtain approval for a greater range of indications.

Table 4.10 Notable US Patent Expirations for Biotech Drugs

Brand Name	Company	Indications	2009 Global Sales ($ Billions)
2012			
Enbrel	Amgen/Pfizer (Wyeth)	Psoriasis, rheumatoid arthritis	6.47
2013			
Cerezyme	Genzyme	Gaucher's disease	0.79[a]
Epogen/Procrit	Amgen/Johnson & Johnson	Red blood cell enhancement	4.96
Humalog	Eli Lilly	Type 1 diabetes	1.96
Neupogen	Amgen	White blood cell enhancement	1.29
Rebif	Pfizer/Merck Serono	Multiple sclerosis	2.14
Remicade	Johnson & Johnson	Rheumatoid arthritis	5.92
2014			
Aranesp	Amgen	Red blood cell enhancement	2.93
Copaxone	Teva	Multiple sclerosis	2.57
2015			
Neulasta	Amgen	White blood cell enhancement	3.36
Rituxan	Roche/Biogen IDEC	Rheumatoid arthritis, blood cancer	5.62
2016			
Humira	Abbott Labs	Rheumatoid arthritis	5.57
2019			
Avastin	Roche	Oncology	5.74
Herceptin	Roche	Oncology	4.86
2020			
Lucentis	Roche/Novartis	Wet adult macular degeneration	2.34

Source: Standard and Poor's, Industry surveys: Biotechnology. August 19, 2010, p. 4. © EvaluatePharma®. Reprinted with permission. All rights reserved.
[a]2009 sales impacted by plant outage.

Before March 2010, when President Obama signed the health care reform law, an important obstacle to bringing copies of biologics to the market in the United States was the absence of a regulatory pathway for approval. The argument was the following: regulators cannot treat biologics like ordinary generics because biologics are made from living source materials (cell lines), which are variable and hard to replicate. As such, generics manufactures would not have access to the exact same lines as the pioneer companies, so the fear was that the generics they produced would not be bioequivalent to the innovative drugs, which is a requirement for any generic drug. This argument is particularly interesting because in Europe, a regulatory pathway for follow-on biologics has been in place since March 2006, when the European Medicines Agency (EMEA) issued the world's first guidelines for regulatory pathways for selected groups of biologics. Since then, Sandoz, a subsidiary of Novartis AG, received European marketing authorization for Omnitrope, its copy of human growth hormone, and launched the product in Germany at a 20% discount to the branded drug. Omnitrope's sales are not expected to be as large as other biotech products, but its importance is more than symbolic because it is creating a precedent. In November 2008, Sandoz received a positive European Commission opinion for biosimilar filgrastim. Filgrastim is indicated for use in treating neutropenia, a condition characterized by a lack of neutrophils—one of the most common types of white blood cells—that is often associated with chemotherapy or bone marrow transplants.[56] The overall positive attitude of Europeans regarding follow-on biologics can be understood if we realize (or take into consideration) that they have a system that is under great rationalization pressure.

According to Jo Walton, pharmaceutical analyst at Credit Suisse:

> *I think that we will continue to accept follow-on biologics .... There was obviously a problem with the follow-on EPO (erythropoietin) product, but very few people had an adverse reaction to the drug. And most people say they didn't notice the difference. But true, there was a difference. Now, I think that European regulators say that's a price worth paying. So we will allow follow-on generics biologics, and OK if it isn't exactly the same. Societally, we are just going to make some more money, we'll save money and be able to treat more people. So yes, one person in 1,000 might die, but 5,000 more people are treated.*

She adds the following:

> *I think there will be fewer problems in Europe, whereas in the States, they want to have the follow-on product characterized because of litigation. Because if you then die on a follow-on biologic, how do you know that it wasn't the fault of the follow-on biologic rather than one of those things that just happens and would have happened anyhow? So I think it's going to take longer in the U.S. Perhaps it is going to get more established here. If it gets more established here and if we have interferon, if we have new more EPOs and there aren't any problems, that will help them in the U.S.*[57]

The real issue with follow-on biologics in the United States is simpler than that. The actual reason is that much money is at stake, especially when one takes into consideration that the United States is the world leader in the biotechnology sector and that several profitable biotechnology products that are already off-patent continue to be sold under the brand name. The number of biologics and the expense associated with them are growing rapidly. Between 2005 and 2009, spending on specialty pharmaceuticals is expected to grow from $40 billion to $90 billion, while traditional drug expenditures should rise from $170 billion to $226 billion.[58]

The biotechnology and generics industries are arguing over how much testing is necessary to prove that a generic biologic is as safe and efficacious as the innovator drug that it copies. Biotechnology industry executives are eager for stringent clinical trials (which are not necessary for traditional generics) for so-called generic biologics, arguing that these products could never be identical to the originals. Those favoring generic biologics say that these trials are unnecessary and burdensome and would raise the cost of developing products significantly. But the pressure from the public is there, and legislative action by Congress is necessary to *implement* a regulatory pathway for biosimilars, just as Congress was responsible for creating a regulatory pathway for generic copies of traditional medicines in 1984.

Although the market penetration of biosimilars remains modest in the European Union and elsewhere, benefiting the branded industry, I expect that penetration will gradually improve, aided by efforts to control health care costs. In the United States, branded biotech drugs are now protected from biosimilars for 12 years after their original launch, as part of the Obama health care reform law. In fact, Merck announced at its annual business briefing on December 9, 2008, that it will form a division called Merck BioVentures to develop follow-on biologics. The company announced that creation of the division was enabled by the 2006 acquisition of GlycoFi, a platform company specialized in the production of therapeutic proteins, because this gave them access to the humanized GlycoFi yeast platform that Merck anticipated could give them a competitive advantage for developing follow-on products. Merck has already started developing its first follow-on product, MK-2578, for the treatment of anemia, which it hopes to launch in 2012.[59]

This debate about biogenerics will become really contentious in the United States, especially after a study published by the *Journal of the American Medical Association* cast a cloud over biologic safety.[60] The study, which is the first to take an in-depth look at safety issues surrounding biologics, suggests that they pose a heightened risk of adverse events compared to other types of drugs. According to the article, 24% of biologics approved in the United States and Europe have prompted safety regulatory actions. This is very important because, as biologics and monoclonal antibodies (mAbs) continue to be widely embraced across the drug industry and, as we have seen, make up an increasingly larger proportion of new drugs approved every year, their safety record is coming under greater scrutiny. In addition, the fact that there is increasing emphasis on the use of biologics as blockbuster treatments for chronic conditions, such as rheumatoid arthritis, implies that significant risk mitigation strategies are likely to continue to be an important facet of regulatory oversight for biotech drugs.

The Biopharmaceutical Industry's Short-Term Solutions to the Crisis

To compensate for the loss of revenue due to massive patent expirations and other costly expenses, the pharmaceutical industry has responded in several different ways. As already discussed, major pharmaceutical firms, such as Pfizer, Johnson & Johnson, Merck, and Novartis, have announced severe cost cuts and workforce reductions. Also, in general, companies have increased the prices of many brand-name drugs, as we saw in Chapter 1; they have taken generics companies into court; and they have forged many strategic alliances and acquisitions with smaller biotech firms to refill their product pipelines. Other companies, especially the European ones, have opted for diversification in the paths that are closely related to the brand-name products, such as the recent acquisition by Novartis of Alcon (a vision company); GlaxoSmithKline's acquisition of Stiefel (focused on dermatology); Sanofi-Aventis's acquisition of Merial (specialized in animal health), Chattem (consumer products), and Zentiva (generics); and Merck KGaA's acquisition of Millipore (life sciences).[61] While several others, such as GlaxoSmithKline, Sanofi-Aventis, and Abbott are invigorating their efforts in emergent markets in many different ways. For instance, GlaxoSmithKline is collaborating with already established generic companies, such as Dr. Reddy (India), to satisfy the high unmet medical needs of these types of markets in areas such as cardiovascular diseases, diabetes, etc. Some companies, among them Bristol-Myers Squibb and AstraZeneca, seem to have one single business focus (i.e., "pure-play") in brand-name drugs, while others, such as Pfizer, are restructuring to reduce costs and exploiting the slow rate of generic penetration (and brand-name erosion) in mature markets outside the United States to sell their brand-name drugs that have fallen into the off-patent category.

A new trend to diminish risk (namely, outsourcing) is gaining momentum as well. In their great urge to diminish costly R&D staff and resources, pharmaceutical companies are relying more and more on contract research organizations (CROs) and, to a lesser extent, contract marketing and manufacturing organizations. It is estimated that in 2007, total pharmaceutical R&D expenditure was $58.8 billion, whereas the CROs market was about $14 billion, or 23% of total R&D expenditures, and is expected to reach $24 billion by 2010.[62] In fact, the annual rate of growth of CROs in the last decade (around 11–12%) has outpaced the rate of growth of the pharmaceutical industry's R&D investment over the same period of time (8%).[63]

During the 1980s and for the greater part of the 1990s, biotechnology was eclipsed by and depended on big pharmaceutical companies for obvious reasons: lack of a track record, lack of experience in running clinical trials, lack of experience in manufacturing and marketing, and inadequate funding. But as relative progress has been made in the field of biotech, and as biotech companies are coming up with the most innovative drugs to come to market, big pharmaceutical companies have embraced biotechnology for several reasons: (1) it is helping them to bring new products to the market through acquisition as they struggle to fill gaps in their product flow caused by generics competition and R&D underperformance; and (2) the pharmaceutical industry believes that biotech will provide a wealth of new products in the future. To gain both in-house expertise and access to promising products, big pharma has established a significant number of acquisitions and strategic alliances with biotech companies. The biotech companies offer efficient, early-stage research and a younger pool of talented and motivated scientists, while big pharma brings in its sales and marketing megastructure, its expertise in running clinical trials, its ability to take promising drugs through the regulatory process, and its capacity to take on great financial risks.

In 2008, the biggest purchase deal was made by Japanese pharmaceutical company Takeda, which bought US biotechnology company Millennium for $8.8 billion. Another example is GlaxoSmithKline's purchase of Sirtris Pharmaceuticals for $720 million.[64] In 2007, acquisitions were worth $22.3 billion, which, although lower in value than in 2006, was still robust.[65] These acquisitions can reduce significantly the years of R&D that are necessary to bring products to the market. Although biotech companies with late-stage clinical trial products have moved to the front of the line, obtaining the highest valuations, large pharmaceutical companies have also become interested in early and very early stage biotech products, creating, in many ways, a valuation inflation for these kinds of companies, some of which do not even have a product in clinical trials yet. It is estimated that some of these acquisitions have boosted the valuation of public early-stage companies as much as 50–60%.[66]

Strategic alliances between biotech and big pharma have reached record numbers in the last couple of years. The number of new partnerships in 2006 and 2007 more than doubled from 2005. Total alliance values in 2006 reached a record of $23 billion, up 69% from 2005, of which $20 billion involved agreements between biotechnology and pharmaceutical companies.[67] Almost 20 of these alliances had potential values exceeding $500 million. Upfront payments (the initial amount given to the R&D partner) increased substantially and are continuing to do so. In 2007, the numbers were even higher.[68] In 2007, a strong partnership to co-develop products took place. Such was the case with RNAi-based drug developer Alnylam Pharmaceuticals, which, in May 2008, followed up its June 2007 nonexclusive technology licensing deal with Roche Holding AG, potentially worth $1 billion, and Japan's Takeda Pharmaceuticals.[69] Another notable example took place between two biotech companies when Genzyme and Isis Pharmaceuticals, Inc., formed a partnership to develop and market the Phase III cholesterol-lowering drug Mipomersen in a deal with a value that could surpass $1 billion.[70] And while the smaller biotech companies were affected in 2008 by the financial crisis, biotech deal making financially dominated the market overall, with 150 deals worth $93.7 billion.[71]

In late January 2009, giant pharmaceutical company Pfizer, the largest pharmaceutical company in the world, announced that it would acquire (out of despair) pharmaceutical company Wyeth, a firm with a strong reputation in biologics and vaccines, for $68 billion,[72] thus creating a supercompany. In buying Wyeth, Pfizer intends to enrich its pipeline (especially in biologics and central nervous system disease drugs) because this company has been hit severely in the past years by the expiration of several of its key drugs and will continue to be hit by the imminent patent expiration of Lipitor, the best selling drug in the world. It is worthy to mention that over the past 2 years, Pfizer has laid off 16,000 employees, closed 15 manufacturing facilities, and severely cut research projects.[73]

In early March 2009, Merck announced that it would acquire Schering-Plough for $41.1 billion in cash and stocks,[74] with the hope of strengthening its chest medicine arsenal because its former blockbuster bone drug Fosamax has gone generic, and in a few years, the same thing will happen to Singulair, its best selling allergy and asthma drug. With this merger, Merck gets access to successful brand-name Schering products with much longer patents, like the prescription allergy spray Nasonex. And Merck could capitalize on Schering's investments in promising biotechnology drugs. Since July 2008, Roche Holdings, which owned 55% of Genentech, made several attempts to acquire the majority of the remaining outstanding shares of the company but was unsuccessful due primarily to mutual disagreements on its valuation. But on March 11, 2009, Genentech, one of the earliest and most successful biotech companies—and one that has not being exempt from several scandals, including the misappropriation of scientific material and information and the marketing of growth hormone for unapproved uses—agreed to be bought by Roche for $95 a share—that is, at a valuation of $46.8 billion.[75] Of course, Sanofi-Aventis could not have fallen behind and, after a nine months pursuit, it acquired Genzyme, in February, 2011, for at least $20.1 billion (Genzyme's stockholders will receive $74 a share in cash as well as so-called contingent value rights that entitle them to payment of as much as $14 a share depending on the performance of Genzyme's experimental multiple-sclerosis drug Lemtrada and production levels of two other products). With this acquisition Sanofi-Aventis gets access to drugs that treat rare diseases.[76] Now even biotech companies are buying smaller biotech firms, as was the case with Gilead Sciences, which, also in March, CV Therapeutics of Palo Alto, California, bought for $20 a share, or $1.4 billion, gaining the rights to drugs for cardiovascular diseases.[77] Another company that is rumored to be bought is Bristol-Myers Squibb.

One may legitimately wonder, with these recent mergers, what is next for the industry? Is the pharmaceutical industry going backward, to the formation of oligopolies (cartels) like the ones in Germany and Switzerland during the first half of the twentieth century, as discussed in Chapter 3? For instance, Norvartis already has a large stake in Roche (more than 20%), which, in turn, owns Genentech. Will it be that the world will end up with a few almighty pharmaceutical players, with a couple in the United States, one in Britain, another in Switzerland, one each in Germany and Japan, and so forth? The fate of Sanofi-Aventis, one of the largest pharmaceutical companies in the world, which has become the next most desirable prey in the pharmaceutical merger and acquisition of food chain, will reveal whether there is a great tendency to form oligopolies at the pharmaceutical industry level.

On top of all these activities, the pharmaceutical industry has become good at the reformulation, patent extension, and expansion of indications of old drugs, making some of its best selling drugs last much longer. The questions that immediately arise are the following: is all this activity enough to sustain growth in the long term? Is the industry heading in the right direction with the new wave of mergers and consolidations? How does big pharma intend to address the large number of unmet medical needs in the world? Finally, given the lack of efficiency of the overall system, is it fair to patients that the industry compensates its revenue losses by increasing drug prices, even though many of the drugs that it is bringing to market are not really innovative? Furthermore, what alternatives can society explore so that cheaper, safer, and more effective drugs reach patients, not only in the developed world, but also in less-developed countries? How will the industry look 5 or 10 years from now?

To answer these questions, it is necessary to examine what is happening at the R&D level in the pharmaceutical industry. But before we delve into that, let us take a look at how medicines are made and marketed. We will explore this topic in the next chapter.

Notes

1. IMS Health, 2010. Global Pharmaceutical and Therapy Forecast. IMS Health, Norwalk, CT. http://www.imshealth.com/portal/site/imshealth/menuitem.a46c6d4df3db4b3d88f611019418c22a/?vgnextoid=4b8c410b6c718210VgnVCM100000ed152ca2RCRD&vgnextchannel=b5e57900b55a5110VgnVCM10000071812ca2RCRD&vgnextfmt=default; Standard and Poor's, Industry surveys. Health care: Pharmaceuticals, 2010.
2. Standard and Poor's, Industry surveys. Health care: Pharmaceuticals, 2006.

3. Standard and Poor's, Industry surveys, 2008.
4. IMS Health, Global Pharmaceutical; Standard and Poor's, Industry surveys.
5. According to the FDA, a new molecular entity or new chemical entity is a drug that contains no active moiety that has been approved by the FDA for any other application submitted under section 505(b) of the Federal Food, Drug, and Cosmetic Act.
6. DiMasi, J.A., Hansen, R.W., Grabowski, H.G., 2003. The price of innovation: new estimates of drug development costs. Journal of Health Economics 22, 151–185.
7. Boston Consulting Group, 2001. A Revolution in R&D: How Genomics and Genetics Are Transforming the Biopharmaceutical Indutry. Boston Consulting Group, Boston. According to Steven Paul, retired head of R&D at Eli Lilly, the average cost per NME is about $1.7 billion.
8. Biological products are approved for marketing under the provisions of the Public Health Service (PHS) Act. The act requires a firm that manufactures a biologic product for sale in interstate commerce to hold a license for the product. A biologics license application is a submission that contains specific information on the manufacturing processes, chemistry, pharmacology, clinical pharmacology, and medical effects of the biologic product. If the information provided meets FDA requirements, the application is approved and a license is issued, allowing the firm to market the product. http://www.babylon.com/definition/Biologic_License_Application_(BLA)/English.
9. Standard and Poor's, Industry surveys, 2008, 4.
10. Pharmaceutical Research and Manufacturers of America, 2009. Pharmaceutical Industry Profile. Pharmaceutical Research and Manufacturers of America, Washington, DC.
11. http://www.fda.gov; see also Hughes, B., 2009. 2008 FDA drug approvals. Nature Reviews Drug Discovery 8, 93–96.
12. Hughes, B., 2010. 2009 FDA drug approvals. Nature Reviews Drug Discovery 9, 89–92.
13. Dooren, J.C., 2010. Drug approvals slipped in 2010. The Wall Street Journal, December 31. http://online.wsj.com/article/SB10001424052748704543004576052170335871018.html?mod=dist_smartbrief.
14. Standard and Poor's, Industry surveys, 2009; see also IMS Health, 2009. IMS Health forecasts 4.5–5.5 percent growth for global pharmaceutical market in 2009, exceeding $820 billion. News Release, October 29. http://www.imshealth.com/portal/site/imshealth/menuitem.a46c6d4df3db4b3d88f611019418c22a/?vgnextoid=9e553599b554d110VgnVCM100000ed152ca2RCRD&vgnextfmt=default.
15. Orelli, B., 2007. Patents shine, but don't be blinded by them. Motley Fool, May 18. http://www.fool.com/investing/high-growth/2007/05/18/patents-shine-but-dont-be-blinded-by-them.aspx; see also Paul, S., 2009. An audience with. Nature Reviews Drug Discovery 8, 14.
16. Standard and Poor's, Industry surveys, 2008.
17. Smith, A., 2009. Big Pharma teaches old drugs new tricks. CNNMoney, March 21. http://money.cnn.com/2007/03/21/news/companies/drug_patents/index.htm.
18. Ibid.
19. Ibid.
20. IMS Health, 2008. IMS Health reports annual global generics prescription sales growth of 3.6 percent, to $78 billion. Medical News Today, December 11. http://www.medicalnewstoday.com/articles/132702.php; Reuters, 2008. Positioning, performance and SWOT analysis of the top 10 generic pharmaceutical companies. Business Wire, September 10. http://www.reuters.com/article/pressRelease/idUS161197+10-Sep-2008+BW20080910; and The top 10 generic pharmaceutical companies: Positioning, performance and SWOT analyses. Business Insight Report, July 11. http://salesandmarketingnetwork.com/reports.php?ID=2670.

21. Doris de Guzman, 2010. Nonbranded drugs are expected to continue their strong growth. But could the dearth of their new branded rivals cause the sector to hit a wall? February 10. http://www.icis.com/Articles/2010/02/15/9333169/generic-drugs-sales-continue-to-climb.html.
22. Top 10 generic pharmaceutical companies.
23. Frost and Sullivan, 2007. US generic pharmaceuticals outlook. April 30. http://www.marketresearch.com/product/display.asp?productid=1487625.
24. DataMonitor, 2008. Generics series: Generics trends in the seven major markets and beyond, November. http://www.scribd.com/doc/10466622/Generics-Series-Generics-Trends-in-the-Seven-Major-Markets-and-Beyond.
25. Top 10 generic pharmaceutical companies.
26. Saul, S., 2008. Wyeth antidepressant is approved. New York Times, February 29. http://www.nytimes.com/2008/02/29/business/29cnd-wyeth.html; see also Women's health: Who can handle the heat for hot flashes? Trokalayjian.com, July 1, 2009. http://www.trokalayjian.com/2009/07/women-health-who-can-handle-heat-for_01.html.
27. Kastelein, J.J.P., Akdim, F., Stroes, E.S.G., Zwinderman, A.H., Bots, M.L., Stalenhoef, A.F.H., et al., for the ENHANCE Investigators, 2008. Simvastatin with or without ezetimibe in familial hypercholesterolemia. New England Journal of Medicine 358, 1431–1443.
28. Standard and Poor's, Industry surveys, 2006; Liptak, A., 2009. No legal shield in drug labeling, justices rule. New York Times, March 4. http://www.nytimes.com/2009/03/05/washington/05scotus.html?scp=1&sq=Supreme%20Court%20Rejects%20Limits%20on%20Drug%20Lawsuits&st=cse.
29. Singer, N., 2009. Merck paid for medical 'journal' without disclosure. New York Times, May 13.
30. Standard and Poor's, Industry surveys, 2007.
31. IMS Health, 2008. IMS Health reports global biotech sales grew 12.5 percent in 2007, exceeding $75 billion. Drugs.com, June 17. http://www.drugs.com/news/ims-health-reports-global-biotech-sales-grew-12-5-percent-2007-exceeding-75-billion-8316.html.
32. Standard and Poor's, Industry surveys, 2008.
33. Nissen, S., Wolski, K., 2007. Effect of rosiglitazone on the risk of myocardial infarction and death from cardiovascular causes. New England Journal of Medicine 356, 2457–2471.
34. Standard and Poor's, Industry surveys, 2008.
35. US FDA, 2008. Warning Letter, March 25. http://www.fda.gov/ICECI/EnforcementActions/WarningLetters/2008/ucm1048360.htm.
36. Home, P.D., Pocock, S.J., Beck-Nielsen, H., Curtis, P.S., Gomis, R., Hanefeld, M., for the RECORD Study Team, 2009. Rosiglitazone evaluated for cardiovascular outcomes in oral agent combination therapy for type 2 diabetes (RECORD): a multicentre, randomised, open-label trial. The Lancet 373 (9681), 2125–2135.
37. Husten, L., 2009. Rosiglitazone goes on the RECORD, but is it a hit? CardioBrief, June 5. http://cardiobrief.org/2009/06/05/1828/.
38. Harris, G., 2010. Controversial diabetes drug harms heart, the U.S. concludes. New York Times, February 20. http://www.nytimes.com/2010/02/20/health/policy/20avandia.html?pagewanted=1&hp.
39. Ibid.
40. Harris, G., 2008. Heparin contamination may have been deliberate, FDA says. New York Times, April 30.
41. Reuters, 2008. FACTBOX: What is melamine, and why add it to milk? September 25. http://in.reuters.com/article/domesticNews/idINT12657320080925>.

42. Liptak, No legal shield.
43. Richwine, L., 2009. U.S. FDA releases list of potential drug risks. Reuters, June 5. http://www.reuters.com/article/healthNews/idUSTRE5540HF20090605.
44. Rapaport, L., 2009. J&J to cut up to 4 percent of jobs, shut facilities. Bloomberg, July 31. http://www.bloomberg.com/apps/news?pid=20601087&refer=home&sid=aOqRDT1rjFaI.
45. In February 2011, Pfizer announced that it would lay off 1,100 workers from its Groton campus in Connecticut as part of a cost-cutting program in order to trim $2 billion from the company's R&D 2011 budget. "Pfizer to layoff 1,100 in Connecticut." UPI, February 1, 2011. www.upicom/Business_News/2011/02/01/pfizer-to-lay-off-1100-in-connecticut/UPI-5131129692156. Rockoff, J., 2009. Pfizer plans lay off in research. The Wall Street Journal, January 14. http://online.wsj.com/article/SB123186230445977567.html.
46. Finance-Trading Times, 2009. Glaxo Smith Kline layoffs job cut: Fires 6000 employees. February 1. http://www.finance-trading-times.com/2009/02/glaxo-smith-kline-layoffs-job-cut-fires.html.
47. Mijuk, G., 2010. Novartis to cut costs, boost productivity to secure growth. Dow Jones, Newswires, November 17.
48. Roche Holding AG (ROG.VX) Wednesday announced its long awaited cost-cutting plan. Dow Jones, November 17, 2010.
49. Standard and Poor's, Industry surveys, 2008.
50. Ibid.
51. Ibid.
52. Alexion sets the price of living well with PNH at roughly $400k a year. Pharma Cutting Edge Weblog. http://www.pharmaweblog.com/?p=276.
53. Beyond the crunch. Nature Reviews Drug Discovery 8 (2009), 3; see also Nature Biotechnology 27 (1), 3–5. Biotech sector ponders potential 'bloodbath'.
54. Ibid.
55. Pollack, A., 2008. Lilly to buy ImClone for $6.5 billion. New York Times, October 6. http://www.nytimes.com/2008/10/07/business/07drug.html.
56. Sandoz receives positive EU opinion for biosimilar filgrastim. Novartis, November 21, 2008. http://www.worldpharmanews.com/novartis/609-sandoz-receives-positive-eu-opinion-for-biosimilar-filgrastim.
57. Interview with Jo Walton, London, May 2007.
58. Standard and Poor's, Industry surveys, 2008.
59. US follow-on biologics debate revived. Nature Reviews Drug Discovery 8 (2009), 8–9.
60. Giezen, T.J., Mantel-Teeuwisse, A.K., Straus, S.M.J.M., Schellekens, H., Leufkens, H.G.M., Egberts, A.C.G., 2008. Safety-related regulatory actions for biologicals approved in the United States and the European Union. Journal of the American Medical Association 300, 1887–1896.
61. Moody's Investors Service, 2010. Industry Outlook. Global Pharmaceuticals, June.
62. The market leader is Quintiles Transnational Corp., with a 14% share of the global market, followed by Pharmaceutical Product Development Inc. and Covance Inc., each with a 10% share, according to http://www.phrma.org/news_room/press_releases/us_biopharmaceutical_companies_r%26d_spending_reaches_record_%2458.8_billion_in_2007/.
63. Standard and Poor's, Industry surveys, 2008.
64. Saul, S., Pollack, A., 2009. Big pharmaceutical companies hunger for biotech drugs. New York Times, August 14. http://www.nytimes.com/2008/08/01/business/01bristol.html?_r=1&ref=business.

65. Biotech has positive year despite weak fourth quarter performance. Burrill News, January 2. http://www.burrillandco.com/news-183-Biotech_has_positive_year_despite_weak_fourth_quarter_performance.html.
66. Standard and Poor's, Industry surveys, 2008.
67. Standard and Poor's, Industry surveys, 2008; Biotech has positive year.
68. Biotech has positive year.
69. Macron, D., 2007. Alnylam inks license, RNAi Rx-Discovery deal with Roche worth up to $1 billion. RNAi News, July 12. http://www.genomeweb.com/rnai/alnylam-inks-license-rnai-rx-discovery-deal-roche-worth-1-billion.
70. Genzyme and Isis announce strategic alliance including exclusive worldwide license of Mipomersen. Isis Pharmaceuticals, News Release, January 7, 2008.
71. Biotech dominates 2008 dealmaking—150 deals announced worth $93.7 billion. Health Care M&A Information Service, January 2009.
72. Sorkin, A.R., Wilson, D., 2009. Pfizer agrees to pay $68 billion for rival drug maker Wyeth. New York Times, January 25. http://www.nytimes.com/2009/01/26/business/26drug.html.
73. Ledford, H., 2009. Pfizer to buy Wyeth in $68-billion deal. Nature News, January 29, 520.
74. Singer, N., 2009. Merck to buy Schering-Plough for $41.1 billion. New York Times, March 3. http://www.nytimes.com/2009/03/10/business/10drug.html?hp.
75. Jolly, D., Pollack, A., 2009. Roche agrees to buy Genentech for $46.8 billion. New York Times, March 11. http://www.nytimes.com/2009/03/13/business/worldbusiness/13drugs.html?hp.
76. Torsoli, A., Tirrell, M., 2011. Sanofi to buy Genzyme for sweetened $20.1 billion after nine-month pursuit. Bloomberg News, February 16. www.bloomberg.com/news/2011-02-16/sanofi-aventis-agrees-to-buy-genzyme-for-74-a-share-in-19-2-billion-deal.html.
77. See Note 75.

5 Understanding Research and Development and Marketing in a Biopharmaceutical Company

Man loves creating and the making of roads, that is indisputable. But why does he so passionately love destruction and chaos as well? Tell me that!

—Fyodor Dostoyevsky,* Notes from the Underground *(1864)

More than anything else, the biopharmaceutical industry's long-term growth and its capacity to overcome expected and unexpected difficulties depend heavily on its ability to bring innovative products to market. This means that a successful, innovative product cannot only be quite profitable and make up for many of the bad decisions that a pharmaceutical company may have made in the past, but it can also overcome many of a company's operational deficiencies. However, no matter how efficient the operations of a company may be and how many operational cost-reduction strategies a company may adopt, growth and high capacity cannot compensate for the lack of productive research and development (R&D), even if, on paper and on a balance sheet, the numbers look nice—at first. As shown in Chapter 4, R&D spending by large pharmaceutical companies has continued to increase over the last several decades; however, investment has not led to a proportionally greater productivity. New products are emerging from the pipelines more slowly than before, while the growing complexity of drug development is increasing the time required to bring new drugs to market, which adds to the costs of doing business. Pharmaceutical companies, on average, spend between 15% and 20% of their sales revenues on R&D, which is perhaps above what other industries (such as electronics, computers, and automobiles) spend on research activities.

The pharmaceutical business model is, indeed, very simple: pharmaceutical companies create new products, launch them, and grow them over a period of time, and finally, these products go off-patent. Bringing a new drug to market is a complex, long, and expensive process, no matter how one looks at it. It takes up to 12–15 years and approximately $0.8–1.0 billion, of which 75% is attributed to failure along the pharmaceutical value chain.[1,2] (Although, according to a venture capital executive, who asked to remain anonymous, the actual expenditure "depends on the drug. I think it can be that expensive, but generally more in pharmaceutical's hands than in biotech's. If biotech takes a drug to phase II, it would not have spent the majority of that money. . . . And a lot of that cash is in sales and marketing anyway, so it is not necessarily R&D. So, I don't think those numbers are accurate for every drug . . . maybe for a few drugs but not for all drugs. . . . But I hope it doesn't cost 800 million dollars[3] for every drug; otherwise, [biotech] will be out of business!")[4]

The World's Health Care Crisis. DOI: 10.1016/B978-0-12-391875-8.00005-6

Many times, new medicines originate from research done in academic centers and research institutes, often in areas that are totally unrelated to the final application or product. Other times, drugs are discovered and developed in-house by pharmaceutical and biotechnology companies. The process of discovering and developing a drug in a pharmaceutical or biotech company is similar, though not identical, as biotechnology products require more complex storage, dosing, and administration regimens than traditional medicines because biotech products are generally large proteins that are difficult for the body to absorb and have to be administered in doctors' offices or hospitals by injection or intravenously. Nonbiologic medicines, in contrast, are generally small, easily absorbed molecules that are administered orally.

One of the major problems that the pharmaceutical industry has to confront today, and which will continue to grow in the coming years, is its large size and constant need to achieve double-digit growth to maintain high market capitalization. Despite the wave of mergers that is currently underway and the constant acquisition of many related technology platforms and potential drug candidates, the success of this industry will always lie in its R&D productivity. And increased R&D productivity can be achieved by (1) lowering production costs and the time required for drugs to reach the market, (2) reducing the failure rates of leading compounds, and (3) reorganizing R&D infrastructure. I will discuss these issues in Chapter 13.

The way in which the biopharmaceutical industry develops drugs now is in stark contrast with the way drug development progressed, say, 20–30 years ago. In the 1970s and 1980s, the most important approach to drug discovery was the chemical modification of existing "lead" candidates[5]. However, from the 1990s on, companies have relied more on high-throughput screening (a robotic/computerized and automated method that allows researchers to test millions of compounds in a day, providing starting points for drug design) and structure-based design (a method by which companies determine the structure of a target receptor and, based on this information as well as theoretical and experimental data, propose potential ligands). Other methods that companies pursue include a greater reliance on genomics (as in the case of Novartis's Gleevec, an inhibitor to Bcr–Abl kinase used to treat chronic myeloid leukemia) and genetics (as in the case of Genentech's Herceptin, a monoclonal antibody used as an adjuvant breast cancer treatment in women who overexpress the Her2 receptor gene), with the goal of identifying new chemical entities that have a more specific (and potent) mode of action and that are less toxic. Though the impact of these new approaches will be discussed in detail in Chapter 13, let me say here that the pressures and the information that exist today are far greater and more complex than in the 1970s and 1980s.

Before reaching the market, drug candidates have to pass successfully through a very large number of stringent stages. We can categorize these stages into two broad categories: the first is a discovery phase, and the second is the development or clinical phase. In this chapter, we will explore the entire process of drug discovery and development because this is paramount to our goal of understanding both the origin of the R&D crisis at the biopharmaceutical level and the causes of the current world health care crisis, discussed, in Chapter 13 (See Figure 5.1, which illustrates the different stages through which a drug should pass).

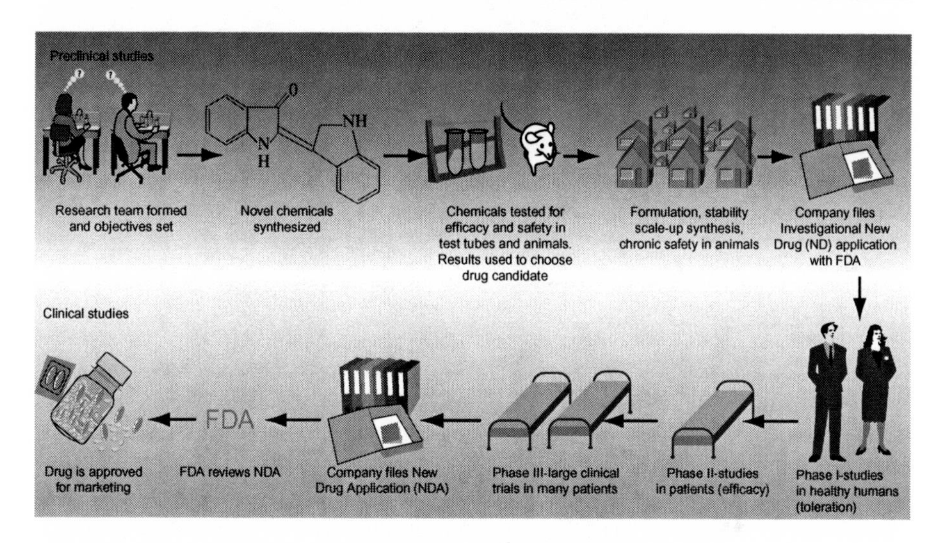

Figure 5.1 The creation of a drug from the laboratory bench to the market.
Before reaching the market, drug candidates have to pass successfully through a very large number of stringent stages. We can categorize these stages into two broad categories: the first is a discovery phase, in which new drug targets are identified, new chemicals are synthesized or developed and tried successfully in animal models; and the second is the development or clinical phase (Phase I, Phase II, and Phase III clinical trials).

Drug Discovery

Target Identification

In general, scientists in companies identify targets (that is, genes and their encoded products, such as proteins) that may be responsible for a particular disease or phenotype.[6] When it comes to infectious diseases, researchers need to isolate, understand, and characterize whatever micro-organism is thought to be the cause of a particular malady. It is estimated that approximately 5,000–10,000 potential drug targets exist, and that current drug therapy is based on approximately 500 molecular targets, of which 45% are G-protein–coupled receptors, 28% are enzymes, 11% are hormones and factors, 5% are ion channels, and 2% are nuclear receptors.[7] Therefore, the number of drug targets that can be exploited for therapeutic applications is at least 10 times the number that are used today in drug therapy. Some of the methods that companies use to identify new targets like genes and proteins and to quantify their expression in normal and diseased cells include classical molecular and cellular biology, genomics (the study of an organism's genome or set of genes), and proteomics (the study of an organism's proteome or set of proteins). The genomics approach of the 1990s, which eventually led to the sequencing of the human genome as well as the genomes of several other organisms coupled to automation and bioinformatics (which allows raw sequence data to be converted into meaningful information such as genes and their encoded proteins and comparative genomic analysis), has played and will continue to play an important role in the identification of clinically relevant biological targets. However, the limitations of genomics have become increasingly evident because it is at the protein level that disease processes become manifest and at which at least 91% of drugs act.[8] It is believed that further discovery of therapeutic targets will result from a better understanding of protein–protein interaction, protein–nucleic acid interaction, and protein–ligand interaction.

Target Validation

Once an area of potential therapeutic intervention has been characterized, companies would proceed to validate the target, which means that they would need to determine the actual role of the target in the disease in question. To validate a target, companies perform knock-out (loss of function) and knock-in (gain of function) assays in animal models to mimic a particular disease state (e.g., gene knock-out in mouse animal models to study cancer). Though time consuming and highly costly, these animal models are very valuable as an approximation of the real situation in humans. Target validation can be highly sophisticated, and in addition to the approaches just described, other methods, such as the use of small molecules (inhibitors, agonists, and antagonists) and antisense nucleic acid constructs (e.g., RNAi, neutralizing antibodies, and information on structural genomics and biology), form part of the biopharmaceutical industry's drug discovery armamentarium. Companies at this stage identify targets by measuring *in vitro* levels of RNA and protein expression and cell-based analysis. Target validation is not so easy to automate and is considered to be a major bottleneck in the process of drug discovery. Furthermore, in addition to the identification of proteins that may be involved in a particular disease state, companies will have to focus on finding ways to determine the "druggability" properties of these targets to decrease attrition and optimize the drug development process.[9]

Lead Identification

At this point, companies aim at identifying compounds that interact with the target proteins and modulate their activities. As such, they develop an assay to screen for drug candidates (using either random screening or a rational design method). Such an assay should be created in a way that would detect the activity that potential treatments would have on the target. Cost-effectiveness, accuracy, high speed and efficiency, and user-friendliness must characterize this assay because the same assay could sometimes be used in other drug development studies, although assays vary from target to target.

Upon development of the assay, researchers proceed by performing a primary screening or tests with a library of chemical compounds that the company already has in stock. The goal is to try to modulate a target that has already been validated, for which scientists would expect a predefined minimum level of activity against the target. Those compounds that meet or even exceed the predefined expectations, which are called "hits," are selected for a secondary screening (see "Lead optimization"), in which the activity of these hits is confirmed while measuring their potency and assessing their selectivity.

High-throughput screening is a popular method used by biopharmaceutical companies to detect the ability of a compound to alter the activity of a protein. This approach allows companies to test between 10,000 and 100,000 compounds per day in libraries containing millions of compounds. These compounds have been generated by using combinatorial chemistry and parallel synthesis, which allows the creation of millions of such compounds. However, the technological tools available today can allow the generation of only 100 million compounds (10^8) with the desired properties. To deal with this problem, scientists are proposing to obtain as much information as possible about the target proteins (such as structure, function, interactions, ligands, etc.) and to design chemical compounds accordingly.[10] Another interesting possibility is to look at natural compounds or derivations thereof, because nature has provided molecules with unique structural and spatial arrangements that can be used effectively to modulate biological activity such as compounds derived from plant, mineral, marine, fungal, and microbial sources. In fact, about one-third of all the drugs available today in the world market belong to this category.[11]

On the basis of the known physicochemical properties of the target (i.e., its three-dimensional structure, atomic composition, and characteristics of the active binding site), companies screen potential lead compounds using computer modeling and sophisticated software in a process called *in silico* (literally, "performed on computer or via computer simulation") screening. *In silico* screening has several advantages, including cost-effectiveness and the possibility of studying compounds that may interact with the target even before such compounds exist or before using expensive synthetic chemistry,[12] and is gaining momentum; but the major obstacle is that to perform some of these screenings or to design structure-based drugs, it is required that the structural data of the target be available already (such as data determined by X-ray diffraction or nuclear magnetic resonance spectroscopy [NMR]) as well as some other biological information such as binding interactions between a ligand (drug) and the target (protein).

Lead Optimization

Once hit compounds have been identified, companies follow up with a secondary screening called *lead optimization*, after which researchers are ready to select those drug candidates that are promising from a pharmacological point of view. This can be a very laborious and time-consuming procedure because it often is performed manually. In fact, lead optimization is considered to be the tightest part of the drug discovery process.[13] During this process, companies chemically modify promising organic molecules with the goal of obtaining compounds suitable to become a drug based on their pharmacodynamic properties (efficacy, potency, and selectivity *in vivo* and *in vitro*), pharmacokinetic properties (absorption and distribution throughout the body, how the drug is metabolized and excreted, etc.), and toxicity. This process is repeated several times until the drug developer selects the candidates that have the best chances of safety and therapeutic efficacy, generating a new library of compounds that have quantitative structure–activity relationships (QSARs). These candidates, through several iterative steps, are optimized even further. At this point, those compounds that demonstrate the greatest activity and the least toxicity, called *leads*, move on to a set of US Food and Drug Administration (FDA) or European Medicines Agency (EMEA) mandated tests or preclinical studies in animals demonstrating their safety (e.g., testing for potential mutagenicity or toxicity) before a human clinical trial can begin. Preclinical testing is also important because it allows companies to assess preliminary effectiveness and other pharmacological properties of the compound. The process of drug discovery varies from drug to drug, but on average, it is estimated that it lasts 7 years. It is remarkable that only a very small fraction of all the drug candidates that make it through preclinical studies go on to clinical trials—only 5 in 10,000—and only 1 in 10,000 make it to market.[14]

Drug Development

After chemical agents have shown promise in animal models or preclinical studies, the company submits an Initial New Drug (IND) application to the FDA Center for Drug Evaluation (CDER).[15] Once the IND application is submitted, the company should wait for 30 days to begin clinical trials to allow the FDA the necessary time to review the application. Assuming that the FDA does not reject the prospective study within 30 days after the application has been received, the sponsor company, following a uniquely and carefully designed protocol (a study plan on which all clinical trials are based) can start human clinical trials for safety and efficacy. Clinical development is the most expensive part of the process and is divided into three or four stages, as follows:

- Phase I clinical trial to test for a drug's safety and efficacy, including dosing range, drug absorption, distribution, metabolism, and excretion in the organism as well as the duration of its action. This test is performed in about 20–100 normal, healthy volunteers. This study takes around one and a half years. Companies may then perform Phase Ib clinical trials,[16] studies that are usually conducted in patients diagnosed with the disease or condition for which the study drug is intended, who demonstrate some biomarker, surrogate, or possibly clinical outcome that could be considered for proof of concept. In a Phase Ib study, proof of concept typically confirms the hypothesis that the current prediction of biomarker or outcome benefit is compatible with the mechanism of action.
- Phase II clinical trial to test for the same effects as in Phase I, with the difference that it is administered to patients suffering from the disease and in a larger population of between 100 and 500 patients. This phase takes around 2 years.
- Phase III clinical trial, usually involving 1,000–5,000 patients in clinics and hospitals. Physicians monitor patients closely to confirm efficacy and identify adverse events. This phase takes three and a half years.

Upon completion of Phase III clinical trials, sponsor companies analyze all the clinical data. If they believe that there is sufficient evidence of the drug's safety and effectiveness to meet the FDA's requirements for marketing approval, companies file for a New Drug Application (NDA)/Biologic License Application (BLA) with the FDA. The applications contain all the scientific information that the company has gathered throughout the drug development process, as well as full information on manufacturing specifications, stability and bioavailability data, the method of analysis of each of the dosage forms that the sponsor intends to market, the packaging and labeling for both physician and consumer, and the results of any additional toxicological studies not already submitted in the IND application.[17] Applications generally contain 100,000 or more pages, and the average review time is approximately 12 months. (We will get to the review time period in Chapter 6, when I discuss regulators in further detail.)

Should the regulators approve the drug, companies are allowed to launch the product and market it for the indication for which it was approved. Sometimes drugs are used for applications other than those for which they were approved; in this case, they are considered to be used *off-label*. For instance, a drug such as Avastin, which was approved by the FDA for colorectal cancer treatment, proved to be very successful in ophthalmology for the treatment of some kinds of macular degeneration and, more recently, in restoring hearing loss associated with a genetic disorder that creates benign tumors in the brain called neurofibromatosis type 2.[18]

Companies generally make production, marketing, and distribution arrangements long before drugs are approved because this gives them a competitive edge should the drug be approved. In the case of biotechnology companies, this is a particularly crucial step that may determine the success or failure of a young biotech firm because the manufacturing process for biotechnology products is more variable, complex, and expensive than the process of making traditional, small-molecule drugs. Making biotechnology products requires huge amounts of living organisms to generate a vast amount of large proteins. Even slight variances in the manufacturing process can have a significant impact in the product, which is the argument that the US biotech companies made to block a regulatory path in the United States for follow-on biologics. Because most startup biotech companies lack experience in the manufacturing process, they need to find ways to manufacture commercial quantities of their therapeutic compounds in a more cost-effective manner, secure financing to construct their facilities, and pass rigorous manufacturing site inspections by the FDA or EMEA. For a product to be successful, clinical development and manufacturing process development need to move together.

Biotech startup firms face the daunting task of deciding whether they should invest in creating a manufacturing facility in advance of potential clinical success, which means that if the product is not approved, the huge financial investment would go down the drain; whether to partner with a large biotech or pharmaceutical company to manufacture a product, meaning that they would have to give up a large part of the profits; or whether to wait until after approval to secure manufacturing capabilities, in which case the company risks suffering delays in revenue. For example, Berlex Laboratories and Chiron Corp had to institute a lottery system after Betaseron was approved for multiple sclerosis in 1993 because Chiron lacked sufficient production capacity. In 2001 and 2002, Immunex (acquired by Amgen in July 2002) was not able to meet demand for its rheumatoid arthritis drug, Enbrel, because of limited manufacturing capacity. Amgen secured additional capacity for Enbrel with a new manufacturing plant that was approved by the FDA in December 2002. But Immunex disappeared.

After drugs have been approved and enter the market, regulators may require companies to perform either a fourth clinical trial (Phase IV Clinical) to determine if the drug is effective against other disease states; to test different ways of taking the drug such as tablets, time-release capsules, or syrups; or to look for adverse events in larger populations over longer periods of time. This process is called *postmarketing surveillance*. In fact, it is through postmarketing surveillance that many of the adverse effects presented by recently launched drugs are detected. But the way in which regulators and companies do this is far from perfect, as some data have shown,[19] and more efforts should be allocated in this direction.

Regulators

In the United States, the FDA regulates the drug industry. In Europe, drug regulation is done by the EMEA, and there are also regulatory agencies in Japan, Australia, and Canada and in other countries as well. As mentioned in Chapter 3, the first regulatory agency in the United States was established in 1906 as part of the Food and Drug Act, which prohibited interstate commerce in falsely labeled and adulterated food, drink, and drugs. The FDA as we know it was created in 1938 when, in response to a number of deaths from the use of a poisonous solvent, diethylene glycol, in a new sulfa drug, the US Congress decided that the government should take more systematic steps to protect the public. The FDA was assigned the specific task of requiring drug companies to prove that their products were safe before they could be sold. It was not until 1952, however, that Congress decided that a doctor's prescription would be necessary to purchase drugs that could not be used safely without medical expertise. In 1962, after it was found that thalidomide (Thalomid), which had been licensed as a tranquilizer in Europe but not in the United States, was responsible for serious birth defects in women who had taken the drug during pregnancy, another requirement was added to the FDA approval process: drug companies had to prove that their products were not just safe but effective. That mandate soon gave rise to rules for carrying out clinical trials as we know them today.

The EMEA (based in London), on the other hand, was created in 1995 by the European Union (EU) and the pharmaceutical industry to harmonize the already existing national medicine regulatory entities of member states. The idea behind this harmonization was both to save drug companies the $350 million annual cost that they spent in winning separate approvals from each member state and to eliminate the protectionist tendencies of states unwilling to approve new drugs that might compete with those already produced by domestic drug companies. In many ways, the EMEA is similar to the FDA, with the exception that it is not centralized. Approximately one-third of the drugs that are approved every year come from the EU.

In 1992, the US Congress enacted the Prescription Drug User Fee Act, which authorizes drug companies to pay user fees to the FDA, with the sole objective of expediting the approval of drugs. The initial fee was $310,000 ($576,000 in 2002 due to terrorism, in the aftermath of the events of September, 2001) per new drug application and soon accounted for half the budget of the agency's drug evaluation center, which created a conflict of interest problem for which the agency has been repeatedly criticized: the FDA is dependent on the industry it regulates.[20]

Sometimes the FDA allows drugs that are still in clinical trials to be administered to seriously ill patients, upon request by the sponsor company, through three different approaches, all with "speed" as a common denominator: fast track, priority review, and accelerated approval.[21] Fast track is a process designed to facilitate development and to expedite the review of drugs to treat serious diseases (such as AIDS, Alzheimer's disease, heart failure, diabetes, depression, and cancer) and to fill an unmet medical need. The purpose is to get important new drugs to the patient earlier. A priority review designation is given to drugs that offer major advances in treatment or that provide a treatment where no adequate therapy exists. A priority review means that the time it takes the FDA to review a new drug application is reduced. The goal is to complete a priority review within 6 months. Often a company requesting fast track designation for a particular drug can also request priority review. Accelerated approval is a procedure (under the Subpart H regulation) through which the FDA may grant marketing approval for a new drug product on the basis of adequate and well-controlled clinical trials establishing that the drug product has an effect on a surrogate end point that is reasonably likely to predict clinical benefit, or on the basis of an effect on a clinical end point other than survival or irreversible morbidity. Approval under this section will be subject to the requirement that the applicant study the drug further to verify and describe its clinical benefit, where there is uncertainty as to the relation of the surrogate end point to clinical benefit or of the observed ultimate clinical benefit.[22]

Many companies focus, however, on the development of orphan drugs. In 1983, the FDA approved the Orphan Drugs Act, designed for drugs to treat rare diseases within patient populations of less than 200,000 individuals. This law provides research grants, tax breaks, exclusive marketing rights for 7 years, and other benefits for companies that develop these kinds of drugs. In 2000, the EMEA passed its own version of the Orphan Drugs Act, but it considered an orphan disease one that affects 5 in 10,000 people.[23] Since then, the EMEA has approved at least 50 orphan drugs.[24]

Intellectual Property

Long before a company begins clinical trials, companies protect the fruits of their R&D through patenting and secrecy, because once clinical trials begin, it is not possible to withhold that information from the public. There are several types of patents, but the one that applies to prescription drugs has a term of 20 years from the date the application is filed with the US Patent and Trademark Office or its equivalent abroad, such as the European Patent Office (EPO). A patent can apply to one of four possible characteristics of a drug: the drug substance itself, the method of use, the formulation, or the process of making it.[25] Drug substance patents simply cover the chemical composition of the active ingredient; method of use patents cover the use of a drug in treating a particular condition such as heart failure or depression; formulation patents cover the physical form of a drug such as by mouth or injection; and process patents cover manufacturing methods. To be patentable, the "invention" is supposed to be "useful, novel, and non-obvious." *Useful* originally meant what it seems to—that it had some practical benefit. *Novel* meant that it was significantly different from earlier inventions, and *nonobvious* meant that it was not simply the next step that any knowledgeable person in the field would take, but rather a remarkably new concept.

Conducting Clinical Trials

Clinical trials are not performed by the drug companies themselves directly (nor by the FDA or EMEA, counter to the widely held belief). Rather, biopharmaceutical companies hire teaching hospitals or private offices to perform clinical trials for them, recruiting their own patient (or volunteer) populations through different means, including some company-sponsored "patient support groups." Several years ago, most trials were done at medical schools and teaching hospitals. In the case of teaching hospitals, companies would provide hospitals or specific faculty members with grants that covered all the expenses of carrying out clinical trials, including medicines, patients' hospitalization, clinical tests, and so on. Though clinical trial costs vary from indication to indication and from drug to drug, according to business intelligence firm Cutting Edge Information,[26] the average cost of a Phase I clinical trial is approximately $15,700 per patient; for a Phase II clinical trial, it is about $19,300 per patient; and for a Phase III clinical trial, it exceeds $26,000 per patient. Roughly, on the basis of the numbers of patients required, this means that a Phase I clinical trial (with 20–100 healthy patients) could cost from a few hundred thousand dollars to $1.5 million; a Phase II clinical trial (with 100–500 patients) could cost around $2–10 million; and a Phase III clinical trial (with 1,000–5,000 patients) could cost from $26 million to $130 million. Larger companies perform, at any given time, several trials simultaneously.

As we saw in Chapter 4, in the last few years, there has been an increase in the number of clinical trials performed worldwide, and companies have relied more and more on for-profit companies called contract research organizations (CROs), which hire physicians (investigators) and organize and carry out clinical trials for the industry. As of today, according to Christopher Milne and Ken Getz[27] of the Tufts Center for the Study of Drug Development, there are about 300 CROs in the United States and about 700–750 worldwide, with revenues from their drug company clients of some $7 billion. Many of these CROs perform clinical studies in countries in Eastern Europe and in Russia, India, and China.

For instance, it is estimated that the Indian clinical research outsourcing market was around $200 million as of 2008, and it was expected to reach $600 million by 2010.[28] Because R&D expenditures are increasing by 15% per year, global biopharmaceutical companies are looking for cheaper options. While the cost of clinical trials varies on the basis of complexity and disease sector, a simple trial in India can cost 15–20% of the US price, and a more sophisticated trial—involving imaging systems—may cost 50–60% of the US price. In 2005, national spending on clinical trials in the United States was nearly $24 billion. In 2006, it rose to $25.6 billion, and it is expected that in 2011, it will reach $32.1 billion—growing at an average rate of 4.6% per year.[29]

As has been indicated elsewhere, an increased demand for the safety of drugs has increased over the years the average number of clinical trials per NDA, for example, 30 in the 1970s, 40 in the 1980s, and 70 in the 1990s. If 1,500 patients were required for an NDA in the early 1980s, the average number of patients is more than 4,000 today.[30] The increased demand for safety is consequently reflected in a prolonged duration of the drug development process. In the 1960s, total development time was 8.1 years. This rose to 11.8 years in the 1970s, to 14.2 years in the 1980s, and finally, to 14.9 years in the 1990s.[31] The National Institutes of Health (NIH) lists 74,470 active trials in 167 countries,[32] recruiting 2.5 million patients; however, the actual number of clinical trials taking place in the world is significantly higher because not all trials are registered with the FDA or NIH. Industry-sponsored clinical trials account for approximately 85% of all clinical trials, at least in the United States, whereas the NIH sponsors only 10%. The remaining 5% are funded by philanthropic groups. One of the greatest limitations when conducting clinical trials is having access to patient populations. For this reason, companies organize many ways to recruit populations through CROs and support groups. It is noteworthy to mention that over the years, the costs of clinical trials have increased significantly (see Figure 5.2).

Once drugs are approved, they have to comply with the regulators' mandates for good manufacturing procedures (GMPs), which require that domestic or foreign manufacturers have a quality system for the design, manufacture, packaging, labeling, storage, installation, and servicing of finished medical devices (or

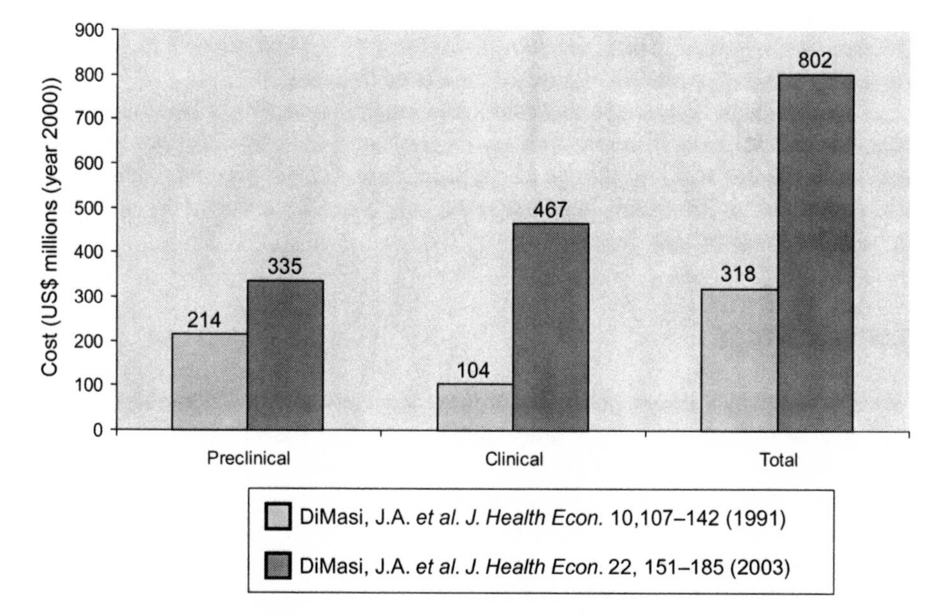

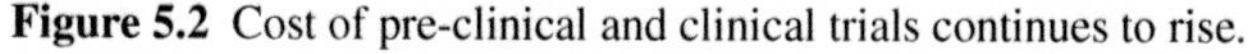

Figure 5.2 Cost of pre-clinical and clinical trials continues to rise.
According to the studies by J.A. DiMasi et al., at the Tufts Center for the Study of Drug Development (TCSDD), between 1991 and 2003 the cost of pre-clinical and clinical trials increased significantly. This is a trend that continues today.

drugs) intended for commercial distribution in the United States, among other things.[33]

Launching of the drug usually takes place a year after the drug is approved and once the company has fulfilled all the requirements and its marketing and sales force arsenal is ready to go.

Types of Drugs

The FDA classifies NDAs by the drugs' chemical types and potential benefits. For "chemical type," the agency determines whether a drug is an active ingredient never before marketed in the United States (a new molecular entity, or NME, assigned the number 1 in the classification scheme) or whether it is a derivative or new formulation or combination of already existing drugs on the market by the same or other manufacturers. The second important classification is made based on the benefit that the drug offers compared to already existing drugs on the market for the same condition. If the drug represents a breakthrough, it may be classified with a "priority review" status, which is for drugs likely to represent "a significant improvement compared to marketed products, in the treatment, diagnosis, or prevention of a disease."[34] These drugs are listed by the FDA with the abbreviation "P." However, NMEs are not necessarily classified as priority review drugs because these new drugs may not be better than already existing ones. Similarly, priority review applications do not necessarily refer to NMEs because they could be modifications of already-existing drugs or new combinations of previous ones. All other drugs receive a standard—or S—review, which, according to the FDA, "is applied to a drug that offers at most, only minor improvement over existing marketed therapies."[35]

A breakthrough drug is one that fulfils two requirements: it is a brand-new drug (i.e., it is an NME) and it receives priority review status. In other words, the drug is a new molecule that will probably be a significant improvement over drugs already on the market. As we have seen, in recent years, only a small number of drugs deserve to be called breakthrough drugs.

Generic Drugs

When a company's patent protection expires, the FDA allows the entrance to the market of generic versions of the drug—that is, a copy of the off-patent drug's active ingredient by other manufacturers. The Hatch-Waxman Amendments of 1984 enabled generics companies to launch a generic product simply by filing an Abbreviated New Drug Application (ANDA) that demonstrates that the generic product is bioequivalent to the brand drug that was already approved, and therefore companies did not have to carry out clinical trials again. (The goal of this amendment of the Hatch-Waxman Act was to simplify the FDA generics drugs approval process for generics companies, whose share of the market rose from less than 20% of prescriptions in 1984 to 75% of prescriptions in the present day, according to some US economists, though their sales are lower because these drugs are much cheaper.[36])

Besides generic drugs proper, there exists another line of generics called *brand generics*, which are medicines that have active ingredients that are *similar*, but not *identical,* to the active ingredients of the brand-name drugs that they imitate (therefore not infringing on patents), and which, for this reason, have the advantage of not having to go through clinical trials. These drugs are priced somewhere between brand-name drugs and true generics, and their market share is growing rapidly, but not without some controversy.

Neither generics nor brand generics are taken lightly by the brand-name pharmaceutical industry. When a brand-name drug goes off-patent, the pharmaceutical company still keeps the high price, and the first generic drugs keep a price that is only slightly lower than the brand-name one, to start eroding brand-name sales. As more generics enter the market, the sales of the brand-name drugs usually plunge to as low as 20% of their peak because generics firms make the drugs at sharply reduced prices. Because pharmacists can substitute brand-name drugs with generics when available (unless indicated otherwise by prescribing physicians), sales of the brand-name drugs erode quite quickly after going off-patent. For those blockbuster drugs (that is, drugs with sales over $1 billion), this represents hundreds of millions of dollars in revenue losses, as we saw in Chapter 4. Some examples include companies like Bristol–Myers Squibb, which lost protection on its $2.3 billion cholesterol drug Prevachol in April 2006; Pfizer, which lost patent protection on the $3.3 billion antidepressant Zoloft 2 months later; and Merck, which lost protection on the $4.4 billion cholesterol drug Zocor that same month.[37]

Companies should not wait until a drug goes off-patent to confront the dangers of the generics industry. In 2006, Bristol–Myers Squibb faced a disastrous blow from a generics firm. The drugmaker Apotex produced generic versions of Plavix, a blood thinner under Bristol's patent protection scheduled to expire in 2011. Apotex produced Plavix without legal clearance to do so, until Bristol managed to get the production blocked by a court ruling. Bristol–Myers Squibb did not handle the situation well, and as such, its CEO, Peter Dolan, was abruptly terminated in September of the same year.

It is important to highlight that although brand-name company losses due to patent expirations may be large, generic drug making is a tough business because the sales that remain are often divided among numerous producers, especially in the case of so-called natural expirations, in which five or six players enter the market right from the beginning. As mentioned earlier, as soon as a drug goes off-patent, a generics maker may be able to secure significant sales, at least for a few months, by successfully challenging patents in court and winning temporary exclusivity. But unless a company gains exclusivity, the margins tend to be low. However, generics sales do add up, even if the profits are much lower than brand-name drugs.

For biologics, becoming generic is a bit tough at present because it is difficult to reproduce what is considered living material, although the EMEA has recently approved such products. Sometimes companies may choose, for strategic and financial reasons, to change a drug's status from prescription to over-the-counter (OTC).[38]

Pricing

As in the case of any other new commercial product that is launched in the market, pharmaceutical companies consider a series of forces that determine the price of medicines. Among the factors that have more weight in their pricing strategies are the relative efficacy and safety profile of a new drug in relation to its competitors, the market size, the competitive landscape, and the costs incurred in the drug's development, which, albeit significant, are very difficult to assess for individual drugs. In general, most drugs are priced according to other established drugs in their class; however, breakthrough therapies for the treatment of life-threatening conditions usually charge premium prices well above those for existing products, such as was the case of Cerezyme, developed by Genzyme for the treatment of Gaucher's disease (at an average cost of $200,000 annually for the patient; see Table 1.5).

Drug pricing, like any other commercial product, varies significantly, depending on who the customer is. Large-scale buyers (hospital chains and other institutional customers) get significant discounts, and they purchase drugs below market price; governmental organizations, such as the Department of Defense, the Department of Veterans Affairs, and Medicaid, get very steep discounts and the best prices, whereas wholesale distributors and pharmacy chains for the retail (or individual physician/patient) market pay higher prices for drugs to compensate for the discounts that drug companies give managed care customers (this is known as *cost shifting*). Not surprisingly, the practice of price fixing, which is what this is, has been a very fertile legal battleground as several pharmacy chains and pharmacy trade associations have sued leading drug manufacturers on this account. On the other hand, ever since Part D was added, Medicare has not been allowed to negotiate discounts from manufacturers, which is one reason why Medicare beneficiaries (just like anyone who buys medicines out of pocket) pay the highest prices.

Actually, companies determine the price for a new pharmaceutical early in the drug development process, which means that several years before the product is launched, it already has a price. The company determines a price threshold above which the return on investment will be sufficient to satisfy its investors. And like luxury items, the more devastating the disease is and the more unique and effective the drug is, the higher the price.

Of course, in setting prices, companies do a great deal of benchmarking; that is, they first compare how other pharmaceutical products already on the market for the same indication are priced, including brand-name drugs, OTCs, generics, brand generics, and devices. This requires a great deal of differentiation: are existing product prices based on daily, weekly, monthly, and yearly doses? Under what conditions? For companies, it is crucial to determine what advantages the new product has over existing products in terms of safety, efficacy, dosing, and convenience, so that they can justify charging premium prices. Positioning any advantages in any of these categories will greatly help market a new product and increase its price. Companies also address the issue of reimbursement for a given indication in their pricing processes—for instance, whether the drug would be covered by managed care organizations, the new Part D drug benefit program of Medicare, Medicaid, Veterans Affairs, and so on—and consider the reactions of insurers, patient advocates, and the government to the price. Companies try to soften the psychological impact that a high price can have on people by instituting a patient access program; that is, providing some poor patients with free medicines or medicines at a substantial discount.[39]

Needless to say, the profit margins for biopharmaceutical companies are extraordinarily high. In many instances, as I said at the end of Chapter 2, the pricing of many drugs is completely unrelated to the benefit to the patient (for example, oncology drugs that cost $100,000 in exchange for only 2 or 3 months more of life), and such prices are completely unrealistic.

Marketing

As described earlier, pharmaceutical companies generally perform extensive elasticity market research to evaluate what the market will bear based on what doctors would prescribe and under what range of prices. If the product is direct-to-consumer (DTC) marketing-intensive, companies consider patients' and private payers' opinions. Pharmaceutical companies analyze hospital formularies, and if the new product is superior to whatever is available on the market, they will waste no time in setting up a premium for it. Contrary to what the industry claims, most companies do not price their products at a level where they can be assured of covering the R&D costs that went into producing the product because it is almost impossible to assess this number for individual drugs. Also, pricing has little to do with the anticipated DTC marketing costs that lie ahead because these are considered sunk costs, in other words, costs that have already been incurred which cannot be recovered.[40] Companies will charge as much money as possible for the drugs to please investors, regardless of whether some ill patients will be able to afford the drugs or not. If the majority of people can pay hefty prices (but not everybody), they will charge what the majority can pay.

Marketing by pharmaceutical companies is under great fire at the moment in the United States, and rightly so. Not only has the pharmaceutical industry gone way too far in pushing drugs by bribing doctors (through special gifts and lavish promotions[41]) so that they will favor prescribing a particular drug over other equally effective and cheaper drugs, but it has also openly lied about its products. The recent scandals involving Merck[42] and Wyeth,[43] discussed in Chapter 4, have exposed a pervasive practice by the industry: ghostwriting reports and presenting clinical data in fake "peer-reviewed" journals to market products—and this is only what we *know*.

In fact, pharmaceutical companies spend significantly more money in marketing than in R&D. DTC advertising, which is the prevalent way in which drugs (and products in general) have traditionally been and are advertised in the United States, has become a double-edged sword. On the positive side, when DTC first appeared in the United States in the 1980s (reaching full maturity in the late 1990s), it was very popular. In fact, it lifted the veil of secrecy around drugs: people used to go to the doctor, who would deliberately write a prescription that the patient could not understand. In many ways, DTC (and the Internet) have educated the public about medical conditions that they would not ordinarily talk about, such as depression, urinary or fecal incontinence, and erectile dysfunction. However, the ads are obnoxious and ubiquitous, and people are really weary of them, especially because some are so repellent and vulgar, emphasizing benefits over harm (and thus interfering in the doctor–patient relationship) to the point that this situation has reached a great level of saturation. The industry has dug itself into a hole and made itself very unpopular because of these ads.[44]

The way in which marketing is performed in the United States will have to change in the years to come. In fact, it is detailing, and not DTC, that really moves drug products in the United States. Furthermore, as doctors become more restricted in what they will write a prescription for (more guidelines, more formulary-driven prescriptions, etc.), DTC will necessarily wane. Now, we should not expect that this will take place as a result of major political action because in the United States, the First Amendment is such that it is going to be very difficult to pass a law through Congress that may actually restrict commercial speech in this area. Congress might be able to do something minor, but because DTC is considered commercial speech, it is protected. It is noteworthy to say that in 2009, DTC pharmaceutical advertising spending increased 3.9%, to around $4.8 billion, following the collapse in 2008 of the world financial markets. This gain was achieved despite a 12% decline in total advertising expenditures.[45]

I think that in the future, the high quality of pharmaceutical products and use of the Internet will, in the end, take care of the market. If a product is really good, who would not want to have it?

Finally, though it is true that companies adjust their prices according to the countries where their products are sold, this in no way means that the drugs will be cheap and affordable for the majority of people in these countries; rather, prices will be "normalized." Products will be cheaper in countries with strict price controls than in countries with none, but only in absolute terms. This price differentiation caused, in past years, big headaches within the pharmaceutical industry, especially in the United States. To control drug reimportation in the United States from Canada and Mexico, pharmaceutical companies decided to establish a quota for the amount of medicines allowed to be sold to Canada and Mexico so that the amount sold would be enough only to satisfy national demands.[46]

I shall conclude this chapter by saying that drug discovery and development is a complex, systematic, and highly scrutinized process. One of the key issues is that as this overall process becomes more sophisticated, it also becomes more complex, and therefore more time consuming, expensive, and difficult to regulate. So the industry depends more than ever on innovation to survive, but abuses on the part of the pharmaceutical industry with regard to the pricing and marketing of their products have tainted their image and created a very fertile battleground for polemic at the societal and public policy levels. In the next chapter, we will explore why.

Notes

1. Boston Consulting Group, 2001. A Revolution in R&D: How Genomics and Genetics Are Transforming the Biopharmaceutical Industry. Boston Consulting Group, Boston, MA.
2. DiMasi, J.A., 2001. Risks in new drug development: approval success rates for investigational drugs. Clinical Pharmacology and Therapeutics 69, 297–307.
3. Ibid.
4. Conversation with a venture capitalist, London, UK, May 2007.
5. Hillisch, A., Hilgenfeld, R. (Eds.), 2003. Modern Methods of Drug Discovery. Birkhäuser, Basel, p. ix.
6. A phenotype is the sum of the observable traits or characteristics of an organism as a result of the expression of that organism's genes and their interaction with the environment.
7. Drews, J., 2000. Drug discovery: a historical perspective. Science 287, 1960–1964.
8. Hillisch, Hilgenfeld. Modern Methods.
9. Ibid, 9.
10. Wess, G., Urmann, M., Sickenberger, B., 2001. Medicinal chemistry: challenges and opportunities. Angewandte Chemie International Edition 40, 3341–3350.
11. Grabley, S., Sattler, I. Natural products for lead identification: nature is a valuable resource for providing tools, In: Hillisch, Hilgenfeld, Modern Methods.
12. Schneider, G., Böhm, H.J., 2002. Virtual screening and fast automated cocking methods. Drug Discovery Today 7, 64–70.
13. Hillisch, Hilgenfeld. Modern Methods.
14. Kaitin, K.I. (Ed.), 2006. Cost to Develop New Biotech Products is Estimated to Average $1.2 Billion, Impact Report 8. Tufts Center for the Study of Drug Development, Boston, MA.
15. Or the equivalent regulatory agency, if the drug candidate is developed in a country other than the United States.
16. There is also a Phase IIb and a Phase IIIb.
17. US FDA. How drugs are developed and approved. http://www.fda.gov/Drugs/DevelopmentApprovalProcess/HowDrugsareDevelopedandApproved/default.htm.
18. Smith, S., 2009. A drug's unintended use restores the gift of hearing. Boston Globe, July 9, 2009. http://www.boston.com/news/local/massachusetts/articles/2009/07/09/a_drug8217s_unintended _use_restores_the_gift_of_hearing/?page=2.
19. Jones, D., 2007. Keeping vigilant about drug safety. Nature Reviews Drug Discovery 6, 855–856.
20. Angell, M., 2004. The Truth about the Drug Companies: How They Deceive Us and What to Do about It. Random House, New York. One should note that EMEA, Canadian regulators, and others have between 75% and 100% user's fee funding.
21. US FDA. Fast track, accelerated approval and priority review. http://www.fda.gov/ForConsumers/ByAudience/ForPatientAdvocates/SpeedingAccesstoImportantNewTherapies/ucm128291.htm.
22. US FDA. Code of Federal Regulations Title 21. http://www.accessdata.fda.gov/scripts/cdrh/cfdocs/cfcfr/CFRSearch.cfm?CFRPart=314&showFR=1&subpartNode=21:5.0.1.1.4.8.
23. European Medicines Agency. Human medicines: orphan medicinal products. http://www.emea.europa.eu/htms/human/orphans/intro.htm.
24. European Medicines Agency, 2008. List of orphan-designated authorized medicines, November 6, 2008, Doc. Ref. EMEA/563575/2008. http://www.emea.europa.eu/pdfs/human/comp/ 56357508en.pdf.
25. Until recently, the process type of patent was considered to lend itself to some ambiguity. Recently, the US Supreme Court has determined, in the case Bilski and Warsaw (http://www.cafc.uscourts.gov/opinions/07-1130.pdf), that there is only one test that should be applied to determine whether a process is patentable: the "machine or transformation" test.

That is, patent claims should either be tied to a particular machine or apparatus or linked to the transformation of an article to a different state or thing. Refer also to the US Trademark and Patent Office. http://www.uspto.gov/web/offices/pac/doc/general/index.html.
26. Center for the Study of Drug Development, 2006. Clinical operations: accelerating trials, allocating resources and measuring performance. Thanks to Chris Milne for this valuable information.
27. Milne, C., personal communication.
28. Jacob, S., 2008. Recession not to hit clinical trials: CROs. Economic Times, November 18, 2008, http://economictimes.indiatimes.com/News/News_By_Industry/Healthcare__Biotech/Biotech/Recession_not_to_hit_clinical_trials_CROs/articleshow/3725055.cms.
29. Fee, R., 2007. The cost of clinical trials drug discovery and development. Drug, Discovery and Development, March 1, 2007, http://www.dddmag.com/the-cost-of-clinical-trials.aspx.
30. Peck, C.C., 1997. Drug development: improving the process. Food Drug Law Journal 52, 163–167.
31. Report issued by the Tufts Center for the Study of Drug Development, Tufts University, Boston, MA, 1988.
32. See the National Institutes of Health Web site. http://clinicaltrials.gov/.
33. *GMP* refers to the Good Manufacturing Practice Regulations promulgated by the FDA under the authority of the Federal Food, Drug, and Cosmetic Act (see Chapter IV for food and Chapter V, Subchapters A, B, C, D, and E, for drugs and devices).
34. US FDA. Guidance for industry available therapy. http://www.fda.gov/downloads/Drugs/GuidanceComplianceRegulatoryInformation/Guidances/UCM071300.pdf.
35. US FDA. Fast track, accelerated approval and priority review. http://www.fda.gov/ForConsumers/ByAudience/ForPatientAdvocates/SpeedingAccesstoImportantNewTherapies/ucm128291.htm.
36. AARP Public Policy Institute, 2008. Trends in Manufacturer Prices of Brand Name Prescription Drugs Used by Medicare Beneficiaries 2002 to 2007, Watchdog Report. AARP Public Policy Institute, Washington, DC.
37. Smith, A., 2006. The big threat to big pharma. CNNMoney, October 31, 2006. http://money.cnn.com/2006/10/31/news/companies/generics/index.htm.
38. Mahecha, L., 2006. Rx-to-OTC switches: trends and factors underlying success. Nature Reviews Drug Discovery 5, 380–386.
39. Gregson, N., Sparrowhawk, K., Mauskopf, J., Paul, J., 2005. Pricing medicines: theory and practice, challenges and opportunities. Nature Reviews Drug Discovery 4, 121–130.
40. Herrera, S., 2006. Price controls: preparing for the unthinkable. Nature Biotechnology 24, 257–260.
41. Hawthorne, F., 2003. The Merck Druggernaut: Inside Story of a Pharmaceutical Giant. John Wiley, Hoboken, NJ.
42. Singer, N., 2009. Trials puts spotlight on Merck. New York Times, May 13, 2009. http://www.nytimes.com/2009/05/14/business/14vioxx.html?scp=2&sq=merck%20 elsevier&st=cse.
43. Wilson, D., 2008. Wyeth's use of ghostwriters questioned. New York Times, December 12, 2008. http://www.nytimes.com/2008/12/13/business/13wyeth.html?_r=1&scp=6&sq=merck%20 elsevier&st=cse.
44. Should prescription drugs ads be reined in? New York Times, August 4, 2009. http://roomfordebate.blogs.nytimes.com/2009/08/04/should-prescription-drug-ads-be-reined-in/.
45. Standard and Poor's, Industry surveys. Health care: Pharmaceuticals, June 2010.
46. Interview with Anita Kidgell, Brentford, UK, May 2007.

6 The Pharmaceutical Regulators

The US Food and Drug Administration (FDA) and the European Medicines Agency (EMEA) are the leading drug regulators in the world. There are, of course, similarities and significant differences between these two entities, as discussed in Chapter 4, but the power that they both exercise over the drug approval process is equally important. And they both, amid severe criticism, continue to implement new initiatives to improve the drug approval machinery.

The relationship between drug regulators and companies has never been a smooth one. Over the years, the pharmaceutical industry has complained that regulators take a very long time to review New Drug Applications (NDAs), that these agencies are too bureaucratic, that their requirements for drug approval are extremely high, and that whenever they need additional data, they request it at the last minute, putting tremendous pressure on companies. In fact, the estimated percentage of new drugs and biologic applications that did not get initial approval from the FDA rose from 63% in 2003 to 93% in 2006. In these instances, the FDA either asked for more data or the companies withdrew the applications.[1] Although a slightly higher number of drugs were approved in 2009, there are no signs that the FDA or EMEA have softened its standards for the approval of new drugs.

As a result of several safety failures, among which Merck's Vioxx was the most notable debacle in recent years, the public has also been severely critical of the FDA. In the particular case of Vioxx, critics have charged the FDA of being too lax when it approved this painkiller, despite the fact that in 2001, there were strong signals coming from the VIGOR trial that pointed toward adverse cardiovascular events associated with Vioxx. In fact, the FDA advised Merck to amend the label concerning cardiovascular risk. But Merck did not believe that Vioxx increased cardiovascular risks and submitted study after study to the FDA until Merck finally detected the cardiovascular signals, at which point it withdrew the drug from the market. However, I have been told that what was known about Vioxx prior to approval is overstated—in other words, that there were suggestive *in vitro* data that it could be prothrombotic and that the VIGOR trial (which the FDA required) was finished *after* approval and showed the clinical signal versus naproxen. Whatever the truth is, the problem is that between 2001 and 2004, the company was advertising the drug without having changed the label and without warning people about increased cardiovascular adverse effects—and consumption of Vioxx was great.[2]

More recently, regarding the case of GlaxoSmithKline's Avandia, a type 2 diabetes treatment that was found to increase the risk of heart attack among patients by 43%, several people, including the authors of the study that brought this finding to light—cardiologist Steven Nissen[3] and his collaborators—have claimed that the FDA

The World's Health Care Crisis. DOI: 10.1016/B978-0-12-391875-8.00006-8

was long aware of the risks associated with Avandia and did not act competently and promptly to investigate these risks.[4] Since then, the FDA advisory committee responded by adding several black box warnings[5] on the medicine's label about the potential risk of congestive heart failure but did not pull Avandia from the market. But in December 2008, the FDA put into place guidelines for industry for the evaluation of cardiovascular risk in new antidiabetic therapies to treat type 2 diabetes mellitus[6] because none of the currently approved antidiabetic agents has been proven convincingly to reduce the risk of cardiovascular disease. In fact, some may actually increase the risk, a situation that is concerning given the fact that type 2 diabetes mellitus treatments usually must be used for life. These guidelines consist of recommendations on how to use clinical trials to show that a new type 2 diabetes mellitus treatment is not associated with an unacceptable increase in the risk of cardiovascular events and provide a detailed approach for acquiring, analyzing, and reporting the necessary safety information from all Phase II and III trials of a novel drug.

Some of the FDA's most radical critics see it as too friendly an agency to the pharmaceutical industry because of the political (and even financial) stake that some of the people in the higher echelons of the FDA (and at the US government level) have in industry. Others, such as Marcia Angell, a Harvard Medical School professor and former editor-in-chief of the *New England Journal of Medicine*, have gone as far as to claim, in a highly critical and criticized book[7], *The Truth about the Drug Companies: How they Deceive Us and What to Do About It* whose notorious lack of objectivity is there for all of us to see—that the FDA is on the pharmaceutical industry's payroll owing to the Prescription Drug User's Fee Act (PDUFA), a device through which the FDA charges companies a user's fee to speed up the processing of drug reviews. (Of course, the author forgot to mention that so do most other regulators around the world, and that this is caused by their legislators, not the agencies.) Of importance, some industrial and public sectors, such as some advocacy and support groups (which, no doubt, are sponsored by industry itself), have blamed regulators for the dearth of new drugs coming to market, claiming that regulators are being "too cautious" at times. Therefore, no matter which front one refers to, the truth is that there is a lot of pressure on these regulatory bodies.

But things, in reality, are not so black and white.

Causes of the Drug Approval Lag

For many years, the FDA and EMEA have observed the declining number of new medicines coming to market, as well as the increasing costs of research and development (R&D). In 2002, when companies experienced a very dramatic drop in bringing new chemical entities (NCEs) to market, both the FDA and the EMEA began to wonder what was happening and held meetings with industry members to analyze the root of the problem.[8] Then, the FDA and the European Commission launched studies to look into this, and after a couple of years of discussion, they concluded that the problem was the high failure rate in drug development:[9] sometimes compounds fail as late as Phase III clinical trials, costing companies a fortune. Therefore, the products that companies bring to market will have a very high price because the industry needs to recoup its financial investment in the all-too-numerous candidates that failed over a long period of time.

Both the FDA and the EMEA agreed that they could not lower the standards for drug approval, which are quality, safety, and efficacy, and that to improve industry productivity, the process of R&D had to change. Regulators then asked themselves what they could do in their official function to facilitate R&D performance, and they concluded that to reach this goal, several initiatives that had been in place since the late 1990s, which resulted from revisions to the PDUFA such as diminishing the administrative burden for the review of drug approvals, needed to be optimized. These agencies also decided to launch some important new initiatives to facilitate better outcomes in clinical trials, while increasing safety before and after launch: the FDA created its "Critical Path," and the EMEA initiated its "Road Map to 2010."

FDA and EMEA Initiatives to Optimize Drug Approval

Before elaborating on the new initiatives by the FDA and EMEA, let us briefly go back to the PDUFA because its importance is paramount. The PDUFA was first enacted in 1992, with the goal of improving the process of drug review. Under this program—which has been subsequently revised in 1997, 2002, and more recently in 2007, as PDUFA II, III, and IV, respectively—the pharmaceutical and biotechnology industries pay certain user's fees to the FDA. In exchange for these fees, the FDA agreed, via correspondence with Congress, to a set of performance standards intended to reduce the approval time for NDAs and Biological License Applications (BLAs).[10]

The PDUFA assesses three types of user fees: (1) fees on applications (NDAs and BLAs), (2) annual fees on establishments, and (3) renewal fees on products. The law includes a set of triggers designed to ensure that appropriations for application review are not supplanted by user's fees. These triggers require that congressional appropriations for such review reach certain levels before user fees may be assessed, and that the FDA devote a certain amount of appropriated funds annually to drug review activities.

As a result of PDUFA I (1992), the agency shortened the review time from an average of 3 to 1.5 years. But since then, clinical trials have become more complex, and to keep the review time short, the FDA took on the initiative of mandating deadlines for the timing of FDA-sponsored meetings, thus increasing scientific interaction between the FDA and the sponsoring companies and aiming to improve clinical trial output (PDUFA II). The goal of these PDUFA meetings was the discussion of clinical points along the regulatory process. There are three types of FDA-sponsor meetings: Type A (meetings for dispute resolution, clinical holds, and special protocol assessments), Type B (pre-IND meetings, certain end of Phase I meetings, end of Phase II/pre–Phase III meetings, and pre-NDA/BLA meetings); and Type C (any meeting other than a Type A or Type B meeting between the FDA and a sponsor or applicant regarding the development and review of a product in a human drug application, as described in section 735(1) of the act, with the exclusion of meetings that do not pertain to the review of human drug applications for PDUFA products, such as most meetings about advertising and promotional labeling for approved drug products, except meetings about launch activities and materials and postmarketing safety evaluation meetings).[11] In fact, prior studies had demonstrated that sponsor-agency meetings have a positive impact on the time required to develop a drug, while leading to a better, safer, and more efficacious overall drug approval process. The FDA holds an average of nine sponsor-requested meetings a day, typically involving 15 FDA staffers and 120−540 person-hours. These meetings have been found to reduce the percentage of product programs experiencing slowdowns during review.[12]

Similarly, the EMEA has also launched important initiatives in this front, among them the New Medicines Legislation (NML), to provide scientific advice to the sponsoring companies both during drug development and once drugs are on the market. Basically, these initiatives have as a goal, among others, to target problems early on during the drug development phase, reducing the risk of subsequent rejection while providing a faster review process. According to Thomas Lönngren, former executive director of the EMEA:

> *You could divide the advice into scientific advice and regulatory advice. You have the quality aspects and the manufacturing aspects. When you look at the questions, [most of them] are on the clinical side: it could be issues from Phase I to Phase II, but normally most of the scientific advice is on Phase III in order to have a discussion about the endpoints of clinical trials and so on.... But more and more the scientific advice is now oriented to the new technologies that are coming... because there are a lot of questions on this front. For instance, if you are manufacturing a cell culture based on stem cells or something like that, you know, how would you demonstrate consistency in manufacturing? How will you ensure [good manufacturing practice] standards? There are completely new kinds of questions that are coming out now... which are in part due to the mapping of the genome and all that derives from it. So we are trying to collect the best expertise in Europe in order to discuss these issues.... So we are in a very early stage in this development of this new science of interaction with companies... [and] we get knowledge from them and think about it from a regulatory point of view and give them advice, you know, and that is the way we are interacting.*[13]

Both the FDA and the EMEA have undertaken several initiatives to gather more safety data on drugs already approved, given the high number of drugs that have been withdrawn for safety reasons. The FDA is trying to accomplish this through PDUFA III (2002), in which it addresses postmarketing commitments and label comprehension and drug interactions in conditions of actual use;[14] the EMEA, through the NML, requires of companies the inclusion of a risk management plan (EU-RMP, created in 2005) within the core dossier of a new marketing authorization application or for significant changes to an authorization such as a new dose, a new route of administration.[15] These policies are particularly important because ever since 1962, when the FDA required companies to perform carefully run clinical trials, the standard parameters for drug approval have been safety, efficacy, and quality. However, over the last several years, these tenets have been subject to closer examination and revision because it has been demonstrated that dosing efficacy can vary by as much as fivefold from individual to individual, while safety has a tenfold range across the normal population curve compared with the standard dose.[16]

Now, the emerging initiatives from the regulators—the FDA's "Critical Path" (see Figure 6.1 a, b, and c) and the EMEA's "Road Map to 2010"—have as a goal to guide the way in which companies perform their R&D so that the clinical trial process is improved and safety is maximized.

FDA Critical Path Initiative

The FDA realized that despite the fact that it had reduced to a great extent the excess time required to review the human clinical trials, the lag in bringing new products to the market still persisted. In fact, more than 80% of potential drug candidates that enter the development phase after filing an IND fail to reach the market.[17] The FDA acting commissioner at the time, Mark McClellan, asked Janet Woodcock, the director of the FDA Center for Drug Evaluation and Research, to look into possible ways to examine the roots of the crisis of affordability and availability of drugs. McClellan's major concern was that even if we got more drugs on the market, they would not be affordable because they would cost so much to develop. According to Woodcock, "I looked into the issue and determined that one of the problems was that although there was tremendous and very up-to-date science in the discovery process, the preclinical and clinical evaluation of drugs were really based back in the mid-twentieth century."[18] So she concluded that the problem was that the applied sciences for medical product development had not kept pace with advances in basic science.[19] According to Woodcock, "the new science is not being used to guide the technology development process in the same way that it is accelerating the technology discovery process. For medical technology, performance is measured in terms of product safety and effectiveness. Not enough applied scientific work has been done to create new tools to get fundamentally better answers about how the safety and effectiveness of new products can be demonstrated, in faster time frames, with more certainty, and at lower costs. In many cases, developers have no choice but to use the tools and concepts of the last century to assess this century's candidates."[20]

For this reason, the FDA launched its Critical Path Opportunity List initiative in 2004, with the goal of improving and accelerating the process of translating experimental leads into approved medicines and creating significant public health benefits in this manner.[21] A crucial part of the Critical Path involves translational medicine, the bench-to-bedside feedback loop mechanism between basic researchers and clinicians that is considered the bridge between discovery and development. In the translational process, which I will discuss in further detail in the next chapters, *biomarkers*—that is, quantitative measures that provide the link between mechanism and clinical effect, assisting in the evaluation of targets (i.e., biological pathways in disease causation and prevention) and matching them to investigational compounds—are extremely important.[22]

Biomarkers are often developed by companies mostly for internal use. Even though biomarkers are the key to model-based drug development, only a few

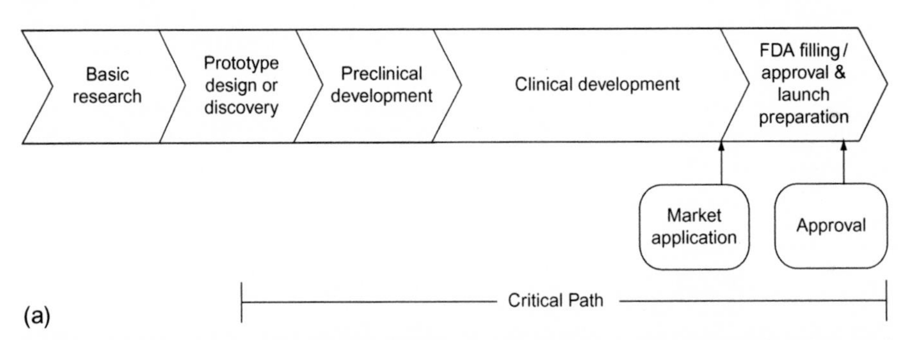

This figure shows an idealized "critical path" that encompasses the drug, biological product, and medical device development processes. At the far left, ideas coming out of basic scientific research enter into an evaluation process (prototype design or discovery). In drug development the "discovery" process seeks to select or create a molecule with specific desired biological activities. Medical device development is generally much more iterative, so that prototypes often build on existing technologies.

The critical path begins when candidate products are selected for development. They then undergo a series of successively more rigorous evaluation steps as they move from left to right along the path . A low percentage of candidates entering preclinical development survive to the market application stage.

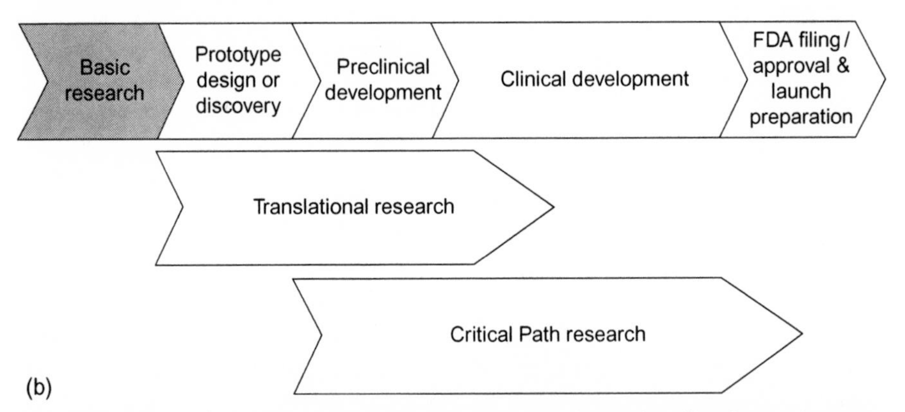

This figures shows how different types of research support the product Development process. ***Basic research*** is directed towards fundamental understanding of biology and disease processes. Basic research provides the foundation for product development as well as translational and critical path research. ***Translational research*** is concerned with moving basic discoveries from concept into clinical evaluation and is often focused on specific disease entities or therapeutic concepts. ***Critical path research*** is directed toward improving the product development process itself by establishing new evaluation tools.

The clinical phase of product development also depends on the clinical research infrastructure. One of the objectives of NIH's "Roadmap Initiative" is strengthening this infrastructure.

Figure 6.1 (a) The Critical Path for medical product development. (b) Research support for product development. (c) Working in three dimensions on the Critical Path.
Source: Challenge and Opportunity on the Critical Path to New Medical Products. US Department of Health and Human Services, Food and Drug Administration, Washington, DC 2004.

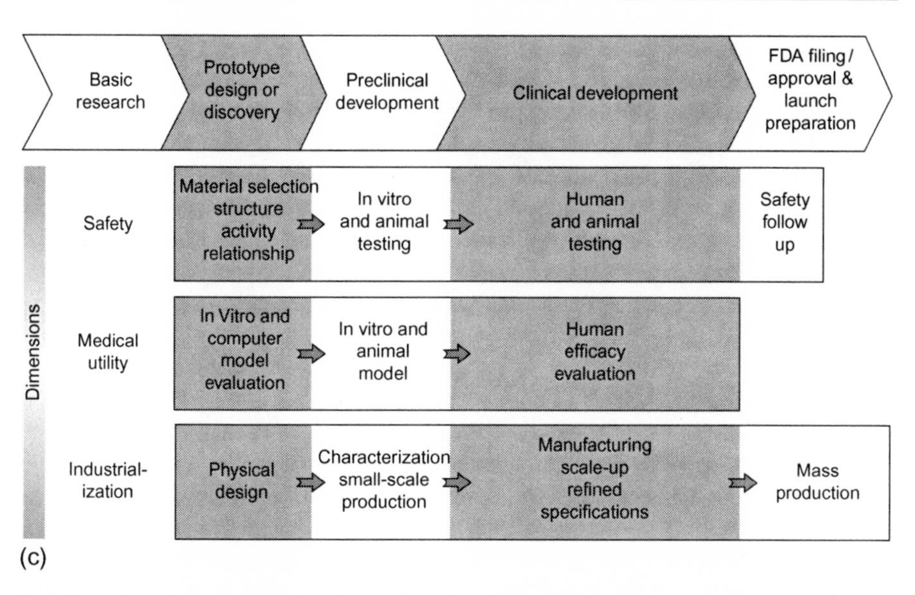

This figure is a highly generalized description of activities that must be successfully completed at different points and in different dimensions along the critical path. Many of these activities are highly complex—whole industries are devoted to supporting them. Not all the described activities are performed for every product, and many activities have been omitted for the sake of simplicity.

Figure 6.1 (Continued)

validated biomarkers exist on the market. For this reason, the FDA is trying to identify end points that are already in use, with the goal of determining what is necessary for new biomark ers to be accepted. In fact, in April 2005, the agency issued its first draft guidance for cancer trials to describe what end points can be used besides survival or irreversible morbidity.[23] The FDA, in collaboration with the National Institutes of Health (NIH) and several US-based universities, is particularly focused on developing biomarkers for proteomics, imaging, immune response, liver toxicity, and QT prolongation (i.e., the risk associated with heart ventricular complications).[24]

But a clinical trial end point is not always easy to determine, as demonstrated in February 2008 by the approval of Genentech's anticancer drug Avastin for the treatment of breast cancer. The drug was approved for this indication on the basis that it temporarily stopped cancer progression in clinical trials; however, the drug did not have a significant impact on lengthening the life of patients while having significant side effects, reasons for which the FDA reversed its Avastin approval decision for the treatment of metastatic breast cancer in December 2010.[25,26]

The FDA has also put into place the voluntary genomic data submission program,[27] which consists of encouraging companies to submit information such as a validation package for genomic expression or data related to the selection of a biomarker that is associated with an adverse drug event, with the objective of leveraging pharmacogenomics[28] and drug-diagnostic codevelopment. The underlying rationale for this activity is to move away from a population-based model, in which drugs are tested on broad pools of patients, to a more targeted approach, in which clinical development focuses on the patients who are most likely to benefit from a drug. It is hoped that these initiatives will increase productivity and create new tools for improving safety while making the FDA approval process more predictable and manageable. The FDA also has proposed the creation of a microdosing stage, or Phase 0, with doses that are not considered to be pharmacologically active because they are less than or equal to 100 μg, to collect pharmacokinetic information or perform imaging studies. However, this initiative came under fire because critics argued that it will make an already-complicated process even more complex by adding an extra step, while exposing patients unnecessarily to some chemical agents.[29]

EMEA's Road Map to 2010

The EMEA, on the other hand, is trying to enhance its regulatory organization and processes through the creation of its "Road Map to 2010"[30] initiative. The plan consists of the creation of a number of programs, such as the establishment of groups of experts in different areas such as gene therapy, pharmacogenomics, and process analytical technology. The goal of the "Road Map" is to facilitate innovation, incentivize small and medium-sized companies, and increase interaction with the agency's stakeholders, while strengthening international collaboration. Another important step that the agency is taking is the improvement of the way in which it deals with the information received from the European Union (EU) member states through several information technology initiatives. For small and medium-sized companies, it has created many incentives by reducing or deferring fees and providing administrative assistance for these companies.[31] In addition, the EMEA has acknowledged that formal interaction with patients has become instrumental for the approval of orphan drugs, and it will expand this interaction in the context of licensing of medicines and guidance development. The EMEA will expand its confidentiality agreement with the FDA, including the pilot program for parallel scientific advice.[32]

Together with the FDA and the European Commission, the EMEA has agreed to expand cooperative activities in several important areas, including pediatric drugs, medicinal products for rare diseases, and risk management, to prevent divergences and ensure the best use of resources.[33] Furthermore, unlike its US counterpart, the EMEA has created a regulatory path for follow-on biologics. It approved the first one, human growth hormone, in 2006, but the feat was not without some challenges: following its establishment, the number of major issues with marketing authorization applications for biotechnological products remains high. For example, the pivotal clinical trials of some late-stage failures have been found not to meet the regulatory guidelines of the EU, and regulators are increasingly concerned that attempts to accelerate the process of biotechnological product development will lead to the neglect of important issues.[34]

The EMEA has proposed a new initiative, the "2015 Road Map," as a continuation of the 2010 Road Map, building on current achievements but also taking account of the agency's business drivers. This new initiative has as its draft title "The Agency's

Contribution to Science, Medicines, and Health," and it was presented to the public for a 3-month public consultation in January 2010.

The FDA Amendment Act of 2007

On the political front, President George W. Bush in September 2007 signed into law the Food and Drug Administration Amendment Act of 2007 (FDAAA),[35] which has had a tremendous impact on the FDA. It reauthorized the 15-year-old user-fee program (PDUFA IV). The fees that the industry pays to the FDA account for one quarter of its budget (the FDA budget is $2 billion). Under the FDAAA, it is expected that user's fees will increase by about $87 million a year, to approximately $400 million in 2008 and continuing through 2012. Similarly, the FDAAA proposed to raise $225 million from industry over a period of 5 years to pay for new drug safety-monitoring initiatives, although this depends on whether Congress authorizes the use of federal funding to accomplish this goal. If successful, these initiatives will be able to boost the FDA's credibility, which has come under fire in recent years owing to many scandals associated with the way this agency has approved some new drugs and how it monitors postmarketing surveillance.

The new law also empowers the FDA to broaden the scope of its safety programs. For instance, now every NDA must have a postmarket risk-management assessment, known as a risk evaluation and mitigation strategies (REMS) assessment, whose full impact on drug approval remains to be determined.[36] Of importance, based on information provided by the NIH, the FDA must create a clinical trials registry that will be posted publicly. Another important issue is that under the FDAAA, the agency must improve the ways in which it detects serious adverse events (SAEs) of medications, which, by definition, are any negative side effects of medication that lead to hospitalization or disability or that are life threatening or irreversible. To accomplish this goal, the FDA must review databases every 2 weeks to find reported SAEs. Also, should the FDA have safety concerns about specific drugs, the agency can request that health care professionals and drugmakers change the way they distribute drugs and that manufacturers revise drug labels—not that the agency did not have safety-based restrictions on drugs through risk management programs in place already. In fact, they have been in place since 2002, but the department in charge of this was understaffed, and many of the agency's actions relied on companies' voluntary cooperation. To illustrate the state of things, only 25% of 130 postmarket surveillance plans submitted in 2006 adhered to FDA demands.[37]

The creation of the FDAAA is the result of a long debate in the political and medical fields concerning the role of the FDA in monitoring the safety and efficacy of drugs, particularly those already on the market. Of course, prior to the passage of the law, the agency had made several attempts to improve its safety review procedures, but it made little progress because of the lack of funding and resources. But after the Vioxx scandal in September 2004, safety came to the forefront in the political arena. As already stated, critics have claimed that the FDA was not stringent enough when it approved Merck's painkiller Vioxx in 2001 despite being aware of data indicating that the drug might put users at higher risk of heart attack. These concerns have more recently extended to other classes of drugs.

So throughout 2006 and into 2007, the FDA required manufacturers to add stronger safety warnings to the labels of selected drugs that are already on the market, such as erythropoietin stimulating agents (ESAs) and, most recently, Avandia, as already discussed. As a result of the Vioxx scandal, the agency created the Office of Drug Safety (ODS), which is responsible for postmarketing surveillance and other drug safety issues. But this received a lot of criticism because this office is not separated from the agency, creating a conflict of interest. Because the FDA does not have the power to order product recalls (such as for homeopathic cold medicines like Zicam, produced by Matrixx Initiatives, which has been the center of controversy recently because this nasal gel could damage or destroy users' sense of smell permanently), it must rely on manufacturers to do so voluntarily. Bills now moving through Congress would give the agency that power.[38] Homeopathic remedies like Zicam, as well as nutriceuticals and other similar drug classes, do not require FDA approval before being sold.

At present, the FDA faces the great challenge of being understaffed (and underfunded), which is reflected in the fact that this agency is struggling to meet the FDAAA goal of reviewing 90% of NDAs and BLAs within 10 months for standard reviews and within 6 months for priority reviews. However, as has been indicated,[39] the fact that the FDA missed its FDAAA review goals in 2008 was because of reorganization and staff recruitment, issues that are currently being addressed.

In my opinion, the major problem with the FDA is that it regulates foods as well as drugs. The FDA should be a medical product agency, like other similar agencies in the world, which do not have foods and other concerns on their tables. Because of this situation, and because it seems that there is a food crisis in the United States almost every week, the leadership of the agency is spread too thin and cannot effectively pay attention to anything. So long as this huge conglomerate continues to exist, it will have difficulty giving a clear message to Congress about its needs. It is interesting that the FDA is part of the Department of Health and Human Services, together with the NIH, the Centers of Medicare and Medicaid, the Centers for Disease Control and Prevention, and other smaller agencies. Furthermore, the FDA's appropriation committee is the senatorial Agriculture Committee, which is really absurd considering that health is not a concern with which this committee is charged. This makes the FDA, which is a regulatory agency, almost an outlier within this governmental conglomerate. So long as the administrative structures are the way they are, I feel that the FDA will continue to be underfunded and suboptimal.

An important factor that has contributed to a crisis in the credibility of the FDA was its lack of an officially appointed permanent commissioner for about 18 months between 2001 and the end of 2006. Some people believe that lack of leadership has caused the FDA to respond more conservatively to safety concerns than it might have done otherwise. While the lack of a confirmed leader did not affect day-to-day operations at the FDA, it affected the agency's ability to defend itself against critics and resolve contentious, broader issues. Some of these issues included weighing better scrutiny of drug safety against the public's desire for access to new medicines and establishing a regulatory path for follow-on biologics. In December 2006, the Senate finally confirmed former President Bush's urologist, Dr. Andrew C. von Eschenbach, as interim commissioner, and later as permanent commissioner, after considerable delay due to partisan maneuvers by both Democrats and Republicans. But his tenure lasted until January 2009, when he resigned with the advent of the Obama administration, and Frank Torti, former principal deputy commissioner and chief scientist at the Drug Administration, became the new FDA acting commissioner. Torti was succeeded by FDA principal deputy commissioner Joshua Sharfstein, who served until Margaret Hamburg was appointed as the new commissioner, in 2009.

Ever since 1962, when the FDA began requiring that companies run clinical trials to prove that drugs are safe and efficacious, the most important legislation in the United States has been the FDA Modernization Act of 1997, which accelerated the approval process of new drugs for life-threatening diseases by giving seriously ill patients easier access to experimental compounds, and provided new incentives for the development of pediatric medicines. While improving the overall efficiency of the FDA, the 1997 law also expanded the drug companies' ability to disseminate information on off-label uses of new and existing drugs.

But in spite of all these initiatives by the regulators, the process of drug discovery and development continues to be challenging. Of course, there is always ample room for improvement. But obviously, there are a series of strict guidelines that ought to be followed, and it is important to acknowledge that there is also something about the products that does not seem to work. Frankly speaking, even if new strategies to review potential drugs faster are implemented by regulators, there is a limit on how much they can achieve. One thing is certain: regulators cannot lower the standards for the approval of drugs, as the biopharmaceutical industry is hoping, and it is necessary to deal with the science and the way in which pharmaceutical and biotech companies develop their drugs. The deficient way in which companies bring drugs to market has been demonstrated by its output hitting a 24-year low in 2007. Clinical costs have risen fivefold in the last decade, and there has been little improvement in the time it takes to develop a drug. At the same time, the attrition rates, especially at the critical Phase III juncture, have climbed to 50%.[40]

It seems to me that for many years, some sectors have been making a lot of noise about regulators' role in the decline of new drug approvals. In my opinion, these sectors, many of which have fallen into the habit of pointing the finger at others, have been looking at the wrong causes. After looking in detail at what the regulators are doing, it becomes obvious that even if some improvement on their part takes place, these initiatives will not make a huge difference in optimizing the process of drug development and approval. The problems that make it so difficult for the pharmaceutical and biotech industries to bring some products to market do not come from the regulators. Rather, they are embedded in the heart of the science performed at the industrial level. In other words, structural and organizational problems at the R&D level are responsible for the productivity crisis that we are experiencing today. Regulators have responded by minimizing the administrative burden associated with drug review and approval and by undertaking initiatives to develop biomarkers to try to help the industry develop medicines in the best way. Because of this, a great many expectations have been laid at the feet of science that will not be easy to meet. Over the last decade, the pharmaceutical industry has been extremely eager to bring products to the market that would be blockbusters, based on a model designed to capture such large markets. But those days are over now, and companies must become more realistic at exploiting any opportunity that they may have. The industry is struggling at the moment to find its way, and it is quite interesting to see how different pharmaceutical companies are shaping their R&D and how they are changing the way in which they are developing their products. So great consideration is going on in the pharmaceutical industry today concerning how the industry will confront its challenges, and one can see differences in the ways companies are approaching this issue.

Notes

1. Standard and Poor's, Industry surveys. Health care: Pharmaceuticals, 2007.
2. Interview with Janet Woodcock, US Food and Drug Administration, March 2009.
3. Nissen, S., Wolski, K., 2007. Effect of rosiglitazone on the risk of myocardial infarction and death from cardiovascular causes. New England Journal of Medicine 356, 2457–2471.
4. Saul, S., Harris, G., 2007. Years ago, agency was warned of a drug's risks. New York Times, May 24, 2007.
5. Black box warnings are a type of warning that appears on the package insert for prescription drugs that may cause serious adverse effects; FDA has requested black box warnings for two Diabetes medications, agency commissioner says at House Committee Hearing. Medical News Today, June 11, 2007. http://www.medicalnewstoday.com/articles/73582.php.
6. US Food and Drug Administration, 2008. FDA announces new recommendations on evaluating cardiovascular risk in drugs intended to treat type 2 diabetes. News Release, December 17, 2008. http://www.fda.gov/NewsEvents/Newsroom/PressAnnouncements/2008/ucm116994.htm.
7. Angell, M., 2004. The Truth about the Drug Companies: How They Deceive Us and What to Do about It. Random House, New York.
8. Lönngren, T., personal communication.
9. Challenge and Opportunity on the Critical Path to New Medical Products. US Department of Health and Human Services, Food and Drug Administration, Washington, DC.
10. Food and Drug Administration, 2005. Prescription Drug User Fee Act (PDUFA): Adding Resources and Improving Performance in FDA Review of New Drugs Applications, white paper. US Department of Health and Human Services, Washington, DC.
11. Food and Drug Administration Center for Drug Evaluation and Research Center for Biologics Evaluation and Research Procedural, 2000. Guidance for Industry Formal Meetings with Sponsors and Applicants for PDUFA Products. US Department of Health and Human Services, Washington, DC. http://www.bcg-usa.com/regulatory/docs/2000/FDA200003B.pdf.
12. Milne, C., 2006. US and European regulatory initiatives to improve R&D performance. Expert Opinion in Drug Discovery 1, 11–14.
13. Interview with Thomas Lönngren, London, April 2007.

14. Food and Drug Administration, Prescription Drug User Fee Act (PDUFA).
15. European Medicines Agency, 2005. Guideline on risk management system for medical products for humane use, November 14, 2005. http://www.emea.europa.eu/pdfs/human/euleg/9626805en.pdf.
16. Milne, US and European regulatory initiatives.
17. Lesko, L.J., Woodcock, J., 2004. Translation of pharmacogenommics and pharmacogenetics: A regulatory perspective. Nature Reviews Drug Discovery 3, 763–769.
18. Woodcock, J., personal communication.
19. Challenge and Opportunity.
20. Ibid.
21. In January 2005, Ray Woosley, MD, PhD, became the first president and CEO of the Critical Path Institute (C-Path), Tucson, AZ, and Rockville, MD, formed by the FDA, SRI International, and the University of Arizona to accelerate the development of safe and innovative medicines; see Ray Woosley, 2008. An audience with. Nature Reviews Drug Discovery 7, 884.
22. It is important to point out here that the Critical Path initiative is not just about biomarkers and is certainly not about surrogate end points for drug approvals. This is a misconception of the program.
23. US Food and Drug Administration, Center for Drug Evaluation and Research, and Center for Biologics Evaluation and Research, 2005. Guidance for industry—clinical trial endpoints for the approval of cancer drugs and biologics: Draft guidance. US Department of Health and Human Services, April 2005. http://www.bcg-usa.com/regulatory/docs/2005/FDA 2005 4B.pdf.
24. Vorchheimer, D.A., 2005. What is QT interval prolongation? Journal of Family Practice, June 2005. http://findarticles.com/p/articles/mi_m0689/is_6_54/ai_n14732743/pg_2.
25. Pollack, A., 2008. FDA extends Avastin use for breast cancer. New York Times, February 23, 2008. http://www.nytimes.com/2008/02/23/business/23drug.html.
26. Hellerman, C., 2010. FDA rejects Avastin as breast cancer therapy. CNN Medical, December 16, 2010. http://www.cnn.com/2010/HEALTH/12/16/avastin.fda/index.html?hpt=T2.
27. In November 2003, the FDA published the "Draft guidance for industry: Pharmacogenomic data submission."
28. *Pharmacogenomics* is the study of the effects of individual genetic variations on drug response aimed at the prescription or development of drugs that maximize benefit and minimize side effects in individuals; see http://pharmacy.ucsf.edu/glossary/p/.
29. US Food and Drug Administration, 2006. Guidance for Industry, Investigators, and Reviewers: Exploratory IND Studies. US FDA, Washington, DC.
30. European Medicines Agency, 2004. EMEA sets out its Road Map to 2010. News Release, April 15, 2004. http://www.emea.europa.eu/pdfs/general/direct/pr/936204en.pdf.
31. European Medicines Agency, 2006. Report from SME Office on its 1st year of operation. Doc. Ref. EMEA/498584/2006, December 15, 2006. http://www.emea.europa.eu/pdfs/SME/49858406en.pdf.
32. European Medicines Agency, 2005. The European Medicines Agency Road Map to 2010: Preparing the ground for the future. Part II. The European Medicines Agency Road Map Implementation Plan. Public EMEA/H/34163/03/Final, March 4, 2005.
33. Hughes, B., 2007. Transatlantic regulatory cooperation expanded. Nature Reviews Drug Discovery 6, 589–590.
34. Schneider, C.K., Schäffner-Dallmann, G., 2008. Typical pitfalls in applications for marketing authorization of biotechnological products in Europe. Nature Reviews Drug Discovery 7, 893.

35. Food and Drug Administration Amendments Act (FDAAA) of 2007. http://www.fda.gov/RegulatoryInformation/Legislation/FederalFoodDrugandCosmeticActFDCAct/SignificantAmendmentstotheFDCAct/FoodandDrugAdministrationAmendmentsActof2007/default.htm.
36. Hughes, B., 2008. Anticipating REMS. Nature Reviews Drug Discovery 7, 963.
37. See Note 1.
38. Harris, G., 2009. FDA warns against use of popular cold remedy. New York Times, June 17, A14.
39. Hay, M., 2009. FDA PDUFA goals missed. Nature Reviews Drug Discovery 8, 10–11.
40. Clinton, P., Wechsler, J., 2006. Whatever Happened to the Critical Path. Pharmaceutical Executive 26, 53–60; see also Milne, US and European regulatory initiatives.

Part III

The Complexity of Innovation

7 The Academia–Industry Relationship

In the fields of observation, chance favours only the prepared mind.

—Louis Pasteur (1822–95)

The academia–industry interface is arguably one of the most fascinating, productive, and important areas in drug discovery and development, even if at times this marriage is not always harmonious and happy. At present, there is a strong outcry in the United States over the influence that the pharmaceutical industry holds over US universities, and a federal investigation led by Senator Charles Grassley (R-Iowa) on the appropriateness of this relationship is underway. Though there are, in fact, many dark areas (and individuals) that deserve a full investigation, overall the academia–industry relationship is necessary for the discovery and development of new drugs, and a negative attitude toward it may not only be unrealistic but actually counterproductive for society. Let us take a close look at this relationship.

Ever since its beginning back in the middle- to late-1800s, the pharmaceutical industry has had an extremely close relationship with academia. To start with, without the chemical, physiological, and biological academic discoveries that took place in Europe throughout the 18th and 19th centuries, the pharmaceutical industry would never have come into existence. Although there is no space here to discuss how an infinite number of academic discoveries has shaped the pharmaceutical industry and guided it well throughout the present day,[1] one thing is very clear: the majority of the targets on which commercial drug treatments are based had their roots in the basic scientific discoveries made by academic researchers all over the world.[2] The pharmaceutical industry has known this since the industry's early years, when universities in France, Britain, and particularly Germany, followed by universities in the United States, provided the industry with an immense wealth of knowledge, ideas, and innovation that were translated by industry into medical products. However, most of these great ideas and findings would have only remained as simple curiosities, dreams, and small-scale applications if an important industrial, profit-driven, and highly organized chemical and pharmaceutical base had not taken the financial risk of creating a platform for the application, commercialization, and marketing of those discoveries.

The impact of academic discoveries has influenced every aspect of drug development, from the initial identification of targets, to the understanding of biochemical and genetic pathways within the cell, to the elucidation of mechanistic paradigms involved in specific diseases, to the creation of diagnostic tools and biomedically oriented devices. So the role of academic research in industry could be categorized into two broader categories: one of pioneering scientific knowledge and the other

The World's Health Care Crisis. DOI: 10.1016/B978-0-12-391875-8.00007-X

of complementing and validating the more focused, sophisticated, and refined work that is performed in industry. Industry, on the other hand, has always taken scientific research to the next level, to applied science or technology, therefore creating great health care and social and economic benefits for society. Industry has also brought back to academia new questions and problems that academia either answers or solves. This is a cycle and a bidirectional interaction that is rarely acknowledged on both sides.

The influence of academic research has been vital to the biopharmaceutical industry in the last few decades, as exemplified by the creation and growth of the biotechnology industry as well as by the way in which long-established pharmaceutical companies are developing new pharmaceuticals, capitalizing on cutting-edge technologies and discoveries that saw daylight in academic settings (e.g., genomics, postgenomics, proteomics tools, nanotechnology, etc.). Although there is no doubt that in the beginning, these academic findings had purely basic scientific purposes—to allow researchers to design better and more sensitive experiments that could increase their knowledge of specific biological issues—it was not too long before scientists found utilitarian applications for these academic developments.

The biotechnology tools that have been created in academia and further developed in industry have facilitated a better and unprecedented knowledge of how the cell works at the atomic and molecular levels, which has had a tremendous impact on our understanding of diseases and the creation of novel drugs. A prime example is the creation of monoclonal antibodies, a work that started out in academia and that later revolutionized medicine when optimized and applied by industry. Though the pioneering work on monoclonal antibodies in cancer drugs, such as Campath, Gleevec, Erbitux, Tarceva, Herceptin, and more recently, Avastin (see Table 7.1), was performed in academia, none would have become therapeutic applications if industry had not taken the financial risk to develop them and contribute their know-how and marketing capabilities. Furthermore, these drugs would not have come to market if it had not been for a very symbiotic relationship, a constant flow of scientists, ideas, experimental results, and materials, between the academic laboratories where these antibodies were originally invented and engineered, and the respective companies that optimized and developed them further.

There are other areas, which are currently shaping drug research, and thus having important beneficial consequences for society, that have been possible only thanks to the academia—industry relationship. For instance, the Human Genome Project, an initiative that was sponsored by the public and private sectors and whose mapping work took place at universities, government-sponsored agencies, and pharmaceutical companies all over the world, has made possible the identification and understanding of diseased genes and genetic markers, with obvious importance in health care. Also, the vast array of genomic and proteomic tools, such as the ever-sophisticated DNA and protein sequencing technologies and DNA-chip technology, to mention just two examples, would never have realized their full scientific and commercial potential had it not been for an uninterrupted osmosis between academia and industry.

Another relevant example is the Single Nucleotide Polymorphism[3] Consortium (SNP), an open and cooperative project created in 1999 by 10 large British

Table 7.1 Monoclonal Antibodies Approved by the Food and Drug Administration

Sample FDA-Approved Therapeutic Monoclonal Antibodies					
Antibody	**Brand Name**	**Approval Date**	**Type**	**Target**	**Indication**
Abciximab	ReoPro	1994	Chimeric	Inhibition of glycoprotein IIb/IIIa	Cardiovascular disease
Adalimumab	Humira	2002	Human	Inhibition of TNF-α signaling	Several autoimmune disorders
Alemtuzumab	Campath	2001	Humanized	CD52	Chronic lymphocytic leukemia
Basiliximab	Simulect	1998	Chimeric	IL-2Rα receptor (CD25)	Transplant rejection
Bevacizumab	Avastin	2004	Humanized	Vascular endothelial growth factor (VEGF)	Colorectal cancer, age-related macular degeneration
Cetuximab	Erbitux	2004	Chimeric	Epidermal growth factor receptor	Colorectal cancer, head and neck cancer
Certolizumab pegol	Cimzia	2008	Humanized	Inhibition of TNF-α signaling	Crohn's disease
Daclizumab	Zenapax	1997	Humanized	IL-2Rα receptor (CD25)	Transplant rejection
Eculizumab	Soliris	2007	Humanized	Complement system protein C5	Paroxysmal nocturnal hemoglobinuria
Efalizumab	Raptiva	2002	Humanized	CD11a	Psoriasis
Gemtuzumab	Mylotarg	2000	Humanized	CD33	Acute myelogenous leukemia (with calicheamicin)
Ibritumomab tiuxetan	Zevalin	2002	Murine	CD20	Non-Hodgkin lymphoma (with yttrium-90 or indium-111)
Infliximab	Remicade	1998	Chimeric	Inhibition of TNF-α signaling	Several autoimmune disorders
Muromonab-CD3	Orthoclone OKT3	1986	Murine	T cell CD3 Receptor	Transplant rejection
Natalizumab	Tysabri	2006	Humanized	α-4 (α4) integrin	Multiple sclerosis, Crohn's disease
Omalizumab	Xolair	2004	Humanized	Immunoglobulin E (IgE)	Mainly allergy-related asthma
Palivizumab	Synagis	1998	Humanized	An epitope of the RSV F protein	Respiratory syncytial virus
Panitumumab	Vectibix	2006	Human	Epidermal growth factor receptor	Colorectal cancer
Ranibizumab	Lucentis	2006	Humanized	Vascular endothelial growth factor A (VEGF-A)	Macular degeneration
Rituximab	Rituxan, Mabthera	1997	Chimeric	CD20	Non-Hodgkin lymphoma
Tositumomab	Bexxar	2003	Murine	CD20	Non-Hodgkin lymphoma
Trastuzumab	Herceptin	1998	Humanized	ErbB2	Breast cancer

Source: http://en.wikipedia.org/wiki/Monoclonal_antibody_therapy (publicly available information).
Waldmann, Thomas A. (2003) Immunotherapy: past, present, future. Nature Medicine 9(3): 269–277.

pharmaceutical companies and the Wellcome Trust Philanthropy (and which later also included the Human Genome Project) to generate a widely accepted, high-quality, extensive, publicly available map using SNPs as markers evenly distributed throughout the human genome, and which has been quite useful to scientists in the public and private domains all over the world in understanding better the genetic causes of important cellular processes and maladies. In the United States, the National Cancer Institute's somatic cell line panel, through which scientists can test the effect of experimental drug agents on 60 cell lines at the same time, has become an invaluable resource for academic scientists, early-stage biotechnology firms, and pharmaceutical companies, especially when determining the initial potential applications to clinical trials based on a specific drug candidate.

One further example of an important academia–industry collaborative project is the establishment of the Critical Path Institute (C-Path Institute) at the University of Arizona, which, in collaboration with the US Food and Drug Administration (FDA), SRI International (an independent, nonprofit research institute conducting client-sponsored research and development for government agencies, commercial businesses, foundations, and other organizations), the National Cancer Institute, and industry, has become a major step in implementing the ideas behind the FDA Critical Path Opportunity List initiative and in helping industry to accelerate the process of drug development via the sharing of research information, the development of drug safety and efficacy tests, and the identification and development of biomarkers.[4] And the list of examples can continue *ad infinitum.*

It may, therefore, be surprising that in spite of the obviousness of the great productivity of the academia–industry interaction, the relationship between academia and industry in recent years has not only not been an easy one but also has been under attack.[5] But there is a reason for this.

Since the creation of the Bayh–Dole Act of 1980, which encourages universities to license discoveries made with federal funds to private industry and benefit financially from this, the university–industry relationship has become very stormy and plagued by multiple scandals. In general, industry has a bad reputation among academic scientists because academic scientists see industrial research as money-oriented, scientifically less rigorous, and compromised by high-stake financial interests: in other words, they see it as the "dark side." For many academics, "industry-sponsored research presents several significant problems for universities. For example, it is not the cash cow that many suppose. In general, companies pay for research that benefits them and their shareholders, not for the undirected curiosity-driven research that is at the heart of the academic enterprise."[6] Furthermore, considerations related to conflicts of interest and the pharmaceutical industry benefiting from public investment in research have generated great debate about the nature of the interactions between industry and academic and public institutions.[7]

On the opposite side, industry considers that some academic scientists have shown a "certain business appetite … and [an] aggressiveness regarding intellectual property issues [that] are about as loud as those from the [industrial] direction"[8] that academics so criticize. And not a few industrial researchers consider academic research as unfocused, lacking in practical sense, and a slave to the personal and political games that characterize the (American) academic settings, not to mention the great lack of regard that many industrial scientists feel toward their academic colleagues.

As a result, today, "officially," the collaborations that seem to work best for pharma are not the ones performed directly with academic groups but rather with the small, entrepreneurial biotech companies that have derived from universities, through which a number of academics who believe passionately in their products will gradually disengage from the university and spinoff companies and commute back and forth from the academic and industrial bases. But even in these types of collaborations, intellectual property concerns become a huge issue and without doubt, judging by events, very fertile soil for all sorts of misappropriation of information and subsequent scandalous and disgraceful legal battles.

Among the most sensitive territories for interaction between academia and industry are teaching hospitals in the field of clinical research because many academic scientists feel that after industry-sponsored clinical trials have become successful, industry does not give them the credit that they feel they deserve—which, not surprisingly, has created the perception that industry is prone to exploitation.

But it is also necessary to say openly—and this comes from my own life experience—that not all academic scientists are angels either, and that a great deal of ruthless and unscrupulous competition goes on in academic labs, often by academics whose sense of self-grandiosity and immunity would make any aggressive and competitive politician or business person blush. In their overriding ambition, many of these academics inflict a great deal of psychological abuse and exploitation on their students and postdoctoral fellows (especially if they are foreigners) and indulge themselves in significant financial conflicts of interest, notwithstanding their incursion into the pervasive (and very permissive) activities of intellectual dishonesty (doctoring scientific research results and stealing information from students and colleagues) and ethical misconduct, which takes place at all levels of the academic hierarchy. As the eminent former Harvard biologist Tom Maniatis said to me:

> *I have worked so closely in both [the academic and the industrial] sides of the issue and I have had arguments with my academic colleagues, on numerous occasions, in which they would argue that because of the financial incentives, the behavior in business is much worse than in academia. And my comment, my response to that is that ego always trumps finance and money. And it does! And the bad behavior in academia—every bit of it—is just as bad as or worse than the [behavior] in business .... I think that the reason for that is that in business over the years, there has been built into the system a very strict legal framework, and that is what patents are about; that is what contracts are about; that is what agreements are about. And so it is on paper, it is written, it is a contract and you have legal recourse for remedy when somebody does something bad. In academia this does not exist. There is no legal system. It is all a matter of trust and power and so people can do things that in business would be considered criminal. So it is their word against yours and that sort of thing.*[9]

Industry, on the other hand, has been excellent at interfering with the normal and ethical development of clinical research in teaching hospitals by subtly providing medical professors a vast array of special gifts (and this is an understatement) in exchange for subtle favors—a situation that has become so obvious and shamefully public that it has become the subject of a federal investigation, as mentioned earlier. Recently, in his ongoing investigation of the drug industry's influence on the practice of medicine, Senator Grassley asked Pfizer to provide all the documentation that it had about payments to 149 faculty members at Harvard University, a school that, more than any other leading US university, has been found to be too much compromised with the industrial establishment. The request for records of Pfizer payments to Harvard Medical School faculty members during the last couple of years is an expansion of the senator's prior investigation of industry money given to three Harvard psychiatrists who promoted antipsychotic medicines for children. On the basis of records that Senator Grassley obtained from drug companies, the professors were accused of failing to properly report at least $4.2 million in payments from 2000 to 2007. As a result, one of the professors was suspended from conducting clinical trials.[10] It has been reported that at Harvard Medical School, 149 faculty members have financial ties to Pfizer, 130 to Merck, and 9 to Baxter International. According to reports, the latter reflects a great conflict of interest: Baxter is the company at which the former dean of Harvard Medical served on the board while overseeing the medical school, and he continues to serve as a director of the company.[11]

In fact, many Harvard Medical students have organized a movement that has as a goal the limitation of the influence of industry at the medical school because conflicts of interest may bias professors' objectivity in favor of the products to which they have financial ties. According to the *New York Times*, "the students [at Harvard Medical School] say they worry that pharmaceutical industry scandals in recent years—including some criminal convictions, billions of dollars in fines, proof of bias in research and publishing and false marketing claims—have cast a bad light on the medical profession. And they criticize Harvard as being less vigilant than other leading medical schools in monitoring potential financial conflicts by faculty members."[12] Some people, such as Harvard Medical School professor Marcia Angell, are even pushing the absurd idea of banning industry outright from providing funding to academia.[13] The situation has become so untenable that in January 2009, Partners HealthCare, the owner of two research hospitals affiliated with the Harvard Medical School, Massachusetts General Hospital (MGH), and Brigham and Women's Hospital, announced the imposition of restrictions on outside pay for two dozen senior officials who also sit on the boards of pharmaceutical or biotechnology companies.[14] All of this, I am sure, is only the very tip of the iceberg.

But aside from these unacceptable, all-too-human, and vicious things that have become second nature to the US academic establishment, the reciprocal negative attitude on both sides of the academia–industry equation is nonsensical from a practical and scientific point of view given the innumerable benefits—targets, genes, and drugs such as insulin; human growth hormone; contraceptives; chemotherapeutic agents Taxol, Gleevec, and Velcade; monoclonal antibodies; statins; and so forth—that have been the crowning achievement of close collaborative efforts between academia and industry. Perhaps a lack of understanding about each player's roles, goals, and interests, which comes from a mutual resentment between the academic front (focused on ego, prestige, and recognition, and sometimes financial profits as well) and the industrial front (focused on productivity, social status, and money), has created this barrier between the two areas, and this is something that needs to be addressed with urgency in our search for better and more efficient ways in which to discover and develop drugs.

It is true that a new target or chemical structure identified by academia is usually hundreds of millions of dollars and years away from ever making it to the market because usually, the original idea or compound is not the one that succeeds in making it through the iterative process of drug development, the process whereby companies test, fail, try again, and occasionally succeed in optimizing a potential drug candidate.[15] However, it would be difficult for industry to come up with such knowledge in the first place because its role is to create drugs, not to pursue basic or open-sky research—this is not only the role of academia, but also the area in which seminal and important knowledge that results in further applications arises.

An important example of how the academia–industry collaboration can affect the fate of a pharmaceutical company is the following: in the late 1970s, when the earliest biotechnology companies were being created in the United States, a number of large and longstanding leading European pharmaceutical companies, especially German ones such as Hoechst and Bayer, failed to take full advantage of this revolution for two reasons. First, German universities had long fallen behind US and British universities; second, despite that these companies established some kind of relationship with the leading US universities, their relationships, as has been indicated elsewhere,[16] were difficult. For instance, in the early 1980s, Hoechst established a collaborative arrangement with a Harvard University affiliate, MGH, through which the company made a 10-year, $70 million investment in a genetic laboratory (the Molecular Biology department) in return for exclusive licensing rights to MGH's inventions. Though this agreement came under fire in the United States because it was considered a foreign firm "skimming the cream off of a publicly built and maintained resource" to which American taxpayers were contributing about $25 million annually,[17] the deal had important consequences for all parties involved. For MGH, this was a beneficial deal because of the creation of a biotech lab supported by the largest and most prestigious pharmaceutical company in the world (even if it gave rise to controversy about the appropriateness of this type of collaboration between an academic institution and a pharmaceutical company). And for Hoechst, it represented a great opportunity to access the most innovative biotechnology research of the time. (We need to remember that because of environmental protests in Germany and elsewhere in Europe, biotechnology research was stalled.)

But a few years later, Hoechst dropped its collaboration with this teaching hospital, which was a key figure in the further development of biotechnology, and thus missed out on a great opportunity: when it tried to catch up on biotech, it was already too late. By the late 1980s, this company had fallen behind and eventually, through a succession of mergers, disappeared into Sanofi-Aventis.[18] In contrast, companies such as Wellcome, Ciba, Roche, Merck, and Lilly pursued the emergent biotechnology[19] and created a platform for biotech startups and learned from them. This strategy immediately placed them at the forefront of research and development and paid off years later.

In recent years, the way in which some companies have approached their collaborations with academia has had mixed results. Some companies, such as Monsanto and Novartis, invested heavily in a direct collaboration with Washington University in St. Louis and the University of California at Berkeley, respectively, with the high expectation of getting some important patents out of their relationships.[20] At the end, though, both companies ended up disappointed because only a small number of patents (and by no means remarkable ones) came from the collaborative partnerships. Other companies have made smaller investments in specific departments or researchers in different universities, and the collaborations seemed to work, as was the case with Amgen and Lilly funding particular labs at the Massachusetts Institute of Technology (MIT). In another approach, companies such as Novartis and Merck have established research institutes close to universities like Harvard; MIT; Tufts; the University of California, San Diego; the University of North Carolina, Chapel Hill; and the University of California, Berkeley; as well as with Cambridge and Oxford universities in the United Kingdom, in the hope of being closer to academia and to keep an eye on what is taking place there.

So now pharmaceutical and large biotechnology companies are importing innovation from academia indirectly, essentially via university technology transfer offices, which act as a liaison in the academia–industry interface, and more so via early-stage biotech enterprises that have derived from academic settings, although recently, in 2008, a novel collaboration between Janssen Pharmaceuticals and Vanderbilt University for the discovery of new drugs for the treatment of schizophrenia took place. Janssen has agreed to pay Vanderbilt University $10 million as an upfront fee for a licensing and research agreement. Janssen will gain access to existing compounds that act on metabotropic glutamate receptors (mGluRs), as well as any additional compounds that Vanderbilt discovers over the next 3 years.

This collaboration, together with several others that took place in 2008, such as Pfizer's Biotherapeutics and Bioinnovation Center at the University of California, San Francisco, has led to the realization on the industry's part that after all, academia–industry partnering is paramount in drug discovery and development,[21] and the reasons for this are simple: without the input of academia's novel ideas and pathways and without this kind of open-minded search for how things function, the development of drugs at the pharmaceutical industry level would too often find itself at a dead end, where companies cannot actually make sense of the data that they observe when testing promising compounds because they are looking too narrowly at the use of a drug they are developing—and a rule of thumb in science is that one usually finds things where one is not looking. It is not surprising that companies often are unable to convert some chemical agents into a useful, patentable product or pass them through clinical trials.

Though at times research in academia can be fiercely competitive, the pressure to show provable performance is much higher in industry than in academia, and this pressure has a negative impact on productivity. To illustrate, if one is pressured to follow a line to the production of a product—for instance, to find an inhibitor for a particular enzyme such as a kinase[22]—one's line of investigation will be so straight and narrow that one may not realize that the inhibitor or its pathway is doing something completely different from what one was seeking. This happens frequently, and it takes someone working with a completely different frame of mind to see the new direction of the inhibitor and say, "Oh! We just did that kinase in flies and worms, and we found that it does something completely different!" Without this kind of information, companies would spend years and millions of dollars finding the right inhibitor. However, despite this, industry curtails expenses by giving deadlines and telling its researchers, "If you don't find a solution by the deadline, throw it out." This is very wasteful, and the history of drug discovery, from aspirin to Gleevec and, more recently, Velcade, all of which were initially put aside by major pharmaceutical companies, demonstrates that this is not a productive way to foster drug development.

The relationship between industrial and academic research needs to be seen as a symbiotic one. Pharmaceutical or applied research is a second stage in science that has as a goal the creation of health care and social and economic benefits for society and that goes along in parallel or together with the more open-ended exploratory research. On the other hand, the exploratory research has to fit in with the more directed applied research to find the proper path. Susan Gasser, director of the Novartis-funded Friedrich Miescher Institute in Basel, Switzerland, expressed this very eloquently:

> *Applied research is like a river that needs to flow downhill from a glacier down to the ocean but that can take many possible valleys to reach there. Basic or open-ended fundamental research guides the river down the right pathway to get it, eventually, to the right destination. So they are very much working hand in hand, and therefore they cannot be two cultures as two cultures only come about in what one is used to, on how people treat one another. Of course, there is a big difference in the way in which people are treated or expect to be treated in a large pharmaceutical company and in academia. But as far as the science is concerned, the act of discovering is very much the same. They completely merge and they feed on each other.*[23]

And in my opinion, nowhere is this more evident than in translational research.

It is my belief that to improve efficiency in the academia–industry interface, basic research students at universities—those who are interested in medical problems—should be trained (and inform themselves) to think about human diseases and human disease phenotypes[24]; in other words, in the course of their studies of mutants of flies or worms or behavioral readouts in mice, they should be trained to ask themselves whether their findings may have some implication for human disease. This is important because in their communication with applied researchers in companies, they could apply the relationship between a target and proteins in pathways to a specific disease. This necessarily implies that scientists would have to read literature that they may not generally read, such as articles related to mutations and targets that are involved in human diseases, and encourage participation in seminars given by medically oriented scientists who are working on clinical research.

The kind of literature on which scientists within this gray area between biology and medicine would be focused includes three sources of information with a medical impact: first, the genetic mapping of heritable human disease; second, the use of model organisms, where a favorite gene is knocked out in a mouse and then characterized and a particular phenotype is observed, which would allow them to make a link to a particular disease; and third, the actual examination of gene families, then finding new members with new phenotypes and trying to correlate them with a particular disease. If a pharmaceutical company is developing such and such kinds of inhibitors (such as a tyrosine kinase or histone deacylases inhibitor), the people at the academic center can look at the phenotypes in animal models either by using those inhibitors or by using gene knock-outs that create a particular disease state or something that would mimic a disease state in animal models and thus allow a better understanding of the biology behind a particular disease, which could have a great impact on the development of drugs to treat or cure them.

This is very important because there is a great need for the understanding of the molecular basis of diseases. Indeed, many drug candidates go to the clinic without companies having a full understanding of the disease, and it is not surprising, then, that when these agents are taken to the clinic, they fail and are subsequently abandoned. The problem is that if something has failed in a clinical trial, it is very hard to rescue unless there is a really strong person in the company who insists that it is possible to do so.

So if scientists were able to better understand the molecular causes of disease, then they would be more successful at creating better patient stratification (or basic patient selection) and also have a better idea of which route they are going to follow. There is certainly a major need for development in this area. And to move in that direction, it is necessary to better understand, for instance, molecular changes in cancer cells and molecular symptoms of diseases; it would be necessary to have a better readout of what genes are and are not being expressed genomewide, more accurate analyses of changes in tumors, better screening for genomic fingerprinting of amplifications and deletions, and so on. This can be done mostly in academia, and if this were done at least for cancer, it would dramatically change the money spent on unsuccessful clinical trials, not only for cancer drugs but also for drugs to treat other diseases. Julian Adams, the CSO of Infinity Pharmaceutical and a scientist, has championed the discovery of two drugs (Velcade, for multiple myeloma; and Viramune, for HIV) and is working on additional drug candidates currently in Phase II clinical trials at Infinity and describes the benefits of the academia–industry relationship as follows:

> *I learned a lot! Every time you develop a drug you learn… because you didn't do everything perfectly…. Even Velcade, which is a great success story today, had five failed Phase I trials in solid tumors that showed no activity until the sixth one showed activity in multiple myeloma, OK? So, my learning from all of that is… having closer contact with academic researchers, making sure that an experiment that is done in the laboratory is repeatable in another laboratory, so it's not like you saw it one time, therefore you are rushing to the clinic. Spend much more time in the preclinical hypothesis to make sure that it is as rigorous as possible. When I say collaborate with academics, I mean a real collaboration; don't just hand them your drug and say, you know, work with their labs, you know, work, you know. I develop a relationship with the professors and the KOLs [key opinion leaders], our lab techs work with their lab techs, make sure that the work is done as rigorously as possible. Those translational experiments are so important in determining dose and*

> *schedule, biomarkers, what disease area you are going to take. By the time you are in the clinic, you are working with largely the same people... with whom you have developed a relationship. And... similarly in clinical trials, the people who do the best work and the most careful work and you spend a lot of time in Phase I, getting it right... getting it and... not getting it perfect, but getting it right! Answering questions. Trying to be very hypothesis driven. Trying to use biomarkers, trying to use early imaging, trying to use tissue biopsies, kind of understanding that the drug is working at least... consistent with what the plan was.*[25]

One of the major challenges that the National Institutes of Health (NIH) and academia in general have to face during this period of transition, which is also affecting academic life, is how to keep a discerning balance between translational science and basic research and how to be realistic about what can be accomplished in academia, as many people, including academic researchers are now looking down on basic research in favor of translational research. And though I am a proponent of more funding going into translational research, I am an even stronger advocate for more funding going into basic research because it is basic research—and not drug discovery and development, something that any company can do better than the best university—that is the quintessential role of academia. Harvard, which for generations has been at the forefront of basic research and medicine under its ousted president Lawrence Summers, vowed to become the center of a new Silicon Valley, meaning that this institution would become the center of biopharmaceuticals, life science, translational research, systems biology, and pharmacogenomics. As a result, this institution has perhaps made several questionable decisions, such as the creation of an undergraduate concentration in stem cell biology. Though stem cells are a highly important field in biology, from a technical point of view, the establishment of an academic major in stem cell biology, according to Maniatis, "is like creating a major in meiosis," or the mechanism by which germ cells (eggs and sperm) divide. Of course, there is great incentive for the university to go in that direction: stem research is a hot topic, and people are pouring money into it. Whenever people can link a disease to anything, that catches people's fancy, they will be willing to give money to such a cause. So right now, Harvard is responding to that, and not to a carefully-thought-through plan of where the life sciences are going to be 10 or 15 years from now. In responding to an immediate financial opportunity, this university is at a risk of becoming a mediocre institution precisely in the area in which it has always been a world leader: fundamental research.

In summary, to make faster and better progress in developing new pharmaceuticals, we have to understand diseases better, and we need to increase our understanding of the basic mechanisms that control their behavior. We need simple models for disease and simple physiological readouts before treating patients; this is why scientists go for inhibitors or their equivalents and try them in cell lines: by doing so, they have acquired a molecular asset. This approach is very important in developing strategies to treat subsets of particular diseases, which is an ongoing process, at least at the pharmaceutical industry level. The pharmaceutical industry has never really grappled with basic problems, and they go all the way from the most primitive screening into what they call discovery research, but obviously, that is a long way from basic research. It is important, therefore, that people in basic research be better prepared to communicate any insight that they have on this front to people who are doing the clinical trials. Companies then should try to characterize disease at the molecular level as much as possible, in collaboration with academia, and be more open and better prepared to accept input from academic scientists.

Before closing this chapter, I would like to touch on a controversial issue that is often discussed in the press: namely, why should taxpayers pay scientists to work on things of little importance (in the minds of many) such as strange plants, fruit flies, little worms, or even protozoans? How does that help us cure disease? Would it not be wiser if this money were directed toward more medically oriented research? To answer this question, let us use small interference RNA (siRNA)—a small, double-stranded RNA that is involved in the RNA interference (RNAi) pathway, where it interferes with the expression of a specific gene (gene knock-out)—as an example. Who would have thought that this type of RNA, first discovered in plants,[26] would become the primary tool for functional analysis in cancer, in neurodegenerative and several other diseases, and an important tool for gene function and drug target validation studies in the post-genomic era? Or take another example, *Tetrahymena thermophila*, a free-living ciliate protozoan that is found in freshwater. Why bother studying this life form? Well, this micro-organism has become a model organism to study gene function *in vivo*. Thanks to *Tetrahymena*, we have learned a great deal about telomeres,[27] the repetitive DNA sequences at the ends of chromosomes that protect them from degradation, among other things; we have learned so much about autocatalytic splicing, about gene expression and regulation, all of which has increased our understanding of cell growth and proliferation (important in cancer), aging (apoptosis or programmed cell death), and so on. In fact, several therapies, especially in oncology, based on information derived from the study of this protozoan are in progress now.

If, 20 years ago, people had held the same narrow view regarding funding fundamental research (for example, in obscure organisms), the great scientific progress that we are seeing today, and most of the therapies now available, would never have come into existence. It is hard for policymakers to understand this—they can be told, and they may have a general idea of a model system, but they do not truly understand the system because they do not have sufficient understanding of biological problems to be able to determine whether the study of any given obscure organism could be fruitful. These kinds of considerations are, in my opinion, the ones on which taxpayers and decision makers should focus.

Notes

1. I strongly recommend the reader refer to Weatherall, M., 1990. In Search of a Cure: A History of Pharmaceutical Discovery. Oxford University Press, New York; Singer, C., Underwood, A., 1962. A Short History of Medicine. Oxford Clarendon Press, Oxford, both of which discuss the issue in great detail.
2. Ibid.

3. Single nucleotide polymorphisms, or SNPs (pronounced "snips"), are DNA sequence variations that occur when a single nucleotide (A, T, C, or G) in the genome sequence is altered. For example, an SNP might change the DNA sequence AAGGCTAA to ATGGCTAA. For a variation to be considered an SNP, it must occur in at least 1% of the population. SNPs, which make up about 90% of all human genetic variation, occur every 100–300 bases along the three-billion-base human genome. Two of every three SNPs involve the replacement of cytosine (C) with thymine (T). SNPs can occur in coding (gene) and noncoding regions of the genome. Many SNPs have no effect on cell function, but scientists believe others could predispose people to disease or influence their response to a drug. http://www.ornl.gov/sci/techresources/Human_Genome/faq/snps.shtml.
4. Woosley, R., 2008. An audience with. Nature Reviews Drug Discovery 7, 884.
5. See for example, Wilson, D., 2009. Harvard Medical School in ethics quandary. New York Times, March 2, 2009. http://www.nytimes.com/2009/03/03/business/03medschool.html? pagewanted=2.
6. Hall, Z.W., Scott, C., 2001. University–industry partnership. Science 291, 26.
7. Lo, B., Wolf, L.E., Berkeley, A., 2000. Conflict of interest policies for investigators in clinical trials. New England Journal of Medicine 343, 1616–1620.
8. Kennedy, D., 2003. Industry and academia in transition. Science 302, 1293.
9. Interview with Tom Maniatis, Cambridge, MA, April 2009.
10. Wilson, D., 2009. Senator asks Pfizer about Harvard payments. New York Times, March 3, 2009. http://www.nytimes.com/2009/03/04/business/04pfizer.html?hp.
11. Ibid.
12. Wilson. Harvard Medical School.
13. Another disgraceful report was given by the *New York Times* on June 18, 2009. According to that publication, Dr. Timothy R. Kuklo, a surgeon in the army and now assistant professor at Washington University, St. Louis, was paid about $800,000 from Medtronic between 2001 and 2008 for a study that claimed that "the use of a Medtronic bone growth product called Infuse had proved highly beneficial in treating leg injuries suffered by American soldiers in Iraq" and that was discovered to be fake. "The British medical journal that published the article retracted it this year after an internal Army investigation found that Dr. Kuklo had forged the names of four other doctors on the study and had cited data that did not match military records." Meier, B., 2009. $788,000 paid to doctor accused of faking study, New York Times, June 17, 2009. http://www.nytimes.com/2009/06/18/business/18surgeon.html?_r=1&hp.
14. Wilson, D., 2010. Harvard teaching hospitals cap outside pay. New York Times, January 2, 2010. http://www.nytimes.com/2010/01/03/health/research/03hospital.html?hp.
15. In fact, it is believed that the average number of small molecules that make it from the chemist to the clinic is 1 in 500 or 1 in 1,000 in terms of synthesis. Although this is already an extremely low number, some scientists believe that for diseases such as central nervous system disorders, the numbers are even lower. Interview with Jackie Hunter, GlaxoSmithKline, June 2007.
16. Chandler, A.D., 2005. Shaping the Industrial Century: The Remarkable Story of the Evolution of Modern Chemical and Pharmaceutical Industries. Harvard University Press, Cambridge, MA.
17. Mattera, P., 1992. Hoechst: the toxic brewmasters. Multinational Monitor 5. http://www.multinationalmonitor.org/hyper/issues/1992/05/mm0592_11.html.
18. Bayer, which imitated Hoechst in this respect, did so too late and was not able to succeed. Nowadays, Bayer is not even among the top 10 pharmaceutical companies.

19. Chandler. Shaping the Industrial Century.
20. Lawler, A., 2003. Last of the big-time spenders? Science 299, 330.
21. Hughes, B., 2008. Pharma pursues novel models for academic collaboration. Nature Reviews Drug Discovery 7, 631–632; see also Novel pharma-academia collaborations continue. Nature Reviews Drug Discovery 8 (2009), 97.
22. A kinase is a type of enzyme that transfers phosphate groups from high-energy donor molecules, such as ATP, to specific substrates.
23. Interview with Susan Gasser, Basel, May 2007.
24. According to Dorland's Illustrated Medical Dictionary, 31st ed. Elsevier, New York, 2007, a phenotype is "the observable morphological, biochemical, and physiological characteristics of an individual, either in whole or with respect to a single or a few traits, as determined by a combination of the genotype and the environment."
25. Interview with Julian Adams, Cambridge, MA, March 2009.
26. Hamilton, A., Baulcombe, D., 1999. A species of small antisense RNA in posttranscriptional gene silencing in plants. Science 286, 950–952.
27. Research on teleomeres in *Tetrahymena thermophila* was awarded the Nobel Prize in Medicine and Physiology in 2009. The recipients were Elizabeth Blackburn, Carol Greider, and Jack Szostack.

8 Translating Academic Innovation into Health Care Products

When it comes to innovation in the biotechnology and pharmaceutical sectors, the United States is the undisputed leader in the field. Not that the quality of the research per se in this country is superior to the equally excellent research performed in Europe and some Asian countries, as testified by the number of patents per million population and research papers produced in those countries (see Tables 8.1 and 8.2). As I shall discuss later, but as has been pointed out elsewhere, in the United States (unlike in Europe and Asia), two historic developments converged to help create this leadership and the excitement about scientific innovation in the biomedical field. The first development emerged after World War II, when the United States became the indisputable technological leader of the world[1] and decided to create a huge national engine of public science. This initiative lent great support to investigator-initiated projects, in particular in academic laboratories. The second development, referred to as industrial-strength basic research, consisted of interdisciplinary teams of scientists working in industry supported by a powerful, highly sophisticated, and well-funded infrastructure,[2] such as in the case of IBM. In addition to this, industry saw in the mid-1970s that ideas caught early in their trajectory had a commercial potential that, with appropriate venture capital, to which tax laws became friendlier, could be further developed and commercialized. Later, the US Congress passed the Bayh–Dole Act of 1980, allowing universities to benefit financially from the patenting and licensing of discoveries made using federal or private funding. The rationale behind this act was to increase patenting of discoveries and the acceleration of economic growth through the creation of high-tech firms that licensed these technologies from the university. Needless to say, the establishment of the Bayh–Dole Act has been instrumental in the further development of the biotechnology industry and in reshaping the academia–industry interface. It has also been adapted by several European countries, and recently by Japan as well.

One of the complications of the Bayh–Dole Act (we will consider a very important intellectual property (IP) complication later in Chapter 10) is that since its enactment, the relationship between academia and industry has generally been perceived as unidirectional, with basic science being translated into applied science. It also helped to create the perception that in the academia–industry relationship, academia is exploited without receiving adequate benefits. However, on close examination, it becomes clear that many scientists see the commercialization of science as a legitimate academic activity and that the academia–industry relationship is bidirectional; in other words, academic research is stimulated by the questions that industry

The World's Health Care Crisis. DOI: 10.1016/B978-0-12-391875-8.00008-1

Table 8.1 Patents and Innovation Worldwide

2004–2008	Innovation Performance			Innovation Enables					
	Patents per M	Innovation Performance Index	Rank	Direct Inputs Index	Rank	Innovation Environment Index	Rank	Aggregate Innovation Enablers Index	Rank
Japan	1,274.533	10.00	1	9.81	9	7.11	23	9.14	11
Switzerland	505.839	9.71	2	9.94	2	8.54	6	9.59	4
Finland	363.298	9.50	3	9.94	2	8.60	3	9.60	3
United States	359.840	9.50	4	9.88	8	8.47	8	9.52	5
Sweden	330.980	9.44	5	10.00	1	8.49	7	9.62	2
Germany	310.695	9.40	6	9.94	2	8.07	13	9.47	6
Taiwan	293.642	9.37	7	9.50	11	7.46	22	8.99	15
Netherlands	212.411	9.16	8	9.56	10	8.45	9	9.28	8
Israel	199.801	9.13	9	9.94	2	6.83	27	9.16	10
Denmark	184.985	9.08	10	9.94	2	8.70	1	9.63	1
South Korea	148.704	8.94	11	9.50	11	6.30	44	8.70	18
Austria	147.317	8.93	12	9.06	17	7.57	18	8.69	19
France	136.223	8.88	13	9.94	2	7.51	21	9.33	7
Canada	132.635	8.87	14	9.50	11	8.25	11	9.19	9
Belgium	116.899	8.79	15	9.06	17	7.88	17	8.77	17
Singapore	111.307	8.76	16	8.81	19	8.66	2	8.77	16
Norway	106.668	8.73	17	8.81	19	7.95	14	8.60	20
United Kingdom	105.211	8.72	18	9.25	15	8.54	5	9.07	13
Ireland	73.814	8.50	19	9.19	16	8.60	4	9.04	14

Australia	73.511	8.50	20	9.50	11	7.92	16	9.11	12
Hong Kong	67.328	8.44	21	8.13	24	8.30	10	8.17	22
Italy	66.909	8.44	22	7.88	27	6.41	39	7.51	27
New Zealand	48.740	8.24	23	8.25	21	8.13	12	8.22	21
Slovenia	22.040	7.74	24	8.25	21	6.29	45	7.76	26
Cyprus	18.237	7.62	25	6.06	40	7.03	24	6.31	36
Spain	15.367	7.51	26	7.94	25	7.51	20	7.83	24
Hungary	9.061	7.18	27	7.69	23	6.78	28	7.46	28
Czech Republic	5.533	6.87	28	8.19	23	6.55	34	7.78	25
Croatia	5.116	6.82	29	6.50	34	5.51	58	6.25	37
Estonia	4.704	6.76	30	7.94	25	7.55	19	7.84	23
Malaysia	4.237	6.70	31	6.44	36	6.55	35	6.46	33
Greece	3.856	6.64	32	5.88	42	6.23	47	5.96	43
Portugal	3.612	6.60	33	7.00	31	6.92	26	6.98	30
South Africa	3.496	6.58	34	5.56	48	6.23	46	5.73	47
Costa Rica	2.429	6.35	35	5.88	42	6.54	36	6.04	42
Slovakia	1.836	6.17	36	7.31	29	6.72	29	7.16	29
Kuwait	1.794	6.16	37	4.75	56	6.01	48	5.06	57
Lithuania	1.563	6.07	38	6.56	32	6.40	40	6.52	31
Russia	1.460	6.03	39	7.13	30	4.61	74	6.50	32
UAE	1.329	5.97	40	5.88	42	6.94	25	6.14	40
Argentina	1.322	5.96	41	6.13	38	5.94	52	6.08	41

Note: Patents data are averaged over 2004–07 and expressed as patents per million population for each country.
The innovation enablers indexes are based on the average for 2004–08.

Table 8.1 Patents and Innovation Worldwide

2009–2013	Innovation Performance				Innovation Enablers					
	Expected Innovation Performance Index	Rank	Growth Expected During the Next 5 Years (%)	Expected Change in Rank	Expected Direct Inputs Index	Rank	Expected Innovation Environment Index	Rank	Expected Aggregate Innovation Enablers Index	Rank
Japan	10.00	1	0.0	0	9.94	9	6.97	28	9.20	11
Switzerland	9.70	2	−0.2	0	10.00	1	8.28	7	9.57	4
Finland	9.53	3	0.3	0	10.00	1	8.52	3	9.63	1
United States	9.44	5	−0.6	−1	10.00	1	7.86	14	9.47	6
Sweden	9.42	7	−0.2	−2	10.00	1	8.41	6	9.60	3
Germany	9.49	4	1.0	2	10.00	1	8.25	8	9.56	5
Taiwan	9.44	6	0.7	1	9.63	10	7.34	21	9.05	14
Netherlands	9.16	9	−0.1	−1	9.63	10	8.22	10	9.27	8
Israel	9.20	8	0.8	1	10.00	1	6.93	31	9.23	9
Denmark	9.06	10	−0.2	0	10.00	1	8.44	4	9.61	2
South Korea	9.05	11	1.2	0	9.50	13	6.73	35	8.81	17
Austria	8.98	12	0.6	0	9.19	18	7.39	20	8.74	19
France	8.96	13	0.9	0	10.00	1	7.66	17	9.42	7
Canada	8.83	15	−0.4	−1	9.50	13	8.10	11	9.15	12
Belgium	8.89	14	1.2	1	9.25	15	7.73	16	8.87	16
Singapore	8.75	16	−0.1	0	8.88	19	8.43	5	8.76	18
Norway	8.75	17	0.2	0	8.88	19	7.82	15	8.61	20
United Kingdom	8.58	19	−1.6	−1	9.25	15	7.93	13	8.92	15

Ireland	8.57	20	0.9	−1	9.25	15	8.74	1	9.12	13
Australia	8.61	18	1.4	2	9.63	10	8.05	12	9.23	10
Hong Kong	8.46	22	0.2	−1	8.06	23	8.57	2	8.19	22
Italy	8.46	21	0.3	1	7.94	26	6.31	45	7.53	28
New Zealand	8.40	23	2.0	0	8.44	21	8.22	9	8.38	21
Slovenia	7.80	24	0.9	0	8.25	22	6.58	37	7.83	24
Cyprus	7.72	25	1.4	0	6.13	43	7.21	23	6.40	38
Spain	7.50	26	−0.1	0	8.00	24	7.28	22	7.82	25
Hungary	7.28	27	1.5	0	7.81	28	6.86	33	7.57	27
Czech Republic	6.79	31	−1.0	−3	7.94	26	6.98	26	7.70	26
Croatia	7.16	26	5.1	1	6.75	32	6.07	54	6.58	34
Estonia	6.82	30	0.9	0	8.00	24	7.64	18	7.91	23
Malaysia	6.57	35	−1.9	−4	6.38	37	6.22	48	6.34	40
Greece	6.75	33	1.7	−1	6.00	45	6.26	46	6.06	45
Portugal	6.79	32	2.9	1	7.25	29	6.98	27	7.18	30
South Africa	6.94	29	5.5	5	5.94	47	6.39	44	6.05	48
Costa Rica	6.69	34	5.4	1	6.19	42	6.94	30	6.37	39
Slovakia	6.19	38	0.3	−2	7.19	31	7.20	24	7.19	29
Kuwait	6.25	36	1.6	1	4.81	60	6.15	52	5.15	58
Lithuania	6.14	40	1.1	−2	6.63	35	6.50	40	6.59	33
Russia	6.14	39	1.9	0	7.25	25	4.74	69	6.62	32
UAE	6.07	44	1.7	−4	6.06	44	6.79	34	6.25	42
Argentina	6.08	42	2.0	−1	6.31	40	5.86	58	6.20	44

Sources: A new ranking of the world's most innovative countries. An Economist Intelligence Unit Report, April 2009, pp. 12–13. © Economist. Reprinted with permission. All rights reserved. http://graphics.eiu.com/PDF/Cisco_Innovation_Complete.pdf.

Table 8.2 Current and Forecast Innovation Index

	2004–08		2009–13		Change in Rank
	Index	Rank	Index	Rank	2009–13/2004–08
Japan	10.00	1	10.00	1	0
Switzerland	9.71	2	9.70	2	0
Finland	9.50	3	9.53	3	0
United States	9.50	4	9.44	5	−1
Sweden	9.44	5	9.42	7	−2
Germany	9.40	6	9.49	4	2
Taiwan	9.37	7	9.44	6	1
Netherlands	9.16	8	9.16	9	−1
Israel	9.13	9	9.20	8	1
Denmark	9.08	10	9.06	10	0
South Korea	8.94	11	9.05	11	0
Austria	8.93	12	8.98	12	0
France	8.88	13	8.96	13	0
Canada	8.87	14	8.83	15	−1
Belgium	8.79	15	8.89	14	1
Singapore	8.76	16	8.75	16	0
Norway	8.73	17	8.75	17	0
United Kingdom	8.72	18	8.58	19	−1
Ireland	8.50	19	8.57	20	−1
Australia	8.50	20	8.61	18	2
Hong Kong	8.44	21	8.46	22	−1
Italy	8.44	22	8.46	21	1
New Zealand	8.24	23	8.40	23	0
Slovenia	7.74	24	7.80	24	0
Cyprus	7.62	25	7.72	25	0

Source: A new ranking of the world's most innovative countries. An Economist Intelligence Unit Report, April 2009, p. 7. http://graphics.eiu.com/PDF/Cisco_Innovation_Complete.pdf.

generates, which usually fall outside the scope, capabilities, and economic interests of the companies, as we have seen. Indeed, it could be suggested that the process of academia producing ideas that are translated into commercial products is cyclical: academia provides answers to the questions created by new commercial products that, in turn, could lead to more commercial products. Although there is secrecy and proprietary knowledge in the process of developing a drug, once the drug is marketed, the mechanisms involved in targeting the disease become public knowledge, resulting in more questions that could be investigated by academia.

In the United States, the National Institutes of Health (NIH), a division of the US Department of Health and Human Services, plays an essential role in fostering innovation by funding purely basic research and some translational research through the NIH Road Map Initiative (2004)—though its strength is, and should be, basic science. In fact, the NIH is the largest governmental funding body in the world. More than 83% of the NIH's funding is awarded through almost 50,000 competitive grants to more than 325,000 researchers at more than 3,000 universities, medical schools, and other research institutions in every state and around the world. About 10% of the NIH's budget supports projects conducted by nearly 6,000 scientists in its own laboratories, most of which are on the NIH campus in Bethesda, Maryland.[3] The NIH comprises 27 separate institutes, of which the first and the largest is the National Cancer Institute, established in 1937. The NIH has been a valuable resource for companies in their quest for new drugs by being very open at maintaining both formal and informal relationships with pharmaceutical companies and early-stage biotechnology companies. Companies with connections to the NIH often gain rights to agents and drug targets discovered by the NIH (usually in conjunction with a leading university). For example, Bristol-Myers Squibb's Taxol anticancer drug originated from NIH research efforts.

In Europe, besides what every individual government and the European Union (EU) invest in research and development (R&D), the EU's chief instrument for innovation is the Seventh Framework Program for Research and Technological Development (FP7), which gathers under a single, common umbrella all the EU's research initiatives over the period 2007–2013, with a budget of €51 billion over 7 years. In 2007, the legal basis for the creation of the Investigational Medicines Initiative (IMI) was approved, with the aim of addressing major bottlenecks in drug development through a joint commitment between the EU individual member states, the European Commission (based in Brussels), and the pharmaceutical industry. According to the plan, €2 billion would be invested over 7 years, with half of that money from the EU budget to support public research and small companies and half from the biopharmaceutical industry. Overall, the IMI expects to expand European expertise and knowledge of new technologies to attract investment for biopharmaceutical R&D in Europe and increase its competitiveness. However, despite the fact that at an EU summit in Lisbon in 2000, the EU set itself the goal of investing 3% of its gross domestic product (GDP) in R&D by 2010 to make Europe "the most dynamic and competitive knowledge-based economy in the world," and despite that since 2000, all European countries have increased their R&D investment, which has been reflected in an increasing number of researchers in science and technology (growing twice as fast as the United States and Japan), their investment, which in 2006 averaged 1.84%, has grown no faster than their growth in GDP. This situation has been identified as "funding stagnation" in Europe[4] (especially if one takes into consideration that Japan spends 3.39% of its GDP on R&D, South Korea spends 3.23%, and the United States spends 2.61%; China spends just 1.42%[5]) (see Tables 8.3 and 8.4).

Although the involvement of academic scientists in entrepreneurial activities might be more evident, even fostered, in areas such as biotechnology and high-tech clusters, such as the ones in San Francisco, Boston, and San Diego (in the United States) and Cambridge, Oxford, Surrey, and Scotland (in the United Kingdom), these clusters are exceptions. Their formation is a complex, expensive, and lengthy process, and their impact on economic acceleration and growth is unknown, or at least not easily measurable. In many respects, the participation of academic scientists in the United States and Europe in commercial activities could still be seen as a distraction or deviation from their academic duties, and many academic scientists prefer not to leave the security and freedom of university circles to pursue opportunities as entrepreneurs because of the risks involved, economic and otherwise. A source in one of the most important charitable research foundations in the world, whose name is withheld upon request, says:

> *True, there are many CEOs of companies and many venture capitalists that started off as scientists. But in general, there are three groups of academic scientists: there are those scientists who are able to adapt to different types of themes and can take on the business and marketing profession very easily; there are those die-hard scientists who are not interested in a very suspicious setting; and there are those groups of scientists in the middle who cannot quite make their minds, and it is a group of people in the middle that can be influenced, and they are going to be influenced by what they see as a result. And so I think what we need are more and more examples to influence that group of scientists, we need more and more examples of good ideas, becoming good products, which they can see may help to make a difference either in health care or in research tools that would not have made a difference if it had not been for that business component, and we need more and more examples of that. The problem that the biotech industry has, actually, is that there are not many products that come out of the industry. There are a number of antibody products, there are a number of chemical entities, but it is difficult for research scientists to associate that with what they do in a basis, so they do not see the connection between those few biotech products and basic science that the business has made a difference.*

This source continues:

> *I think that incentivization is important. But it is getting the balance right, so you don't want to distract scientists from their basic, core work. Nonetheless, they should be rewarded for the extra effort that goes into producing and commercializing the technologies. It is balance that you have to achieve there, and overall, I think what we need to do is provide the resource and environment whereby scientists get more and more exposed to the benefits of seeing their ideas commercialize*

Table 8.3 R&D as % of GDP: Sweden Tops List of OECD Countries

	1998	1999	2000	2001	2002	2003	2004	2005	2006	2007
Sweden	–	3.605	–	4.169	–	3.848	3.624	3.795	3.741	3.634
Finland	2.864	3.16	3.344	3.302	3.355	3.43	3.448	3.479	3.449	3.473
Japan	3.005	3.021	3.043	3.123	3.165	3.199	3.167	3.323	3.394	–
South Korea	2.342	2.252	2.393	2.59	2.532	2.631	2.847	2.98	3.225	–
United States	2.61	2.664	2.746	2.761	2.66	2.656	2.587	2.619	2.658	2.684
Germany	2.272	2.395	2.454	2.461	2.49	2.52	2.486	2.485	2.536	2.528
Denmark	2.045	2.177	–	2.387	2.508	2.575	2.485	2.452	2.463	2.538
Austria	1.781	1.9	1.941	2.067	2.14	2.258	2.255	2.443	2.456	2.565
France	2.139	2.159	2.148	2.197	2.23	2.168	2.15	2.099	2.097	2.081
Canada	1.758	1.795	1.912	2.088	2.041	2.031	2.051	2.014	1.941	1.893
Belgium	1.863	1.938	1.972	2.076	1.943	1.885	1.865	1.838	1.885	1.893
United Kingdom	1.785	1.856	1.848	1.823	1.821	1.779	1.71	1.757	1.779	–
Netherlands	1.895	1.959	1.825	1.804	1.724	1.756	1.782	1.737	1.732	1.727

Source: A new ranking of the world's most innovative countries. An Economist Intelligence Unit Report, April 2009, p. 10. http://graphics.eiu.com/PDF/Cisco_Innovation_Complete.pdf.

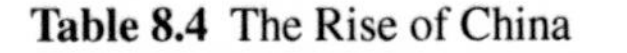

Table 8.4 The Rise of China

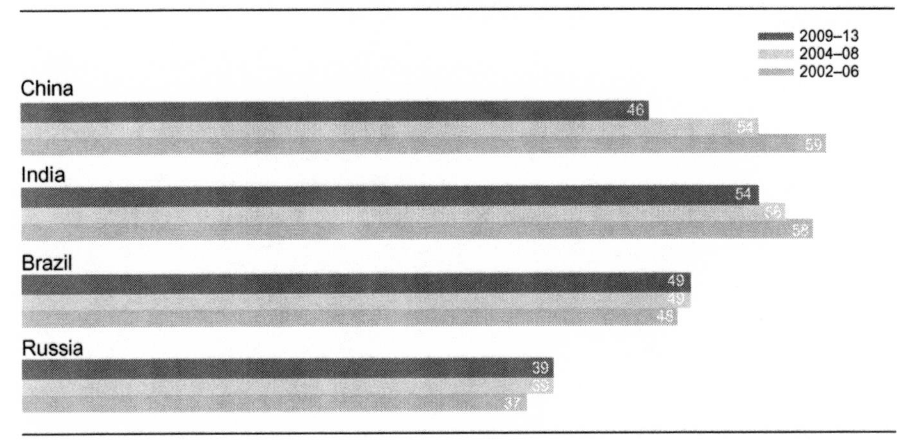

Source: A new ranking of the world's most innovative countries. An Economist Intelligence Unit Report, April 2009, p. 8. © Economist. Reprinted with permission. All rights reserved. http://graphics.eiu.com/PDF/Cisco_Innovation_Complete.pdf.

> *or translated. I think pushing academics or forcing them is the wrong approach. I think they have to be shown how to work and be led by success. And I think they will become much more. … Their hearts and minds will be won over. … So I am not necessarily sure that training is what is required. I think that is more having the support infrastructure around them so that it's easier for them to do the commercialization.*[6]

As we have discussed already, the pharmaceutical industry is going through some difficult times and is turning to wherever it can for innovation and potential products. Pharmaceutical companies understand that from the total amount of money being spent on R&D, any one drug company is going to have a small amount of the total. So it is clear to them that they are never going to have a total monopoly on good ideas and that they all need to have an externalization strategy to pick up on the good ideas that serendipitously appear. Then they have to be able to operationalize an inventive way to bring these products in and champion them and develop them. Therefore, there will always be a balance between internal and external development.

Pharmaceutical companies have had great success in going after the small biotech companies and university spinouts to bring in their compound leads to build their pipelines in this sector (see Tables 8.5 and 8.6).[7] With the hope of benefiting from the innovation that takes place in major universities, several pharmaceutical companies have installed research institutes in important high-tech and biotech clusters (near top universities) to keep an eye on what is going on there, which is very important to their life science groups. So companies try to interact with universities by sponsoring studentships and research in laboratories that they think are on the right track. Under the terms of this kind of sponsored research, firms have an option to license technology that results from it. Universities, on the other hand, are also in touch with all the major pharmaceutical companies and their representatives on a regular basis. But so far, this approach has not quite worked because there are too

Table 8.5 Selected 2009 M&As

Company	Country	Acquired or Merged Company	Country	Value (US$M)
Dainippon Sumitomo	Japan	Sepracor	United States	2,600
Bristol-Myers Squibb	United States	Medarex	United States	2,400
Gilead Sciences	United States	CV Therapeutics	United States	1,400
Johnson & Johnson	United States	Cougar Biotechnology	United States	970
H. Lundbeck	Denmark	Ovation Pharmaceuticals	United States	900
Onyx Pharmaceuticals	United States	Proteolix	United States	851
Celgene	United States	Gloucester Pharmaceuticals	United States	640
Endo Pharmaceuticals	United States	Indevus Pharmaceuticals	United States	637
Novartis	Switzerland	CorThera	United States	620
Alcon	Switzerland	ESBATech	Switzerland	589
Sanofi-Aventis	France	Fovea Pharmaceuticals	France	514
Sanofi-Aventis	France	BiPar Sciences	United States	500

Source: Ernst and Young, 2010. Beyond Borders: Global Biotechnology Report, p. 76.

many conditions that need to be fulfilled on the academic side, which makes academics wary of pharmaceutical firms.

However, the entrepreneurial interactions between university spinoffs, big pharma, and private investors have worked quite well. In fact, there is certainly, in the life science area, a very healthy mergers and acquisitions (M&A) market, as seen in Figures 8.1a and b, and 8.2a and b. Therefore, companies and investors who are willing to invest in the riskier deals of the early stages and have the appetite for them, have some reasonable access to those deals through acquisition by larger pharmaceutical companies, as many of them are acquiring products at Phase I, preclinical, or even earlier stages. Now it is interesting to look at the trends in that area because for a while, pharmaceutical companies were definitely not interested in early deals. Today, both large biotech companies, such as Amgen and Biogen/Idec, and small biotech companies, such as Infinity Pharmaceuticals (based in Cambridge, Massachusetts), certainly have an M&A group, a group that is destined for specific research projects and a group that acquires companies, and they all work very closely together. That is the best way to obtain the technology and fill their gaps. Other companies, however, may decide not to license a technology and instead work with a small company, waiting until a large portion of their risk is removed before acquiring them. Some others buy technologies that are at an earlier stage and play the odds.

Table 8.6 Alliances Between Pharma and Biotech

Company	Country	Partner	Country	Potential Value (US$M)
Novartis	Switzerland	Incyte	United States	1,310
AstraZeneca	United Kingdom	Tangacept	United States	1,240
Sanofi-Aventis	France	Exelixis	United States	1,161
AstraZeneca	United Kingdom	Nektar Therapeutics	United States	1,160
Bristol-Myers Squibb	United States	ZymoGenetics	United States	1,107
Takeda	Japan	Amylin	United States	1,075
Bristol-Myers Squibb	United States	Alder Biopharmaceuticals	United States	1,049
GlaxoSmithKline	United Kingdom	Chroma Therapeutics	United Kingdom	1,008
GlaxoSmithKline	United Kingdom	Concert Pharmaceuticals	United States	1,000
Johnson & Johnson	United States	Elan	Ireland	875
Wyeth	United States	Santaris Pharma	Denmark	847
Bayer Schering	Germany	Algeta	Norway	779
Astellas	Japan	Medivation	United States	765
Amgen	United States	Array Biopharma	United States	726
GlaxoSmithKline	United Kingdom	Prosensa	Netherlands	668

Source: Ernst and Young, 2010. Beyond Borders: Global Biotechnology Report, p. 77.

This has led some observers to consider biotech startup companies as the research arms of the pharmaceutical industry.[8] But under the light of the microscope, this concept does not actually hold because biotech can do research only in terms of specific drugs or drug products; it cannot spend its limited resources (time and money) doing mechanistic research, which belongs to the realm of academia and fundamental research. Biotech has become the bridge between academia and fundamental research and big pharma (I have described these types of interactions elsewhere).[9] This is not surprising because most such companies originate from academia: an academic lab has an idea that it believes is important and wants to spin it out and create a small company around it. It is often an idea that, by itself, cannot attract big pharma, or that academia cannot sell directly to pharmaceutical companies because it is perhaps too novel or its niche is not yet established. So universities provide an incubator, so to speak, for that idea to be matured, and in some cases a biotech idea

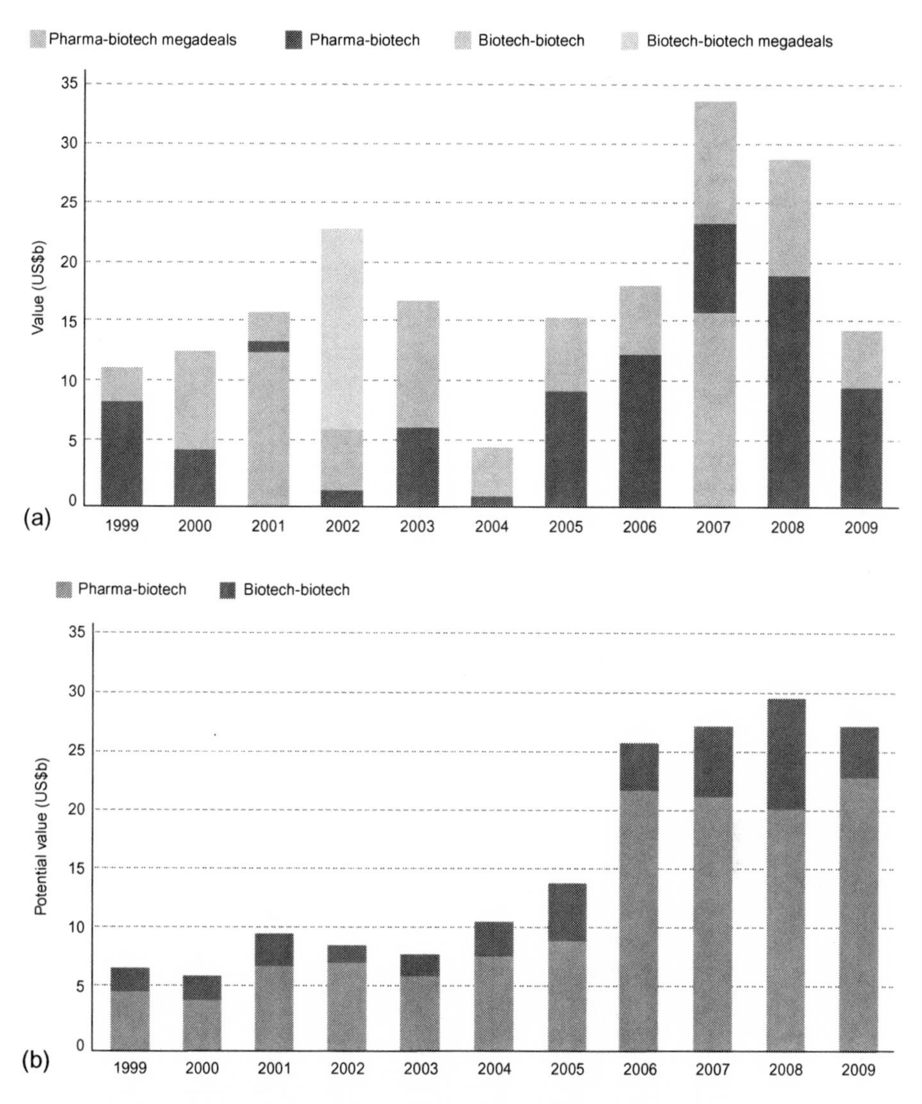

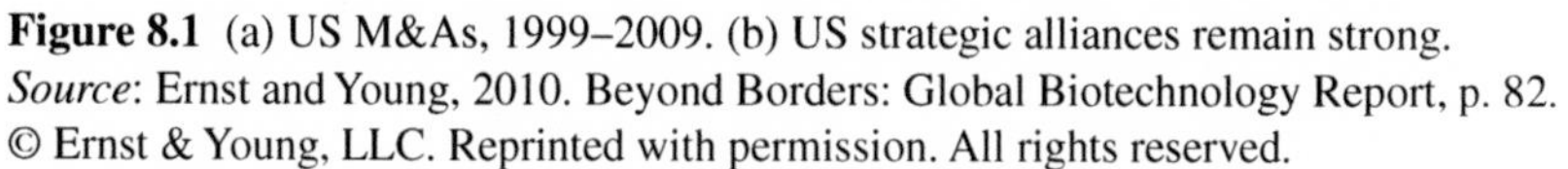

Figure 8.1 (a) US M&As, 1999–2009. (b) US strategic alliances remain strong.
Source: Ernst and Young, 2010. Beyond Borders: Global Biotechnology Report, p. 82.

may itself take off if it gets enough venture capital and if there are the resources to be able to take the idea through becoming a compound that could go to market. It is rare to see a biotech idea go from an academic bench—that is, from a concept—to the clinic, and even if that were the case, chances are that it would eventually fail. So the fact that universities act as incubators for ideas is a reasonable model that simply provides society with another mechanism for capturing intellectual output, scientific output, and taking it to a point that it could eventually lead to medical benefits.

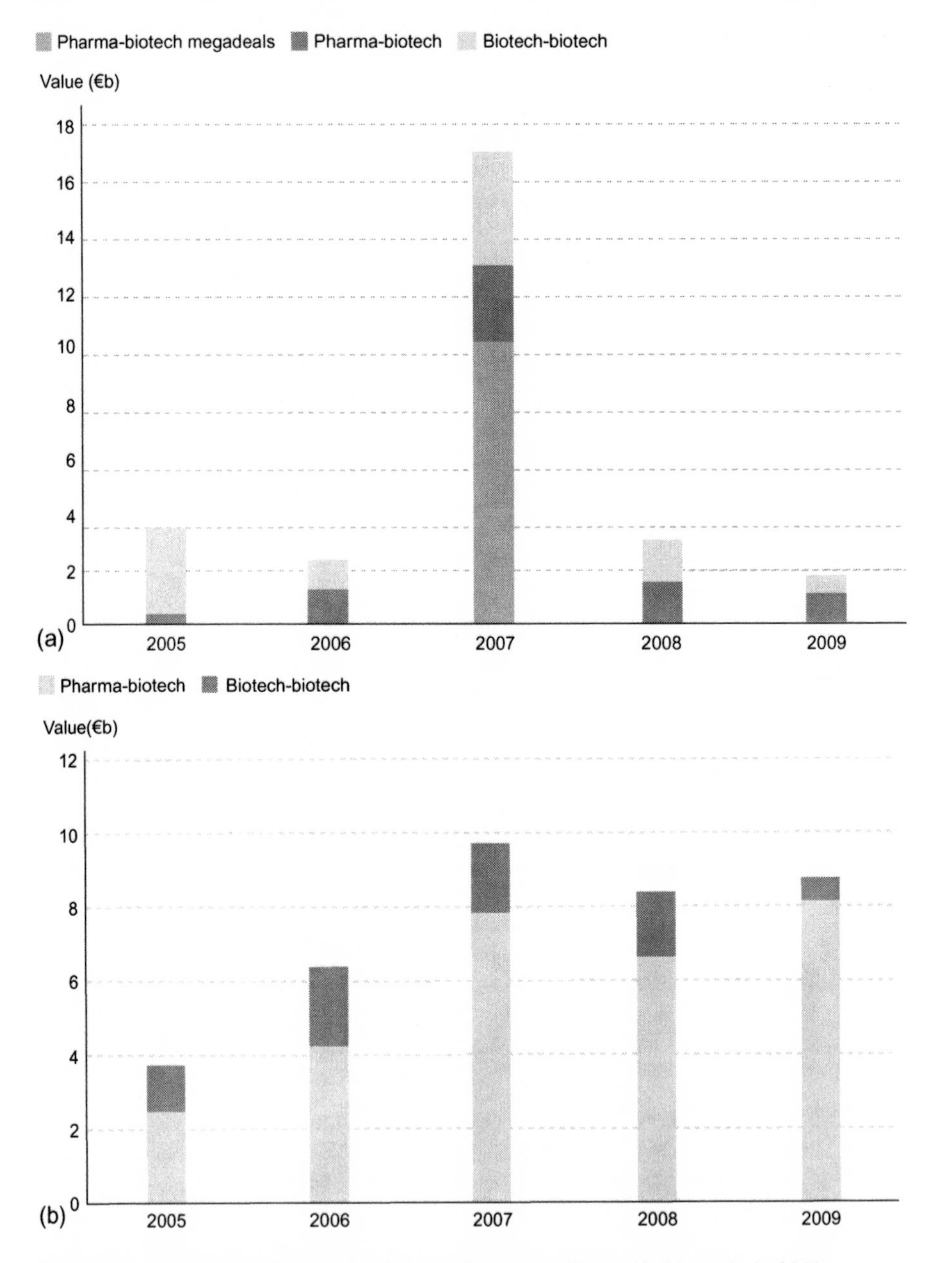

Figure 8.2 (a) European M&As, 2005–9. (b) European alliances held steady in 2009. *Source*: Ernst and Young, 2010. Beyond Borders: Global Biotechnology Report, p. 83.

Tom Maniatis, now at Columbia, summarizes this well:

I think that it has evolved into a system that works reasonably well. The biotech companies, if you will, have become sort of the intermediate station for development, so it takes this vast academic knowledge which is funded by the government and funnels it into these new entities that are very hungry and very new and have the incentives and drive to make things happen. And it is clear that each of these companies cannot then be a fully integrated company and succeed as a long-term thing. And it seems as if there is going to be this constant evolution of new entities that are going to be financially controlled by the larger pharmaceutical companies. And you can see that happening right now.... They are merging, and part of the reasons for that merging is that they are consolidating their strengths into one entity. So they will take the best marketing people, they will take the best pharmacology people—that's the idea—and make these basically strong organizations that could take a Phase I target from a biotech company and bring it to the point of having an FDA-approved drug. I think that that is the way in which things are going to continue to run over the short run, as you can't have all the elements with one biotech company, and I believe that Genentech was the last example of that: they actually had the combination of recruiting academics within the company and maintaining those interactions within academia.[10]

Translating Basic Discoveries into Commercial Products

The agreements made between universities and external parties, such as companies and investors, and the relationships between universities, their startups, pharmaceutical firms, and investors can sometimes be very fluid, dynamic mechanisms that work well, but sometimes they can be quite awkward and nasty. According to the CEO of a prestigious European university's spinout tech transfer office, whose name is withheld upon request, when negotiation problems occur,

they are mostly relationship management issues. It is difficult, when you get a lot of cases going on, to spend the time that you would really like with the academics to make sure they really understand what they are doing, that they are comfortable with the process, that they understand the company's point of view, that the company understands the academic's point of view, so that if there is something exciting that the academic wants to publish it, you don't want to delay their publication, but you want to make sure that the company is comfortable that we are filing patents on time so that we are not losing time, so a lot of it is that type of relationship management and then with the contract area as we get more and more industry relationships. It is better to have multiple relationships than one big one, but then that adds complexity to what we call a gap ground right.[11]

The overall process works as follows: once researchers see the potential for the commercialization of an idea, they go to the tech transfer office of their university. As soon as it receives a new idea, the tech transfer office evaluates it internally and begins to seek advice from the business community—usually external people who had had major successes in a given field—that could help them conduct a rapid assessment of the technology and its viability as a commercial enterprise. So they could decide to license out the technology to scientists, to entrepreneurs to form a company, or to a third party such as a big pharmaceutical firm. Should scientists, entrepreneurs, and the universities form a company, they create a business plan with the patented technology (or pending patent approval). Usually, together with their universities, they work with different angel groups; that is, wealthy investors who provide the seed money to begin the project in exchange for equity in the startup company. On some occasions, universities work with the different consultancies in town that have deep industry relationships with companies and know what those companies are looking for. Usually, this is a very open and supportive business community. Those who are involved with these networks are usually very generous with their time. Even if they have no intention to invest, they would still look at the technology and give the university feedback. Whereas venture capital groups are more selective with their time, individual venture capital organizations are very helpful because this idea could be in their own interest. Then the entrepreneurs, often in collaboration with the universities, prepare a business plan, and then companies and universities find investors, generally venture capitalists (VCs).

As illustrated in Table 8.7, there are many VC groups (and angels), especially in technology and biotechnology clusters such as San Francisco, the greater Boston area, and Cambridge and Oxford (United Kingdom), although this is also happening in Japan, China, India, and some other East Asian countries such as Singapore. Some of them are early-stage investors, and universities generally give them an early look into some of the companies they are working on with small seed funding that the universities themselves have provided to incubate the technology. Because early investors could invest before most people, this is a good way to get their feedback so that the universities and entrepreneurs know how to structure their deal in the best manner while taking the company to the point where other people may want to invest. This is also a good opportunity to get entrepreneurs and investors together so they can get to know each other, which could encourage a strong syndicate of coinvestments, which is very important in managing financing risks in these early-stage companies. Early-stage investors also constitute a window on hot deals, and universities may find them valuable for targeting coinvestors with whom they can work. In general, the early-stage investors invest $250,000–500,000 initially, usually up to $3 million over the life of the deal, and the larger funds will want to make an investment between $2 million and $5 million, up to $20 million during the life of a deal.

Venture Capitalists

The relationship that VCs establish with universities and entrepreneurs is very close. VCs generally have sessions with universities and bioincubators where they meet with the leading professors in a given space to learn what is happening, what is new in the space, what the hot new companies are, what the hot new targets are, and what the hot new areas are. They go to the universities, meet the entrepreneurs and

Table 8.7 Selected List of Venture Capital Firms Around the World

Name	Location	Founding Date	Specialty	Capital Managed (Approximate)
Accel Partners	Palo Alto, CA	1983	Technology	
Atlas Venture	Cambridge, MA; London, England	1980	Technology and life sciences	$2.0B
Azione Capital	Singapore	2006	Interactive digital media, mobile communications, wireless technology, energy, maritime	
Bain Capital Ventures	Boston, MA	1984	Infrastructure software and services, communications, new media, business services, health care	$1.4B
Benchmark Capital	Menlo Park, CA	1995	Technology & financial services	$2.3B
Bessemer Venture Partners	Menlo Park, CA; Larchmont, NY; Boston, MA; Herzliya, Israel; Mumbai, India	1911	Technology & services	$2.5B
Canaan Partners	Menlo Park, CA; Westport, CT; Gurgaon, India; Herzliya, Israel	1987	Technology and health care	$2.3B
Charles River Ventures	Menlo Park, CA; New York, NY	1970	Technology	$2.1B
Clearstone Venture Partners	Santa Monica, CA; Menlo Park, CA; Mumbai, India	1998	Internet, consumer, communications, software	$650M
Draper Fisher Jurvetson	Menlo Park, CA	1985	Technology and technology services	$3.5B

(Continued)

Table 8.7 (Continued)

Name	Location	Founding Date	Specialty	Capital Managed (Approximate)
Enterprise Partners	San Diego, CA	1985	Technology and life sciences	$750M
Fidelity Ventures	Boston, MA	1970	Information technology	$1.5B
Galen Partners	Stamford, CT	1990	Health care technology, medical devices, specialty pharmaceuticals	$1.0B
General Catalyst	Cambridge, MA	2000	Technology, clean energy, software, and new media	$1.6B
Greylock Partners	Cambridge, MA; San Mateo, CA; Israel; India	1965	Consumer Internet, enterprise IT, and clean tech	$2.0B
Highland Capital Partners	Boston, MA; Menlo Park, CA; Geneva, Switzerland; and Shanghai, China	1988	Consumer, health care, information and communication technology, and Internet and digital media	$3.0B
Index Ventures	London, England; Geneva, Switzerland; Jersey, UK	1996	Consumer Internet, communications, media, enterprise IT, clean tech, biotech	$2B+
Insight Venture Partners	New York, NY	1995	Software and Internet	$3.25B
Kleiner, Perkins, Caufield & Byers	Menlo Park, CA	1972	Alternative energy, technology, and life sciences	$1.5B
Lux Capital	New York, NY	2000	Emerging technologies, physical and life sciences	$100M

Matrix Partners	Boston, MA; New York, NY; Boston, MA; Palo Alto, CA; Mumbai, India; Beijing, China; Shanghai, China	1977	Software, communications, hardware, Internet, consumer, semiconductors, clean technology, wireless	Latest fund $600M in 2009
Mayfield Fund	Menlo Park, CA	1969	Wireless, consumer, software, semiconductors	$2.4B
Menlo Ventures	Menlo Park, CA	1976	Private communications, Internet infrastructure, software, semiconductors, data storage, computer hardware companies	$4.0B
New Enterprise Associates	Menlo Park, CA; Baltimore, MD; Reston, VA	1978	Information technology and health care	$6.0B
Nexit Ventures	Saratoga, CA; Helsinki, Finland; Stockholm, Sweden	1999	Mobile and wireless	$180M
Oak Investment Partners	Westport, CT; Palo Alto, CA; Minneapolis, MN	1978	Information technology and health care	$8.4B
Point Judith Capital	Providence, RI	2001	Communications, Internet, health care, and software	$100M
Quicksilver Ventures	Saratoga, CA	2001	Secondary venture capital (acquire existing corporate and venture portfolios). Investment focus: emerging technologies such as video and imaging; networking and mobility; data management, services and security; storage components and systems; enterprise applications	$ Evergreen, portfolio acquisition value from $1 M–250 M
Rho Ventures	New York, NY	1981	New media, information technology & communications, cleantech, health care	$2.5B

(Continued)

Table 8.7 (Continued)

Name	Location	Founding Date	Specialty	Capital Managed (Approximate)
Santé Ventures	Austin, TX	2006	Health care	$130M
Scottish Equity Partners	London, England; Glasgow, Scotland	1991	Information technology, health care, and energy technology	$500M
Sequoia Capital	Menlo Park, CA	1972	Components, systems, software, and services	$4.0B
Sevin Rosen Funds	Dallas, TX; Palo Alto, CA; Austin, TX; San Diego, CA	1981	Technology	$1.6B
Tenaya Capital	Menlo Park, CA; Boston, MA	2009	High technology: software, semiconductors, consumer Internet, communications	$1.0B
Union Square Ventures	New York City, NY	2005	Technology	
Viking Venture (sic) Management	Trondheim, Norway	2001	Electronics, software, oil and gas, materials, clean technology	Unknown
Wellington Partners Venture Capital	Munich, Germany	1991	Technology, digital media, life sciences	$700M under management

Source: Wikipedia. http://en.wikipedia.org/wiki/List_of_venture_capital_firms (publicly available information).

spinouts, and talk to technology transfer people. They have to do this because that is where the largest part of new technologies comes from.

The stage at which a VC is interested in investing in a company depends on the technology, and the equity stake could range anywhere between 8% and 60%, depending on the company. Generally, VCs do not take a majority of the shareholding, but that is generally where they end up in terms of equity. The stage of the company in which they invest could be as late as Phase III or even on the market. Others could be much earlier and in the discovery phase. But generally speaking, most of the companies tend to fund companies that are between late discovery or preclinical through Phase II. Needless to say, VCs need to diversify investments to mitigate risks. According to Zina Affas, former principal at Atlas Venture, one of the largest life science VC firms in the world:

> *Sometimes we make investments into lower risk cases like life cycle management type, specialty pharma type cases, where they take a drug from the United States that has been approved and marketing is in Europe or vice versa and so on, but doing this sort of lowers risk. But potentially, you lower the reward type investment. But also on the other hand, doing the higher risk/higher reward, so early-stage discovery programs that could fail, you know. So very easily the probabilities are higher for failure; however, if they do make it the rewards are higher. So by diversification, you try to help that, mitigate that market and general industry risk that you have.*[12]

This is how VCs operate at the time of investment and throughout the development process.

At the time of investment, VCs work out the valuation going back from the company's exit. They ask themselves the following questions: how novel is the technology? What market can it capture? How long will it take the company to exit? Will the company need another finance round between now and its exit? How many rounds? Would that be a step-up valuation? Will there be value creation between now and the exit? This aspect is particularly important because companies need to create value between now and the exit because that is how they and their investors get the step up. So investors always have a view of when the company will be exiting, at what price, and whether it will be by an initial public offering (IPO) or M&A. As such, they have different scenarios, so they calculate a likely case, a high case, and a low case; that is, they calculate the worst-case scenario, the best-case scenario, and what is most likely to happen. Based on that, VCs work out the investment thesis and whether it makes sense for them as an investment. Once they make an investment, the hard work starts because investors begin to work with their companies. It takes at least 5–8 years to exit the company, and many things can change or go wrong. For example, if the company has only one product and that product fails, they and their investors have to consider whether to get rid of the company, whether to bring in another product, or whether anything can be done to try to salvage something that could give the company value, such as intellectual property or something similar. As such, there could be things along the way that could change the initial strategy, so companies and investors have to be flexible and prepared to form partnerships to raise more cash. (An interesting example is Actelion Pharmaceuticals, a Swiss company whose first product failed but which found a way to succeed with a second product and eventually became a $1 billion company.)

As said earlier, most VCs are typically lead or colead investors. As such, they pay significant diligence up front to really understand the risks, and they truly understand the company and what needs to be done. They also visit the company's board, either by serving in a full board position or by being a board observer. In that way, they are very proactive. Some VCs only give their money and let the companies run on their own. Others like to be more proactive, so they help the company in many different ways, including trying to help with business development activities. Some VCs add value to their companies by meeting annually with the top 50 pharmas at least once a year to help their portfolio companies. They also help them to recruit senior managers within their companies as well as board members, and they aid them with strategies on how to find different types of financing, including venture debt or grants; when they will be able to IPO; how they could get the right banks on board; who to include, how to do it, and with which exchange. Many VCs, such as Atlas Venture, Oxford Biosciences, and MPM Capital, have an in-house support team so they have lawyers, human resources people, and finance people who can help companies in terms of building on their expertise. That is how they add value: they provide added service apart from money. Once a company goes public, there are different ways in which it can finance itself, as illustrated in Table 8.8.

The financial situation of VCs in the last years has been on the weak side. Even before the collapse of Lehman Brothers (September 2008) triggered a domino-effect global banking crisis, VC firms were struggling to raise new capital, judging by the numbers. In the 9 months from January to September 2008, US VC firms raised only $19.7 billion from their limited partners, compared with $32 billion for the entire previous year and $30 billion in 2006 (Dow Jones Venture figures). It is estimated that of the total amount of funding raised in venture capital, 25–30% is allocated to the health care sector.[13] Although in 2008, VC investment deployment in the health care sector held steady compared to 2007, the global financial crisis has changed the structure of VC investing. Nowadays, some of the larger and more mature VC firms are increasingly infusing more of their cash into their existing portfolios at the expense of startups. Furthermore, the smaller and less-experienced VC firms are struggling to raise capital, while others have put on hold seed or early-stage financing for months or even years, and others are having trouble meeting their fund-raising targets (see Figure 8.3a and b raised by leading VCs in the United States and Europe).[14] In addition, the potential imposition by the government that all private pools of investment capital be registered with the Securities and Exchange Commission (SEC) may have a negative impact on the creation of early-stage biotech firms.[15]

For biotech companies, VC funding has become essential, and this is true in the United States, Europe, and Asia. According to Affas:

> *I think that the science is solid on both sides of the Atlantic, there is no doubt about it. The United States has been doing VC for much longer and therefore they have managers and entrepreneurs who have been doing this time and time again who*

Table 8.8 US Yearly Biotechnology Financings, 1998–2009 (US$M)

	2009	**2008**	**2007**	**2006**	**2005**	**2004**	**2003**	**2002**	**2001**	**2000**	**1999**	**1998**
IPOs	697	6	1,238	944	626	1,618	448	456	208	4,997	685	260
Follow-ons	5,165	1,715	2,494	5,114	3,952	2,846	2,825	838	1,695	14,964	3,680	500
Other	7,617	6,832	12,195	10,953	6,788	8,964	8,306	5,242	3,635	9,987	2,969	787
Venture	4,556	4,445	5,464	3,302	3,328	3,551	2,826	2,164	2,392	2,773	1,435	1,219
Total	**18,034**	**12,998**	**21,391**	**20,313**	**14,694**	**16,979**	**14,405**	**8,699**	**7,930**	**32,722**	**8,769**	**2,766**

Source: Ernst and Young, 2010. Beyond Borders: Global Biotechnology Report, p. 66.

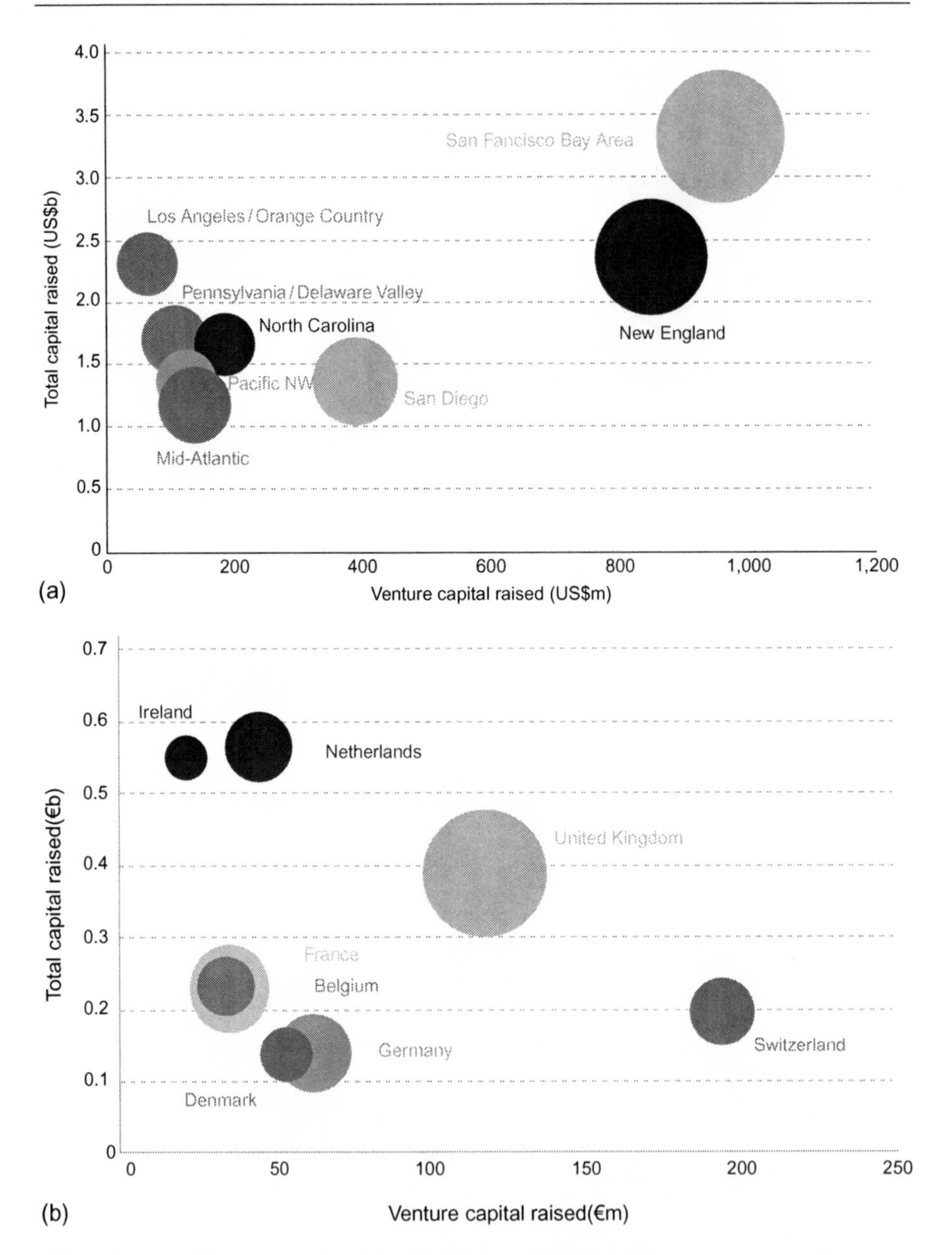

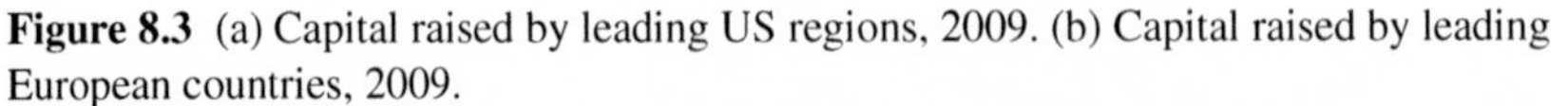

Figure 8.3 (a) Capital raised by leading US regions, 2009. (b) Capital raised by leading European countries, 2009.
Source: Ernst and Young, 2010. Beyond Borders: Global Biotechnology Report, p. 69 and 70.

have failed and learned, who have succeeded and learned much more. Europe is now getting there. But it has been behind the United States. We have found it much harder to get good management here in Europe than in the States. However, on the flip side, there is far less competition here in Europe than there is in the States for good deals because there are very few VCs at the same time. In terms of the companies themselves, science is good on both sides. Different styles of working, yes, and the United States is much more used to the entrepreneurial and VC environment. They understand how ventures work. The Europeans, perhaps, need a little more educating, from time to time, depending on who you deal with and whether they have done it before.

Affas adds:

China and India could be seen as one or separate, depending on how you want to see them. China has been very strong on the biology side and India has been very strong on the chemical side. India has been very strong on the generics side as well. China has been difficult and fraught with governmental issues, FDA issues with corruption and so on ... and India had different issues with IP and so on. But now they are getting sorted, and India is seeing more innovation, China is seeing more innovation. China is seeing more globalization. They are bringing drugs in from outside, you know, and there are a lot of deals that have been done, you know, the Cubist deal with AstraZeneca, for example, that are bringing drugs to China. So this market ... will be the fourth largest market in the next few years. So, you know, it's huge, so there is a lot of potential to it. I would say, to make money in China, if you can do it correctly, you have to be very careful and you have to deal with the issues of the corporate structure of the company. So there are more legal and governmental type issues to deal with rather than scientific at the moment.[16]

Challenges in Translating Innovation into Commercial Products

One of the big challenges that universities face when working with very early-stage drug targets is that these targets are a long way from becoming products that the pharmaceutical companies may be willing to license out directly from the university, or in which VCs may be interested in investing. Thus it is necessary to ask: what can universities do while they are waiting for research to bear fruit? One potential solution could be to have some VCs pool resources for subcontracting out different types of work so they could move a drug development idea along a little further, to answer some questions in advance that pharma and biotech may have before they engage. This does not mean that it is impossible to engage VCs or the biopharmaceutical industry earlier so that the technology transfer offices obtain input from them, but it may make sense to have that resource in place because there is a big gap in getting things into the pharma pipeline.

Now, as far as pharmaceuticals are concerned, perhaps the biggest challenge is to find a balance between the economic profitability of a potential drug product and the impact that product has on society. Though it is important for universities to think constantly about improving the probability that a new idea will be attractive to license or will be appropriate for creating an interesting company, and to consider how the returns come back in, it is definitely important to think that this product will meet an unmet patient need. But that is not going to happen if the financial incentives are not set up and if they are not aligned with how the capitalist system works. For instance, if a university thinks that it has found something that cures renal disease—a really difficult target to address—then universities need to understand that market, they need to figure out who the best people are with whom to work, and they need to know if they could realistically wash the risk out of the idea to get the right partner involved to take it forward. There is, then, something they could reasonably do with their resources: they can learn the technical, basic knowledge and hope that the next thing to come along will answer the questions, and they can take those resources and put them to work so that they can treat patients. Universities' biggest challenge while being involved in this kind of early-stage technology development is to keep being highly optimistic. The odds that a basic and original idea will succeed are very rare, so a challenge at the tech transfer level is to say no to things because they see potential in everything. In this way, universities have a hard time setting priorities and thinking not just about out-of-pocket expenses but also about opportunity cost when working on potential deals. This is a big issue for people who work at that level and also for investors and the pharma companies.

Having the industry involved sooner rather than later is always going to have a positive impact. As Tom Hockaday, the CEO of ISIS Innovation (Oxford University's tech transfer subsidiary), has rightly pointed out, "There is a specific trend that we are seeing at the moment, which is that the attitude of companies to innovation is changing and that the open innovation model is real, relatively new and different; company attitudes are changing as they realize they need to go out to talk to others, they need to be more open, they need to bring in other people's ideas because they are unlikely to generate enough themselves."[17] This is of great importance for universities because in such a scenario, companies are more willing to decide to fund specific projects or specific laboratories. For this reason, it is important that tech transfer makes sure that scientists have all the resources to do what they think is right. In exchange, companies want a chance to look at technologies when they come out, and if a technology looks reasonable, they want an option to license it. From a practical point of view, it is better for a university to have as many relationships as possible with different companies than to have one strong relationship with any one company. It is important to have what is called gap or proof-of-concept money, which is not money for patenting but rather money to validate an idea or address technical problems. Proof-of-concept funding does not take too much money (maybe $20,000 or $200,000), but it is quite important because it could make a difference in the attractiveness of a technology to pharmaceutical companies so that they will pick it up and take it forward. These are very critical resources that gap funding people count on, but it is not really research funding and not really venture capital investment; rather, it is funding that can be deployed to optimize a promising technology before commercializing it. And this is a funding gap at present.

Thus society has to look for and create alternative funding sources to bridge this gap. The Medical Research Council (MRC) in the United Kingdom, which is the UK equivalent of the NIH and the Wellcome Trust in London, is perhaps the paradigm in this new direction and may deserve imitation. According to Martin Wood, retired director of licensing and agreements at MRC Technology (which is the commercialization company affiliated with the MRC), and Robert Lang, MRC Technology Director of corporate resources:

> *MRC is able to put funds into validating things. We have set a new thing called the MRC Development gap fund, which is designed to do exactly what it says: to fund the additional research that is necessary to take an invention, an early-stage invention, into something that is more attractive as a licensing opportunity to industry or indeed as the basis of a start-up company. So that means that we will fund additional work because we own the work if it is an academic program since the scientists are already funded by MRC Technology to do the extra work and put in extra staff to do additional research. ... We look to maximize the benefit to society as well as the income of MRC. MRC is in the business of improving human health as well as achieving economic benefits, but often there is no conflict between those objectives.*[18]

The primary focus of the Wellcome Trust is to fund basic scientific research. The trust also assists in the translation of basic academic research or any basic science into commercial products regardless of whether it is commercial or not for profit, whether it targets an orphan disease or blockbuster indication. In the words of Richard Seabrook, head of business development at the Wellcome Trust, "our mission is to improve human and animal health through scientific research, and the trust wants to fund the best science or the best project. We do not prioritize a particular therapy area. So if the best projects happen to be in malaria, or leishmaniasis or Chagas' disease, we would fund them. We are not put off from a project by the fact that it is a niche or orphan disease."[19]

In addition, the Wellcome Trust has a Technology Transfer Division, whose objective is to add value to basic scientific findings when those basic scientific findings can be developed into a product. By adding value, I mean that this division reduces the risk, the proof of concept, and makes it attractive to follow-on investors. Those follow-on investors may be existing companies, so that the division creates something attractive from a licensing perspective, or they may be the financial community, so that they make something attractive from the point of view of forming a business. In the case of orphan or neglected diseases, it might be that the division makes something that is attractive to a nongovernmental organization or a public–private company.

In general, there are two types of agreements between these partners and with people outside this organization. The first type of agreement is a funding agreement; that is, the basis on which the division is to provide its funding to another party. The division's philosophy is that it does not want to spend a great deal of time negotiating all the terms on which it is to provide funding.[20] It can live with those terms and conditions or find them inappropriate, and it knows not to apply to the trust.

The second type of agreement is typified by those cases in which the trust is responsible for the transaction after its funding, whereby it is transacting with another party to further develop the product that is using some of its funding. Then they have license agreements and they get involved in the formation of new companies, and those are very much context-specific. They are tailor-made, and it is very difficult to generalize; however, because the trust is a charity, and because it is providing funding for health care benefits, it does require certain provisions in its agreements. So if the trust is transacting with a commercial company, it will need protection should it decide not to develop the product; those rights should go back to the trust, and it will also need the right to develop the technology in any part of the world where the company chooses not to develop the technology. Obviously, certain countries are more committed in practice than others, but their responsibility is global, and therefore, if a company does not develop a technology in some of the poorer countries, then the trust would like to have the right to work to see if there is a way in which that technology could be made available to those areas.

In terms of the relationship between the trust and some of the companies with which it deals, it is not possible to generalize. In the trust's experience, once a company has decided it wants to work with the trust, the trust needs to go through the legal agreement and establish the principles under which the two parties will work together. But it is very important from the outset to make the company aware of the specific requirements of the charity so that it can be decided at an early stage whether the company can accommodate the trust's requirements.

But the case of the Wellcome Trust is an isolated one. In the United States, there are a large number of philanthropic organizations and some advocacy groups that contribute a large amount of funding to biomedical research, but these organizations, with the exception of the Bill and Melinda Gates Foundation, are focused on particular diseases. Also, especially now with the credit crunch, their funding is very limited. Another limitation of the smaller funding agencies is that some money usually goes to areas where there is already funding, whereas in some other areas, there is no money. It is not surprising to find duplication in the allocation of funding and power battles between philanthropies that cover the same disease, as is the case between the Multiple Myeloma Foundation and the International Myeloma Fund, whose CEOs vie for the spotlight. Nonetheless, all these organizations play an important role in educating and providing additional funding and, in the case of some advocacy groups, small funding for research in specific sectors within a disease category. It would be good, though, to establish an international fund that would make money readily available to fill in areas where there is a funding gap.

Intellectual Property Rights

With the Bayh–Dole Act, patenting, licensing, and material transfer agreements (MTAs) became an important part of translating basic innovation from university settings into commercial products. This has created a situation in which intellectual property constraints may have a negative effect on scientific communication and the use of such discoveries, in a situation described by legal scholars as knowledge anti-commons or "the tragedy of the anticommons."[21] In fact, intellectual property rights, although doubtless necessary, can be an impediment to the process of translating basic science into commercial products.

Of course, most companies and investors will not finance translational science and develop drugs without a strong intellectual property position to protect their investment. But after collaborative conversations have started, the terms and conditions of the licensing and technology transfer agreements can often reach absurd levels for either or both parties, and interesting and highly viable projects can reach an impasse, slowing down the translational process. Indeed, there is a perception among people working in academic biotechnology spinoff companies that a significant number of the obstacles they encounter come from the universities themselves, especially when dealing with issues related to ownership and economic dividends. Many times, university tech transfer offices, companies, and VCs cannot agree on valuations for their deals. It is very common that many deals are not realized because of this. While universities tend to overvalue their technologies, VCs and pharmaceutical companies tend to undervalue them. Regarding this point, a source at a prestigious charitable institution in Europe, whose name is withheld upon request, says that

> *there are all sorts of reasons why particular transactions get delayed. And it's not easy to generalize, but some people would say that in the university environment, universities tend to overvalue their intellectual property and therefore the negotiation process gets elongated because of unrealistic expectations. The problem the universities have is that they don't have a reference point to compare against so that they would know what their technology is worth. Because companies are around taking transactions all the time, they know what they can afford to pay for a technology. The universities, because of the diversity of the technologies (which are in the early stage), are in the dark. They don't know what it's really worth, so therefore they have a tendency to overvalue it, as you were selling a house, and overvalue it, and expect the company to cut them down. So I think the solution to the problem would be some form of database in which, which would provide a reference point so the universities know what their technology is worth.*[22]

Material transfer agreements, for instance, are the bane of everyone in the tech transfer business. At the same time, they are necessary. For instance, someone could come in with a disclosure of his invention, and he used an antibody to create the invention, which probably came from somewhere else. So it is necessary to have some written agreement on who gets to use what material for what purposes. There are some cases in which materials are exchanged freely between academia and industry, but at other times, the donor considers the transfer as proprietary material. Though the donor may be aware that the material is important for further research, the donor may allow its use under the condition that the donor is informed of whatever inventions are made when the transferred material is used and that the donor is given the right of first refusal. So universities need to have a written agreement in which they get permission from the company to use the material, or vice versa. But the system is far from perfect, as seen by the significant number of suits and countersuits on this front and by the many conflicts of interest seen in the academic sector.

Taxpayers' Money for Innovation and Commercial Applications

In the United States, there is a debate about taxpayers' money being invested in research and the biopharmaceutical industry benefiting from it. As we explored when discussing the relationship between Hoechst and the MGH, this is a sentiment that has cycled its way through. Certainly when the first policies were put in place, intellectual property was being developed with taxpayers' dollars in the United States. To give an example, the patents were sitting and no one would use them, so they were given away. If one can give the ideas away, one can publish them, or no one develops them. There is no reason to invest the time, effort, and risk. If anybody can do it, one has to do it within a monopoly where one can earn interest, and so the premise is that the taxpayer dollars are squandered unless one creates a commercial incentive for someone to take something forward. Otherwise, sure, one can read about it, but the drug is not going to be available to treat the patient, so what good is it? And because the drug companies have to invest substantial sums and time for a return on investment that is 20 years old or longer, one has to be in an exclusive position. But at the same time, it is an issue more in the pharmaceutical industry because of health care costs and pricing than it is in different industries. And time and time again, it becomes clear that when we look at the products that are on the market today and that had their origin in academia, these products would never have been available to the public without a private intervention that, at an early stage, created value and a limited monopoly on the licensed inventions.

So the argument is that taxpayers, in both the United States and Europe, would be rather angry if there were no effort to make an economic impact with the research that is performed with their money. And the way one has an economic impact is by making sure that there are products and services on the market based on research that has been developed with those funds. That the innovators are capturing a return is fair: without an economic incentive, it would be difficult, if not impossible, for them to participate in the commercialization of innovation, on top of their demanding academic duties. That the institutions owning the inventions (that is, the universities) capture a return on their investment so that this return is put back into teaching and research and in protecting additional ideas is completely fair. It would actually be irresponsible for them not to do so. The commercialization of innovation derived from university settings makes economic and policy sense.

In contrast with the United States, Europe is much more oriented toward economic impact. If universities have an asset or idea, they have to make sure that the idea will have an impact on society. In fact, this was the rationale behind the Bayh–Dole Act: universities had ideas that were being shelved and not used because they were not aligning interests properly. But we can align interests by allowing both the universities and the federal government to own ideas, making sure that in their licensing deals, universities give preference to small firms and manufacturing companies in the United States so that the benefits generated, financial or otherwise, become recycled in the national economy.

Important Implications for the Developing World

On top of the bleakness of the prospects for new drugs, the decline in prescription drug sales, the lack of investors' confidence, the large number of corporate layoffs, and the high pricing of many innovative drugs, there is the need to deal with the demands from poorer countries to gain cheap and immediate access to new drugs. Although the Third World situation, with regard to pharmaceuticals, will be discussed to a fuller extent later in the book, one of the issues that needs to be resolved is how universities in scientifically innovative regions such as the United States and Europe can help other countries that do not have access to mainstream medicines and where their prices are very high. Because rich countries attract and capture talent from poor nations, as exemplified by the large number of successful foreign students and scientists in the United States, they should give something back in return.

One way to deal with this has been suggested: whenever possible in the licensing process, universities should seek preferential pricing and benefits for underserved patient populations.[23] Universities are in a negotiating position with the pharmaceutical industry where they could expect to get the regular royalty rate on drugs sold to the United States and Canada, but they could say that they would like a commitment from the company if they are supplying products to specific regions of the world so that the university waives its royalties and cooperates with the company in other ways, if the pharmaceutical firms lower prices in those areas of need. Of course, universities and companies are not going to be able to work in this way at times because doing so may prove to be a deal killer, but if it is possible to do so, for instance, 1 out of 10 times, it will have an impact. And there are certainly pharmaceutical companies, such as GlaxoSmithKline and Novartis, that are embracing this now, too, and this remains a good deal for them.

There are many fine universities in the less-developed regions of the world, with excellent human capital and with great potential to develop their R&D infrastructures if only institutions such as the World Bank, which has some programs on innovation, financing, and intellectual property exploitation for the benefit of the regions they cover, were more proactive, efficient, and effective. Needless to say, for whatever reason, and judging by results, the World Bank has been quite ineffectual in helping universities in developing countries to raise their R&D performance. Intellectual property is vital, so we must talk about these issues, about the core principles within it, and about the setting up of expectations around the world. This is very important because if one cannot give people this limited monopoly and enforce intellectual property rights in these countries, then it is hard to create the necessary incentives for companies to do business in them. So we come full circle: intellectual property rights continue to be crucial in this respect.

Countries like China and India and the entire surrounding region, which is booming especially in biotech, are quite interesting. Their potential cannot be ignored. Certainly, seeking intellectual property protection in China was difficult a decade ago, and at that time, rights were not enforceable. When companies do business with these countries, they should look at it not from the point of competing head-to-head, but from the standpoint of developing skills and capabilities and assets, and they should see what they can learn from each other, which is a prosperous way to think about the issue. Some of the more conservative politicians in the United States and Europe want to put up trade barriers and the like against these countries, which may not be the right approach. There is a lot to learn. Instead, policy perspectives in this sector should focus on the cost of licensing, allocating more funding for proof-of-concept in academia and clarity in ownership, always remembering that it is only through the efficient translation of innovation into commercial and useful medical products that we can not only accelerate progress in health care but also create more than remarkable benefits for society.

Notes

1. Mowery, D.C., Rosenberg N., 1991. Technology and the Pursuit of Economic Growth. Cambridge University Press, New York, p. 123.
2. Kennedy, D., 2003. Industry and academia in transition. Science 302, 1293.
3. Refer to the National Institutes of Health Web site for further information at http://www.nih.gov/.
4. European Communities, 2008. A More Research-Intensive and Integrated European Research Area: Science, Technology, and Competitiveness Key Figures Report 2008/2009. Office for Official Publications of the European Communities, Luxembourg. http://ec.europa.eu/research/era/pdf/key-figures-report2008-2009_en.pdf; see also Meyer, D., 2009. European R&D levels "stagnating." ZDNet UK, January 27, 2009. http://www.zdnetasia.com/news/business/0,39044229,62050353,00.htm.
5. A country such as Russia cannot even be discussed here because this nation, despite its long scientific heritage (especially in physics) and recent heavy investment in nanotechnology, is marred by funding shortages, an old-fashioned scientific establishment, and a profound lack of productivity in the life sciences.
6. Personal interview, London, UK, May 2007.
7. Edwards, M.G., Murray, F., Yu, R., 2003. Value creation and sharing among universities, biotechnology and pharma. Nature Biotechnology 21, 618–624.
8. Drews, J., 2000. Drug discovery: a historical perspective. Science 287, 1960.
9. Sánchez-Serrano, I., 2006. Success in translational research: lessons from the development of bortezomib. Nature Reviews Drug Discovery 5, 107–114.
10. Interview with Tom Maniatis, Cambridge, MA, April 2009.
11. Personal interview with a technology transfer officer, UK, May 2007.
12. Interview with Zina Affas, London, UK, May 2007.
13. Mitchell, P., 2009. Venture capital shifts strategies, startups suffer. Nature Biotechnology 27, 103.
14. Ibid.

15. Patricof, A., Dinallo, E., 2009. Stopping start-ups. New York Times, August 30, 2009. http://www.nytimes.com/2009/08/31/opinion/31patricof.html.
16. Interview with Zina Affas, London, UK, May 2009.
17. Interview with Tom Hockaday, Oxford, UK, May 2007.
18. Interview with Martin Wood and Robert Lang, London, UK, May 2007.
19. Interview with Richard Seabrook, London, UK, May 2007.
20. The Wellcome Trust's funding agreements, as well as all the grant conditions of the trust, are freely available on the Wellcome Trust's Web site (http://www.wellcome.ac.uk/Funding/index.htm), so that anyone who wants to apply for funding with this charity can see what the terms and conditions are.
21. Heller, M., 1998. The tragedy of the anticommons: property in the transition from Marx to markets. Harvard Law Review 111, 621–688.
22. See Note 6.
23. "Nine points to consider in licensing university technology," white paper signed by the California Institute of Technology, Cornell University, Harvard University, the Massachusetts Institute of Technology, Stanford University, University of California, University of Illinois–Chicago, University of Illinois–Urbana-Champaign, University of Washington, and the Wisconsin Alumni Research Foundation. http://www.mcgill.ca/files/senate/IP_Policy_9_points_to_consider.pdf.

9 The Biotechnology World and Its Challenges

As discussed previously in this book, biotechnology has gained a preeminent position in the pharmaceutical industry. It has become an industry in its own right as well as an important source of products and innovation for the long-established but ailing pharmaceutical companies (see Figure 9.1). Biotechnology products account for approximately 20% of the pharmaceutical industry's revenues and it is estimated that in the year 2014, 50% of the top 100 drugs will be of biotechnology origin.[1] Biotechnology has also become a bridge between academia and big pharma as pharma struggles to access academic research directly. Albeit most of the biotechnology products approved in the last several years have come from a small handful of already-established large-cap US biotech companies, such as Amgen, former Genentech, Genzyme, and Gilead Sciences, which rank among the top biotechnology firms in the world in terms of sales and market capitalization (see Table 9.1 for a ranking of the top 10 biotechnology firms; Table 9.2 is a list of the top biotech drugs), we can see to a lesser extent that smaller players are getting some market share as well, especially in highly specialized areas (see Figure 9.1).

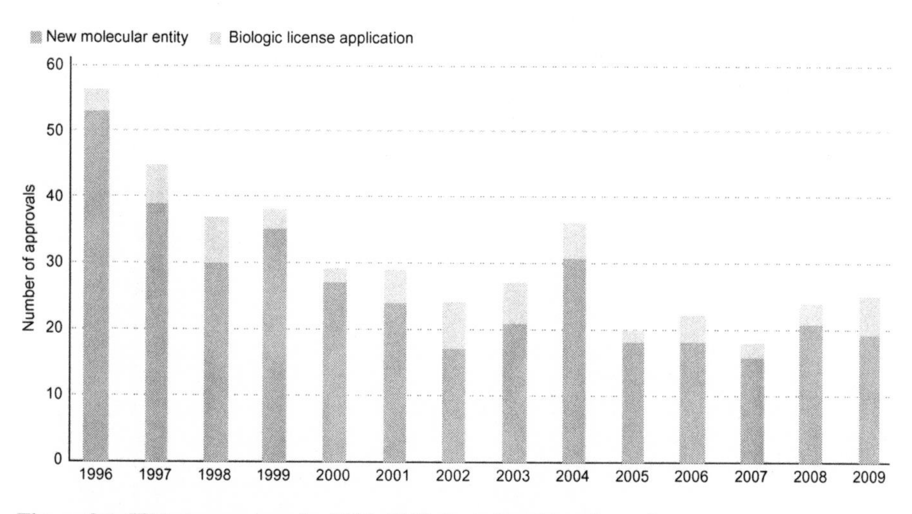

Figure 9.1 FDA drug approvals, 1996–2009, including biotech products.
Source: Ernst and Young, 2010. Beyond Borders: Global Biotechnology Report. 2010, p. 88.
© Ernst & Young, LLC. Reprinted with permission. All rights reserved.

The World's Health Care Crisis. DOI: 10.1016/B978-0-12-391875-8.00009-3

Table 9.1 Research and Development Expenditures of Leading Public US Biotech Companies (in Millions of Dollars, Ranked by 2009 R&D Expenditures)

Company	R&D Expenditures			Revenues			R&D as % of Revenues	
	2008	2009	% CHG.	2008	2009	% CHG.	2008	2009
Amgen	3,030	2,864	(5.5)	15,003	14,642	(2.4)	20.2	19.6
Biogen-Idec	1,097	1,283	17.0	4,098	4,377	6.8	26.8	29.3
Gilead Sciences	733	940	28.3	5,336	7,011	31.4	13.7	13.4
Genzyme	1,308	865	(33.9)	4,605	4,516	(1.9)	28.4	19.2
Celgene	2,671	795	(70.2)	2,238	2,677	19.6	119.4	29.7
Cephalon	404	442	9.3	1,975	2,192	11.0	20.5	20.1
Vertex Pharmaceuticals	360	401	11.3	176	102	(41.9)	205.4	393.8
Regeneron Pharmaceuticals	278	399	43.4	238	379	59.1	116.6	105.1
Exelixis	257	235	(8.8)	118	152	28.8	218.4	154.7
Amylin Pharmaceuticals Inc.	293	185	(36.9)	840	758	(9.7)	34.9	24.4

Source: Standard & Poor's, 2010. Industry surveys. Biotechnology. August 19, 2010, p. 19.

Table 9.2 Top 10 Biotechnology Drugs (Ranked by 2009 Global Sales)

Product	Company	Indicated Use	Sales (mil. $)		
			2008	**2009**	**%CHG.**
1. Enbrel	Amgen/Pfizer/ Takeda	Rheumatoid arthritis/ psoriatic arthritis	6,199	6,469	4.4
2. Remicade	J&J/Merck	Rheumatoid arthritis/ Crohn's disease	5,302	5,922	11.7
3. Avastin	Roche	Oncology	4,818	5,744	19.2
4. Rituxan	Roche/Biogen IDEC	B-cell non-Hodgkin's lymphoma/rheumatoid arthritis	5,481	5,620	2.5
5. Humira	Abbott Labs	Rheumatoid and other forms of arthritis	4,540	5,566	22.6
6. Epogen/ Procrit	Amgen/J&J	Red blood cell enhancement	5,163	4,964	(3.9)
7. Herceptin	Roche	Oncology	4,712	4,862	3.2
8. Lantus	Sanofi-Aventis	Diabetes	3,600	4,293	19.3
9. Neulasta	Amgen	Restoration of white blood cells	3,318	3,355	1.1
10. Aranesp	Amgen	Red blood cell enhancement	3,457	2,930	(15.2)
Total, top 10			46,590	49,725	6.7

Source: Standard & Poor's, 2010. Industry surveys. Biotechnology. August 19, 2010, p. 18. © EvaluatePharma®. Reprinted with permission.

The United States is the leader of the biotechnology industry, although there are a large number of important biotech companies in Europe (see Table 9.3; in fact, there are more public and private biotechnology companies in Europe than in the United States) and, there are also some in Asia, Canada, and Israel. The reasons for this are simple: as we saw in Chapters 3, 7 and 8, when biotechnology was born as an industry in the United States, the country created a formidable industrial, financial, and regulatory infrastructure similar to the one that Germany had created a century earlier with the pharmaceutical industry, which was quite ahead of Europe's response in embracing the new technology. This was the case despite the fact that it was in Europe where a large number of the key basic research findings that led to biotechnology were made (such as the discovery of the structure of DNA by James Watson and Francis Crick and the elucidation of the Operon Model by Jacques Monod and his colleagues). Furthermore, US universities, the federal government, and the long-established pharmaceutical firms, such as Roche, Merck, Lilly, and GlaxoWellcome, invested heavily in the nascent technology in the United States and created a cross-fertilization between

Table 9.3 Number of Biotechnology Firms, 2008 or Latest Available Year

	Biotechnology Firms	**Dedicated Biotechnology Firms**	**Year**	**Type of Firm**	**% Dedicated**
United States	3,492	2,325	2007	Biotech R&D firms	67%
France	1067	676	2008	Biotech R&D firms	63%
Spain	942	305	2008	Biotech firms	32%
Japan	925	..	2008	Biotech firms	N/A
Korea	833	358	2008	Biotech firms/Dedicated biotech R&D firms	43%
Germany	645	531	2009	Biotech firms	82%
Australia	**527**	**384**	**2006**	Biotech firms	73%
United Kingdom (*)	487	..	2010	Biotech firms	N/A
Switzerland (**)	288	184	2008	Biotech R&D firms	64%
Netherlands (***)	206	72	2008	Biotech R&D firms	35%
Italy	197	117	2008	Biotech R&D firms	59%
New Zealand	186	93	2009	Biotech firms	50%
Ireland	167	71	2009	Biotech R&D firms	43%
Norway	161	..	2007	Biotech R&D firms	N/A
Belgium	**145**	**122**	**2006**	Biotech firms	84%
Finland	**141**	**77**	**2007**	Biotech R&D firms	55%
Denmark	124	79	2007	Biotech R&D firms	64%
Austria	**121**	**111**	**2006**	Biotech firms	92%

Portugal	120	55	2008	Biotech R&D firms	46%
Sweden	100	58	2009	Biotech R&D firms	58%
Czech Republic	93	69	2009	Biotech R&D firms	74%
South Africa	78	38	2006	Biotech firms	49%
Poland	37	16	2009	Biotech firms	43%
Estonia	30	25	2008	Biotech R&D firms	83%
Slovak Republic	11	8	2009	Biotech R&D firms	73%
Slovenia	10	3	2008	Biotech R&D firms	30%

Source: OECD, Biotechnology Statistics Database, January 2011.
There is no new data for countries in bold.
1. Biotechnology firm: a firm that uses biotechnology to produce goods or services and/or to perform biotechnology R&D. These firms are captured by biotechnology firm surveys. Biotechnology R&D firms: a firm that performs biotechnology R&D. These firms are captured by R&D surveys. 2. Dedicated biotechnology firm: a biotechnology firm whose predominant activity involves the application of biotechnology techniques to produce goods or services and/or to perform biotechnology R&D. These firms are captured by biotechnology firm surveys. 3. Dedicated biotechnology R&D firms devote 75% or more of their total R&D to biotechnology R&D. These firms are captured by R&D surveys.
*For the United Kingdom, results exclude firms outside the medical and industrial biotechnology sectors e.g., agri-biotech and aquaculture-biotech firms; however, it is estimated that the majority of biotechnology companies in the UK are included.
**For Switzerland, dedicated Biotechnology R&D firms are defined as firms that have dedicated 100% or more of their total R&D to biotechnology R&D.
***For the Netherlands, results of the Dutch R&D survey are grossed up to the total target population which corresponds to all firms with 10 and more employees. However, due to the special way the survey population was established (i.e. some firms which were identified as biotechnology firms based on registers were added). The number of 206 biotechnology R&D firms also includes some firms with less than 10 employees. Their results were not grossed-up.

academia and industry that was fundamental in the translation of academic innovation into commercial biotechnology products. In addition, there are important cultural differences between the United States and (for example) Europe that may help explain why the United States is the leader on this front. For instance, entrepreneurial zest is far stronger in the United States than in Europe. As the Latin American joke perfectly frames it, "Americans make one cow to produce the milk of four cows; one day, when the cow suddenly drops dead, Americans become upset and irritated and ask, why has the cow died?" In addition, American business practice, more than any other in the world, is based on the concept of efficiency ("We want things here and we want them now!") and on a pragmatic approach and positive attitude toward failure ("If I fail, at least I gave it shot") that are in a strong contrast with the attitudes of their European counterparts, despite the fact that the extraordinary pool of highly talented minds in Europe is (at least in my opinion) far more creative and subtle than the American pool.

One of the major problems with Europe in this sector is that its history and its long-established structures cannot allow either the dynamism that is required to keep ahead of the game in this kind of cutting-edge business or the implementation of innovative fiscal policies that are considered normal in the United States. On the other hand, attitudes toward entrepreneurship between Europe and the United States could not be more different. Whereas Americans are ready to jump off a cliff to get whatever they want (many times at the expense of quality and mindless of the potential spillover effects of their risky behavior), Europeans are risk-averse: they value comfort and quality over risk. They wait for the Americans to jump off the cliff, and if all looks OK, they jump too; but if it does not look OK, then they will find another way to descend to the waters with enviable elegance.

Attitudes toward commercialization are different between the United States and Europe. As Mark McGrath, former head of technology transfer at the Friedrich Miescher Institute in Basel (now at Novartis, Switzerland) and someone who has worked on both the academic and private sides of research and development (R&D) in Europe, the United States, and Canada, has said, "I think that American scientists would have far fewer problems, by and large, about commercializing their research and exclusivizing it for commercial development. I think that there is this feeling among some European researchers that to put any sort of structure on their research is somehow bad, even though, of course, it's almost absolutely true to see that patenting something would only protect it for commercial development: it doesn't stop academic work on it."[2] One of the major problems in Europe is that the continent is inherently too divided—with its individual countries sometimes too unwilling to work together beyond what is strictly necessary—to reach a common goal. And as we have seen, Europe does not invest enough on its R&D or offer the same financial incentives to entrepreneurs as the United States does, so it cannot come close to the United States in terms of leadership in commercial biotechnology.

Of course, there are other players. Countries such as Canada and Israel (and even Cuba) are doing quite interesting things in biotechnology, as exemplified by the number of biotech companies that exist in these countries (or that have gone public, in the case of Canada) or the products they have launched, but they are just too small to compete with the United States or even Europe. China and India are waking up; their governments are investing in their best asset, their human capital; and important developments are taking place. For instance, the Chinese government announced in 2006 that it was going to increase its investment in biotech R&D to bring its technology R&D into a position of global leadership by 2020. India, too, is going through heavy industrialization, not only in high tech, but also in the area of pharmaceuticals and biotechnology. The development of this region will greatly depend on its economic growth and the solution of many of its key social, political, and economic issues—which are many—although it seems to me that they are, more than anything, a mine of golden opportunities for the West (in terms of R&D, access to human capital and naive patient populations, and of course market size[3]). But again, things may shift as these economies continue to grow and gain power. China, for example, is the biggest creditor of the United States,[4] holding foreign reserves of more than $2 trillion, about two thirds of which are assets that are denominated in US dollars.[5] And interestingly, as was recently reported in July 2009:

> *Chinese officials asked their American counterparts detailed questions about the health care legislation making its way through Congress. The president's budget director, Peter R. Orszag, answered most of their questions. But the Chinese were not particularly interested in the public option or universal care for all Americans. They wanted to know, in painstaking detail, how the health care plan would affect the deficit… Chinese officials expect that they will help finance whatever Congress and the White House settle on, mostly through buying Treasury debt, and like any banker, they wanted evidence that the United States had a plan to pay them back.*[6]

But in spite of its great promise, the biotech industry, like pharma, faces serious challenges worldwide—some of which, such as funding, have been exacerbated by the current credit crunch. Among these challenges, financial and commercial success is the most serious and deserves discussion. Biotech is not necessarily a "big commercial failure," as has been portrayed,[7] but it is true that even though some of these companies have good management, good science, huge budgets, and hundreds of people and biotech partners, they have been working in a vicious vortex for a while now in that they have never returned money to their shareholders. And this is very common in biotech. So why, among the thousands of biotech companies that have been created since the beginning of the industry and the huge amount of money that has been poured into it all over the world, have only an extremely small number of biotechnology companies succeeded in bringing products to the market or in becoming fully integrated firms?

The answer to this question is not at all straightforward because it is necessary to consider that the biotech industry is still a relatively young and, more important, highly innovative, sophisticated, and diversified industry that needs to go through a learning cycle, not only from an R&D point of view but also from a financial and managerial perspective, before it realizes its full potential. It is also necessary to have a maturing stage in science and technology, whereby scientific knowledge (across related scientific disciplines) reaches convergence. As Mark McGrath, from Novartis, reminds us:

> *I agree with the fact that it has taken [biotech firms] a long time to take [their products] to market, but I don't agree that that is a problem or in any way surprising.*

> *You know, monoclonal antibodies—the original protection for that, which was missed—would have expired by more than ten years now.... But, anyways, nothing was brought into the market for over twenty years after the initial discovery of monoclonal antibodies.... That's just the nature of 'innovation-to-the-market' process, and that just takes a long time. If you invented, for instance, a new gadget, it doesn't have to be tested as rigorously. And of course, when there is a bad result in biotech, then the issue is that that bad result could put the whole industry back and you have to take a step back, reassess what trials need to be done because of these disasters, and smoothly refollow again. And I think that the industry ran straight ahead as you would as there are always pioneers, and after the early discoveries, the making of the first plasmid and the recombinant proteins, recombinant insulin, EPO, some of the other things, some of them got to market, some of them won't, but of course, there are big problems when you try to engineer human proteins, put them back into human beings, in mammalian cells... I mean there're just a lot of technical hurdles to overcome, so it doesn't surprise me.*[8]

Furthermore, terms such as *failure* and *success* are very difficult to use in absolute terms in this particular industry because very few companies have actually succeeded in all respects. For instance, a company may succeed on its own in demonstrating proof of principle[9] in man of a particular drug but fail at becoming a fully integrated biotechnology firm or, worse, at returning money to its shareholders. Likewise, a company may succeed in returning money to its shareholders through products that it has developed or marketed through acquisition but fail at developing drugs on its own. What we can safely say is that failure, in a broad sense, in biotech obeys two major forces: scientific issues (attrition, deficient development, wrong therapeutic application, and novelty) and structural/organizational problems (incompetent management, weak funding base, and a crippled business model).

For example, when it comes to scientific reasons, the science of a large number of biotech companies fails to deliver because of attrition. And one sees attrition at every phase in the drug discovery and drug development process. The best companies have early attrition where they have made the least amount of investment (usually before Phase I); in other words, they kill a compound if it is not good enough in preclinical activity. Others, however, experience attrition in Phase I, usually owing to unexpected safety problems that they did not pick up on in animal studies, which is not surprising as one can never be a perfect predictor of what is going to happen when one moves from animal studies to human studies. This type of attrition is rare, but it happens. In addition, companies could also have poor or variable pharmacokinetics in humans such that a subpopulation of humans responds very poorly to the drug because metabolism issues could lead to toxicity. This is a problem because Phase I is about safety in a small number of patients. If one does a Phase I trial and enrolls, say, 60 patients, and the incidence of the safety signal is half a percent, one might miss half a percent of the total population that would have a very bad toxicity outcome because safety has been assayed in such as small population. This is not easily predicted and one cannot monitor for it, and as a result, one has a very serious problem when going to bigger trials. This was part of the problem in the development of drugs such as Vioxx (Merck) and Tysabri's (Biogen-Idec). It is generally claimed that the companies developing these drugs did not pick up the key safety signals arising in Phase I and Phase II. However, the idea that Vioxx's myocardial infarction (MI) excess or Tysabri's progressive multifocal leukoencephalopathy (PML) problem could be picked up in Phase I or II is *wrong*. Vioxx required a large randomized trial, and PML is so rare that it would be found only after approval.

Lack of efficacy in Phase II (in other words, when the drug does not hit the right target) is the most common cause of attrition in drug development. But sometimes biotech companies succeed in demonstrating efficacy in Phase II, albeit in a second or third line of treatment. The problem is that very often, companies that have been developing second- or third-line therapy drug studies in Phase II become greedy and say, "Well, it's working, so let's go for the big market. Let's open up the front-line therapy in Phase III!" The problem is that if a company is in frontline therapy, then it has a big population; if it is in a third-line therapy, however, then the company will have a much smaller population with a shorter duration of treatment. Therefore, companies that treat third line in Phase II and then want to go on the front line in Phase III are calling for trouble because this is a different population; not surprisingly, the drug fails.

This happens all the time. Syntex is a clear example of a company that failed for exactly this reason. So drugs fail in Phase I owing to lack of safety; they fail in Phase II because of a lack of efficacy; and then they fail in Phase III because of incompetence, because a drug should never make it to Phase III if it does not have robust data behind it, and a great deal of detection of potential problems depends on the rigor with which these studies are conducted. But because the probability of success increases to about 70% in Phase III (and so do the stocks of traded companies when they move their clinical programs from Phase II to Phase III), not all companies want to evaluate the clinical data *too* critically.

When it comes to the application of a potential drug to a particular disease, sometimes companies fail because they are targeting the wrong disease. This was the issue with Regeneron, a biotech company that developed powerful platforms based on targeted genomics, functionomics, and designer protein therapeutics but that suffered a major clinical failure in its early days because, as Roy Vagelos—the former luminary CEO of Merck, who later became chairman of Regeneron's board—has said, "The problem was that Regeneron had focused this sophisticated science on the most difficult diseases in the world: those poorly understood at the molecular level."[10] After Vagelos joined the board of the company, Regeneron reshaped its objectives and disease targets and managed, many years later, to bring a product to the market [Arcalyst (rilonacept)] for the treatment of a rare genetic inflammatory disease, cryopyrin-associated periodic syndrome (CAPS).[11] Or take a look at Exelixis, a company with a great discovery engine but very unremarkable development.

Other times, the technology of some start-up biotech companies is so novel and different that most people, including scientists, investors, and big pharma, fail to recognize their potential and make the life of such companies quite miserable. These types of companies have a hard time fund-raising. Such is the case of Myogenics/ProScript (in Cambridge, Massachusetts), which I have discussed elsewhere (see also preface and Chapter 13).[12] This company had in its hands a highly successful product (a boronic acid agent) in which no one believed. As such, this company was sold twice before being acquired indirectly by Millennium Pharmaceuticals (now part of the Japanese company Takeda), which initially was not interested in the company's leading compound, either. Luckily, Myogenics/ProScript had a very first-rate scientific staff that secured powerful and productive collaborations with other academic groups, with government agencies such as the National Institutes of Health (NIH)/ National Cancer Institute (NCI) and with cancer advocacy groups, that eventually, once within Millennium Pharmaceuticals, made a case to promote and rescue the anticancer agent bortezomib (Velcade). The story of how Myogenics/ProScript developed bortezomib makes one wonder how many companies with breakthrough technologies, such as this one, have perished because of a lack of understanding by the pharmaceutical industry and investors.

On the structural/organizational front, companies with promising products have failed not because of their science or because of the lack of financial backup, but because of poor and inexperienced management. Take, for example, Millennium Pharmaceuticals, a company that had the best science in the world but that never brought a single product to the market on its own. It did market Velcade, for the treatment of multiple myeloma, but this was through the acquisition of ProScript, as I discussed earlier in this chapter.[13] The problem with Millennium is that it grew too big, had too many research projects, and did not focus. As a result, it lost a great deal of money, and finally, by the time Velcade came to the market, there was a loss of confidence in the management of the company, and there were concerns about its size and future direction. So the company had no option except to be bought, which eventually happened when Takeda came to its rescue.

Even a few of the largest companies today (in terms of market capitalization) could hardly be considered "unquestionable" successes, as they struggled during their early days. Biogen, for instance, despite its initial powerful R&D and the financial resources committed to it, would have been doomed to perish in its early years had it not been for its board of directors. Distressed by the more than incompetent way its founder and CEO, Nobel laureate Walter Gilbert, was managing the company, the board decided to replace him with a more competent CEO. Since that time, the company has managed to bring most of its products to market via acquisition (and, according to some people, luck). Similarly, Genzyme would have not become the company that it is today had Henri Termeer, an experienced executive at Baxter, not come on board as the CEO and steered the company in the right direction. Termeer has done a fantastic job in managing this company and recognizing a niche in human genetic diseases, where the company has relatively little competition. Genzyme is a very successful company, and it made it completely on its own.

Amgen, the largest biotech pharmaceutical company in the world, was not exempt from managerial problems in the beginning, either. In fact, Amgen has made lots of money based on two products that were developed in academic labs: erythropoietin and granulocyte colony-stimulating factor (GCSF; Neupogen). This company has never really developed a powerful, in-house scientific team. It has become a big pharma-like company.

Even the biotech company that some consider the most successful and innovative enterprise of its kind, Genentech, had to be rescued by Roche, Lilly, and Merck in its early years.[14] One important characteristic of the Genentech-Roche relationship was that before Roche bought Genentech in its entirety in 2009, Roche was very hands-off with Genentech. Now that Roche has acquired Genentech completely, it is feared that the value and culture of this first-rate research biotech company will be destroyed, as happened in 1970 when Parke-Davis was acquired by Warner-Lambert (which in turn was acquired by Pfizer) and when the promising Genetics Institute was acquired by American Home Products.

In fact, the current wave of mergers and acquisitions that has taken place in the pharmaceutical industry has created a great deal of concern, not only for the disruptive effect that this has on the pharmaceutical companies themselves but also for the effects that this has on smaller biotech companies. Many biotech people are concerned that the partnership with pharma is at risk right now because if pharma is losing profits, if pharma is laying off people, and if companies are merging, there will be fewer and fewer companies to partner with biotech and to underwrite some of its research.

Even more concerning is the fact that with the mergers, new managerial structures are created, which jeopardize the survival of some promising pharma and biotech projects. And these fears are not without some foundation because the biotech companies that collaborate with big pharma now have to find a way to figure out their new politics. And so, if a given biotech company has a drug that is in the hands of a mega-merged pharma firm, and they have a portfolio of, say, 50−70 molecules, smaller biotech companies cannot know where they stand in the pipeline because the bigger pharma firm will not tell them. The project manager in the big pharma firm will tell the smaller biotech company that it should not worry. Yet the fact that it cannot deliver probably means that the small biotech company is not very important at all. This creates a lot of tension and great disincentive. One cannot do this kind of work with complicated managing structures where the incentives are not perfectly aligned: it just implodes on itself.

I also believe that in addition to all I have said, there is some kind of barrier to entry in biotechnology (similar to the one that exists in the pharmaceutical industry). In other words, once a handful of successful companies that have survived through natural selection (and whose origins can be traced back to early stages in the history of the commercialization of biotechnology) take the leadership, the system becomes locked so that it becomes very difficult, if not impossible, for newcomers to succeed. Indeed, many biotech companies, such as Modern Bioscience in London, have developed a business model whereby they have no expectations to become fully integrated firms carrying out discovery, development, and marketing. Instead, they license interesting leads from university settings, take compounds through proof of principle in man (Phase I and Phase II), and then sell them off to big pharma. According to Tom Maniatis,[15] a brilliant former Harvard scientist who pioneered the recombinant DNA technology and who has seen the complete development of biotech and participated on both the academic and entrepreneurial sides of this field:

> *Nowadays the situation with biotech companies is completely different from years ago. So basically, what happened is that after the big biotech companies, type Amgen, Genentech, Genzyme...became established, it became clear that that template, the goal of becoming a fully integrated firm from discovery research all the way to drug approval, would no longer work. And it wouldn't work because a*

combination of impatience of the investors: venture capitalists don't like to wait fifteen years to get a return.... And also it is a combination of resources, both financial and human: you can't generate all these companies that are fully integrated and have high quality people in every position, within pharmacology, and preclinical, and all that kind of stuff. So what began to happen, the combination of the constraints in venture capital and, you know, in a sense the lack of enough trained people in all these different areas, biotech companies became really discovery companies, and that's really what it is today: it is that the biotech companies make the discoveries, they outsource much of the preclinical science and pharmacology, and so on, to get to the point where they are attractive, and then they either partner with a big company and codevelop or they are bought. And you know, Sirtris is a perfect example of that, where they create a lot of buzz about an interesting new area. They do some very basic discovery and then they are bought. And that is probably the extreme example on one side.

Maniatis provides a full explanation for this:

I think what is happening today is that the in-house discovery research efforts of big pharma have shrunk, and almost every big pharmaceutical company has made major cuts in their discovery research. Obviously, they still have very large efforts in the downstream part, in the development part, from pharmacology through animal testing through clinical trials. And that seems to be the current configuration of the industry, is that little biotech companies that raise capital and partner are sold, and I don't know how long this is going to last.

Now that decisions are made so early on, it is going to be so extremely rare that a biotech company actually becomes a fully integrated firm. First of all, there will not be fully integrated companies, and second, they are unlikely to exist for a very long period of time, because if they don't succeed, they are going to disappear, and if they do succeed, they are going to be bought, because I think that big pharma has concluded that they can actually, as a financial model, do much better by buying off *mature and productive and demonstrated successful biotech companies than by having this enormous in-house research, and it makes sense for the way that happens ... what you realize is that the biotech companies have a much more direct access to the cutting-edge research in academia than big pharma.... Well, first of all, the biotech companies are usually generated through founding by academics, so ... it is mostly the connections of the academics to the broad field that brings the strength to the biotech company. Again, Sirtris is an example. What Christoph Westfall did was to capture an entire field in sirtuins. Their scientific board is enormous! But part of their strategy was to really get all the thought leaders in the field pouring all their ideas and critical insights into the company. And big pharma cannot do that. One, there is no incentive. You know, getting paid $1,200 for spending a day in Merck is very different from actually being engaged in an exciting start-up, both financially and otherwise.*[16]

And for big pharma, this works out perfectly, as Timothy Wright, vice president and global head of Translational Research at Novartis, told me:

I think this approach would work mainly because with the expanding knowledge of the genome and the fact that no single pharma could work on all of the new targets *that they're going to find. There is a need for a lot more work being done on the early targets, early phase work on the targets ... and I can see that being done to some degree in academia or bridge, in a hot tech area, and I think that it is very viable to be able to generate enough capital to test out these ideas, much less viable to get the capital to take it through the clinic all the way, as the latest number is somewhere around $800 million on average to $1 billion to develop a drug. It's not likely to be able to do that within a biotech.*[17]

Though we are in an economically depressed time (something that is not going to last forever), the venture community and a highly sophisticated capital market structure continue to exist, which makes it relatively straightforward to start a biotech company with seed funding. The problem is that there are too many biotech companies (ranging from around 1,500 to 2,000) that compete for limited funding, and seldom do these companies have good businesspeople, good discovery people, and good development people under the same roof.

Given this scenario, it is legitimate to ask, then, the following question: what does it take for a small biotech company to succeed nowadays? But here the answer, again, depends to a great extent on the background of the company (see Table 9.4 for the different types of biotech firms that exist today) and what we define as success.

For Jo Walton, a Credit Suisse pharmaceutical analyst, "if the biotech company has a platform, what it could do is to develop the first product in the platform and then sell it off incredibly cheaply. So they make it really easy for big drug companies to know them."[18] As a good example, Walton cites Cosmo Pharmaceuticals, an Italian company that has developed a technology for delivering drugs to the transverse colon.[19] This company licensed their first product to Shire for a very small amount of money. Shire gave them validation and a bit of money, and then Cosmo went on to develop their next product. They hoped to keep this next product for a bit longer, to maintain a bit more of the value. Then they licensed it to the next company in the food chain, Forest Labs. Cosmo received some m oney back and then hoped that this platform would keep generating products.

Table 9.4 Types of Biotechnology Companies

— Therapeutics
— Diagnostics
— Genomics, proteomics
— Enabling technologies
— Industrial biotech
— Drug discovery technologies and services
— Drug delivery
— Agbiotech
— Other

One might object that the problem with this strategy is that small companies run the high risk of giving away too much of their intellectual property, but it is important to point out that platform companies have to understand that investors need to diversify risk. They need other companies to sign on to that technology and give them money and then hope that the platform will deliver the company enough products so that by the third or fourth product, everybody appreciates that it is going to work and the company receives a big slice of the action and copromotional rights.

Now if one looks at general practitioner-based products (i.e., drugs), the preceding strategy is never going to work, and success will depend greatly on the type of drug and how well these companies can partner with larger companies. A small biotech company developing a drug for a large market that needs a large number of reps will never be able to maintain 1,000 reps on its own, so it will have to work in partnership with a big pharmaceutical company to reach its market and will have to give up many of its rights, including copromotional rights. But small oncology companies (specialty companies) can, in contrast, afford to partner their products: they can keep the rights to copromotion because they only need 100–200 sales representatives.

For example, a few years ago, UK-based Celltech Group, during the clinical development phase, gave its rights to Pfizer on its CDP-870, for the potential treatment of certain autoimmune and inflammatory diseases, including rheumatoid arthritis and Crohn's disease, in exchange for royalties and milestone payments; but then Celltech got full support from Pfizer for the subsequent marketing of the drug.[20] Had the company remained on its own through the trials, then in the next stage (i.e., filing for registration), it would be looking for a partner to market the drug. But that partner, for providing 150–200 reps, would ask for a large slice of the pie. Should the company wish to pursue going it alone on its first product, then it will risk disappearing, as Immunex did when it tried to market Embrel alone, for which it had no production capacity. Amgen had to come to the rescue.[21]

In general, many observers argue that the main issue is to have the right idea, the right target. But having the right target is not enough, as we have seen. Many early-stage biotech companies may have the right idea, but they need to figure out how they could convert great ideas and targets into effective and valuable therapeutic products. They also need to foresee what the future business and therapeutic trends may be and attempt to minimize costs and maximize the acquisition of knowledge of particular drug targets via effective collaboration with academic centers, greatly using connections with particular academic labs in a process that I have described elsewhere as a *trade of assets*.[22]

Early-stage biotech start-ups may want to avoid spending their limited resources on animal facilities and on doing an unnecessary number of animal models. What they need to do is focus their energies and resources on identifying their target, screen it as effectively as they can, show that the mechanism works in animals, and then move on to a small patient population study because if they get something that *really* works, they will be able to pick it up quickly. Now, if an agent shows some promise, then companies will have to carry out further assays in larger patient populations.

Jackie Hunter, from GlaxoSmithKline, says, "I'd be thinking if I wanted to be really successful in biotech, there are these patient groups that I know I can test these mechanisms in very easily, therefore working backward from the patient, so I spin on this disease and apply my targets to that disease. So one would focus basically up to proof of concept in man, Phase I clinical trials or Phase II. I'd pick a disease area where I could use my patients to try what I am actually thinking."[23] And according to Julian Adams, the CSO of Infinity Pharmaceutical, "the few biotechs that succeeded managed to harmonize the business, the science, and the drug development, and even the commercialization with excellent execution."

Adams augurs success for those companies that manage their growth: "Companies that are working on some smaller portfolios and are doing innovation not only at the level of discovery, but also rigorous clinical developments to figure out what subset of disease can be targeted … and with this, we get to personalized medicine and other aspects that I think will be the future. I think there will be a lot of technologies in the future that'll allow us to do clinical trials in smaller populations so you can get an approval with a very narrow level and your label expansion will happen in the Phase IV and … once you have a marketed product, but at least you have a proven mechanism and a proven pathway that isn't questioned as if the drug works, you know it! It's a question of what is the breath of the indication."[24]

Of course, some therapeutic areas present more complexities than others. For instance, a biotech start-up that would focus on the development of drugs to treat central nervous system ailments, such as Alzheimer's disease, would find a great many challenges owing to the complexity of the disease and the fact that a great deal of knowledge about it remains to be unveiled. Crucially, the time that clinical trials for this kind of disease would take is certainly beyond the capacity of most small biotech enterprises and the patience of their investors, while the end points are very difficult to determine. On the other hand, diseases like migraine or cancer are better biotech targets. In the case of cancer, many small biotech companies, such as Amgen in the beginning and now Celgene, have proved that they could make it big by bringing oncology drugs to the market. In the case of migraine, a small company could easily do a very effective acute migraine study with 60 people. It can be done with an adaptive design. Some drugs for the treatment of migraines have actually shown their effects in the first 10 patients in a short time.[25]

Though US biotech companies are the leaders in the field, some little biotech companies in Europe are not ineffective; for instance, look at Almirall (Spain) and Actelion (Switzerland). They are strong players with a domestic heritage, and they have kept more of the value to themselves as well as scientists. Almirall spends roughly only €70 million a year on R&D. How did they manage to develop three new compounds in 10 years, which is very unusual? The answer is that there were many good Spanish scientists who had done some work internationally but then wanted to return to Spain. They also have cheaper bench hours because European scientists usually do not have such high debt levels when they get out of university, as people have graduating from US universities. And the science is strong in Europe, so that is not a problem. This is probably how Europeans can compete.

German companies tend to have a problem with their educational system because it is very long, so that scientists end up being relatively old before they come out of the university system. For instance, at the English firm Glaxo, the head of combinatorial chemistry should be in his early 30s, and he has risen high in his specialization in a very large company in a short period of time. That would not happen at a German firm such as Bayer, where the head of combinatorial chemistry would be much older. However, a common trait between US and European biotech firms is that they are characterized by a small number of young and highly enthusiastic scientists (see Table 9.5 on the percentage of biotechnology firms with fewer than 50 employees in OECD countries). In every biotech company, employees have a stake in the company, so the "biotechies" have a proportionally larger stake in the success of that company. And attracting this kind of motivated talent is a major problem in big pharma and part of the reason why biotech is outperforming and will continue to outperform big pharma.

As has been reiterated before, pharmaceutical companies are always open to input from biotech, and biotech companies should take advantage of this fact. Accordingly, and independently of the financial crisis (which should, in theory, represent a bonanza for the pharmaceutical industry given the large number of cash-hungry biotech start-ups that are in peril of extinction today), the early strategic alliance teams of big pharma companies need to be perhaps even more active in engaging biotech start-ups to see what they may have and how to facilitate interaction with these companies.

Some companies, such as Novartis, have an internal venture capital fund that can be used to help support novel ideas, and that is one way in which a pharma company could help in the biotech area. Novartis also has the Genomics Institute of the Novartis Research Foundation, based in La Jolla, California, which has a very collaborative partnership with the nearby Scripps Research Institute. This collaboration is very innovative and entrepreural. The foundation has the ability to spin out new companies with the capacity of generating compounds for which the foundation has the right of first refusal. In 2009, Merck, too, announced its own BioVentures program.[26] This is another interface model between biotech, pharma, and academic institutions, especially nowadays, when the financial crisis that afflicts the global markets has given rise, perhaps exaggeratedly, to the speculation that a large portion of venture capital funding may be drying up[27] or at least diminishing. And funding, or lack thereof, is always a latent human concern.

Providing adequate financial resources for biotech is always important because while biotech, among several other functions, exists as a bridge between academia and big pharma, it also provides a broad incubator space for ideas, some of which will eventually reach a point where they could attract enough capital on their own and become a source of revenue but more likely be moved into big pharma for full development. Government agencies, too, especially during these times of financial turbulence, should come to the rescue of early-stage biotech companies.

Before closing this chapter, let us examine the following case scenario, which illustrates something that is very important to understand. As I said earlier, even though

Table 9.5 Percentage of Biotechnology Firms with Fewer than 50 Employees, 2008 or Latest Available Year

	Less than 50 Employees (%)	Year	Type of Firm
New Zealand	90.0	2009	Dedicated biotech firms
Estonia	90.0	2009	Biotech R&D firms
South Africa	**89.0**	**2006**	**Dedicated biotech firms**
Germany	87.8	2009	Dedicated biotech firms
Austria	**86.0**	**2006**	**Dedicated biotech firms**
United Kingdom	84.0	2010	Biotech firms
Spain	**81.0**	**2008**	**Dedicated biotech firms**
Denmark	81.0	2007	Biotech R&D firms
Slovenia	80.0	2008	Biotech R&D firms
Belgium	**78.0**	**2006**	**Dedicated biotech firms**
United States	76.0	2007	Biotech R&D firms
Poland	75.0	2009	Dedicated biotech firms
Canada	**75.0**	**2005**	**Dedicated biotech firms**
France	71.7	2008	Biotech R&D firms
Finland	**71.0**	**2007**	**Biotech R&D firms**
Italy	69.0	2008	Biotech R&D firms
Ireland	67.8	2009	Biotech R&D firms
Portugal	65.0	2008	Biotech R&D firms
Switzerland	64.0	2008	Biotech R&D firms
Korea	60.9	2008	Biotech R&D firms
Czech Republic	60.2	2009	Biotech R&D firms
Norway	59.0	2007	Biotech R&D firms
Slovak Republic	54.5	2009	Biotech R&D firms
Netherlands (*)	47.9	2008	Biotech R&D firms
Sweden	44.0	2009	Biotech R&D firms
Japan	42.5	2008	Biotech firms

Source: OECD, Biotechnology Statistics Database, January 2011.
Note: The majority of biotechnology firms in OECD countries have fewer than 50 employees.
There is no new data for countries in bold.
*For the Netherlands, results of the Dutch R&D survey are grossed up to the total target population which corresponds to all firms with 10 and more employees. However, due to the special way the survey population was established (i.e. some firms which were identified as biotechnology firms based on registers were added). The number of 206 biotechnology R&D firms also includes some firms with less than 10 employees. Their results were not grossed-up.

funding could be a major limitation for small biotech enterprises, there are instances in which biotech companies are well funded, yet they still fail. Besides management, I mentioned science, but I need to be clear about what I mean. Because companies often have a single purpose in whatever particular target they are going after, they seriously need to plan for failure because the number of ideas and compounds that fail in the clinic is high and the rule for drug development is attrition; in other words, success is the exception. So if one sets up a company based on one or two ideas—and many of these biotech companies are based only on one or two ideas—even though they are novel and they may have many merits, the probability is that they will fail. Before setting up a biotech company, entrepreneurs should make sure that they have enough ideas and a broad collection of intellectual property that they can pursue in parallel, to a point where one of them could be fully developed (one at a time, perhaps, because the cost of taking things forward is very high), keeping in mind that if that one product fails, the others could quickly come to the fore. And that is the key.

Companies should also make sure that they have sufficiently plentiful revenue streams. If one looks at many of the more successful companies, it becomes clear that they had a revenue stream early on, either because of some intellectual property that they had licensed or because of some niche compound or other product that they could market. One example of this is Celgene with thalidomide, which can be used for the treatment of multiple myeloma as well as other diseases. As cited earlier, the Swiss biotech company Actelion Pharmaceuticals failed in its first program but was able to manage with another program so that they became a $1-billion company. So having a revenue stream is key, as is having an array of ideas that allows one to test one idea at a time. In addition, because it is often too costly to bring more than one product forward at a time, companies sometimes need a backup plan for a better succession of potential products.

An important element that needs to be addressed is the performance of big clinical trials. Most early-stage biotech companies are not familiar with how really good clinical trials should be done. Thus, not only do they refrain from doing big clinical trials, but they also refrain from doing definitive clinical trials. Most of them would not have what one would consider translational medicine; in other words, they have not developed in-house capabilities to obtain information on how a patient is responding to a specific treatment at a given time. Instead, they often bring in consultants to help them design the trials. The aforementioned case of Myogenics/ProScript was exceptional because without enough financial resources, this company secured translational medicine of the highest order thanks to collaboration with academic basic science and clinical groups and the support of federal agencies such as the NCI.[28]

Because of the likelihood for attrition in their first compound and because their initial clinical trials may contain flaws, many companies may have to go back into the lab to bring in a backup. Most of the time, these companies do not have the luxury of backups because of their limited funding. If a big company has a target that gives it great confidence based on preclinical biology, in human genetics, it will have a series of compounds from different chemical structures and series to make sure that it has the ability to test out the compounds and the concept in the clinic. And when the company gets information from the clinic about the first compound, it often will go back and come up with separate series of different experiments that will address any block found, and it will also invest in preclinical testing to determine whether a block is a problem of toxicology or pharmacokinetics, which it will then be able to address. But as everyone knows, many biotechs, especially now, have one shot and if they do not succeed, they are done. Many of these companies are thinking from a registration standpoint, but they are not thinking how the company can generate the biology around a specific compound or how it is going to make a go/no-go decision. Because most of these companies are often operating on a shoestring, they do not have the ability to generate the biomarkers. They lack the biomarkers to show whether their compound is hitting the target or has the appropriate biology in the indication or in healthy volunteers. They are missing pieces in their early development program, and so many times, they end up with incomplete data or fail simply because they went for a study design that did not cast their compound adequately. As said already, sometimes small companies go for a big market indication, whereas if they had chosen a small niche market indication with the appropriate scientific input, they might have been able to show that their compound worked.

Finally, another problem with smaller biotech companies is that they often misunderstand the attitude of the regulators. In other words, the fact that regulators may encourage them to develop a certain agent is far removed from the approval of such agents. However, as Thomas Lönngren, former executive director of EMEA, has said, "If I were a scientist in a company and started to develop a clinical program in order to develop a product, I would seek scientific advice with the regulators as early as possible—absolutely. Then I would try to attract the best expertise, of course, that I could get in this area… and then design my clinical trials in a way that answers all the questions that are being asked." He continued to say that companies should avoid "making the mistake of believing that the clinical trials will answer all the questions for you. So you need to have the perspective that even if you are designing the clinical trials in this quite artificial environment, and when you are selecting the patients in this way and so on, … you need to have an understanding of what will happen with this product when it is coming out of the clinical reality… that I should probably have a look into it, and this is why EMEA is asking companies now to submit a risk-management plan."[29]

To keep things in perspective, success in bringing new drugs to the market in the biotech sector depends greatly on maintaining a fine balance between drug discovery, development, fund-raising, external partnerships and collaborations, and marketing capabilities.

Notes

1. Standard and Poor's, Industry surveys. Health care: Pharmaceuticals, June 2010.
2. Interview with Mark McGrath, Basel, May 2007.
3. Wallack, T., 2008. Drug makers stick by China. Boston Globe, March, 14, 2008. http://www.boston.com/business/articles/2008/03/14/drug_makers_stick_by_china/.

4. Setser, B., 2008. China: creditor to the rich. China Security 4 (4), 17–23. http://www.cfr.org/content/publications/attachments/CS12_3.pdf.
5. Evans, T., 2009. China–U.S. relationship called "most important" in world. CNN, November 17, 2009. http://edition.cnn.com/2009/WORLD/asiapcf/11/16/china.us.relations/index.html.
6. Cooper, H., Wines, M., Sanger, D.E., 2009. China's role as U.S. lender alters dynamics for Obama. New York Times, November 14, 2009. http://www.nytimes.com/2009/11/15/world/asia/15china.html?hp.
7. Pisano, G., 2006. The Science Business: The Promise, the Reality, and the Future of Biotech. Harvard Business School Press, Boston, MA.
8. Interview with Mark McGrath, Basel, May 2007.
9. The clinical confirmation that an investigational product possesses a desired pharmacological effect in patients with the disease of interest.
10. Vagelos, P.R., Galambos, L., 2004. Medicine, Science, and Merck. Cambridge University Press, New York.
11. Refer to Regeneron's Web site: http://www.regeneron.com/arcalyst.html.
12. Sánchez-Serrano, I., 2006. Success in translational research: lessons from the development of bortezomib. Nature Reviews Drug Discovery 5, 107–114.
13. Ibid.
14. Chandler, A.D, 2005. Shaping the Industrial Century: The Remarkable Story of the Evolution of Modern Chemical and Pharmaceutical Industries. Harvard University Press, Cambridge, MA.
15. Interview with Tom Maniatis, Cambridge, MA, April 2009.
16. Ibid.
17. Interview with Timothy Wright, Basel, May 2007.
18. Interview with Jo Walton, London, UK, May 2007.
19. I owe this information to Jo Walton.
20. Litterick, D., 2004. Celltech poised for deal to market $1.2bn drug. Telegraph, March 17, 2004. http://www.telegraph.co.uk/finance/2880245/Celltech-poised-for-deal-to-market-1.2bn-drug.html.
21. Robertson, D., 2001. Immunex takes premature step to guarantee Enbrel market share. Nature Biotechnology 19(2), 108–109.
22. Sánchez-Serrano, Success in translational research.
23. Interview with Jackie Hunter, Harlow, UK, June 2007.
24. Interview with Julian Adams, Cambridge, MA, March 2009.
25. Interview with Jackie Hunter, Harlow, UK, June 2007.
26. Bethencourt, V., 2009. Merck joins the biotech game. Nature Biotechnology 27(2), 104.
27. Schonfeld, E., 2008. The end of venture capital as we know it? TechCrunch, December 6, 2008. http://www.techcrunch.com/2008/12/06/the-end-of-venture-capital-as-we-know-it/.
28. Sánchez-Serrano, Success in translational research.
29. Interview with Thomas Lönngren, London, UK, April 2007.

10 Causes of the Pharmaceutical Crisis

Fallacious is the idea, which has become diffused by the existence of scientific specialization itself, that the progress of any science is to be measured by the mass of observations that its followers have succeeded in accumulating.... The advance of a science is measured by the degree with which it succeeds in bringing a multiplicity of observations under general laws.

—***Charles Singer and E. Ashworth Underwood,***
A Short History of Medicine *(1962)*

No se puede vivir eternamente en la revolución, que es un análisis *enloquecido. Lo que necesitamos es la* síntesis *verdaderamente libertadora, o sea equilibradora y tranquilizante.*[1]

—***Vintila Horia,*** **Introducción a la literatura del siglo *XX (1976)***

Overall, when we look at the improvement of our health care over the last century, it is undeniable that the pharmaceutical industry has made an extraordinary contribution to the world in saving and improving the quality of people's lives, especially if we consider that the way in which most drugs have come into being has not been easy. For an innovative drug to come to the market, many years of basic academic research and the collaboration of many scientists across different disciplines throughout the world are necessary, along with many years of research and funding at the pharmaceutical industry level. As science makes inroads into an even better understanding of the cell and informs us about the molecular mechanisms at play in many diseases, one might expect that the process of bringing innovative drugs to the market to treat human diseases would be quicker and more efficient than in the past. But unfortunately, this is not the case. As covered in Chapter 6, when discussing pharmaceutical regulators, it has been suggested that the key reason that we have observed a decline in the approval of novel pharmaceuticals is that medical applications of scientific research have not kept pace with progress in basic science. But this is not the only reason, and we need to explore the issue more deeply because a satisfying answer to this question is key to understanding the current global health care crisis and will enable us to find better ways to deal with it.

Drug Discovery and Development Before Biotechnology

If we think carefully about the evolution of drug research,[2] say, between c. 1850 and c. 1950, we realize that it was actually during this period that most of the better-known or "popular" diseases that afflict humans—such as microbial and viral

The World's Health Care Crisis. DOI: 10.1016/B978-0-12-391875-8.00010-X infections; deficiency and metabolic diseases; and chronic ailments such as diabetes, hypertension, and cancer—became understood and characterized. In fact, by the end of World War II, drugs to cure or treat such diseases had already been found.[3] Many of these drugs were discovered and developed in Europe, but many were discovered and developed in the United States as well. When World War II ended, Europe (with the possible exception of Britain) lost its leadership in the biological and medical sciences, yielding significantly to the United States. Germany and France, the countries that had created the strongest and most formidable bases for the pharmaceutical industry, lost many of their smartest people, either to death or to exile in Britain and other European countries, the United States, or the Americas. As World War II concluded, companies, especially in Britain and the United States, which by this period were fully focused on the production of antibiotics, had to find different strategies to sustain growth because it was no longer necessary to produce antibiotics in the same way that was required during wartime. The production of new drugs at the industrial base leveled off, and price controls for medicines loomed on the horizon in the United States. As a result, most companies in the United States opted for diversification in other areas, such as consumer products, fine chemicals, and cosmetics, to keep growing. While European companies struggled to make a comeback after World War II (which, eventually, they did), the US firms, such as Merck and Pfizer, emerged as leaders. US companies had very close ties to US universities, which, year after year, were becoming the world's leaders in biomedical innovation, and this relationship was very important in defining the future direction of the pharmaceutical industry.

After World War II, great progress was made in basic research, most notably in bacteriology, biophysics, biochemistry, and genetics, and a new type of scientist, the specialist, and a new discipline, molecular biology, emerged. Molecular biology was so revolutionary and so novel that in the beginning, some of the world's best minds were focused entirely on the genetic and molecular understanding of the mechanisms by which the cell works, without establishing a link between what they observed at the molecular level in bacteria or viruses or worms or insects and human disease. But before long, the progress experienced in the life sciences began to permeate the clinical sciences and the practice of medicine. And thus there was a natural and increasing emphasis on trying to understand many of nature's best-kept secrets based on a molecular biological approach—a totally different approach compared to how drug research was done before World War II, which was largely, though not always, based on trial and error.

An example of this targeted approach is James Black's discovery, at the SmithKline Laboratories in Britain in the late 1960s, of a molecule that resembled the structure of histamine that suppressed the secretion of stomach acid, which eventually led to the medicine Tagamet.[4] Though random screening of potential drug candidates was the prevalent way to develop medicines well into the late 1970s, Black's method had a great impact on the way companies would develop their drugs from the mid-1970s through the mid-1990s. The way in which Merck developed its anticholesterol drugs (Mevacor, Zoloft) based on statins (discovered by Akira Endo, who, while an employee at the Japanese pharmaceutical company Sankyo, discovered statin compounds and realized their clinical potential)[5] is another clear example of this targeted approach.

Impact of Biotechnology in Drug Discovery and Development

The biggest changes in drug discovery and development occurred when molecular biology and molecular genetics and biochemistry fused to give rise to biotechnology in the early 1970s, which, from a health care perspective, truly revolutionized medicine, as epitomized by the production in the late 1970s and early 1980s of monoclonal antibodies, genetically engineered insulin, human growth hormone, a hepatitis vaccine (Recombivax HB), and other medical breakthroughs. Biotechnology also allowed scientists to gain a much better understanding of the genetic and mechanistic causes of cancer and many other diseases and has permitted a much better characterization of most diseases. At present, the potential of this technology seems to have no limits.

But ironically, as scientists began to better understand the science behind diseases, the scientific hurdles grew higher and the complexity of diseases began to seem greater, therefore making it more difficult to develop safer and more acceptable and efficacious drugs. It is not surprising, then, that the pharmaceutical industry is having difficulty maintaining the terrific track record that they had achieved for more than 150 years, at a time when there are unprecedented opportunities.

Most pharmaceutical executives and even academics complain that the pharmaceutical industry's problem is lack of innovation. I entirely disagree because if anything, this is an unprecedented time in history, one in which we actually have an excess of innovation. And it has become very difficult to find ways to make all this knowledge converge so that all the knowledge being generated somehow begins to make sense and becomes useful to society in the form of better technological tools and, specifically, better drug products.

So scientific specialization has made it more difficult for scientists to integrate effectively the scientific knowledge that is generated in the world on a daily basis: there is simply too much information to be processed and fully integrated into a coherent whole. The knowledge and new technology amassed in the last decades has been growing exponentially, yet the conversion of that knowledge into fundamental scientific paradigms that will explain the behavior of the cell (and tissues and organs and systems) and then the use of this holistic understanding in the creation of concrete commercial products has lagged. I think this is the root of all the problems in research and development (R&D) productivity that the industry has at present and the reason why no health care system will work, no matter how many billions are infused into reforming it, unless this issue is fully addressed.

It is also not surprising, therefore, that as more technological tools have become available and the pharmaceutical industry has become more dependent on them to discover new drugs, the results have been more than disappointing. For instance, when the pharmaceutical industry's pipelines emptied around the mid-1990s, companies thought that introducing new technologies, such as combinatorial chemistry and high-throughput screening, was going to solve all the problems that they were facing, and they envisaged the period (now) during which they were going to have many new ideas and new product introductions. But this approach had too many flaws. For example, for a few years, companies were moving away from traditional animal models and pharmacology, as they tried to get to the nuts and bolts of the causes of disease by looking at the genetics and relying increasingly on new technologies. The problem is that the new technologies have not delivered what was expected of them. Of course, they have improved their efficiency in performing drug assays; they have delivered a better-educated workforce of young scientists who look at things differently; but they have not yet delivered more leading candidates—although there are some signs that things are improving. Of importance, there has certainly been a change in the standards of what can be a major seller because companies are more open now to focusing on therapies that will work, regardless of what the initial market size appears to be.

As I have said earlier, the main problem that the pharmaceutical and biotech industries must deal with is the high failure rate in drug development. During the process of drug discovery and development, companies have a huge amount of drug candidates, but too few of them come down the funnel, a phenomenon that is called *attrition*. The high failure rate in drug development is costing the industry, which in turn passes the costs to the patients. For example, if a firm has 50 candidates at the beginning of Phase I clinical trials and only 2 reach the market (meaning that the other 48 candidates perished between Phase I and Phase II, and sometimes even as late as Phase III), after very large investment, the 2 successful products have to cover the costs of the other 48 failed ones. Not surprisingly, these products will have a very high price.

Let us take Pfizer as an example. Pfizer is the largest pharmaceutical company in the world, and it would be fair to compare it to a dinosaur that needs a great deal of food to survive. A $50-billion company like Pfizer needs at least six financially successful drugs every year to keep its pipeline alive. This means that to achieve this goal, the company needs at least 60 promising compounds every year coming into clinical trials. But what if I told you that they have never done better than 15, never mind 60? They have never done more than 15 or 20 compounds, year in, year out, just like a budget deficit. And people ask, why are they not producing six drugs?

Specifically, companies have difficulties in determining the right target, and as such, there are two big courses of attrition in Phase I and Phase II, one being a lack of efficacy, which means that the company is hitting the wrong target. Though lack of efficacy sometimes may be the result of a wrong dose, the usual reason is that scientists have no clue what the important target really is. The other cause of attrition is that scientists cannot assess what combinations of targets exist so that they can be exploited into combination products. A third issue is toxicity—unpredictable toxicity, that is, the other biggest killer. It is interesting that Gleevec, which works beautifully in some types of chronic myelogenous leukemia (as well as in other cancers), is ineffective in some kinds of chronic myelogenous leukemia, and again, the reason is that there are very idiosyncratic conformations in the protein targets of some of these leukemias that render them more or less vulnerable to the medicine.

Without this kind of fundamental scientific information, it is very difficult to develop new drugs. If one looks at the indications for which drugs have been registered over the past 50 years, and if one were to look at the sheer number of drugs and improvements of drugs that were introduced early on for things like hypertension, diabetes, and pain, one would see that there were a great many drugs registered between 50 and 10 years ago for such indications. But what has happened in the last 10 or 15 years is that by and large, drugs often reach a market in which they are considered the best of their kind and difficult to improve. The statin Lipitor is an example: it is difficult to improve, so people have moved beyond Lipitor to develop combined modes of action, such as Crestor. And if one looks at that field, people may rightly say that the low-hanging fruits are gone, with the big indications now covered by drugs that are very satisfactory. Not that there could be no improvements for the treatment of hypertension or diabetes, but these areas are reasonably well covered for the general population—so much so that it has become difficult to come up with something that is significantly much better. This would require a major breakthrough, and breakthroughs occur infrequently in these areas. So the differences between curing drugs that are hitting previous targets and the next generation of drugs will greatly depend on our understanding of the genome and the relationship between diseased genes and phenotypes. That is going to take a while.

The pharmaceutical industry is at an inflection point, a phase in which the genome has been mapped and in which scientists are beginning to understand the biology of the proteins that are encoded by the genome. As such, one might predict that there will be a lag between basic scientific and mechanistic models and the initial ways in which new high-level drugs are brought to market. So one should expect a large number of fantastic new drug introductions in the future at which point both the biotech and pharmaceutical industries will have changed beyond recognition. But in the meantime, there is not much to sustain growth. It used to be that large pharmaceutical companies could still make money by launching drugs that were third, fourth, or even fifth in their class, such as statins (Mevacor, Zocor, Lipitor, Zoloft, etc.), selective serotonin-reuptake inhibitors (Prozac, Celexa, etc.), or histamine H2 blockers for ulcers, because those markets were vast and side effects varied from drug to drug depending on the specific type of patient. Therefore, if a specific drug did not work for a particular patient subpopulation, it would work for another, and so on. The problem is that those drugs have come out of patent, and the huge sales in those large markets have been lost to generics, so that money will soon run out. According to Sam Williams, former European biotech leading analyst and now CEO of Modern Bioscience in London, "If you look at the eighties and the first half of the nineties, the pharma industry did just brilliantly selling me-too drugs. There were no incentives to innovate, and maybe that's the reason why the pharma companies' pipelines are suffering and have been suffering throughout the last ten years—because they stopped trying to innovate." Williams continues to say that "Nowadays, there is an economic harsh reality which is if you are a me-too drug, or the fourth, or fifth, or seventh in the class, you are not going to be reimbursed, you won't get in the formulary unless you have a particular pricing advantage, a dosing advantage, or a safety advantage. A sexy product has to be one that has a novel mechanism of action. So it can't be another 'ACE' inhibitor, for example, because you could be the thirteenth of fourteenth, so there is no interest in that... . And I mean there is the whole economics of that."[6]

Again, Pfizer, the largest cardiovascular pharmaceutical company in the world, recently announced that it will get out of the cardiovascular field. The largest cardiovascular drug company in the world has gone out of business in that sector.

Anita Kidgell, Vice-President of Corporate Strategy at GSK, summarizes the situation in the following manner:

> *In the past, when people saw the great potential of inhibiting enzymes, everybody focused on enzymes and tried to inhibit enzymes, and accordingly, there was a change in R&D based on that approach; then people understood that you can block a receptor with some particular drugs, and so people started developing drugs based on receptor blockers—Zantac is a good example of a drug for the treatment of gastric ulcers—and now we are at a stage where everybody is looking for the next step and there is a lot of hope now with genomics and proteomics and things like that... but they tend to be more like tools rather than actual products.*[7]

In the meantime, most companies will continue to focus on targets that have been fairly well tried already, that is, the targets that have been used by many companies to improve on existing drugs to keep a stream of revenue coming in while they developed new products. The strategy is the following: 30 or 40 years ago, many drugs had significant side effects, but as time has passed, companies have improved them. Similarly, for many drugs that produced severe side effects, it was very common to have the drugs administered two or three times a day. Now these drugs, in compliance with the safety and efficacy required by regulators, can be given once a day or much less frequently, with reasonable side effect profiles. Biphosphonate, for the treatment of painful osseous metastatic cancer, is a clear example. This drug, which was to be administered once a day initially, now is limited to once a year when approved for osteoporosis. This is the new concept of improvement, but once companies reach a certain threshold, the gold standards of drugs will be hard to improve. And until companies come up with new products based on new targets, the pharmaceutical industry is in peril of extinction because generics companies benefit from drugs that are off patent but do *not* innovate. Who is going to come up with new drugs to treat diseases if biotech is struggling, too? And the truth of the matter is that no company today has enough new medicines in development to market enough new products to sustain growth in light of the patent expirations that are occurring like clockwork and which, by 2016, will reach a total of $200 billion in lost sales. It is, therefore, no wonder that the major pharmaceutical players have consolidated out of despair.

From a commercial point of view, as we saw in Chapter 3, in the past, companies were very diversified, counting not only on a prescription drug line but also on over-the-counter (OTC) drugs and, in some cases, other business lines such as cosmetics, soaps, medical devices, oil and gas, chemicals, and food products. This meant that they did not rely only on the results of scientific innovation (i.e., new drugs) to keep their businesses growing. For patients, this meant cheaper drugs because companies were not so dependent on their prescription drug sales. Nowadays, pharmaceutical companies depend exclusively on how many new prescription drugs they can bring to the market, which ultimately depends on how quickly basic scientific discoveries can be translated into commercial products—something that is not easy and that cannot simply happen overnight. Furthermore, most of the time, there are no real indicators of when a scientific breakthrough will take place.

During the 1990s, the pharmaceutical industry went through a wave of mergers and acquisitions arising from the lack of productivity of major pharmaceutical companies and from a shortfall in short-term earnings. In fact, every one of the major European companies, with the exception of Roche, which for family reasons did not merge (until recently, with Genentech), was formed from a merger. Subsequently, a large number of drugs were approved, and obviously, companies had a huge number of representatives as a result of these mergers, which created multibillion-dollar drug sales and subsequently led to the creation of what has been called *blockbuster syndrome*; that is, the industry became dependent on large sales to sustain growth. Though all these mergers worked quite well from a marketing point of view, they also created major disruptions and additional layers of management that were not conducive to good research. In fact, if we look at overall productivity every year, the pipeline in the industry has been descending from 1996 up until now (see Figure 9.1).

Because companies can grow either by keeping existing products going for longer, by lining up extensions and reformulations, or by introducing new products, sales have gone down due to the shortfall of new product introductions. So for more than a decade now, companies have pursued only things that they thought was going to be big and neglected many of the areas that constituted the biotechnology industry's niche market: drugs for small patient populations. However, now the industry is trying to capture that market as well and is making great efforts to stratify patient populations (so-called personalized medicine) for the reasons we have discussed. If we go back 25 years and look at the number of major pharmaceutical companies that existed and then compare that number with the number of companies that we have now, it is obvious that the number has decreased. Over that period, most of the large pharmaceutical firms have been bought, acquired, or merged. Today, we have eight of those companies left of which two are mid-sized: Lilly and Bristol-Myers Squibb. Every one of the other companies has consolidated. We have seen another wave of consolidation in 2009, and it is not clear to anyone what this industry may or may not look like 10 years from now. Will we have only four companies or five companies in a couple of years? Are we going back to the formation of pharmaceutical trusts and oligopolies as happened in Switzerland (Basel Syndicate) and Germany (IG Farben) in the interwar period? Are the pharmaceutical companies going to become big marketing engines for biotechnology? No one knows, but the changes that are taking place are enormous and reflect that the pharmaceutical business model is no longer working.

According to Janet Woodcock:

> *People are still sick.... Actually, our population for the first time may be getting sicker rather than getting healthier. And so people are going to need interventions. In general, I think that industry needs to get comfortable with the fact that the day of the blockbuster drug is over and that the day of being able to advertise drugs into blockbuster status is probably over. What they need to focus on—and I have told this to the industry multiple times, ever since I published the white paper on [the critical path initiatives list], is value. If they produce an innovation that is valuable, the public will demand it! And that historically has been true. For example, in the U.K., when people feel that medicines are going to be valuable to their health and they are not going to be able to obtain them, they become very unhappy! If a new drug*

hasn't been shown to add any additional value, compared to existing alternatives, it is probably not going to be paid for. So, the name of the game may have shifted for pharmaceutical development. But it doesn't mean the market isn't there. There is a tremendous market. There are so many unmet medical needs.

When asked what drove this blockbuster syndrome in the first place, Woodcock stated:

I think it has to do with what happened in the United States in the financial sector and a lot of other areas where the leadership was driven by corporate boards and investors. As the companies were all public, they were focused on short-term returns, and they lost sight almost of their mission: they were focused on short-term profits and the financial markets for their companies, and that worked for a while, just like it did in the other sectors. But now the whole thing is coming and crashing down. I think it was a gradual shift-over from scientific medical leadership at the companies to marketing leadership, and you can see that in the CEOs and the senior management of the companies and also the stock market, where the pressures were extremely high. If you take a company that has 100,000 employees, they can't just focus on short-term returns. They have a huge infrastructure and they need to have a robust pipeline and produce value or they are not going to survive.[8]

Christopher Milne, assistant director of the Tufts Center for the Study of Drug Development, has a similar view:

I think that pharmaceutical companies have to be concerned. I mean, if there is a point where there are only five or six major super-pharmas, then they are going to become like public utilities, and they may well be regulated that way. But at the same time, they are doing this because they know that they have to do this to survive. But I think that they are also realizing that once they do—and there is probably a downside to it, in terms of inertia and dealing with all... and keeping their staff—they realize that they have to break back down, so they build up and they realize that they need to reorganize in some way to keep that innovative system alive, or innovation alive by having systemic changes that permit a small organization. If a company has 60,000 people and buys another company with 40,000 people, then the new company will have 100,000 people! And just prioritizing resources is not going to deal with it.[9]

From a policy point of view, the Bayh-Dole Act of 1980,[10] which entitled US universities to benefit from the intellectual property (IP) rights of their discoveries made using federal funding, has had a great impact on the pharmaceutical industry, which has shifted more toward a prescription drug path and a focus on financial profit. Although the goal of Bayh-Dole was to foster innovation by allowing US universities to license their technologies to university spin-off biotech companies or to the pharmaceutical industry, it also created a different culture at the university level. From this point onward, scientists saw themselves not only as scientific researchers but also as managers, entrepreneurs, and, more recently, investors as well. In creating or joining biotech companies, scientists soon realized that in just a matter of years, by assuming the risks of becoming an entrepreneur, they could not only become multimillionaires but they might also become celebrities. Given their close link to academia, where innovation really is, biotech firms, thanks to a great deal of funding by investors and the financial know-how support of the pharmaceutical industry, have become the most innovative sector of the health care industry. Looking to benefit from their earlier investment in the nascent biotech industry, the pharmaceutical industry embraced biotechnology to a point at which it became increasingly dependent on it to bring products to market, as demonstrated in Chapter 4.

But the Bayh-Dole Act also created serious IP problems (and IP means money) that, instead of fostering translation, have become obstacles to it, as demonstrated in recent years by the enormous number of legal suits and countersuits in the United States among pharmaceutical and biotech firms and universities—which in these matters tend to act more as corporations than centers of knowledge. As mentioned earlier, because of the focus placed on potential economic rewards from IP as related to health care, a curious philosophy called the *anticommons paradox hypothesis* points out that property rights in certain fields—notably biotechnology—can be equally counterproductive.[11] As a result of the increasing complexity in the IP negotiations that have to be done, it has taken longer for pharmaceutical firms to license in and develop those technologies directly from the universities, so now they have to wait for an incubation period in the biotechnology industry.

Furthermore, the expectations of biopharmaceutical companies' shareholders and investors are so high now that it is difficult for those companies to satisfy what their shareholders want as a return, without making some sacrifices that have a direct and indirect impact on drug development productivity. Of course, this raises the following questions: why should pharmaceutical industry shareholders expect a double-digit return? Is it unfair if the pharmaceutical industry, after recovering its high-end investment, were normalized to all other industries in which returns of 3–5% are adequate?

Over the years, the pharmaceutical industry has complained that the biggest hurdle and delay in getting new biopharmaceuticals to market was the time that regulators took to evaluate drugs. But regulators have done their homework and diminished the paperwork burden that created delays in the drug approval process, which has shortened the time required for approval even if the process is still imperfect. Still, the lag in innovative drug approvals remains. The actual fact is that as regulators are getting cleverer about what they are prepared to approve, they are going to demand more and more data, making it more difficult for companies to register small improvements. And instead of just saying that everything must be shown to be an improvement as compared to a placebo, if they say instead that everything should be compared to the current gold standard, which is what the European regulators are doing, then it will get increasingly difficult to register products because the hurdles are very high. Also, with the large number of safety scandals that have taken place in recent years, payers, too, are becoming smarter about what they are willing to pay and whether they will pay for small improvements—and, in fact, they still pay for small improvements; they are going to demand higher safety and efficacy and put pressure on the regulators to be more stringent in their drug approval process.

The overall public expectation in the developed world is that people in these countries should live in a very safe and comfortable environment. As living standards have increased, overall expectations regarding the safety of medicines have increased as well. In many respects, the media and many a high-profile scientific journal, such as *Nature* and *Science* (both "Príncipe de Asturias" Award, 2007), among others, have done something that governments and the pharmaceutical industry have failed to do: they have educated people, alerted them, and turned their attention toward the positive and negative effects of medicines. Nowadays, the press dedicates much more time to medicines, or practically anything in the medical field, than they used to. Every day, it seems, some new fact or discovery related to health care comes to light—and this was not so in the past. So it is in the context of well-being that we can see the expectations for safer or completely safe medicines.

The industry itself has also been responsible for the public's high expectations regarding the potential of R&D, clinical trial results, and new drug product launches—which end in great disappointment most of the time. In fact, when biotech and pharmaceutical companies write their press releases, they often emphasize the "potential" of some drug product and play down the side effects and risks associated with it. Of course, besides satisfying and attracting investors while boosting stock prices, companies are well aware that they are creating the market in advance: people start thinking about the product well before the product is launched. But the truth of the matter is that there is not a single pharmaceutical that is 100% effective or safe as organisms react differently to the same drugs.

In certain cases, the industry itself has damaged the prospects of its own products. Looking at the Merck case of Vioxx, the COX-2 mediator removed from the market, one could say that if the different parts of the company had worked in a more coherent and honest way, they would have made less profit, but the product would still be alive. So, in the hunt for extreme effectiveness and productivity and profits, companies start to kill their own children, as the big marketing machine inside tells them, "Press the product very powerfully to anyone who can ingest it, to anyone who can pay the bill, despite serious contraindications."

This situation has created another challenge for the pharmaceutical industry, as regulators have tightened the regulatory environment on safety. Safety in the post-Vioxx era is a very big deal. Extra studies and lots of increased pharmacovigilance, which is very expensive and costs lots of people lots of time, are undergone to find idiosyncratic toxicities that sometimes are overrepresented in the press. Then, litigators get involved with lawsuits: some have merit, some do not, but all have made the enterprise of discovering the drug not just more costly, but much more lengthy and difficult.

Marketing takes many shapes and forms, of course, and it is very interesting that the present business model in the pharmaceutical industry is extremely market-intensive, which is very dangerous because there are always long-term effects. If biopharmaceutical companies do not build some mechanism to balance this, they will suffer in the long term. Maybe it is very good for investors in the short term, but it turns out not to be in the long term, as patients are becoming increasingly critical of and unhappy about this approach, which may lead to the imposition of heavy regulation on pharmaceutical marketing and advertising. Too-aggressive marketing may realize quick profits but could also lead to major disasters—and there is a lot of such speculation going on in the stock market. There are also a large number of powerful world financial instruments that have interfered with the R&D of pharmaceutical products, which formerly was not the case.

Using television ads and similar marketing schemes seems ridiculous to me because that is an extremely expensive way to market drugs and consumes a huge percentage of budgets, regardless of whether one considers marketing as a sunk cost. In the past, costs used to be two research dollars would be paid for every marketing dollar; but now the situation is inverted. One could argue that this may not even be ethical because companies should not market prescription medicines to consumers; rather, they should market them to physicians—without trying to bribe them or provide them with fake clinical data—because physicians are trained at understanding medical conditions and medicines and how to dispense medicines to patients. Pharmaceutical firms are basically subverting the role of physicians and hurting the medical profession through their use of these marketing practices.

Steven Paul, retired president and head of R&D at Eli Lilly, reminds us that "R&D expenses as a percentage of sales in the industry run somewhere between 15 and 20 percent. Lilly is at the higher end; we are at 20 to 25 percent. We have a very strong commitment to our R&D, but remember sales and marketing and manufacturing both are much higher than R&D. So we do spend twice or three times in selling, marketing, and promoting our drugs than we do discovering! But we have to find more cost-effective and effective ways of selling and marketing our drugs because if you get better drugs, these products will speak for themselves."[12]

All this creates a benefit–cost paradox. As people's expectations grow, they want very specific drugs, they want drugs that do not have side effects, and so forth. Of course, this pressure is passed on to the regulators, who in turn pass it on to companies. Now, if one looks at some of the most effective medicines on the market today—for instance, haloperidol, paracetamol, aspirin, and several established diabetes products—all of them have side effects that would have prevented the drugs from making it to the market today, considering the current standards for drug approval, because the way in which these drugs came to market was completely different.[13] One could say that many patients are being deprived of very effective medicines today because of the high approval hurdles that need to be overcome regarding safety. But these hurdles would not have reached their current levels had the biotech and pharmaceutical industries been more transparent to start with. In fact, many drugs, during clinical trials or once they are on the market, show deleterious effects in patients (sometimes years after the drug has been approved), even when companies have done everything correctly. Sometimes drugs would show side effects no matter what.

For example, a drug called Tysabri, a VLA-4 antagonist, used in the treatment of multiple sclerosis and Crohn's disease, was withdrawn voluntarily from the market by Biogen-Idec/Elan Pharmaceuticals after a report of a progressive brain condition that can be fatal in some patients: progressive multifocal leukoencephalopathy (PML). The US Food and Drug Administration (FDA) and the company did everything correctly, yet there were reports of side effects, which required more research data and which put the progress of other VLA-4 antagonists on hold. Because there were no further reports of patients developing PML, Tysabri was brought back to the market in 2006 with stricter prescribing guidelines—designed to minimize the risk of contracting the disease—and a warning that 1 in 1,000 patients could develop

PML. A couple of patients presented with PML while taking Tysabri in 2008, which seems to fit with the statistics provided on the drug's label. Despite the chance of developing the disease, however, many patients have been willing to use Tysabri to treat serious forms of multiple sclerosis and Crohn's disease when other treatments have failed. As of the end of September 2009, more than 35,500 patients were taking Tysabri, and Biogen-Idec estimated that 100,000 were using the drug by 2010.[14] Had Biogen-Idec not been proactive about Tysabri, the drug would have been buried, which would have been very unfortunate for many patients.

How many people who actually obtained real benefits from Vioxx are now deprived of the drug and condemned to suffer while moving around because of the pain they feel, simply because things were not done correctly? Many radical changes at the pharmaceutical industry level need to take place with great urgency—and we will get there soon.

Notes

1. "We cannot live eternally in a revolution, which is a maddening, *analytical* state. What we need is a truly liberating *synthesis*, which is both equilibrating and tranquilizing."
2. Refer to Weatherall, M., 1990. In Search of a Cure: A History of Pharmaceutical Discovery. Oxford University Press, New York; Singer, C., Underwood, A., 1962. A Short History of Medicine. Oxford Clarendon Press, Oxford; Maxwell, R., Eckhardt, S.B., 1990. Drug Discovery: A Casebook and Analysis. Humana Press, Clifton, NJ.
3. Weatherall, In Search of a Cure: A History of Pharmaceutical Discovery.
4. Ibid., and Singer and Underwood, A Short History of Medicine.
5. Stossel, T., 2008. The discovery of statins. Cell 134 (6), 903–905.
6. Interview with Sam Williams, London, UK, May 2007.
7. Interview with Anita Kidgell, Brentford, UK, May 2007.
8. Interview with Janet Woodcock, Silver Spring, MD, March 2009.
9. Interview with Christopher Milne, Boston, MA, March 2009.
10. Bayh-Dole Act, 35 USC 200-212.
11. Heller, M., 1998. The tragedy of the anticommons. Harvard Law Review 111, 621–688.
12. Interview with Steven Paul, Indianapolis, IN, April 2009.
13. In 1952, the FDA created clinical trials. In 1962, clinical trials were required to prove that drugs were safe and efficacious, therefore increasing the standards for drug approval. Prior to these regulatory landmarks, drugs were applied directly to humans, and then to animals followed by humans in a more or less trial-and-error manner. See Weatherall, In Search of a Cure, and Singer and Underwood, A Short History of Medicine.
14. Wallack, T., 2008. Another Tysabri patient has PML. Boston Globe, October 30, 2008. http://www.boston.com/business/healthcare/articles/2008/10/30/another_tysabri_patient_has_pml/.

Part IV

Morality and Duty on a Lonely Planet

11 Wealth versus Poverty

Life is an island here and now in a dying world.
—Norbert Wiener,* The Human Use of Human Beings: Cybernetics and Society *(1954)

But what are principles? What are ideas ... before the facts?
—Joachim Fernau,* Hail, Caesar! *(1971)

As far as having access to pharmaceuticals is concerned, there are significant imbalances in the world. First, there is the imbalance of excess because most medicines are consumed in the developed world, but this does not necessarily mean that most sick people are in the developed world. Second, there is an imbalance in terms of the regulatory capacity of the developed and underdeveloped nations. The developed world has created extremely sophisticated regulatory systems, but most of the developing countries cannot even implement the most simple, straightforward regulatory systems. Third, there is also a research and development (R&D) gap between the two worlds because in many areas with public health importance, there is very limited ongoing R&D, whereas in some other areas, there is a significant amount of duplicate and ineffectual R&D going on. Let us understand how this works.

Medicines for the Developing World: Yes, This Is Our Problem

The public expectation in the developed world is that people (therein) should live in a very sheltered and protected environment—after all, this is the ideal behind economic, social, and cultural progress. Thus, anything that the biopharmaceutical industry proceeds to develop is highly dependent on what people are paying or willing to pay. Therefore, the biopharmaceutical industry has great economic (and to some extent social) incentive to produce novel drugs for a wide range of diseases—it simply pays to do so. Now, because a great deal of the most important R&D that takes place in the world is driven by commercial interests and is relatively less influenced by public health needs, the pharmaceutical market's needs may not necessarily be the same in the developed and underdeveloped worlds. Whereas in the rich nations, there is great need for innovative drugs to *prolong* life or *improve* living conditions (with the exception of orphan diseases), in the poor nations, there is great need for both existing generic drugs (which are easily available in the developed world) and innovative medicines to *save* life. In fact, people in tropical and subtropical regions, where most of the world's poverty is concentrated, have to deal with the same diseases that afflict the developed world and, on top of that, with many other

The World's Health Care Crisis. DOI: 10.1016/B978-0-12-391875-8.00011-1

diseases for which there is no treatment at all or insufficient ongoing research into them. The economic resources of the poorer nations are extremely limited, and if the money is not there, the market is not there, either. Consequently, if there is no money and there is no market, then there are few economic incentives for pharmaceutical companies to pursue research in these regions.

When it comes to having access to the right medicines, the developing world confronts two major problems (having access to doctors, nurses, medical technology, and so on, is another issue). First—and this is a very big problem that should be addressed before anything else—these people lack access even to the well-proven, well-established medicines that we take for granted in the developed nations, many of which are already out of patent. According to the "Essential Medicines List" compiled by the World Health Organization (WHO), 95% of the diseases in the developing world could be treated, cured, or both if patients had access to medicines already available off patent[1]—but of course, there is the financial burden. Second, these countries have to face very difficult decisions about how to use their limited economic resources. For example, if generic medicines could solve more than 90% of the developing countries' problems, at least satisfactorily, if these medicines are of good quality, available, and accessible, this means that the remaining 10% of diseases would require innovative medicines. So, when these countries need to make crucial decisions on how to allocate funding to purchase medicines, they have to struggle between buying generics—which would represent saving the life of many people with common diseases and letting people with rare disorders or more complex diseases, such as cancer, die—or purchasing innovative medicines. Of course, countries choose to purchase generics because more lives can be saved that way. This raises the following questions: how much is human life worth? Should saving the life of a person depend on how much money is invested?

Many people in the developed world, including pharmaceutical companies and biotech enterprises, may ask: why should we invest in the developing countries if their health is not our problem? The issue is that the world environment has changed and there are emerging diseases appearing everywhere, such as the A(H1N1) flu pandemic that we are currently facing but for which we were totally unprepared. Initially, governments thought that the A(H1N1) virus would not mutate quickly, but Tamiflu-resistant strains have appeared in Europe and the United States, which hints at unforeseeable consequences. But can we imagine what would happen if these viruses were of a different, more harmful, nature? In addition, we also face the imminent threat of an avian flu pandemic, among several others. Now, the developed world could then say, "Ah! OK. If the developing countries are the primary points where pandemics break out, what can we do? We can help them now because in helping them, we can help ourselves too." However, that mentality is not there yet, despite what is happening and judging by the areas on which the pharmaceutical companies have chosen to concentrate.[2]

When it comes to an avian flu pandemic, to mention just one example, many of us feel safe because we rely on the claim that there will be a vaccine out there to deal with a potential epidemic outbreak. But this is far from being the case, and we should know better by now given the disastrous way in which the so-called swine flu has been handled. If there were an avian flu pandemic, most likely there would not be enough vaccine available, and countries would have to scramble to make it available quickly. In other words, they would have to come up with a plan on how to protect themselves and the developing countries as well. When there was only Oseltamivir available, a drug to be used for this disease, a large number of countries wanted to stock it. This, however, would have been very ineffective because not every country would have needed the drug in the case of an epidemic outbreak, especially if one thinks that once the medicine expires, it needs to be thrown away, which means a waste of resources and millions of dollars. Why not think of a win–win situation? Why not compile a global stock? With present-day military planes and logistics, one can take anything anywhere on earth within 12h. So why not concentrate our efforts in a global way and send vaccine where it may really be needed? The rich countries and the biopharmaceutical industry seem to forget that many of the drugs that could be developed for the underdeveloped world could actually save lives in developed nations as well.

But the "that's not my problem" attitude does not end here. Many people think that the problem of having access to anti-HIV drugs in developing nations is going to be alleviated in the near future because many of the anti-HIV drugs that were created a while ago will become generics soon. But this is not completely accurate. It is true that the first HIV drugs have started to go off patent, but unfortunately, if someone starts treatment with these drugs, after a couple of years, theoretically, the patient will develop resistance and need the second line of treatment. And the erosion continues because after the second line, the patient, after a couple of years, may need a third line. And so it goes on because resistance is developing relatively fast with all the existing drugs, considering the overall lifespan of the patients, not to mention the fact that these drugs have secondary effects on the liver and kidneys. And it is important for the patient to start with the appropriate treatment on a timely basis to increase his or her chances of survival. Unfortunately, there are already populations coming up with strains that cannot be treated easily even with the first line.

HIV is a good example of how a disease can spread globally so easily, having unforeseen complications. Many years ago, people in the developed world would not even have heard that people were dying in Africa of a strange disease. In fact, why should they have heard of it if, after all, it was not their problem? But the problem came to them—and quickly. Another growing problem is multiresistant tuberculosis, and there is no solution to it because there is not much innovative research ongoing in this area. Again, even if it is basically still the problem of the developing world, the developed world is not exempt from it because there are multiresistant cases in the United States already. Because we are so globalized, there will be many more cases elsewhere; it is just a matter of time.

The case of HIV/AIDS should teach us to create greater cooperation globally to invest more in R&D in infectious diseases. It can also teach governments, biopharmaceutical companies, and private funders a great deal on how to create markets in the developing world. For instance, for many years, people have talked about prevention in Africa because they thought treatment was too expensive and they could not manage to deal with it. However, as soon as brand-name anti-HIV drugs, such as Triomune, became generics, competition among generics companies began, and anti-HIV drug prices started dropping quickly. Soon, international funds became available. While Africans still pay $300 per year to be treated with high-quality antiretrovirals,[3] we must remember that international funds artificially created a market where there was no market at all. They helped the situation because they created incentives for developed and underdeveloped countries to engage in this kind of business. And this situation could be quite useful if applied to a large number of diseases treatable with generic medicines.

Though African countries suffer the most in terms of access to medicines, Latin America, India, China, and a large number of other Asian countries face serious problems as well. Though China and India are making great progress not only in the development of a generics industry but also in innovation at the R&D level, Latin America still lags on this front owing to a lack of investment in science and technology, old-fashioned political systems, corruption, and a lack of solidarity and cooperation among Latin nations.

Bridging the Gap?

So what can be done to bridge the gap, to facilitate access to more and better medicines in the developing world? This is, of course, a trillion-dollar question for which there is not a simple answer because, first, drug discovery and development is a business, and people invest in this costly, time-consuming, and risky process because they seek economic reward, while creating health care benefits. Second, the research financing mechanisms that could serve as a model, such as the US and European systems, are too highly sophisticated to be implemented easily in developing countries.

Public–private partnerships (PPPs) are now the modern trend. PPPs consist of joint initiatives between the private sector (i.e., pharmaceutical companies) and public funders to develop drugs that satisfy an unmet medical need in the developing world. In an influential report sponsored by the Wellcome Trust,[4] Mary Moran and colleagues discuss the success of this type of enterprise in bringing some medicines to the market more rapidly and at very low cost, without local governments creating additional incentives for the pharmaceutical industry in terms of tax breaks. The report provides a list of at least eight or nine of these products that are at very advanced stages in clinical trials; some of them are coming up the pipeline as well, and some smaller biotech companies are finding a niche for this kind of market.

Now, this needs some discussion because this is important. According to Lembit Rago, director of health technology and pharmaceuticals at the WHO:

> *You can change certain things only if you can bring them to the level of having common denominators. You can't compare things that are incomparable. Now, if you look at the public–private partnership outcomes, outcomes should be medicines that meet the international standards for quality, safety, and efficacy. How you can prove it? You can prove it if you go through a stringent regulatory authority abroad. If you don't go through that, then you could say, "Yes, the medicine is there but probably*

different standards have been used, and you can't compare either the expenses or the other things because they are incomparable things." Now people may respect the logical error because if you have the medicines passing much less stringent regulatory processes, probably a lot of research has not been done because it has not been requested by these authorities either, because of not having enough knowledge or regulatory requirements in place, and there might be many other things. … But you can't compare this.[5]

This situation is very similar to the one in which people who are trying to compare the prices of medicines say, "Oh! I saw Viagra in tablet form for one cent. It's wonderful!" Yes and no. The price is wonderful, but if one does not know anything about this product, then the price has no value because one does not know if the product meets the quality, safety, and efficacy criteria. And many people in the less developed world do not know that the low price alone is not of value, that it is not an indicator of the quality of the pharmaceutical product.

According to Rago, there is an antimalarial drug in the market that is clearly not meeting the standards to pass any regulatory scrutiny in Europe, the United States, Canada, Australia, or Japan. But it was developed with a PPP. In many other countries, which have very limited regulatory capacity to assess the quality of the product or where there is practically no regulatory capacity, of course, this product has been approved. When I asked Rago what was happening, his answer was as follows:

Nothing is happening. Everybody is, of course, happy, especially those who have created the product because it goes. Now, again, is it moral to have a product for which we have one set of standards for the, let's say, rich countries, and we have another set of standards for the poor countries. Is it moral and ethical? I would question this. And second, I think people don't want to record history and reality as they are, because real life is at times uglier than it seems. Sometimes, we don't like to look in the mirror because we may not like the picture we see, but it is still there. So, for a long time there has been a sort of silent approach, a silent attitude toward medicines for poor people! And it was not so long ago that respectable organizations were procuring medicines for the developing world for which they only had one indicator: price! The cheaper, the better! And no question about quality! Now, there are, of course, trends to change this scenario, but it hasn't changed completely. If you talk about research and development, I think there is a lot of it also in research communities. Some sorts of aspirations that all these bad, bloody regulators are making everything so complicated that if we go to the developing countries, we can bypass them! Let's put something together and let's go! So, it's not an option for me, and also it's not an option that is, in the long term, sustainable![6]

Though the concrete example just discussed is an antimalarial (malaria is not in Europe, the United States, or Canada but is mostly in developing countries), there are also many other drugs for neglected diseases that affect the developing countries that face the same issues. There is now a regulatory mechanism in place to address this problem through the new Article 58, which is the regulatory pathway for medicines that are exclusively meant to treat diseases and public health problems outside the European Union (EU).[7] Through this article, the European Medicines Agency (EMEA) provides scientific advice to companies involved in the manufacturing of these types of drugs using EMEA's procedures, norms, and standards at no charge. The goal is to provide incentives for the development of drugs for the developing world. The negotiations around Article 58 started at the European Commission and the Enterprise for Pharmaceutical Units (at that time, it was still pre-EMEA). So EMEA is now asking PPPs to seek regulatory advice from them, especially nowadays, when it has become a common practice to get regulators involved during the early stages of R&D. So companies meet regulators, have discussions, and try to seek advice on how to develop new drugs and whether their strategies would be acceptable from the regulatory point of view. Recently, it was asked how many PPPs had asked for regulatory advice, and it became known that almost none had.

To bridge the gap in developing drugs for the developing countries, it will be necessary, to start with, that drugs approved via PPPs go through stringent regulatory hurdles that would ensure their quality, safety, and efficacy. Then, one may legitimately ask, "What is the issue with that?" The private sector will legitimately say that they will do so much. But it will also be a matter of the other party (the public one) being very proactive in implementing the rest. And this is the problem—the standards that are required in a pharmaceutical company and the ones required in PPPs are not the same, and in this case, industry certainly is not motivated to invest huge amounts of money because the financial stakes are not there. Of course, the biopharmaceutical industry would like to obtain a positive image from PPPs because their reputation in the world is not very good and they are constantly under fire by the media. In entering a PPP, they are trying to give people a clear message about their corporate responsibility. But as said earlier, industry has one little trick that people do not realize: industry does as much as required and no more. And this is understandable because if one is in business, one does as much as required.

When R&D turns out to be very costly, sometimes some industries do more when going into the developing world, but then they have other incentives for that and perhaps longstanding strategies that they hope will pay off. But there are no freebies, and companies engage in PPPs knowing that the products that get out of PPPs do not have to go through the stringent regulatory authorities, cutting significant regulatory costs in this manner. And the reason is that these products, not being needed in the developed world, will never get to the United States or the European Union.

As a large portion of the public side is untrained and unqualified, they cannot follow the process because they do not have the necessary training. It would therefore be necessary for public funders to carry out significant due diligence before executing any R&D project. And if the research is not scientifically solid, they should then say, "Good luck, guys! Bye-bye!"

So what does all this tell us? Unfortunately, it tells us that current strategies are not working. Some public funders, and in fact, some companies, may have good intentions, but they may have unqualified people who still have a lot to learn. Perhaps with a learning curve, people will begin to become more efficient. Also, coordination between PPPs and funding mechanisms is not functioning because in certain areas, duplicated research is carried out, and in certain areas, there are gaps and no one puts in money. Globally, what is missing is a more coordinating road for the R&D gaps: in certain areas, there seems to be competition in which everybody rushes to get involved, whereas in others, there is only emptiness and no one is involved. One of the very good examples is pediatric medicines. The European Union has recently changed its pediatric medicines legislation to give companies not only more obligation and responsibility but also more incentive to advance, although it is still too premature to say how this will work in the end. One could say that of the medicines used in the world, in certain settings, 90% are used off-label; there is not enough R&D in this sector, and pediatric indications represent a huge research gap. This gap persists substantially, even in the developed world, and until recently it has been underestimated. Now people are talking more about it, and that will help things move along. The United States is more advanced because it established that legislation early on and came up with some additional incentives. The European Union is following a different approach: if a company develops a medicine that could *potentially* be used in pediatric populations, it is required to disclose to regulators all the studies done using pediatric populations and submit pediatric applications as well. But it remains to be seen how this will work in real life.

Going Beyond Business

It is clear by now that the business sector will do only as much as is required to make as much money as possible. Now, let us stop here and ask: what could be done in other sectors to create a balance between public and private interests when it comes to medicines for the developing world and for neglected areas in the developed world?

It is quite unlikely that one could realize a perfect balance because as far as R&D is concerned—and because, as we have seen, most of R&D is determined by expected profits—companies certainly go after mostly profitable market niches. Having said this, public intervention, though difficult to implement, can at least take on certain initiatives. First, governments should be more open to financing research that, though not representing lucrative market niches, may still be important for public health (see Table 11.1 and Figure 11.1). Second, governments should put more effort into training regulatory experts and engaging in more dialogue with regulatory experts between the industries and also academia to sort out what could be done in regulating (though not excessively) what needs to be regulated.

Regarding the development of the regulatory standards for new chemical entities, it is assumed that regulators are equal partners in industry. But in examining this carefully, this is no longer true because in certain narrow expertise areas, there is much more expertise in the industry nowadays than in government. Therefore, there is already an imbalance, and this is not very healthy because it means that although, formally speaking, it is a balanced process, there is a clear danger that industry will drive the process, which is not ideal. Historically, drug regulators have been more reactive than proactive. Usually, regulations start to come out when there is a catastrophe or when it is too late. When there was a quality catastrophe in the United States

Table 11.1 Priority Medicines List*

Ranking	Disease
1.	Infections due to antibacterial resistance
2.	Pandemic influenza
3.	Cardiovascular disease (secondary prevention)
4.	Diabetes (Type 1 and Type 2)
5.	Cancer
6.	Acute stroke
7.	HIV/AIDS
8.	Tuberculosis
9.	Neglected diseases
10.	Malaria
11.	Alzheimer's disease
12.	Osteoarthritis
13.	Chronic obstructive pulmonary disease
14.	Alcohol use disorders: alcoholic liver diseases and alcohol dependency
15.	Depression in the elderly and adolescents
16.	Postpartum hemorrhage

Source: Kaplan, W., Laing, R., 2004. Priority Medicines for Europe and the World, November, p. 45. http://www.femeba.org.ar/fundacion/quienessomos/Novedades/medicamentos_prioritarios.pdf.

*These diseases/conditions have been identified as demonstrating pharmaceutical gaps. Their ranking here is based on the relative importance of these diseases/conditions based on the findings of this study, and on the potential for publicly funded research to have a major impact on reducing the burden of disease.

in the late 1930s, a great deal of quality assurance, including the Food and Drug Administration (FDA), was established. Then the thalidomide crisis created significant enough damage to prompt US regulators to require companies to improve the safety and efficacy of medicines. More recently, a recent catastrophe, although smaller in scale, with monoclonal antibodies in Europe in 2006[8] led to new drug guidelines at the EMEA level concerning first-in-man use and how to manage the risk.

How could we break the cycle and ensure that regulators are not too reactive, but rather are acting proactively when dealing with innovative drugs? When something is new, when we have an emerging technology, there is always a risk of overregulation. If one starts to regulate these innovative technologies too heavily in the beginning, one risks curtailing their full development or blocking it altogether. Regulators therefore need to be very cautious in trying to observe very closely the development of the technology and in trying to obtain, step by step, more knowledge of the new technologies and the risks and benefits associated with them. On the basis of that knowledge, they could then establish appropriate regulatory guidelines. This

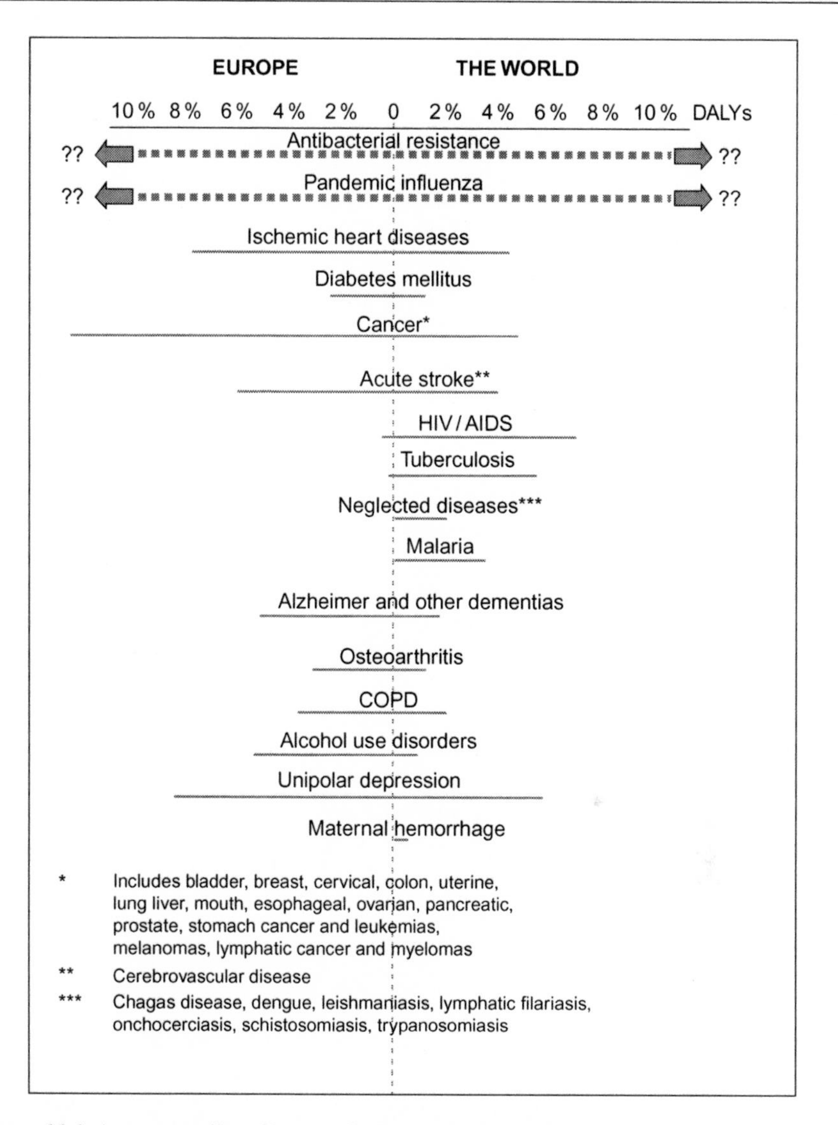

Figure 11.1 A commonality of interest for Europe and the world.
Source: Kaplan, W., Laing, R., 2004. Priority Medicines for Europe and the World, November, 2004, p. 37. © World Health Organization. Reprinted with permission. All rights reserved. http://www.femeba.org.ar/fundacion/quienessomos/Novedades/medicamentos_prioritarios.pdf.

means that it would be necessary to create general regulatory guidelines and move toward more specific guidelines as we learn more. In this sense, the regulators' new approach of starting conversations with industry at very early stages—which was formerly unthinkable because companies did not go to regulators until the product was already developed—represents significant progress. Companies can go to the regulators and say, "Look, guys, this is our plan, and we would like to develop a product for this and that disease, and we are here now because we would like to bring it to your attention because this is something new."

There needs to be more pressure to establish very early dialogue in the process of R&D—very early dialogue between regulators and sponsors—especially concerning innovative approaches, innovative technologies, and other new things. This could be done, but it would mean more resources for the regulators. If it is not done, then a bottleneck on the regulatory side will occur, and this can certainly slow down innovation, especially when people do not fully understand or when people are not trained well enough.

Another fundamental issue that needs discussion regarding the development of medicines for the developing world is that of the "license to operate" that pharmaceutical companies have to earn in these markets. Although, in theory, the Agreement on Trade-Related Aspects of Intellectual Property Rights (TRIPS and TRIPS+)[9]—an international agreement administered by the World Trade Organization (WTO) that sets down minimum standards for many forms of intellectual property (IP) regulation as applied to nationals of other WTO members—stipulates that essential medicines should be affordable in these markets, discussion should explore the need to relinquish IP in some markets and let generics exploit their low-cost manufacturing so that a volume/price trade-off can develop. Furthermore, many pharmaceutical firms are recognizing that pursuing the Western model and creaming the wealthy is not a sustainable option—judging by what is happening in Thailand and Brazil. Companies are also beginning to explore open innovation as a way to encourage more people to work on pre-competitive ideas.

So progress in the Third World will largely depend on the establishment of regulatory infrastructure, more investment in R&D (which implies the need to improve and enforce intellectual property laws in those countries), prevention and education, and better use of the funding that comes from international donors. And we, in the developed world, can certainly contribute to this effort.

Notes

1. WHO model list of essential medicines, 15th list, March 2007. http://www.who.int/medicines/publications/essentialmedicines/en/index.html; see also Worrall, M. (Ed.), 2007. Global health and the pharmaceutical industry. Association of the British Pharmaceutical Industry, July. http://www.who.int/phi/public_hearings/second/contributions_section1/Section1_RichardBarker_ABPI_Full_Contribution.pdf.
2. It is disgraceful that at the Hunger Summit of November 16, 2009, held by the Food and Agriculture Organization (FAO) in Rome, Italy, all the G-8 leaders except Italy were absent. This fact alone says a great deal about how much they care about the 17,000 children who die every day because of hunger. "Los 'grandes' se ausentan de cumbre contra el hambre." La Prensa de Panamá, November 17, 2009. See also http://edition.cnn.com/2009/WORLD/europe/11/17/italy.food.summit/index.html.
3. Interview with Lembit Rago, Geneva, June 2007.

4. Moran, M., Ropars, A.-L., Guzman, J., Diaz, J., Garrison, C., 2005. The New Landscape of Neglected Disease Drug Development. Pharmaceutical R&D Policy Project. Wellcome Trust/London School of Economics, London.
5. See Note 3.
6. Ibid.
7. Article 58 of Regulation (EC) No 726/2004. http://www.emea.europa.eu/htms/human/non_eu_epar/background.htm.
8. Ho, M.-W., Cummins, J., 2006. London drug trial catastrophe—collapse of science and ethics. Institute of Science in Society, July 4, 2006. http://www.i-sis.org.uk/LDTC.php.
9. Uruguay Round Agreement: TRIPS. Trade-Related Aspects of Intellectual Property Rights. http://www.wto.org/english/docs_e/legal_e/27-trips_01_e.htm.

12 Social Responsibility, Governmental Role, and Nongovernmental Organizations

Ferdinand Gonseth: My conclusion, my belated evidence is the following: human beings are entities created with the purpose of being bearers of moral obligations. Man is, by his very nature, a moral being. If we ever arrive to the point where we would know everything, then we would no longer be moral beings.
Vintila Horia: We would find ourselves in a position beyond good and evil.
Ferdinand Gonseth: That is right. You have formulated this very well. It is against our "creature statute" to be beyond good and evil.

—*Ferdinand Gonseth (Swiss mathematician and philosopher) interviewed by Spanish-Romanian novelist Vintila Horia (*Viaje a los centros de la tierra*, 1971)*[1]

Some pharmaceutical companies, such as GlaxoSmithKline, Merck, Novartis, and AstraZeneca, are taking their social responsibility very seriously (see Figure 12.1). In fact, some pharmaceutical companies have responded to criticisms regarding their lack of interest in the developing world by making donations to underserved countries (more than $7 billion a year), selling drugs at cost, and so on. For instance, Merck, under the leadership of Roy Vagelos, donated for perpetuity the drug Mectizan, for the treatment of river blindness disease caused by a parasitic worm.[2] Companies such as GlaxoSmithKline have set up research institutes with the goal of focusing on neglected diseases and an oncology center in Spain and Peru, respectively. In early 2009, the company pledged to cut drug prices by 25% in 50 of the poorest nations, release intellectual property rights for substances and processes relevant to neglected diseases into a patent pool to encourage new drug development, and invest 20% of profits from the least-developed countries in medical infrastructure for those countries.[3] Though GlaxoSmithKline's initiative was not accepted unconditionally (e.g., some medical charities had mixed, negative reactions,[4,5] while others, such as Médecins Sans Frontières, had a positive attitude toward it but criticized GlaxoSmithKline for failing to include HIV patents in their patent pool and for not including middle-income countries in the initiative),[6] it has encouraged other companies to take on similar initiatives.

And GlaxoSmithKline is not alone. Novartis has its Tropical Disease Institute in Singapore, which is working on a number of tropical diseases. AstraZeneca has a facility in Bengaluru, India, that is dedicated to research in tuberculosis. Other pharmaceutical companies, in one way or another, have embraced corporate social responsibility, but as was said before, they can do only so much because in the end, their CEOs have

The World's Health Care Crisis. DOI: 10.1016/B978-0-12-391875-8.00012-3

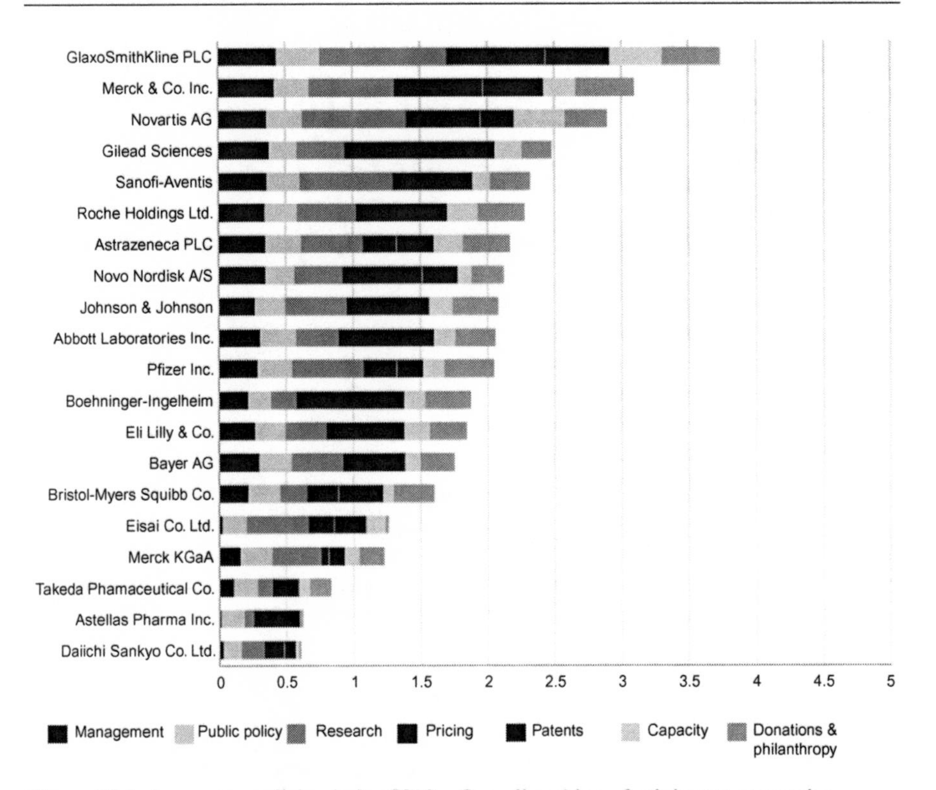

Figure 12.1 Access to medicine index 2010—Overall ranking of originator companies. *Source*: Access to Medicine Index, 2010, p. 18. © Access to Medicine Index. Reprinted with permission. All rights reserved. http://www.accesstomedicineindex.org/sites/; http://www.accesstomedicineindex.org/files/publication/Access_to_Medicine_Index_2010.pdf.

to stand in front of Wall Street institutions to justify what they have done, which is not easy to do. This is why society has to find complementary and alternative ways to invest in research and development (R&D) and to make progress in facilitating access to pharmaceuticals to people who cannot afford them. But of course, this must be a shared responsibility among pharmaceutical companies, international organizations, philanthropic groups, and especially the countries receiving the international aid.

What the Wellcome Trust (to mention only one of the best-funded and dynamic philanthropic organizations in the world) is doing,[7] and what some governments are trying to do in terms of providing complementary funding for R&D, funding neglected disease research, and creating an infrastructure in the developing world that may be sustainable is the way to go. Of course, some organizations have contributed more than others, but what we need is more government involvement in this direction; in particular, the US and European governments should start following up on that commitment to make a new pharmaceutical system in the developing world a reality. Emerging economies, such as India and China, are becoming much wealthier, so they need to start doing more for the have-nots in these societies (see Table 12.1 for a list of

Table 12.1 Seeking Sustainability Health Care Reform in Major Emerging Markets

Country	Pharmaceutical Market Size	Reforms
China	• US$25.5 billion • Projected to reach US$35.3 billion by 2014	• "Healthy China 2020" plan to realize universal access to essential health care services. • Phase I to realize universal coverage of essential health care. Allocates US$124 billion to curb medical costs, urban–rural gap. • Phase II (2010–2015) to boost services beyond those of other developing countries. • Phase III (2015–2020) to complete a robust essential health care system with universal coverage.
India	• US$8.4 billion • Projected to reach US$16.5 billion by 2014	• Recently established a system to track supply trends of drugs in the market, to allow the government to forecast drug supply shortages. • The new drug tracking system may increase prices to incentivize pharmaceutical companies to relaunch their versions of drugs in local markets. • Boosting regulatory regime to increase competitiveness of exports and outsourcing providers.
Brazil	• US$16.6 billion • Projected to reach US$24.9 billion by 2014	• Pharma is one of our pillars of new industrial policy. • Federal government has created a special financing program to increase the local production of medicines, facilitate R&D developments and encourage M&A. • Government plan to boost investment in biotechnology R&D through 2017.
Russia	• US$7.9 billion • Projected to reach US$13.6 billion by 2014	• Reforms to expand coverage for prescription drugs by 2010. • Universal prescription drug coverage will expand demand for retail prescription drugs (mostly paid out-of-pocket at present).
Mexico	• US$13.2 billion • Projected to reach US$17.0 billion by 2014	• Plans to cover 85% of the country's population under the public health care system by 2012. • Pledged to invest US$9.5 billion investment to improve infrastructure.

Source: The World Pharmaceutical Markets Fact Book, 2009; Ernst & Young, 2010. Global pharmaceuticals industry report. Progressions. Pharma 3.0., p. 6.

health care reform initiatives in emergent markets). In Latin American countries, such as Chile, Brazil, Argentina, and Mexico,[8] whose R&D structures are among the most developed on the subcontinent (Panama, whose economic growth has been remarkable, even during a world recession, could become an important logistic center for Latin America[9]), great effort should be directed toward R&D investment and the observance of intellectual property laws so that they become a model for the region. Cuba, which unfortunately is trapped in an outdated and repressive political system, has a very interesting scientific infrastructure, with an important number of talented scientists and physicians and the creation of several biotechnology drugs.[10] But again, the limitations of Latin America, in spite of its first-rate minds and tremendous potential in the pharmaceutical sector, are constituted by the great corruption and lack of vision that is pervasive from Mexico to the tip of Argentina. One could find highly intelligent people, geniuses, even in the most rural areas of these countries, but how could all this talent develop its full intellectual potential and become a tremendous asset for society in an environment that is so brutally antagonistic to self-realization and so deprived of opportunity? How could these countries expect to be less dependent on richer nations if they do not invest in an R&D platform, if they do not exploit their human capital, if there is not a radical change in their mentality, and if they do not make an effort to deal with their problems in an intelligent and systematic manner? These are not rhetorical questions in any way. This is a summary of my own life, of my own existence.

There are important players in the world, such as the Global Fund, that are not driving R&D themselves but that are helping developing countries to buy drugs, creating a mechanistic market where there was no market and complementing the work being performed by the organizations mentioned earlier. HIV and tuberculosis are well-known cases of diseases that afflict tropical and subtropical regions, but there are also other lethal diseases caused by worms, for instance, where a market needs to be created so that pharmaceutical products are brought to these regions. In this respect, there is one flow of this funding to purchase medicines and another flow that is in tune with financing R&D gaps. And what the world needs is to continue to increase and synchronize both types of funds. However, it is important that these funds be different and complementary; in other words, one type of fund should focus on education and R&D and the other on purchasing and financing drugs, which is not happening at present. Though the Global Fund has now made a separation between R&D and drug purchasing, there are still many development aid funds in developed countries that have not done so. In these funding activities, two key aspects must be kept in mind: first, the ethical dimensions of development aid and, second, conflicts of interest; those entities that buy the drugs or finance their assessment should not be the same as those that finance R&D.

The World Health Organization (WHO) plays a huge role in the processes mentioned and has done quite a few things. But WHO should also be strengthened in certain roles to assume the maximum amount of responsibility because it could be in an excellent position to do certain things that other parties cannot. What are these things that other parties cannot do? WHO still enjoys a very strong reputation among many developing countries. A good example is the swine flu: WHO has been brokering to encourage all countries that have cases of swine flu to make biological samples available to the industry. Had WHO not brokered certain of these initiatives, it would have been much more difficult to get the samples out and do further research in countries with more sophisticated research infrastructure. So there is something of a coordination role for WHO in trying to bring different parties together. But again, WHO should be very cautious not to enter conflicts of interest, which unfortunately, they are doing already. Now, WHO should be much stronger in pointing out the research gaps and much more vocal in pointing out what drug research needs to be done to help certain populations that face a particular health care hazard, and also in ensuring that someone will produce these drugs.

There are now antimalarials produced by generics manufacturers based on the Chinese experience with artemisinins, a drug used to treat multi-drug-resistant strains of *falciparum* malaria. The generics manufacturers have started to do *de facto* new drugs: they can put it together with the quality of the tablets, but if one asks questions about safety and efficacy, these companies cannot answer, but they have the tablets. Now, there are pressures to accept it, which is not correct. There should be a way of saying, "OK, antimalarials are not a problem of the West, except for tourists. Therefore, there are no incentives for a research-based industry. Fine!" Then, there is a public funding mechanism to do the necessary R&D, and generics companies can do it. If one has the elements for the safety and efficacy of a drug, then these generics manufacturers can come in and do the job. This could lead to an interesting mixture of R&D from public funds and collaboration with generics companies that could be quite productive. This activity could create revenues that could act as an incentive to generics manufacturers in developing countries, which would allow them to improve their business. There are many interesting opportunities in developing countries.

Countries like China should put in much more governmental effort toward training their people in regulatory affairs and science, in quality control, and in how to make medicines properly. If they do not do so, they will serve neither their population, the long-term financial perspectives, nor the global community. Chinese medicines are now increasing in number; they are going to developing countries because they are already catching up economically, but they still have a lack of knowledge. What is then a very interesting trend is that although the patent owners are in the developed world and most of the patients are still there, a large number of clinical research programs are being held nowadays in the developing countries, which is a clear shift: more and more patients are being enrolled in developing countries for clinical trials. The industry is happy about that, not only because it is so cheap to run clinical trials in developing countries, but the patient populations in the developing world are interesting because some of them are unique or even naïve populations (meaning that they have never been exposed to a particular kind of medicine before). In the case of some diseases in Europe, where one gets disease treatment guidelines, everybody gets certain drugs. If one has the disease, one receives the drug because one is reimbursed there. Now, if one wants to study something in a population that has not been exposed to this drug, one cannot find such a population in Europe anymore, so one has to go to developing countries where there are many populations for untreated naives. In countries like China, where there are so many people, companies can recruit patients easily, so there are many incentives for companies to work there.

Another important trend is starting to take place in the developing world: namely, contracting out clinical trials and the involvement of smaller R&D pockets that never create the final product but that contribute to its development. Thus, it would be extremely positive if R&D of this sort were to go to the developing countries because it helps create a national knowledge base and allows for the appropriate training and use of a highly educated workforce to accomplish its ends. Though neglected at present, teaching local people regulatory science at the highest possible level today, with all the scientific and development input, is extremely important, especially in countries like Brazil, as I mentioned earlier. Governments could have a more responsible role in this, and they should ensure that they understand that job and create an infrastructure.

There are certainly avenues to creating infrastructure with adequate personnel to work on R&D as related to medicine. But again, there needs to be some sort of incentive or commercially viable concept for countries to invest in the creation of this type of initiative. Who may need them? National regulatory authorities would need them; pharmaceutical and local industries would need them because there are a significant number of local industries all around the world, and most of them would need better-qualified staff than they have today. Having any government take over the manufacture of pharmaceuticals is a call for disaster, as exemplified by the diethylene-glycol poisoning case that took place in Panama in 2006. In this case, the government prepared cold syrup with a batch of contaminated solvent that was acquired from China and sold as propylene-glycol when in reality it was diethylene-glycol, a poisonous agent used as antifreeze,[11] killing hundreds, maybe thousands, of people. (At least, this is what the *New York Times* reported; the Chinese manufacturers were executed, but no justice has been made in Panama by the local authorities. The government has not provided adequate help and follow-on treatment to the surviving victims nor to the families of the deceased ones, which, not surprisingly, belong to the humbler strata of society). Governments instead should be involved in the control and organization of the process and in the creation of incentives for local manufacturers to carry out the manufacture of the drugs. And in the case of counterfeit drugs, a pervasive and prevalent problem in the developing countries, the culprits should be taken to an international criminal court and be dealt with.

Donors also have powerful tools to get these things done, and the key issue is to invest in qualifying people and in creating a platform that would become sustainable over time. Donors can encourage underdeveloped countries to work together. What is now happening in Africa is that every country wants to have local manufacturers, but unfortunately, this is not financially and commercially viable: they end up producing expensive, low-quality products.

Of the African nations, probably the one that can become a model for the rest is South Africa because it is the biggest and most developed. But South Africa is not really typical of Africa because it has a developed infrastructure, educated people, universities, and manufacturing. But like in Brazil, the great social and economic inequality that exists in South Africa is a barrier to progress.

It is, therefore, necessary to foster the convergence of efforts among and cross-talk between the biopharmaceutical industry, academic institutions, public funding agencies, investors, nongovernmental organizations and advocacy groups, and regulators to solve the health care crisis that afflicts not only the developing countries, but also the developed world.

Notes

1. "—Ferdinand Gonseth: Mi conclusión es la siguiente, mi evidencia tardía: que el ser humano es un ser hecho con el fin de ser portador de unas obligaciones morales. El hombre es, por naturaleza, un ser para lo moral. Si llegáramos a conocerlo todo, dejaríamos de ser un ser para lo moral.
   —Vintila Horia: Nos encontraríamos más allá del bien y del mal.
   —Ferdinand Gonseth: Justo. Usted acaba de formularlo muy bien. Está en contra de nuestro estatuto de criaturas esto de poder ser más allá del bien y del mal."
2. Vagelos, P.R., Galambos, L., 2004. Medicine, Science, and Merck. Cambridge University Press, New York.
3. Drug giant GlaxoSmithKline pledges cheap medicine for world's poor. Guardian, February 13, 2009. http://www.guardian.co.uk/business/2009/feb/13/glaxo-smith-kline-cheap-medicine.
4. UNITAID statement on GSK patent pool for neglected diseases, February 16, 2009. http://www.unitaid.eu/en/resources/news/158-unitaid-statement-on-gsk-patent-pool-for-neglected-diseases.html.
5. Baker, B.K., 2009. GSK access to medicines: the good, the bad, and the illusory. Health GAP, February 15, 2009. http://www.healthgap.org/bakeronGSK.htm.
6. MSF response to GSK patent pool proposal. Médecins Sans Frontières, February 16, 2009. http://www.msfaccess.org/media-room/press-releases/press-release-detail/?tx_ttnews[tt_news]=1532&cHash=f8c0eca3b4.
7. Unfortunately, the Bill and Melinda Gates Foundation cannot be discussed here as, in spite of several attempts, they refused to be interviewed for this book.
8. In January 2010, Mexican billionaire Carlos Slim announced the donation of $65 million for a 3-year joint collaboration between the Instituto Nacional de Medicina Genómica de México and the Broad Institute in Cambridge, MA (MIT/Harvard), to study the genomics of seven different types of cancer, diabetes mellitus, and renal failure. "Slim donará 65 millones para investigación de medicina genómica," La Prensa de Panamá, January 21, 2010. http://mensual.prensa.com/mensual/contenido/2010/01/21/uhora/cienc_20100121100957 58.asp.
9. In fact, at the end of October 2009, Genzyme announced the creation of a subsidiary in Panama. Philips, BMW y Genzyme establecerán sedes en Panamá. Panama América, October 29, 2009.
10. Cuban biotechnology products in 58 countries of the world. Cuban News Agency, February 8, 2009. http://www.cubaheadlines.com/2009/02/08/15729/cuban_biotechnology_products_58_countries_world.html.
11. Bogdanich, W., Hooker, J., 2007. From China to Panama, a trail of poisoned medicine. New York Times, May 6, 2007. http://www.nytimes.com/2007/05/06/world/americas/06poison.html.

Part V

Reinventing Research and Development

13 Time for Reorganization

One must be constantly changing, renewing, rejuvenating oneself so as not to become boring.

—Johann Wolfgang von Goethe in a letter to Chancellor von Müller, April 24, 1830

At the beginning of this book, we saw that the health care crisis that is afflicting the world like an epidemic has two dimensions: the world's health care systems are inadequate to provide people with appropriate access to health care, and importantly, they are unable to provide them with medicines. For decades, prominent people, notably politicians and economists in the United States, have praised the European and Canadian health care systems for being "universal" (which means that every citizen is insured) or for having a single payer (i.e., the government becomes responsible for providing health insurance to its citizens). In the United States, there have been several attempts to adopt a health care system similar to the ones in these regions, the most recent being President Bill Clinton's failed endeavors in this direction and President Barack Obama's current bumpy efforts. These attempts, in my opinion, have been performed without a full understanding of how the world's health care systems work, which may, in the long run, create very serious and undesired effects that will be opposite to what is being sought. In the end, the so-called cure may be more harmful (and expensive) than the diseases left untreated.

This book has been based on the idea that regardless of whether the US health care system becomes a universal (or single-payer) system, having access to more effective, safe, and innovative drugs will continue to be a problem—as supported by evidence that in those countries (Europe, Canada, Japan, etc.) where there has been a single-payer system for decades, health care systems are highly dysfunctional. Take Britain, for example, a country where, back in 2008, a patient wanting to be reimbursed for a course of Lucentis, a drug used to treat macular degeneration of the eyes, had to lose one eye before getting reimbursed.[1] Or take as an example the high inefficiency of the Canadian or Japanese health care systems, which are characterized by long waiting lists for what they consider nonemergency treatments; or the case of France, where overconsumption is driving the system toward collapse.

A health care system based on a single payer, given the depredatory capitalistic mentality of the United States, is not only anathema to this country, where people always demand what they think is the best for them, but economically, it is unsustainable. The same holds true for the alternatives currently being explored by the US government. We need to look no further beyond Medicare and the health care reforms enacted in states such as California and Massachusetts to get a taste of what is coming. Even insured people, as we saw in Chapter 1, are having problems affording some

The World's Health Care Crisis. DOI: 10.1016/B978-0-12-391875-8.00013-5

very expensive drugs. As Anita Kidgell from GlaxoSmithKline has pointed out, "The U.S. vision is a very consumer-focused country. And I mean for pharmaceuticals, the U.S. is the key market because people demand the best treatment. In Europe, they are much more laid back. If the doctors say this is the best one, they take it. Whereas in America … the competitive spirit in terms of commercialization is much greater." When comparing the US and British systems, Kidgell says, "But the U.K. is different … I think it is very restrictive in terms of drugs. So in the U.K., you don't get a lot of choice, you kind of get what you are given, and some areas in the U.K. are denied life-saving cancer therapy. In the U.S., that would never exist. People would be out in the streets … but here you are seeing people complain, some patient groups saying 'This isn't right!' but not in the way you would get in the U.S. … and that sort of restrictive aspect is just not the mentality of Americans: they want choice, they want to make their own decisions and they want to get the best whereas here is different."[2]

I am not a pessimistic person, and far be it from me to oppose a health care overhaul. I am a firm believer that every country should provide its citizens with adequate health care insurance to cover their health needs. But I am also realistic, and I believe that no country can provide its citizens with adequate health care without a mixture of public and private benefits and incentives and without careful study and planning. So a health care overhaul is not something that one can improvise or try to accomplish in one year or during a presidential term. It is a lengthy, carefully thought-out process that needs to suit the economic, political, sociological, psychological, health, cultural, and historical conditions of the country where such reforms are to be implemented.

The key issue that is missing from the equation in the current health care debates is the following: how will people have access to the best medicines in the world, and who is going to pay for them? Economists and politicians in the United States say that that is not a problem because nearly 80% of prescriptions written in the United States are for generic drugs, which are easily affordable. But after reading this book, and examining this situation carefully, we realize that this is indeed a problem because generics companies are *not* innovators. In other words, they make money from drugs that have already been discovered and developed by other companies and that have gone off patent, and effective though these drugs may be, there is always room for improvement in terms of dosing, effectiveness, or safety. Not only that, but consider the large number of unmet medical needs, such as those requiring antibiotics, that exist today and that will continue to increase, as well as the increasing incidence, diversity, and complexity of chronic ailments among the world population. Furthermore, it has recently been acknowledged by regulators that some generics really are not equivalent to the branded drugs that they are imitating, which has prompted the U.S. Food and Drug Administration (FDA) to consider (and adopt) tougher new standards to make sure "there is less variability" among generics, which has certainly concerned the generics industry.[3]

We can ask an even more provocative question: if generics companies are not innovators, then who is going to produce the next generation of drugs?

And here we hit a wall. The answer to this question is obvious: the biopharmaceutical industry will be responsible for creating the next generation of drugs. But at this point, we need to emphasize that the pharmaceutical industry will do this so long as there are economic incentives for it because the biopharmaceutical industry is a business, and any business, especially in the United States, exists to make money. So businesses need a monetary incentive to bring new and better products to the market (take as an example Apple's iPod and iPhone, or Microsoft, or BMW—they all do this). If this incentive is not on the table, then there are no incentives to take on the financial risks that biopharmaceutical companies do to bring new drugs to market, which, as we have seen throughout this book, is a highly complex, lengthy, expensive, and sophisticated endeavor.

The major issue that we encounter with the pharmaceutical industry is that it has been abusive on all fronts, and people know it. But at the same time, it is necessary to remember that there are many risks looming on the horizon if our attitude toward the biopharmaceutical industry becomes too negative. For instance, there is the risk that price controls will be imposed in the United States, which may represent a real disaster, not only for the pharmaceutical industry but for everyone, because there will not be great enough incentive to innovate, and as a result there will be no wonder drugs to treat cancer, Alzheimer's, Parkinson's, HIV, arthritis, and other serious diseases that plague the human race.

Luckily, the pharmaceutical industry is going through the deepest crisis in its 150-year history—with a severe lack of productivity and loss of sales to generics, not to mention shorter patent exclusivity time, poor public image, and great concerns from regulators about safety issues, among many other issues—which makes it more receptive to external input and forces it to consider some real internal metamorphoses. As we thoroughly explored in the book, the bottom-line problem with the pharmaceutical industry is research and development (R&D) productivity, which is a direct function of how basic scientific knowledge becomes translated into commercial products and how applied research is guided by fundamental research. As Christopher Milne, at the Tufts Center for the Study of Drug Development, says:

> *[T]he scientific problems that the pharmaceutical industry is confronting are particularly challenging. And I think that now they feel like they have exceeded their capacity to deal with them, so you are getting a lot more talk, and it's probably the reason why you are getting the companies buying each other up, you know, trying to buy more later-stage research products, etc. But it is also the reason why you are getting people interested in public-private partnerships. And industry is also more willing to do what they call "free-competitive collaboration" or working together to the point called "specific utility." Because they realize that the only way they are going to be able to deal with some of the scientific challenges is through pooling resources, and now I think that they are going to think about pooling data too, again because of the problem with patient recruitment. The industry is learning as it goes, and so are the regulatory agencies as well. So that's a hurdle, but you can see that also as an opportunity.*[4]

From a global society point of view, the main issue is how people can have access to more affordable and better medicines. And this ultimately depends on how efficient the biopharmaceutical industry becomes from now on so that prices go down. Thus, we come full circle. More government-funded health insurance will help, but people need to know that this is neither an "overhaul" nor a real solution to the problem. In the best of cases, it will become a short-term palliative. Outside the United States, where the majority of the world population lives, health care services are comparatively cheap, but for a large percentage of this population, having access to *adequate* medicines represents the most expensive part of health care spending because it is an out-of-pocket expense for individuals (see Figure 2.1b). And some of the poorest countries in the world have neither adequate health care services nor access to medicines. It is about time that we think about these issues from a global perspective.

Health care reform, therefore, should be not only about health insurance reform but also about biopharmaceutical industry reform, intellectual property law reform, regulatory system reform, university–industry collaboration reform, basic science reform, pricing reform, prevention reform, tort reform, and other types of reform—all of which contribute directly and indirectly to the cost of the health care system (see Figure 13.1). On the basis of all that has been said in previous chapters of this book, there are several areas of focus for industrial initiatives and for public policy-making that could contribute to the bringing of better drugs to the market more rapidly and affordably for patients and help the pharmaceutical industry deal with the problems that it is currently confronting. We will consider these areas of focus in the remainder of this chapter.

Reorganization of Research and Development at the Industrial Level

As we have discussed extensively throughout the book, the major problem that the pharmaceutical industry faces is its lack of R&D productivity. Steven Paul, formerly at Lilly, agrees with this perspective:

> *My own perspective is that if you basically cut through the bottom line, the big problem, the one fundamental argument, the most important problem that industry faces is this problem of R&D productivity. All our ills will be corrected. I mean, if we behave ourselves, we do the right thing, etc., to our patients, for our patients, if we could solve the problem of how do we enhance the amount and quality of innovation in our pipelines, that one thing alone would change the whole. Of course, the irony is we are dealing with, as you know as a scientist, an actually incredible unprecedented time in scientific biomedical research. I think what is happening today is that the in-house discovery research efforts of big pharma have shrunk and almost every big pharmaceutical company has made major cuts in their discovery research. Obviously, they still have very large efforts in the downstream part, in the development part, from pharmacology through animal testing through clinical trials. And that seems to be the current configuration of the industry, is that little biotech companies that raise capital and partner are sold, and I don't know how long this is going to last.*[5]

But in a pharmaceutical firm, R&D productivity is not only a function of how much money is put into it, how big an R&D infrastructure is, or how sophisticated

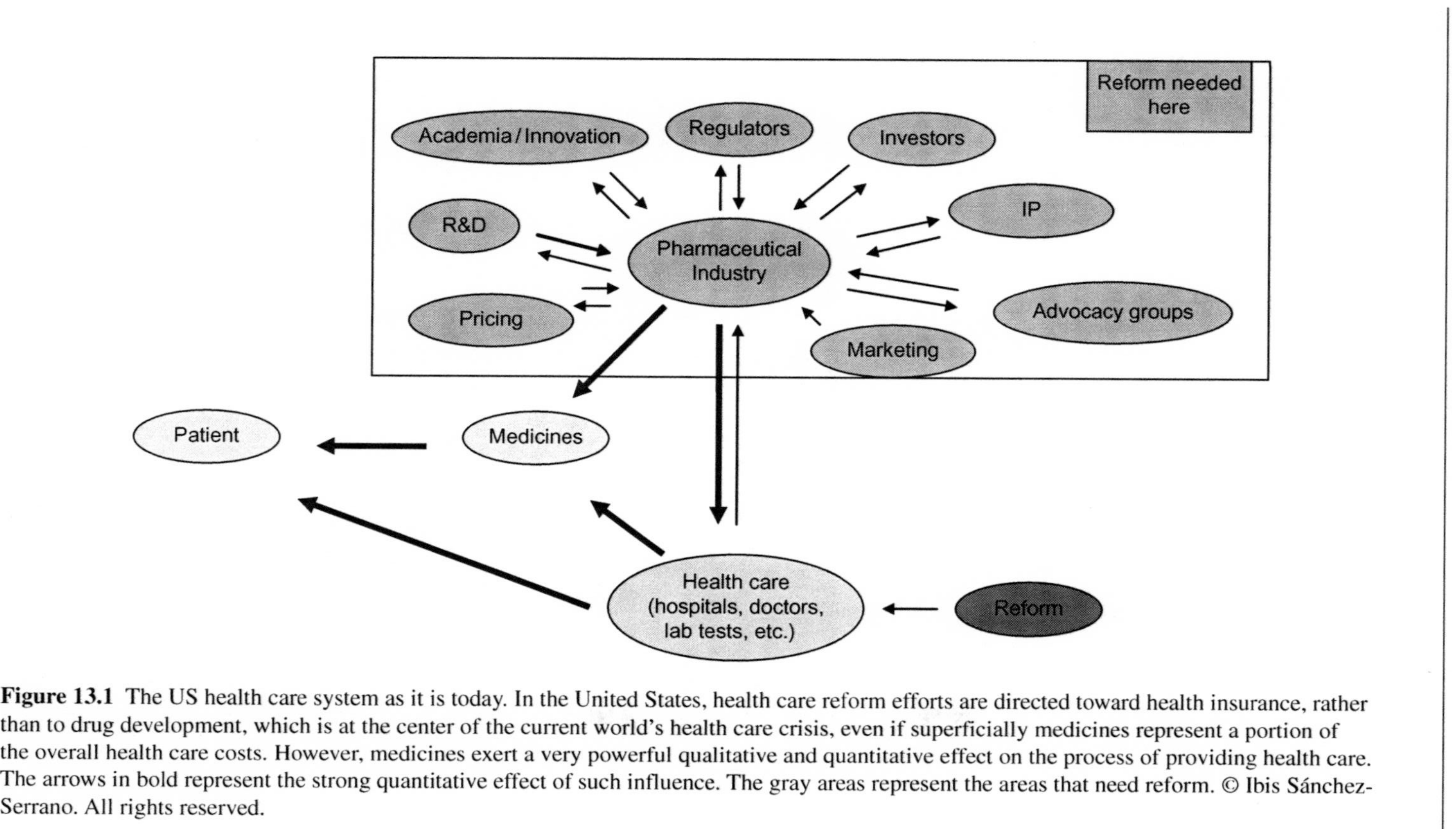

Figure 13.1 The US health care system as it is today. In the United States, health care reform efforts are directed toward health insurance, rather than to drug development, which is at the center of the current world's health care crisis, even if superficially medicines represent a portion of the overall health care costs. However, medicines exert a very powerful qualitative and quantitative effect on the process of providing health care. The arrows in bold represent the strong quantitative effect of such influence. The gray areas represent the areas that need reform.

the scientific tools being used to discover new drugs are; rather, it is a matter of how R&D is organized and how the top management of a company creates a research-focused culture within the company. When Roy Vagelos became the CEO of Merck in 1985 after being head of its R&D division for almost a decade, not only did he preserve the R&D culture that had characterized this company for many decades but actually improved it. He created an almost "academic" environment in this company and a large number of incentives so that it could attract very talented people who would work very hard to make the company the best in the United States. For that reason, for 7 years in a row (1987–1993), Merck became not only the number one pharmaceutical company in the world, but the number one company across all industries.

But those days are gone. Nowadays, companies are much bigger and decentralized, people work significantly fewer hours, and the bigger economic incentives for young and talented scientists are not in big pharma but in early-stage biotech firms, where scientists can amass a large fortune if their company becomes successful—which is a very big incentive for people to do their best and to work long hours. As a leading European biotech CEO, who prefers to remain anonymous whose name is withheld upon request, put it:

> *The cost of drug discovery depends upon how efficient your process is and also how good you are at what you do, and I suspect the soonest you start discovering things in very large organizations, the social systems and the cultures put increasing difficulties on the scientific process, so that I am sure it is much more costly. Well, it is much more costly in the pharmaceutical [industry] than it is outside in biotech. And all this has to do with the scale of the organization and the efficiency... If you have twenty people working together in a small biotech company, that's going to be far more efficient than having a research department of three hundred people. I don't think that's a criticism of the pharmaceutical companies that got more expensive, it is a result of having that critical mass and all those different functions and systems and layers of management to coordinate it all, which makes it more expensive.*[6]

The last wave of mergers, far from solving the pharmaceutical industry's problems, has compounded them, and in the years to come, these mergers will certainly create not only more managerial layers but also great disruptions in the cultures and programs of these large firms. As a result, it will be impossible to manage them directly from the top, as used to be done, or in a "closed innovation" fashion, in which ideas in these companies were generated internally and taken from concept to commercialization using vertically integrated resources.

Instead, an "open innovation" model—one in which new product innovation originates from both internal and external ideas—may be the way to go.[7] So, companies will have to reorganize and fragment their operations, especially their R&D infrastructures, into smaller units, and they will have to focus on the effective feedback between basic scientific information and commercial research via translational science. The good news is that several reorganizational models to accomplish this are emerging, notably at companies such as Lilly and GlaxoSmithKline (although Johnson & Johnson has restructured in a way similar to GlaxoSmithKline) and at Novartis, a company with a very powerful translational research program, to mention just a few firms. As Steven Paul, formerly at Lilly, says, "the transformation, by the way, that has to occur in this industry is first and foremost a transformation of R&D. So you have to approach the whole problem of R&D. The whole approach to R&D has to change. Unless the industry changes its approach to R&D, it will go out of business! We need the drugs! But second, we need to transform the business model. The business model is not a good model, and so all of that has to be done!" Let us discuss these approaches in some detail because I think a great deal can be learned from them.

At Lilly, R&D efforts are directed toward what the company refers to as an unprecedented target—in other words, a target for which a mechanism of action for that potential medicine has not yet been unequivocally established to produce a desirable clinical benefit.[8] This strategy, which on the positive side might be very rewarding—because it could give rise to medicines that could change the standard of care for a given disease and which, in turn, could replace older and less effective drugs—has the disadvantage of high risk and time consumption. In addition to a strong focus on developing drugs based on entirely new targets (more than 60 programs going on at present), the company is exploring a set of different organizational arrangements, such as outsourcing their toxicology unit, establishing cooperation with other firms to share R&D information and financial risk, and outsourcing some leading compounds until they have demonstrated proof of principle in man[9] and taking them back for full development in-house. Similarly, GlaxoSmithKline has radically changed its R&D organization after two consecutive mergers with the creation of the Centres of Excellence for Drug Discovery (CEDDs), which consisted of fragmenting the company's R&D platform into smaller units similar to biotech companies.

Eli Lilly has also realized that it was costing the company an average of $26 million to get a drug from the point of lead optimization to the end of Phase I, and that this was taking them 40 months to accomplish. To speed up this process, Lilly decided to experiment with minimizing the infrastructure around several promising agents and, as such, created an independent entity named Chorus. This unit, located six miles away from the Lilly campus in Indianapolis to give it a physical and bureaucratic distance, hired outside consultants and experts in the field to take these likely-to-succeed leads to Phase I clinical trials; in other words, to establish proof of concept on the company's drug candidates as quickly and inexpensively as possible so they could give them back to Lilly at the end of Phase I. This strategy allows the company a great deal of flexibility because Chorus can assemble quickly the consultants that they need to work on specific projects or wholly different therapeutic areas; in this way, they can move faster than from within the company organization.

The key issue in this strategy is the fact that Chorus works from lead optimization through Phase I and Phase II, which are the trials where scientists generally look for safety and proof of concept (i.e., efficacy), where most of the attrition in drug development takes place. This system is also suitable for post-Phase I or even Phase II studies in which companies are interested in better understanding the mechanisms of disease or the use of biomarkers in areas such as cancer, inflammation, or infectious disease, which are very appealing for this strategy.

As a result, Lilly has reduced the average cost of going to the end of Phase I from \$26–30 million to \$3.4–5 million, and the time from 40 to 18 months, and then to 12 months. In addition, the company has increased its R&D productivity from candidate selection to proof of concept by as much as five- to tenfold over more traditional pharmaceutical development.[10] There have also been some positive results in using this strategy. For instance, Lilly has produced in this way some positive proof of concept into man, as illustrated by analgesic activity in human pain models. This type of data helped the company reduce Phase II attrition from roughly 75−50% and, if sustainable, will by itself reduce the cost of developing a new molecular entity (NME) by almost \$300 million.

So Lilly, as they say, is moving from being a fully integrated pharmaceutical company (FIPCo) to a fully integrated pharmaceutical network (FIPNet) in which the company uses resources by outsourcing some work (such as toxicology work from preclinical to Phase I) and by partnering very costly, late-stage projects to mitigate financial risk (i.e., Phase III clinical trials in Alzheimer's disease) in collaboration with other companies (see Figure 13.2).[11] Despite some criticisms, these models are being adopted by other large companies and also by some biotech start-ups (such as

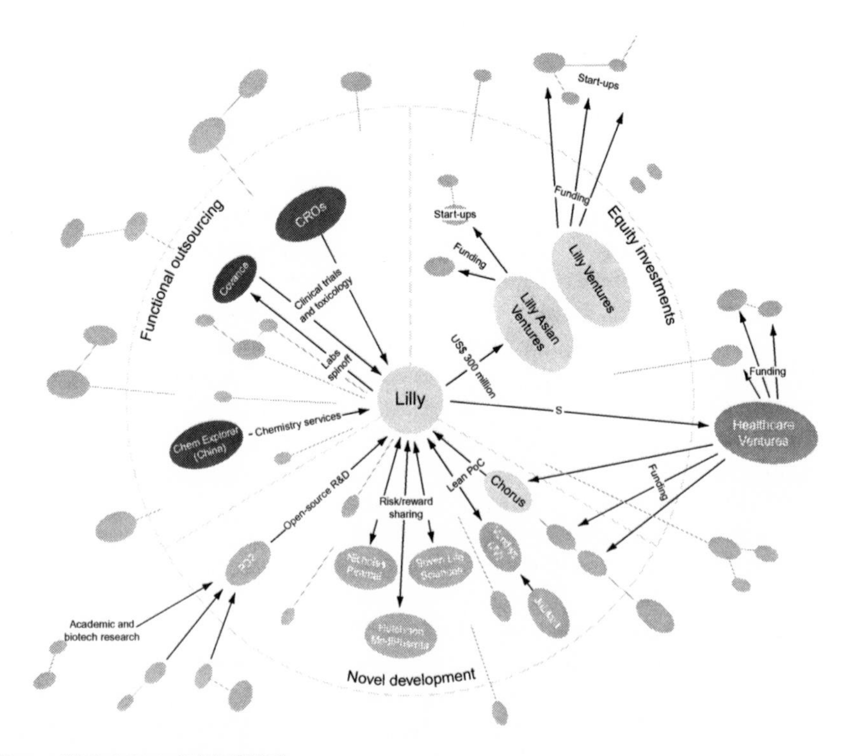

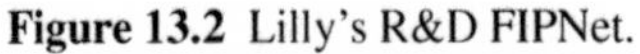
Figure 13.2 Lilly's R&D FIPNet.
Source: Ernst and Young, 2010. "Beyond Borders: Global Biotechnology Report," p. 32.

Modern Biosciences in London), which takes potential drug agents from academia, moves them through proof of concept, and then sells them to pharma.

GlaxoSmithKline's case is more complex. After its last merger (in 2000), the company realized that it was spending about $4 to 5 billion a year in R&D and still was not performing it effectively. After two mergers, Glaxo's R&D pyramid posed a big problem: all the work was concentrated at the bottom of the pyramid, while at the top, there was the head of R&D, and between the top and bottom, there were 23 layers of management, which certainly was not conducive to good research. So Glaxo fragmented its R&D into smaller R&D units known as the Centres of Excellence for Drug Discovery (CEDDs), which are like small organizations and therefore easier to manage. The heads of the CEDDs are like the CEOs of small biotech companies: they decide whether to in-license or out-license products, whether to use their own research or have research done by outsiders, which research direction to take, and so on. They have the power to do that because they have their own budget to do so; and therefore they have the same degree of accountability and flexibility of a biotech, where scientists also have some accountability for target validation and certainly pick what targets to work on. At the CEDDs, they are buying in, licensing out, making the best possible deals, and have access to the best research and use it, regardless of whether it is developed internally or licensed from a competitor. They are trying to develop the best portfolio they can, and it does not matter whether all of it comes externally because so much of it is collaborative.

Clearly, it is impossible to be a biotech company in a big organization. But in taking a biotech-like approach, the company aims at playing big and small at the same time. On the front end, Glaxo wants to have all the advantages of a large multinational organization, such as large-scale sequencing and high-throughput screening, and on the back end, it is interested in deploying effectively its expertise in regulatory affairs and, on the toxicology front, in conducting large-scale clinical trials. The company now has a very big early-drug discovery setup, which is big machinery, where right at the start, it carries out high-throughput screening. Then these leads move to the CEDDs, where they select the right candidates before they go on to full development. So the goal of taking the leads to the CEDDs is to create a very nimble process to allow the company is able to make decisions very quickly and get the best of those groups. As a result, once they get to the big areas like Phase III clinical trials or Phase IV, after launch, they need massive investment to get all that going. So it starts with big screening using the company's large infrastructure, then small, nimble optimization, and finally big development. And that is the way this company is structured.

The bulk of the CEDDs' work takes place from lead optimization through proof of concept. Whereas before, the company would have a discovery organization and they would throw molecules all over the world to develop them, in a CEDD, if scientists select a candidate molecule, they must be sure that it is going to deliver a proof of concept. Now it might not deliver a positive proof of concept, but the person in charge of the CEDD would like to be able to make a decision at the end of the day about that proof of concept. And if it does not work in the target, then that indication is dead. Now, how is that different from how research is organized in some companies, such as Roche and other companies, that are organized by therapeutic area? According to Jackie Hunter, senior vice president of Science Environment Development and former head of GlaxoSmithKline's Neurology and Gastrointestinal CEDD:

> *The difference is that in the CEDDs, not only do I have the accountability for a portfolio, my portfolio, but I can decide how to run it because I know the budget for it. I know the budget for the preclinical studies. I know the budget for the clinical studies. I know the money I expend early on and the reason that's important is the following: if Glaxo's assessment wants to do a huge, big prioritization and say, "We only got some internal reasons … we're going to have to put your project dead," fine. I can make a decision. I can make the tradeoffs in my projects, in my portfolio, and make sure that my top projects don't get lost in some global miasma. Now, some other companies are actually organizing what they call CEDD-like lines, but they are not getting the budgetary accountability in the same way because of the other parts of the organization they have. And it is not just about having the accountability for the portfolio. It is about having the budget as well.*[12]

So actually it is necessary to have more control—not only over the science, but also over the budget. This, bringing financial control and research to a convergence point, would address one of the major problems of the industry, which is efficiency. A CEDD's head, who is a champion for the portfolio he or she is developing, is going to be judged on whether the portfolio makes it. Thus far, some CEDDs have had a number of failed proofs of concept, which could be a success because at least those indications were killed and no further investment was made in them.

One of the potential risks associated with the approach taken by GlaxoSmithKline is that it fosters competition between CEDD units. However, Glaxo created means to incentivize people within their basic CEDDs, while making people realize that they get paid and funded only as a whole company. Doing this in this way creates every incentive to cooperate and therefore increase the flexibility of the CEDDs, which more than offsets the elements of competition. In terms of management, despite the fact that it is challenging for a big company to manage these kinds of things, GlaxoSmithKline manages to have all this collaboration and all these little CEDDs and still keeps a very organized structure.

Indeed, there are many areas that overlap. Infrastructures like human resources and information technology are shared across the CEDDs. In terms of the actual management of the groups, they have a variety of CEDD meetings that look across all CEDD groups, and with that, they get access to a review by a board of people in R&D to decide what priorities should go where, which possibilities are most exciting, which possibilities have the most supporting evidence, where the most resources should be allocated, and so on. So there is an overseeing board that is responsible for assigning resources to the best projects.

In picking the right targets at the CEDDS, GlaxoSmithKline clearly has invested heavily in genetic studies (sometimes in collaboration with outside groups) to develop more sensitive and flexible medicine models in humans. For example, in the pain arena, they routinely carry out a battery of tests in volunteers in their Phase I studies—normal pain threshold or opioid-valid induced pain or capsacin-induced irritation—to see whether they can target their patient population better in Phase II trials or select doses to take forward into Phase II. So they are trying to allow them to pick the best targets and ask the right questions in Phase II clinical rounds. This is important not only for looking at the preclinical validation and developing better techniques like RNAi or inducible capsules, but also for looking at humanity and trying to get as much information about it as possible.

At Glaxo, their efforts are beginning to bear fruit, given the number of interesting leads they have in different areas. In May 2008, after becoming the new CEO of GlaxoSmithKline, Andrew Witty continued the company's strategy of restructuring research around CEDDs. Each CEDD will have to pitch a three-year business plan to Glaxo's Drug Discovery Investment Board—composed of six members from Glaxo, two venture capital bosses, a former executive of the UK National Health Service, and the chief of a biotechnology firm—to ensure an objective decision-making process for project selection. An important component of the CEDD model is external collaboration with academic institutions. For instance, in June 2008, GlaxoSmithKline established a $25-million collaboration between Glaxo and the Immune Disease Institute of Boston for the development of immunoinflammatory drugs. It is interesting that this collaboration is intended to be more like a partnership than the traditional model in which the pharmaceutical industry simply provides funding for multiple academic laboratories, which corroborates our impressions about the academia-industry interface.

Translational Research

In addition to reorganization, companies should continue to have a strong focus on R&D. Translational research, in other words, the transformation of basic scientific discoveries arising from laboratory, clinical, or population studies into clinical applications in humans—often referred to as research "from bench to bedside" or from laboratory experiments through clinical trials to the actual point of care in patient applications[13]—has been identified as an important step in accelerating the process of drug discovery and development. The typical approach in big pharma is if one compound fails in the first trial, it may sometimes get approval in the second trial; but if it fails in the second trial, then usually the company loses interest in it and says, "Well, that is a bad compound. Just put it away." What people in translational research are trying to do is build their knowledge from the biological response that the compound creates so that they can discover whether supposedly failed compounds may actually work in subpopulations. With this kind of approach, scientists conduct a gatekeeping study whereby they prove the safety of the compound and probe for druglike properties in terms of pharmacokinetics, and that is key. They do not want to go forward with a compound that, for whatever reason, does not hit its appropriate target, but if they have evidence of modulating the biological activity in humans—and this could be a clinical readout or a biochemical readout—and they have that assay set up, then based on that, they will expand into these kinds of indications.

One of the major differences between translational research and traditional pharma drug development is that in translational research, promising compounds, granted that they have a safe profile, are administered early on to patients instead of healthy volunteers. In addition, translational medicine generally requires access to two critical types of information about patients: first, clinical information, including data contained in hospital systems and medical records, pathology reports and diagnostic labs, clinical trial systems and study participant questionnaires; and second, biomolecular information, including genomics, proteomics, medical imaging, and other high-throughput molecular and cellular research data.

If one looks at the management of common diseases, they presently are well managed, at least under current standards—and that is not saying that one could not develop a better drug for diabetes or hypertension, for instance, but the new drugs in these areas would have to be much, much better to be cost-effective. Therefore, for a company to invest in such research, it must understand much more about the biology of diseases (something that will probably occupy pharmaceutical companies in the next decade), but with that long barrier also comes the understanding of the relationship between the genome and the phenotype, that is, understanding genes and their products.

When one speaks about the biology of a disease, it is necessary to specify what biology means in this context. Biology could mean many things: it could be the proteins and how they work in the cell, but at the same time, it could be broader than that because there are some other physiological aspects and there are also some external environmental factors that could have an impact on the behavior of organisms (epigenetics). In fact, it can be even more complicated than that. And so the first thing is to understand the protein function in the cell. Then one needs to understand the function of that protein in the context of the organism. Finally, one needs to understand the relationship between the organism and the environment. So there are all kinds of complications that will occur over time in terms of our understanding becoming deeper. It is within this context that translational research is evolving to provide that understanding between the genotype and the phenotype.

As I have pointed out already, the crucial problem in developing a new drug is the high rate of attrition of compounds. Unfortunately, many compounds undergo attrition, especially early on, before scientists know very much about them, because of safety or pharmacokinetic issues (such as rate of excretion, duration of effect, etc.) or simply because of their first lack of efficacy in a given patient population. What scientists are trying to do in companies that have a translational research program, such as Novartis, is to get as much information as possible about compounds (even about failing compounds) early on, with the goal of understanding the pharmacokinetics and the safety parameters. For this reason, they perform the relevant studies as quickly as possible by taking the agents into a patient population, either in the first or the second study, so long as the compound has appropriate safety parameters, so that they can identify a population that will provide them with biological parameters or clinical readouts that would allow them to develop a biomarker.

In that way, the company would get a sense of whether the drug is going to have some impact on the biological pathways that may be linked to a disease. At the same time, this approach gives the company an earlier view on the potential for the compound. Even though that compound may initially fail, scientists can determine at least whether they are targeting a valid pathway or a good pathway with which to take the agent (or its class) forward. If the company decides that a specific compound does not have a value based on hitting (or not) the human target *in vivo*, then they will drop it, and a great deal of time and money is saved in not pursuing something that will not work. According to Timothy Wright, vice president and global head of Translational Medicine at Novartis:

> *It's important in the process of translational medicine to understand that we quietly have a great relationship with our research colleagues, and in fact early on, it is that partnership that distinguishes us from other companies because the bench scientists are the ones that are profiling the new compounds, doing the high-throughput screenings, coming up with compounds to take forward, and there is an interaction at a very early stage between translational medicine and the bench scientists. That interaction helps to guide preclinical studies as far as in vitro and in vivo testing, and then in preparation in going to humans, a series of things need to be done in terms of a toxicology package, the pharmacokinetics in other species need to be established, and then the final estimate for the human trial, to design the human trial; and translational research plays a role all the way through that, and again in some companies that's done primarily by the clinical pharmacology group, and to get it into humans, there is a very standard package that can be generated. We try to adapt that in considering what would be our first testing of patients, and that's one of the things that we do differently is try to get our compounds into patients as quickly as possible.*[14]

Translational research programs have their scientists do significant brainstorming to find what other indications may be there in addition to the initially targeted population, and in fact, they often try to consider whether there are well defined, genetically defined, or disease subset populations that can be examined first with the compound. The reason for this is that they can best understand the scope of the potential for the compound. As we discussed earlier in the book, in many cases compounds are eventually registered for several indications different from the one that was initially identified, but this usually occurs in what is called *life cycle management*, that is, after the compound becomes a drug and has entered the market.

A great advantage of translational research, given the fact that compounds are taken directly into a patient population, is that it allows scientists to address the potential for multiple applications earlier, so that the patients take some benefit from the compound and have the ability to use this new compound as an indication much earlier than is traditionally possible. For the company, there is also a side benefit in the sense that the company expands the scope of benefits earlier, which means that the revenues for these sorts of indications will also have earlier results. It is an opportunity to increase revenues, as well as expand to appropriate medical needs if the compounds seem to have promise outside their initial indications.

The selection process of a drug candidate is not always easy for companies because scientists must make important decisions constantly regarding the viability of one program over another. Translational research is very important in drug selection because it allows companies to choose at an earlier stage the programs they think are more likely to be taken to the point of proof of concept.

In general, the drug selection process in companies doing translational research happens as follows: scientists discuss their compounds in regular meetings, so knowledge of these compounds does not reside within one single group but in the company, and suddenly it becomes known that they have a good compound. They acknowledge these compounds, and the fact that they are heading toward the clinic is acknowledged and shared very early. Scientists ask the following questions: "Should we quit that work somewhere else? Is that compound that is targeting autoimmunity likely to work in cancer, in neuroscience?" So they begin to discuss things with one another and suggest that they take the compound back to the lab and do some additional preclinical studies to verify the translational research group's ideas. If they get verification or if, in some cases, there are illnesses for which there are no good animal models, the translational research group will propose a clinical plan to their management board. Then, if the management board gives the OK, the next step will be to propose a clinical study and then a clinical plan that would go along with the clinical study, in case it turns out to be positive. This is all happening sometimes even before the first proof-of-concept study is ever approved. Likewise, at this early stage, scientists may be thinking about what they call *parallel indications;* in other words, how a single agent could be used to treat different diseases. With small molecules, that is, organic compounds that are biologically active (biomolecules) but not polymer molecules (as in the case of proteins), there is great potential for failure because the rate of attrition of these molecules is very high because many of the molecules are highly insoluble. Therefore, scientists usually stagger these molecules in the sense that they begin with some confidence about safety in humans and the pharmacokinetic and druglike properties of the compounds, and then soon after that, they follow up with additional indication studies. In some cases, they might say, "Wait for the first proof of concept, and we'll have the second, the third, and the fourth lined up just behind it."

Compounds that have single indications most of the time are interesting in their own right and in fact satisfy an unmet medical need. In other cases, companies have compounds that could go into multiple indications, which creates great excitement among scientists. Many times, those multiple indications are small, but companies are aware that several small indications could make up for the lack of a single, broad one. There are probably many compounds on the shelves of pharmaceutical companies that do have applications, but they all need initial indications, and they are put aside even though they may have a reasonable safety profile and reasonable druglike properties, precisely because people do not know what they could be used for.

In setting up their clinical programs, companies certainly take into consideration the input of a large number of leaders in the field—also known as *thought leaders*—in terms of clinical trial design and, in particular, what patient population may be targeted and the appropriate duration of the study looking for clinical effects. In general, companies have internal expertise in disease areas; they filter the information that comes from outside and retain the key information. Many outside experts are very useful to pharma, especially in designing late registration trials, which are large, so thought leaders address the registration end points, which are large clinical populations. What companies are trying to do in early studies in translational medicine is to identify key populations in which compounds could be tested and come up with a study that could be anywhere from 5 to 100 patients that will give the company a definitive answer as far as the value of the compound to take forward. So they take a great deal of input from opinion leaders and challenge them to determine whether they are using the compounds in the better populations, whether there are subpopulations, and whether there is a genetically defined group that would allow the company to test the agent very quickly so it can make a go/no-go decision. Companies usually present through that group of experts a broad proposal, something that they think may be an approach to a clinical trial, and then they have the group of experts dissect it to assess whether the approach is appropriate and what type of populations may be tried. Companies also educate the experts about their needs in terms of whether they want to do a short study, a small study, a definitive study. If all goes well, they send compounds into a subsequent clinical trial. There should, in general, be a short study to give a first notion that the compound has good clinical benefits, and then they follow up by looking at the longer-term benefits and address many times the big issues that relate to potential for registration.

As we discussed already, biomarkers are key in all this work. The biomarkers that companies are talking about, by and large, are the ones they have to develop internally, and many of these will never see the light of day, either as a diagnostic or something commercially viable, because they are for internal decision making. Biomarkers allow scientists to look at a tissue or look at a blood sample and ask, for instance, whether they have modulated up or down the target of interest based on administering their drug or compound. That is the challenge because getting the biomarkers in place requires more than a year, or sometimes it may even take 2 years, in terms of development time; it also takes significant resources. Importantly, the biomarker work needs to be done in parallel with getting the compound prepared to go to the clinic, and thus, this work is done in collaboration with translational medicine research and their biomarker development group.

There are some compounds for which companies have good, quick clinical readouts; for example, psoriasis (inflammation of skin cells), a clinical disease in which companies can look for a clinical response to a specific compound or determine whether the compound is hitting the right target in as short a time as 2 weeks. This is because the company can easily measure, from a clinical outcome, the response of the skin cells to the use of a given compound. In this case scenario, though biomarkers could be helpful in modulating the effect of the drug in skin cell inflammation, they are not necessary for decision making.

But there are other disease models that are often much more complex and long ranging, for which companies do need a biomarker to give them an early reading of whether they are having any positive effect in targeting a disease, such as imaging in multiple sclerosis. In the case of some cancers, developing biochemical biomarkers is important because this would allow scientists to pick a cancer-associated biomarker fairly early to see whether the molecule or the compound that the company is using is hitting the target in, for example, the tumor.

Though *biomarkers* is a buzzword in clinical trials now, in reality, they are much more complicated than people think. People see that the classic biomarkers are things that are laboratory-tested in a clinic. But what we are talking about is a whole spectrum of markers across different platforms, whether they are blood-based, tissue-based, or imaging-based, and each one of them has been used appropriately in an early-stage study to give scientists decision-making capabilities.

In spite of its great promise, translational research at the pharmaceutical industry level (as in academia) faces a significant number of challenges. For one thing, the recruitment and retention of the talent within this group is very difficult. Many of the people have come from academia, and it is hard to get individuals to come from academia into industry because industry is still perceived as "the dark side." At times, industry is perceived as the place where people, perhaps, are less scientifically rigorous and more focused on profit as opposed to science, which is perhaps a totally incorrect concept. Wright himself, a scientist who arrived first at Pfizer from the Johns Hopkins University, and then went to Novartis, says it clearly:

> *Originally, I thought that industry would be very confining and would restrict your activities to research that would only be devoted to the big-market products, but that is entirely not the case, and in fact there is encouragement to explore new ideas that might be to break through a handful of unmet medical needs, and then the concept would be to address it in terms of the market. That was one of the first things that really struck me in the very beginning about industry, was basically that they seem to have a lot more resources to get things done compared to academia, where NIH grants were on the down side depending on the percentile of funding, and at the same time, my perception was that there was a lot more academic freedom in industry than I anticipated, many more opportunities to pursue new ideas.*[15]

So companies need to bring the right kind of people to do this work, and most companies have few people like this.

In addition, conducting translational medicine studies is significantly more expensive than traditional drug development, even considering that it is a more time-consuming effort. One of the reasons why many companies are not taking this approach is that compared to traditional drug development, where the drugs are tested initially in healthy volunteers, some people believe that putting compounds into patients early will definitely slow down their programs. In traditional drug development, single-dose, multiple-dose, escalating, safety, tolerability, and pharmacokinetic studies are classically done in healthy volunteers. Then, companies proceed to a Phase I study, and then they perform a Phase IIa definitive trial in patients. But what the translational research groups are trying to do is blend Phase IIa into Phase I and get the patients into dose escalation, or there is an expansion phase of that study. Therefore, it is creating something like a hybrid trial.

Translational research certainly costs more than traditional drug development because the company is recruiting patients and measuring patient outcomes, but it is not extraordinarily expensive during these early studies. What some companies have, in fact, found in many cases is that they can skip Phase IIa and go directly into a dose-range-finding Phase IIb study, and in that sense, they could save money. The key is to take attrition early, so by doing that study combined with a Phase I study, getting it to the patient as a component of that, they can stop the compound for that indication. After this, they actually save a lot of money and time because they do not need to conduct a big Phase II study.

Of course, the need to recruit patients may slow things down. This is true if companies do a large Phase IIa study as part of the process. But if they can design the studies with critical internal decision making end points for which they have predefined go/no-go criteria and have them paralleled by biomarkers that allow the company confidently to say, "Yes, this is hitting the target, we have good modulation of the biological target," then the company could recruit a relatively small number of patients to make its decisions. There is a natural tendency in any situation to try to expand the size of the study, and part of the goal in translational medicine is to push back and say, "The general rule here is attrition; as much as we are excited about the compound, it is still likely to fail. So let's keep it small. Let's keep it definitive, and we will get a good answer, yes or no, and then we can go and do the big study."[16]

Suggestions for Improving the System

To become fully effective, R&D reorganization and translational research should be coupled to changes in other domains as well. In the case of regulators, several changes should take place, starting with more funding at the level of the FDA so that this agency could modernize its operational infrastructure and hire more people. But this will not take place until the US Congress fully understands the value of doing it, as we saw in Chapter 6. The separation of foods from drugs at the FDA is a major change that needs to take place so that this agency focuses on medicines alone. More collaboration, harmonization, and exchange of information between the FDA and other regulators, such as the European Medicines Agency (EMEA), and the creation of more clinical trial research networks should also take place to facilitate enrollment of patients and better monitor the development of clinical trials, which could certainly contribute to optimizing the drug development and approval processes. Regulators should strengthen their pharmacovigilance programs and should be allowed to take stronger measures to make sure that companies comply with warnings related to the safety of particular products.

According to Janet Woodcock, "I think harmonization is very positive for the developers, because having disparate regional standards is the worst of all possible worlds. Companies have to meet the requirements in multiple different regions, usually without any scientific rationale for the differences. This is why ICH [International Conference on Harmonization of Technical Requirements for Registration of Pharmaceuticals for Human Use] was started long ago. The regulators all supported ICH because we saw that having multiple standards was wasteful and possibly unethical (e.g., because of the need to duplicate animal and human testing). The ethnic and cultural differences, at least between Europe and the United States, are not so great that there is much difference in drug effects. The health care systems are different and that may make a difference on whether a drug is approved or not. But the requirements for development are not all that different. And I will predict that in other emergent regions the same dynamic will occur. So that eventually it will be desirable to have worldwide standards."

She continues, saying:

> *I don't think there is a single problem in drug development. I think drug development is very hard. We haven't made a concerted effort, in the pre-clinical and clinical development sphere, to bring the newest science in: the development process still involves a lot of guesswork. The developers start with identifying an effect on a target … Some effort may be made to look at off-target effects in vitro, but this is not systematic. The animal models are not predictive of certain side effects that occur in people. There is not a good set of safety biomarkers that bridge between animal and human testing. So we are missing many of the predictive tools that are needed. If you look at drug development as an engineering process, and you are trying to do quality design, your problem is that you only know a few of the important parameters such as "on target effect" and perhaps solubility and permeability, but that's all you know! The rest of the drug performance has to be determined empirically. And you expect to succeed! Human biology and disease involve extraordinarily complex biological systems. So, I think that is the problem! And currently, with chronic diseases being targeted, the complexity is much higher. And the performance expectations are higher, in particular, the safety standards are significantly higher each decade!*[17]

In fact, we are limited by what a clinical trial situation demonstrates, as this is a very artificial environment and only a prediction of what may happen. For Woodcock, "we can't make reliable predictions. We don't have good predictions from discovery of what's going to happen in the clinic; we don't derive good predictions in the clinic of what is going to happen in the market. And we have to fix all of those."[18]

In addition to changes at the FDA level, greater funding for basic research should be allocated to the National Institutes of Health (NIH), especially given the fact that during the George W. Bush administration, the funding of this agency stagnated for many years. Though the NIH pursues translational research in addition to basic research, it should be said that its focus *must* remain on basic research. A way in which the NIH can greatly contribute to the discovery and development of drugs, while keeping its great commitment to fundamental research, is by the creation of an NIH-based tissue bank, setting national standards on how to collect tissues, how to measure DNA, how to measure RNA, how to do proteomics, and so on.

Also, the way in which people collect tissue (paraffin-imbedded and formalin-fixed tissues) is not standardized. The rules for doing transcriptional profiling are not standardized either, and every institution has its own computer program with its own algorithm. Denmark, for instance, has DNA samples and a bank of tissues for every one of its citizens. This is very important because first, it would allow scientists to look at population health so that they are not looking at 40 specimens, but hundreds of thousands of them, which is very handy, especially in oncology, where one could select subpopulations based on genotypic and phenotypic information. There are hundreds of genetic abnormalities and lesions in the genome that cannot be known if one has only 200 specimens, but that would be identified with 60,000 specimens. This could be extremely useful to academics, to small biotech companies, and to large pharmaceutical firms, which cannot obtain tissue specimens so easily. But the NIH can create a national resource so that researchers in the public and private sectors can have access to tissue specimens. We have to get back into the relevant organism (humans) and start studying disease and genes and proteomes and every single interaction. To do that, it is necessary to create a broad platform because this is not something that can be done in one organization's lab. I do not see that happening. But as Julian Adams pointed out to me during a conversation, this initiative has to come from Congress and from President Obama.

Similarly, the creation of more consortia between public and private sectors that could generate a large and common pool of information and technologies, which could be shared among members, would have a significant impact on the translation of basic discoveries into commercial products. As Thomas Lönngren said to me, "One of the hurdles in drug development is the issue of sharing of information. There is so much research now going on that more and more data will be generated, you know, huge amounts of data will be generated in individual pharmaceutical businesses ... small and big ones, and they all want to bury this in their archives in order not to share it with their competitors ... and I don't think the world can afford to put so much money into research when more or less all this research will be hidden in some archives somewhere ... It does not fly in the future."[19] I think that companies should find ways like the one I just mentioned to facilitate the sharing of important data. This issue should also be part of intellectual property reform in which still important information cannot be used because some specific types of patents block its usage.

The government may want consider granting the drug companies market exclusivity for a longer period of time, say, 10–15 years after the drug has first reached the market. If this is done, companies should not be allowed to perform tricks such as reformulations, patent extensions, presenting drugs in other forms (powder form, liquid form, etc.), creating new isomers, or making generic versions. The reason why this is worth considering is that companies may be keeping drugs on the shelves that are very good, but they will not develop them because it is not commercially viable. For instance, Lilly has a drug that it thinks could be effective to treat diabetes retinopathy complications.[20] Lilly cannot develop this drug any further because the FDA wants the company to do another study, which will take 5 years to complete. The company will then have only 5 years of data patent exclusivity once the drug hits the market. So guess where is it staying? On the shelf! But these kinds of changes should be granted on the condition that prices will go down. If prices will not go down, then why bother?

So the problem is not intellectual property. Intellectual property, like any kind of property, is owned by someone. The problem, rather, is how the owner should manage intellectual property, in the same way that an owner of a building must manage that building. I believe that attacking the intellectual property system is the wrong approach. I think it is about having rules and guidelines about how people can use intellectual property. And there is a balance that has to be attained between commercial incentives and making intellectual property available for the public good. Overall, the intellectual property system, which has been around for 400 or 500 years, works very well. In the case of patents of discoveries made using federal or charitable funds, it is expected that the people who exploit patents will be involved in development and that they will not use those patents to prevent other people from doing research. In a paper published in 2006 in *Nature Reviews Drug Discovery*, I proposed an R&D model, named the *core model*, to deal effectively with these intellectual property issues.[21] This model is based on my theory that progress, economic growth, and development are the direct result of a "trade or exchange of assets" (information, knowledge, technology, materials, resources, money, personal connections, etc.) and *not* driven by the state of technology itself, as was proposed by Nobel laureate in economics Robert Solow.[22] Therefore, I think that this model can not only be a solution to the "tragedy of the anticommons" but also have a very powerful impact if applied to broader economic problems, to business organization, and to international public policy issues. It may even explain how wealth is created (see Figure 13.3).

Pharmaceutical companies should also find new models for the marketing of their products: models that would be less expensive and provide patients and doctors with more accurate information. Direct-to-consumer advertising has reached its limit of tolerability, and companies should realize that in the final analysis, the high quality of their pharmaceutical products should speak for themselves. If any given company, today or tomorrow, were to find a wonderful, safe, and effective drug for a particular type of cancer, would not people want to be treated with that drug based on its inherent benefit–cost ratio?

Finally, more involvement of the public, advocacy groups, and private foundations in the drug development process should be promoted through educational programs. Advocacy groups can be important when recruiting patient populations for clinical trials and can have a considerable impact on the drug-approval process at the FDA level. The public needs to consider that it plays an active part in the drug development process rather than being simply a passive consumer of prescribed medicines. It is important that the public better understand the complexities, potential, limitations, and purposes of each step in drug development and the role of the institutions and agencies involved in this process. The implementation of educational programs by the government for the general population regarding all aspects of the process of drug development, as well as more information and transparency on the part of the biotechnology and pharmaceutical industries, will have a positive effect on society's understanding and cooperation. Failed clinical trials, drugs withdrawn from the market because of harmful effects, the high price of prescription drugs, and the lack of adequate drugs to treat (even mild) maladies in the developing world create public resentment and skepticism, and this situation urgently needs to be addressed.

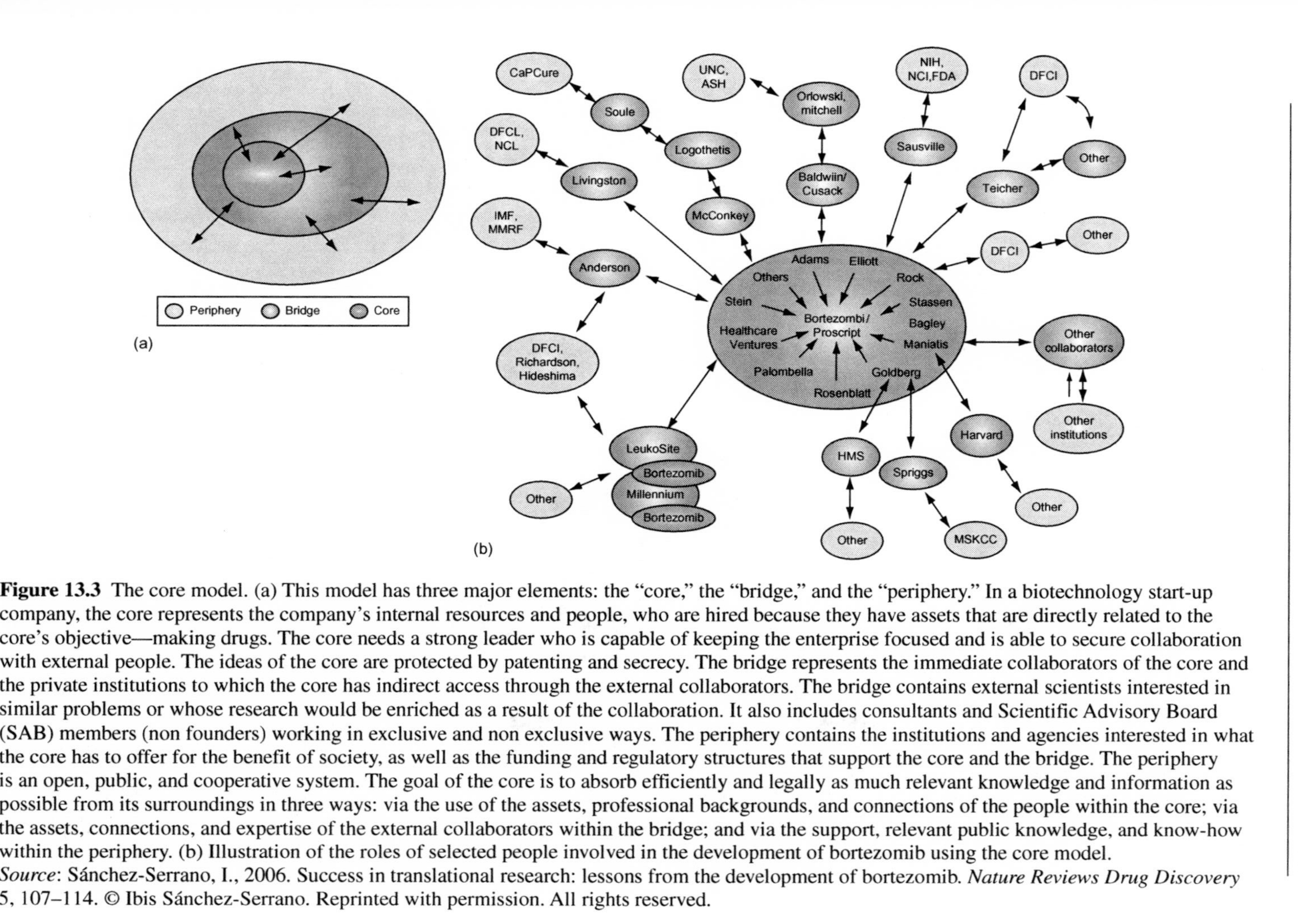

Figure 13.3 The core model. (a) This model has three major elements: the "core," the "bridge," and the "periphery." In a biotechnology start-up company, the core represents the company's internal resources and people, who are hired because they have assets that are directly related to the core's objective—making drugs. The core needs a strong leader who is capable of keeping the enterprise focused and is able to secure collaboration with external people. The ideas of the core are protected by patenting and secrecy. The bridge represents the immediate collaborators of the core and the private institutions to which the core has indirect access through the external collaborators. The bridge contains external scientists interested in similar problems or whose research would be enriched as a result of the collaboration. It also includes consultants and Scientific Advisory Board (SAB) members (non founders) working in exclusive and non exclusive ways. The periphery contains the institutions and agencies interested in what the core has to offer for the benefit of society, as well as the funding and regulatory structures that support the core and the bridge. The periphery is an open, public, and cooperative system. The goal of the core is to absorb efficiently and legally as much relevant knowledge and information as possible from its surroundings in three ways: via the use of the assets, professional backgrounds, and connections of the people within the core; via the assets, connections, and expertise of the external collaborators within the bridge; and via the support, relevant public knowledge, and know-how within the periphery. (b) Illustration of the roles of selected people involved in the development of bortezomib using the core model.
Source: Sánchez-Serrano, I., 2006. Success in translational research: lessons from the development of bortezomib. *Nature Reviews Drug Discovery* 5, 107–114.

Notes

1. Triggle, N., 2008. Lucentis: an NHS dilemma. BBC News, August 27, 2008. news.bbc.co.uk/2/hilhealthy/7582740.stm.
2. Interview with Anita Kidgell, Brentford, UK, May 2007.
3. Staton, T., 2010. Woodcock: FDA may tighten generic drug rules. FiercePharma, October 21, 2010. http://www.fiercepharma.com/story/woodcock-fda-may-tighten-generic-drug-rules/2010-10-21.
4. Interview with Christopher Milne, Boston, MA, March 2009.
5. Interview with Steven Paul, Indianapolis, IN, April 2009.
6. Personal Interview, London, UK, May 2007.
7. Hunter, J., Stephens, S., 2010. Is open innovation the way forward for big pharma? Nature Reviews Drug Discovery 9, 87–88.
8. Paul, S., 2009. An audience with. Nature Reviews Drug Discovery 8, 14.
9. The clinical confirmation that an investigational product possesses a desired pharmacological effect in patients with the disease of interest.
10. See Note 4.
11. Paul, S.M., Mytelka, D.S., Dunwiddie, C.T., Persinger, C.C., Munos, B.H., Lindborg, S.R., et al., 2010. How to improve R&D productivity: the pharmaceutical industry's grand challenge. Nature Reviews Drug Discovery 9, 203–214.
12. Interview with Jackie Hunter, Harlow, UK, June 2007.
13. Sánchez-Serrano, I., 2006. Success in translational research: lessons from the development of bortezomib. Nature Reviews Drug Discovery 5, 107–114.
14. Interview with Timothy Wright, Basel, May 2009.
15. Interview with Timothy Wright, Basel, May 2007.
16. I must say that while I believe that academia, pharma, and biotech are at the root of scientific innovation, they are not yet successfully optimizing for success. My interviews with people at Eli Lilly, GlaxoSmithKline, and Novartis represent the personal attempts of some highly visionary people to address this issue of efficiency and success, but the economic incentives to individual performance simply do not attract the best middle management. What I described in the preceding section are noble experiments still in progress, but I would like to submit that no company has demonstrated an exemplary organizational model yet. The only possible exception to this is the now-defunct Genentech. But even Genentech would not have been as successful as it was if not for its CEO, Art Levinson, who, like Roy Vagelos at Merck, was a unique individual at the right moment and in the right place. Perhaps no other current biopharma CEO has that kind of talent or vision. Therefore, much of a company's success comes down to the leadership of the businesspeople involved.
17. Interview with Janet Woodcock, Silver Spring, MD, March 2007.
18. Ibid.
19. Interview with Thomas Lönngren, London, UK, April 2007.
20. See Note 4.
21. Sánchez-Serrano, I., 2006. Success in translational research: lessons from the development of bortezomib. Nature Reviews Drug Discovery 5, 107–114.
22. Solow, R.M., 1956. A contribution to the theory of economic growth. Quarterly Journal of Economics 70, 65–94.

Conclusion: Future Trends

— How awful for you! By the looks of it, you have developed a soul.
— A soul? D-503 responds. But that is a strange, ancient and long-forgotten word! We some times said "heart and soul," "soulful," "lost souls"... but soul? That cannot be true! Is it ... is it very dangerous? D-503 babbled.
— It is incurable, the doctor replies.

— Yevgeny Zamyatin, **We** ***(1920)***

Human perfection and technical perfection are incompatible. If we strive for one, we must sacrifice the other: there is, in any case, a parting of the ways. Whoever realizes this will do cleaner work one way or the other.
Technical perfection strives toward the calculable, human perfection toward the incalculable. Perfect mechanisms—around which, therefore, stands an uncanny but fascinating halo of brilliance—evoke both fear and a titanic pride which will be humbled not by insight but only by catastrophe.

— Ernst Jünger, **The Glass Bees** ***(1957)***

The current economic recession is demonstrating that the world is fundamentally changing, that new clusters and centers of power are emerging. We can already see a clash between the old and the new structures, not only in the economic order but also in the scientific arena. It is necessary to ask ourselves what can be done so that these transitions are as smooth as possible. After more than a decade of delocalization (i.e., globalization), the world has fallen into a demoralizing economic crisis that has had a very powerful and negative impact on society. As such, the global economy has to adapt to the consequences that a large number of bankruptcies in the United States have brought forth. Many businesses that just a few years ago seemed mighty and unshakable have either disappeared or reshaped themselves to survive. Similarly, as basic science, research and development (R&D), and the pharmaceutical industry have become more globalized [regulators, too, are following that line, for example, there is increasing cooperation between the U.S. Food and Drug Administration (FDA) and the European Medicines Agency (EMEA)], important research clusters have become visible in Asia, most notably in China and India. We saw in Chapter 3 that the drug industry shifted from Europe to the United States once Germany, for economic and political reasons, lost its leadership in this sector. As health care reforms are implemented in the United States and as this country, which is in different ways heavily indebted to China and Israel, tries to find its way out of the mess in which it is immersed, will we see a shift of the pharmaceutical industry back to

Europe, or perhaps to new locations such as India and China? As the US health care reforms are implemented, and as the pharmaceutical industry becomes less productive, will we eventually see more consolidation, less competition, and even eventual partial nationalization of the drug industry in the United States, just as in the financial sector? It is hard to say.

There is an aspect about China and India and other developing countries that is not taken as seriously as it should by the pharmaceutical industry: the importance of traditional or even primitive drugs and natural medicine in these cultures. Although there is plenty of room for charlatanism in this area, some of these drugs, which have come down to us from ancient knowledge, rituals, and local medicine in developing countries, have proven to be extremely effective throughout the centuries and are becoming very popular in the Western world as the cost of medicines and health care continues to rise. After all, before the creation of the pharmaceutical industry, this was the way in which people were treated, and it was precisely because of quinine, isolated from South American cinchona bark and used to treat malarial fevers, that the pharmaceutical industry was born. In fact, one third of all drugs are derived from natural resources, as I indicated earlier. So the capacity to find new active elements in plants, tropical forests, minerals, and so on is an asset that the developing countries will have to develop if they cannot get access to Western drugs.

The United States is a country that, since World War I, has had the great capacity to introduce a series of economic, political, social, and cultural innovations that have spread quickly and deeply (and not necessarily positively) throughout the globe, to be then the first to retract from the path on which they led the world. Sometimes that has occurred when it was already too late, as is happening now with the global economic recession and climate change. The lift of the ban on federally funded stem cell research in the United States may seem a great scientific and political conquest, but have the ethical, and even scientific, implications of this research been thoroughly examined?

The world will have to adapt not only to progress in stem cell research but also to the transformation of the drug industry, once we make our transition from biotechnology—which still promises much—to nanobiotechnology or nanomedicine; in other words, as the new discipline of nanotechnology (which creates devices that are submicron in size) makes growing inroads into biotechnology and medicine, opening an enormous field of opportunity to humankind in areas such as biomaterials, drug delivery, and therapeutics; smart medical devices; biosensors; tissue engineering; *in vivo* molecular medicine, and so on.[1] Companies that have a strong biologics angle may in fact perform well because if we look at the life cycle of a biologic, it appears longer than the life cycle of traditional drugs. So companies get an extra net present value (NPV) for a biologic, which implies that the companies that invest in the development of biologics and vaccines will be better off in the future. The area of monoclonal antibodies is promising in the future, as is the development of antibiotics. More important, brain research, which will be by far the most interesting field of research in the years to come, will answer many questions about diseases such as Parkinson's and Alzheimer's and processes such as learning and memory and will also tell us a great deal about human evolution, intelligence, states of mind such as consciousness, or even the existence of the soul. This research—in contrast to the present state of biology, which is highly dominated by the deterministic and positivist mentality of the 19th century—will open up to the world a more spiritual and less materialistic and deterministic vision of nature, inasmuch as we become capable of learning from science's past mistakes, especially on those occasions when it has been consciously misused and vilified itself in the service of economic and political power, but always in the name of humankind.

In the developed world, if we carry on as we are, the cost of health care is going to become unaffordable. Therefore, we ought to have a much smarter way to diagnose and prevent illness, and people should take more responsibility for their well-being. We need to strive for a change of attitude in the general population regarding the preservation of people's own health, but we also need to give them the devices and tools that they need to measure their well-being and take preventive action, to be responsible for their health. That is a long-term goal, and I think that there is a lot of scope for new technology and new products in that process. The impact that our increased knowledge of the genome has on our present ability to target drugs to those who really need them is a tremendous asset, for instance, one person's asthma might not be the same as another person's asthma, which requires the creation of different treatments for the same disease category. Again, there will be a wealth of diagnoses, of detection technology, in making sure that we are not wasting money giving someone the wrong treatment, allowing us to manage patients in a more intelligent and sensitive way. Although the individual technologies and drugs are getting more expensive, if we become smarter in the way we do things, the overall costs of health care may not be as expensive as projected. Finally, the practice of medicine should become more sensitive to the psychological, emotional, spiritual, in short, *anthropological* conditions of patients and their families to help them cope with and fight against a particular disease. But this requires *true* medical vocation ... and no one talks about this.

I would not like to end this book without confessing that to me, the future is preoccupying, as evidenced by the enormous and often lethal inequalities that exist in today's world, at all levels. This is a world, it is true, of great scientific advancement and unprecedented communication, but also one of great stupidity, of absolute selfishness, in which trillions of dollars every year go to senseless and *unjust* wars that take away the lives of thousands of innocent people in a few seconds, that destroy civilizations that man has painfully constructed over thousands of years ... in the name of what? And it is ironic that while society wastes its time, money, and resources in the most abominable, frivolous, and superficial consumerism, more than 17,000 children—the very hope of humankind—die of hunger every day, while many others die without dignity because of the lack of access to medicines. The increasing, and perhaps irreversible, contamination of the environment and the misuse, abuse, and destruction of our natural resources, precisely by those countries that should be the role models in this sector, call for a profound and cathartic act of contrition and self-examination. As George Orwell used to say *(1984)*: we live in a world in which "the truth" is a lie, and where "a lie" is the truth. We live in a time of universal deceit, in which telling the truth becomes a revolutionary act.

And it is not the current economic crisis where we must look to find the "turning of the tide," paraphrasing the great Dutch historian Johan Huizinga.[2] It is in the decay of spiritual, moral, and ethical values, in the unnecessary automation of man because of the misuse of science, and in the great materialism that has rotted the foundations of our society where the real and imminent perils are. And nothing escapes this. The challenges that the biotech and pharmaceutical industries confront today—and even academia, when it comes to that—are part of this decadence, even if the environments within which they continue to evolve are very different from prior decades. And at times, it is not easy to realize this.

But there is always hope because "where danger is, grows the saving power also," *if we choose to believe* in the words of the German poet Friedrich Hölderlin.[3]

I personally believe that the world is going through a historic transition period (an unprecedented inflection point) in which everything is being reshuffled, in which we could choose either to move forward and survive or to perish. Within this context, it is not surprising that people feel lost and pessimistic; that our old beliefs easily succumb to the new forces that rule the world now, which carry their own momentum and weight. For these reasons, I believe that the *role* of this generation (*my* generation) is to make sure that we manage this transition in the most intelligent and careful way so that our children inherit from us a livable planet and the possibility of living in a better, more fraternal, and humane society.

Notes

1. Wagner, V., Dullaart, A., Bock, A.-K.K., Zweck, A., 2006. A global survey of companies pursuing "nanomedicine" indicates that nanotechnology is taking root in the drug and medical device industry. Nature Biotechnology 2 (10), 1211–1217.
2. Huizinga, J., 1936. In the Shadow of Tomorrow. W.W. Norton, New York.
3. Friedrich Hölderlin, Patmos, 1802–1803.

List of Terms

bioinformatics The application of information technology to the field of molecular biology and genetics.

biomarker A specific biological trait, such as the level of a certain molecule in the body, that can be measured to indicate the progression of a disease or condition.

biopharmaceutical industry An industry composed of the biotechnology and traditional pharmaceutical industries.

biosimilar *See* follow-on biologic.

brand generics Medicines that have active ingredients that are *similar*, but not *identical*, to the active ingredients of the brand-name drugs that they imitate (therefore, they do not infringe on patents), and which for this reason have the advantage of not having to carry out clinical trials.

Centres of Excellence for Drug Discovery (CEDDs) With the goal of sharpening productivity gains and infusing into its large organization well-defined accountability and entrepreneural drive, pharmaceutical company GlaxoSmithKline created a new model for pharmaceutical research and development named Centres of Excellence for Drug Discovery (CEDDs). There are several CEDDs around the world, each of which is dedicated to a specific therapeutic category, such as Antibacterials and Host Defence; Cardiovascular, Cancer and Urogenital; Metabolic, Muskuloskeletal and Viral Diseases; Neurology; Psychiatry; Respiratory Inflammation and Respiratory Pathogen.

combinatorial chemistry Technique by which large numbers of structurally distinct molecules may be synthesized in a time and submitted for pharmacological assay. The key of combinatorial chemistry is that a large range of analogues is synthesized using the same reaction conditions, the same reaction vessels. In this way, the chemist can synthesize many hundreds or thousands of compounds in one time instead of preparing only a few by simple methodology.

commercial biotechnology The use of biotechnology in the creation of for-profit products.

co-payment In general, a fixed fee paid by subscribers to a medical insurance plan every time they are treated or receive health care services, in addition to an insurance plan's membership fee.

cost shifting When wholesale distributors and pharmacy chains for the retail (or the individual physician/patient) market pay higher prices for drugs to compensate for the discounts that drug companies give managed care customers.

coverage gap *See* doughnut hole.

detailing In the pharmaceutical business, a process in which pharmaceutical representatives visit doctors to provide them with information about specific drugs (also called *sales visits*).

differential pricing When identical products are priced differently for different types of customers, markets, or buying situations.

discovery by design A drug discovery approach in which scientists, based on biochemical and crystallographic studies, design drugs that would interact specifically with the active site of molecules inside the body involved in a specific malady. Also known as *rational design.*

doughnut hole The difference between the initial coverage limit and the catastrophic coverage threshold; within this coverage gap, the patient is responsible for all prescription drug costs.

follow-on biologic The term used to describe officially approved new versions of innovator biologic or biopharmaceutical products after patent expiration. *See* biosimilar.

genomics The branch of genetics that studies organisms in terms of their genomes (their full DNA sequences).

health management organization (HMO) An organization in which a group of doctors and other medical professionals offer health care to voluntary subscribers within a particular geographic region, for a flat monthly rate. In general, an HMO covers only visits to professionals within its network unless specifically approved. A primary physician within the network handles limited referrals to outside specialists.

high-throughput screening A robotic/computerized and automated method that allows researchers to test millions of compounds in a day, providing starting points for drug design.

in silico In the pharmaceutical industry, this term (which literally means "performed on computer or via computer simulation") refers to the use of computer modeling and sophisticated software to identify potential lead compounds.

in vitro Literally meaning "in glass" in Latin, this term refers to testing or action outside an organism (e.g., inside a test tube or petri dish).

in vivo Literally meaning "in the living" in Latin, this term refers to experimentation done in or on the living tissue of a whole, living organism rather than a partial or dead one.

knock-in assay A genetic technique that involves the insertion of a protein-coding cDNA sequence (a gene) at a particular locus in an organism's chromosome, which creates a "gain of function."

knock-out assay A genetic technique in which an organism is engineered to carry genes that have been made inoperative (have been "knocked out" of the organism). This implies a loss of function.

lead optimization In drug discovery, a term used to describe the stage at which pharmaceutical companies follow up with secondary screening compounds that have already been selected as biologically active. After this stage, researchers are ready to select those drug candidates that are promising from a pharmacological point of view.

Medicaid The U.S. government's health insurance program for the needy.

Medicare The U.S. government's health insurance program for people aged 65 and older or who meet other special criteria (such as disability).

me-too drug A term used to describe a drug that offers little or no benefit over a similar drug that has already been approved by the U.S. Food and Drug Administration (FDA).

naive population A patient population that has never been exposed to a particular disease or medication.

nanobiotechnology The use of nanotechnology; the technique used to create devices that are submicron in size to solve problems in biotechnology or medicine, also known as nanomedicine.

nanomedicine See nanobiotechnology.

net present value (NVP) A term that refers to today's value of future costs and benefits.

nongovernmental organization (NGO) A legally constituted organization that is not part of local, state, or federal government. It is almost synonymous with *nonprofit* or *voluntary organization*.

nuclear magnetic resonance (NMR) spectroscopy A technique used to study the physical, chemical, and biological properties of matter, exploiting the magnetic properties of certain nuclei.

off-label The use of a prescription medication by a physician to treat a condition other than that for which the drug was approved by the U.S. Food and Drug Administration (FDA).

orphan drug An FDA designation for drugs developed to treat a rare disease (one that afflicts a U.S. population of less than 200,000 people). There are few financial incentives for drug companies to develop therapies for diseases that afflict a small market population, so the U.S. government offers additional incentives to drug companies (i.e., tax advantages and extended marketing exclusivity) that develop these medicines.

over-the-counter (OTC) A term referring to a drug that can be purchased without a doctor's prescription.

pharma A term referring to the traditional pharmaceutical industry.

phenotype A term used for the sum of the observable traits or characteristics of an organism as a result of the expression of that organism's genes and their interaction with the environment.

pill A medicinal dosage form consisting of a small round or oval mass meant to be swallowed. Pills often contain a filler and a plastic substance, such as lactose, which permits the pill to be rolled by hand or machine into the desired form. The pill may then be coated with a varnishlike substance. Pills preceded tablets and capsules, though today tablets, caplets, and capsules are collectively referred to as *pills*.

postmarketing surveillance The practice of monitoring a pharmaceutical drug or device after it has been released on the market.

price shifting The result of cost shifting; in other words, the phenomenon of increasing the price of a service to another payer (i.e., a private insurer) to compensate for the reduction in fees imposed by the initial payer (i.e., Medicare).

proof of concept The clinical confirmation that an investigational product possesses a desired pharmacological effect in patients with the disease of interest. Also known as proof of principle.

proteomics The branch of genetics that studies the full set of proteins encoded by a genome.

public–private partnership (PPP) A joint venture between community members and government or business or between corporations and government.

Research and Development (R&D) Creative work undertaken on a systematic basis in order to increase the stock of knowledge, including knowledge of man, culture and society, and the use of knowledge to devise new application (OECD definition). R&D is often scientific or geared towards developing particular technologies. It is usually perform at government and corporate settings.

random screening A method used by the pharmaceutical industry for many years in which compounds were tested in a bioassay without regard to their structures. This method now has largely been replaced by varying combination of combinatorial chemistry and rational design.

rational drug design *See* discovery by design.

rationing Government policies that impose controlled and restricted distribution of scarce resources.

rDNA Stands for recombinant DNA; in other words, the DNA formed by combining segments of DNA from two different sources.

reference pricing Any reimbursement rule used by a third-party payer or regulator that sets the maximum reimbursement for one product by referring to the price of a comparable product in the same market.

sales visits *See* detailing.

single-payer system A health care system where a government-run organization or entity collects all health care fees and pays out all health care costs. In other words, a single payer finances the delivery of universal health care to a given population as defined by age, citizenship, residency, or any other demographic.

specialty drug Prescription medication that requires special handling, administration, or monitoring. These drugs, which are usually biotechnology-derived products, are used to treat complex, chronic, and often costly conditions such as multiple sclerosis, rheumatoid arthritis, cancer, HIV/AIDS, and hepatitis C.

structure-based design A method by which companies determine the structure of a target receptor and, based on this information as well as theoretical and experimental data, propose potential ligands.

tablet A pressed, compacted, and solid mixture of active substances and excipients, usually in powder form, used as a dosage form. *See* pill.

translational research In this book, this term is used to refer to the translation of findings from the "bench to the bedside"; that is, translational research takes basic and preclinical findings and applies them to humans.

unprecedented drug target A completely novel drug target.

X-ray diffraction A method of studying microscopic crystal form and structure.

Bibliography

AARP Public Policy Institute, 2008. Trends in manufacturer prices of brand name prescription drugs used by medicare beneficiaries 2002 to 2007. Watchdog report. AARP Public Policy Institute, Washington, DC.

AARP Public Policy Institute, 2009. Drug prices continue to climb despite lack of growth in general inflation rate. Watchdog report. AARP Public Policy Institute, Washington, DC.

AARP Public Policy Institute, 2010. Trends in retail prices of brand name prescription drugs widely used by medicare beneficiaries 2005 to 2009. Rx Price Watch report. AARP Public Policy Institute, Washington, DC.

An audience with Ray Woosley, 2008. Nat. Rev. Drug Discov. 7, 884.

An audience with Steven Paul, 2009. Nat. Rev. Drug Discov. 8, 14

Angell, M., 2004. The Truth about the Drug Companies: How They Deceive Us and What to Do about It. Random House, New York.

Bethencourt, V., 2009. Merck joins the biotech game. Nat. Biotechnol. 27 (2), 104.

Beyond the crunch, 2009. Nat. Rev. Drug Discov. 8, 3.

Boston Consulting Group, 2001. A Revolution in R&D: How Genomics and Genetics Are Transforming the Biopharmaceutical Industry. Boston Consulting Group, Boston, MA.

Campbell, E.G., 2005. Sharp critique of industry's influence. Science 307, 1049.

Challenge and Opportunity on the Critical Path to New Medical Products, 2004. U.S. Department of Health and Human Services, Food and Drug Administration, Washington, DC.

Chandler, A.D., 2005. Shaping the Industrial Century: The Remarkable Story of the Evolution of Modern Chemical and Pharmaceutical Industries. Harvard University Press, Cambridge, MA.

Clinton, P., Wechsler, J., 2006. Whatever happened to the critical path. Pharm. Exec. 26, 53–60.

Danzon, P.M., Towse, A., 2003. Differential pricing for pharmaceuticals: reconciling access, R&D and patents. Int. J. Health Care Finance Econ. 3, 183–205.

DiMasi, J.A., 2001. Risks in new drug development: approval success rates for investigational drugs. Clin. Pharmacol. Therap. 69, 297–307.

DiMasi, J.A., Hansen, R.W., Grabowski, H.G., 2003. The price of innovation: new estimates of drug development costs. Journal of Health Economics 22, 151–185.

Dormont, B., Huber, H., 2006. Causes of health expenditure growth: the predominance of changes in medical practices over population ageing. Ann. D'Econ. Statist. 83/84. http://www.adres.ens.fr/anciens/n8384/vol8384-08.pdf

Doyal, L., Doyal, L., 1999. The British National Health Service: a tarnished moral vision. Health Care Anal. 7, 363–373.

Edwards, M.G., Murray, F., Yu, R., 2003. Value creation and sharing among universities, biotechnology and pharma. Nat. Biotechnol. 21, 618–624.

Fortune 500. The most profitable industries. May 4, 2009. http://money.cnn.com/magazines/fortune/fortune500/2009/performers/industries/profits/.

Gardner, W.M., 1915. The British Coal-Tar Industry: Its Origin, Development, and Decline. William and Norgate, London.

Giezen, T.J., Mantel-Teeuwisse, A.K., Straus, S.M.J.M., Schellekens, H., Leufkens, H.G.M., Egberts, A.C.G., 2008. Safety-related regulatory actions for biologicals approved in the United States and the European Union. J. Am. Med. Assoc. 300, 1887–1896.

Green, D., Irvine, B., 2001. Health Care in France and Germany: Lessons for the UK. Institute for the Study of Civil Society, London.

Gregson, N., Sparrowhawk, K., Mauskopf, J., Paul, J., 2005. Pricing medicines: theory and practice, challenges and opportunities. Nat. Rev. Drug Discov. 4, 121–130.

Hall, Z.W., Scott, C., 2001. University–industry partnership. Science 291, 26.

Hamilton, A., Baulcombe, D., 1999. A species of small antisense RNA in posttranscriptional gene silencing in plants. Science 286, 950–952.

Hawthorne, F., 2003. The Merck Druggernaut: Inside Story of a Pharmaceutical Giant. John Wiley, Hoboken, NJ.

Hay, M., 2009. FDA PDUFA goals missed. Nat. Rev. Drug Discov. 8, 10–11.

Heller, M., 1998. The tragedy of the anticommons. Harvard Law Rev. 111, 621–688.

Herrera, S., 2006. Price controls: preparing for the unthinkable. Nat. Biotechnol. 24, 257–260.

Hillisch, A., Hilgenfeld, R. (Eds.), 2003. Modern Methods of Drug Discovery. Birkhäuser, Basel.

Hughes, B., 2007. Transatlantic regulatory cooperation expanded. Nat. Rev. Drug Discov. 6, 589–590.

Hughes, B., 2008. Anticipating REMS. Nat. Rev. Drug Discov. 7, 963.

Hughes, B., 2008. Pharma pursues novel models for academic collaboration. Nat. Rev. Drug Discov. 7, 631–632.

Hughes, B., 2009. 2008 FDA drug approvals. Nat. Rev. Drug Discov. 8, 93–96.

Huizinga, J., 1936. In the Shadow of Tomorrow. W.W. Norton, New York.

IMS Health, 2008. Global Pharmaceutical and Therapy Forecast. IMS Health, Norwalk, CT.

International Trade Administration, 2004. Pharmaceutical Price Controls in OECD Countries: Implications for US Consumers, Pricing, Research and Development, and Innovation. U.S. Department of Commerce, Washington, DC. http://www.trade.gov/td/health/DrugPricingStudy.pdf

Jürgen, D., 2000. Drug discovery: a historical perspective. Science 287, 1960–1964.

Kaitin, K.I. (Ed.), 2006. Cost to Develop New Biotech Products is Estimated to Average $1.2 Billion. Impact report 8. Tufts Center for the Study of Drug Development, Boston, MA.

Kaplan, W., Laing, R., 2004. Priority Medicines for Europe and the World. World Health Organization, Geneva.

Kastelein, J.J.P., Akdim, F., Stroes, E.S.G., et al. 2008. Simvastatin with or without ezetimibe in familial hypercholesterolemia. New Engl. J. Med. 358, 1431–1443.

Kennedy, D., 2003. Industry and academia in transition. Science 302, 1293.

Lawler, A., 2003. Last of the big-time spenders? Science 299, 330.

Lesch, J.E. (Ed.), 2000. The German Chemical Industry in the Twentieth Century. Kluwer Academic, The Netherlands.

Lesko, L.J., Woodcock, J., 2004. Translation of pharmacogenomics and pharmacogenetics: a regulatory perspective. Nat. Rev. Drug Discov. 3, 763–769.

Lieberman, T., 2008. Cautionary healthcare tales from California and Massachusetts. The Nation, March 25. http://www.thenation.com/doc/20080407/lieberman

Lo, B., Wolf, L.E., Berkeley, A., 2000. Conflict of interest policies for investigators in clinical trials. New Engl. J. Med. 343, 1616–1620.

Lopes, C., 2007. Health care in France: facing hard choices. Can. Med. Assoc. J. 177. http://www.cmaj.ca/cgi/content/full/177/10/1167?ck = nck

Mahecha, L., 2006. Rx-to-OTC switches: trends and factors underlying success. Nat. Rev. Drug Discov. 5, 380–386.

Mazzola, L., 2007. Commercializing nanotechnology. Nature 449, 1137–1143.

Mitchell, P., 2009. Venture capital shifts strategies, startups suffer. Nat. Biotechnol. 27, 103.

Moran, M., Ropars, A.-L., Guzman, J., Diaz, J., Garrison, C., 2005. The New Landscape of Neglected Disease Drug Development. Pharmaceutical R&D Policy Project. Wellcome Trust/London School of Economics, London.

Mowery, D.C., Rosenberg, N., 1991. Technology and the Pursuit of Economic Growth. Cambridge University Press, New York.

Nakajima, H., 1995. World Health Organization annual report 1995. World Health Organization, Geneva.

Nissen, S., Wolski, K., 2007. Effect of rosiglitazone on the risk of myocardial infarction and death from cardiovascular causes. New Engl. J. Med. 356, 2457–2471.

Novel pharma-academia collaborations continue, 2009. Nat. Rev. Drug Disc. 8, 97.

O'Dowd, A., Coombes, R., 2008. Government will not meet its health inequalities targets in England. Br. Med. J. 336, 633.

Peck, C.C., 1997. Drug development: improving the process. Food Drug Law J. 52, 163–167.

Pisano, G., 2006. The Science Business: The Promise, the Reality, and the Future of Biotech. Harvard Business School Press, Boston, MA.

Richmond, J., Fein, R., 2005. The Health Care Mess: How We Got into It and What It Will Take to Get Out. Harvard University Press, Cambridge, MA.

Robertson, D., 2001. Immunex takes premature step to guarantee Enbrel market share. Nat. Biotechnol. 19 (2), 108–109.

Sánchez-Serrano, I., 2006. Success in translational research: lessons from the development of bortezomib. Nat. Rev. Drug Discov. 5, 107–114.

Schneider, C.K., Schäffner-Dallmann, G., 2008. Typical pitfalls in applications for marketing authorization biotechnological products in Europe. Nat. Rev. Drug Discov. 7, 893.

Schneider, G., Böhm, H.J., 2002. Virtual screening and fast automated cocking methods. Drug Discov. Today 7, 64–70.

Schneider, M., 2003. Structure and Experience of German Opt-Out System of Statutory Health Insurance (GKV). World Bank, Washington, DC. http://194.84.38.65/files/esw_files/gkv_health_eng.pdf

Setser, B., 2008. China: creditor to the rich. China Security 4 (4), 17–23.

Singer, C., Underwood, A., 1962. A Short History of Medicine. Clarendon Press, Oxford.

Stevens, A., Milne, R., 2004. Health technology assessment in England and Wales. Int. J. Technol. Assess. Health Care 20, 11–24.

Stossel, T., 2008. The discovery of statins. Cell 134 (6), 903–905.

US follow-on biologics debate revived, 2009. Nat. Rev. Drug Discov. 8, 8–9.

Vagelos, P.R., Galambos, L., 2004. Medicine, Science, and Merck. Cambridge University Press, New York.

Wagner, V., et al. 2006. A global survey of companies pursuing "nanomedicine" indicates that nanotechnology is taking root in the drug and medical device industry. Nat. Biotechnol. 2 (10), 1211–1217.

Weatherall, M., 1990. In Search of a Cure: A History of Pharmaceutical Discovery. Oxford University Press, New York.

Wess, G., Urmann, M., Sickenberger, B., 2001. Medicinal chemistry: challenges and opportunities. Angew. Chem. 40, 3341–3350.

Wilking, N., Jönsson, B., 2005. A Pan-European Comparison Regarding Patient Access to Cancer Drugs. Karolinska Institutet, Stockholm. http://ki.se/content/1/c4/33/52/Cancer_Report.pdf

CPSIA information can be obtained at www.ICGtesting.com
Printed in the USA
236070LV00001B/4/P